Praise for *Pelosi*

"A smart, solid biography with a lesson: Despite our current fixation on political showmanship, politics works best in a complicated democracy like ours when its practitioners can navigate their way through the byzantine cloakrooms of power."   —Joe Klein, *The Washington Post*

"Even dedicated political junkies will learn something new about the controversial figure in this comprehensive look."

—Lizz Schumer, *Good Housekeeping*

"Even after years spent covering the House, and three different Speakers, I have a far richer and more intimate understanding of Nancy Pelosi after reading Molly Ball's masterwork. Molly Ball's achievement with *Pelosi* is telling us what makes the most powerful woman in American history tick. With that knowledge, we can now examine the Speaker's every accomplishment—political and personal—in the sweeping, elegant context her legacy demands."

—Tim Alberta, *New York Times*–bestselling
author of *American Carnage: On the Front Lines of the
Republican Civil War and the Rise of President Trump*

"Immersing . . . Equal parts high drama and supreme wonkiness."
—Nell Beram, *Shelf Awareness* (starred review)

"A great read about a great woman. *Pelosi* is timely and valuable, not only for women who will be inspired by her ability to sequence a career from motherhood to national power but for all Americans who still believe that politics is not only the 'art of the possible' but also a path to lasting progressive change."   —Anne-Marie Slaughter, CEO of New America

"An entertaining and balanced biography of Nancy Pelosi . . . Ball offers plenty of insightful anecdotes, presenting events within historical perspective so that readers can fully appreciate their import."

—Kathleen McBroom, *Booklist* (starred review)

"A top-notch political biography." —*Kirkus Reviews* (starred review)

"Read this book, not just to understand how Nancy Pelosi operates as Speaker of the House but to understand how she became the first female Speaker in American history. Molly Ball, one of the most perceptive political reporters in the country, takes readers on a journey through Pelosi's formative political experiences that parallels the transformation of the political process over the last sixty years."

—Amy Walter, national editor for the *Cook Political Report*

"[A] sharp, lively biography . . . With deft political analysis, the author charts Pelosi's rise in the ranks, her relationships with George W. Bush, Obama, and Trump, and her record."

—Barbara Spindel, *The Christian Science Monitor*

"An engrossing and deeply reported political biography of an astute and powerful woman. Molly Ball's lively portrait of Nancy Pelosi, twice Speaker of the House, is packed with sage insights and telling anecdotes. This sparkling new take on Pelosi makes us understand how this 'San Francisco liberal'—often the only woman in the room—has become America's most consequential legislator since the days of LBJ."

—Kai Bird, Pulitzer Prize–winning biographer

"Molly Ball's *Pelosi* is the inspirational political book we've all been waiting for. In this dark season, Ball shines a light on the nearly heroic Speaker and her unwavering commitment to truth, justice, and well-tailored jackets. This is the definitive bio of an icon."

—Vanessa Grigoriadis,
author of *Blurred Lines: Rethinking Sex, Power, and Consent on Campus*

"A lively and detailed portrait . . . Ball's accessible review of recent legislative history and behind-the-scenes coverage of congressional matters provide valuable insights for political junkies. Even readers who don't entirely agree with Pelosi's agenda will gain respect for her accomplishments and tenacity."
—*Publishers Weekly*

"There's a delicious scene in *Pelosi* where she chases down a Republican congressman who had disparaged her and shouts, 'You are an insignificant person!' at him again and again. Whether taking on a low-level backbencher in the House or President Trump in the Oval Office, Nancy Pelosi could never be called insignificant, as Molly Ball so revealingly documents in this absorbing book."

—David Maraniss, Pulitzer Prize–winning
author of *First in His Class: The Biography of Bill Clinton*

Molly Ball

PELOSI

Molly Ball is *Time* magazine's national political correspondent and a frequent television and radio commentator. She has received numerous awards for her political coverage, including the Everett McKinley Dirksen Award for Distinguished Reporting of Congress, the Gerald R. Ford Journalism Prize for Distinguished Reporting on the Presidency, and the Toner Prize for Excellence in Political Reporting. She grew up in Idaho and Colorado and lives in the Washington, DC, area with her husband and three children.

PELOSI

Molly Ball

PICADOR

HENRY HOLT AND COMPANY
NEW YORK

Picador

120 Broadway, New York 10271

Illustration credits can be found on page 323.

Library of Congress Control Number: 2020930617

Picador Paperback ISBN: 978-1-250-79845-9

Designed by Meryl Sussman Levavi

Our books may be purchased in bulk for promotional, educational, or business use. Please
contact your local bookseller or the Macmillan Corporate and Premium Sales Department at
1-800-221-7945, extension 5442, or by email at MacmillanSpecialMarkets@macmillan.com.

For book club information, please visit facebook.com/picadorbookclub
or email marketing@picadorusa.com.

picadorusa.com • instagram.com/picador
twitter.com/picadorusa • facebook.com/picadorusa

1 3 5 7 9 10 8 6 4 2

For David

"If you think a woman can't beat Donald Trump,
Nancy Pelosi does it every single day."

—Senator Amy Klobuchar (D-MN)

Prologue

It was sometime around 5 a.m. when Nancy Pelosi decided she might as well just give up.

January 3, 2019, was a day she had been looking forward to for a long time, the day she would, for the second time, become Speaker of the House. The previous day had been a whirlwind of ceremonial and official duties: a meeting at the White House about the ongoing government shutdown, a tea in honor of the women of Congress, a celebratory dinner at the Italian embassy, where Bill and Hillary Clinton toasted her and Tony Bennett sang. And then she went home, to her airy penthouse apartment overlooking the Georgetown waterfront, to put the finishing touches on the "rules package," the sixty-page document that sets out the changes to how Congress governs itself.

Most of the package had already been agreed to, but Pelosi wanted it to be perfect. She had been up until 2 a.m., calling colleagues, tweaking this clause and that, refreshing herself as she did so with a watermelon-lime seltzer. At seventy-eight, she found her preternatural energy undiminished. She never drank alcohol, rarely had caffeine that wasn't from her beloved dark chocolate and didn't need more than a few hours' sleep per night. But there must have been something in the seltzer she sipped, because when she finally lay down to sleep, Pelosi—two-time Speaker of the House, second in the line of succession for the

presidency, the most powerful woman in American political history—
was wide awake.

She lay there for three hours, until the dull sun began to stream
through the windows and melt the dirty clumps of snow on the ground.
She tried to put the time to productive use, organizing her thoughts for
the big day ahead. It was impossible not to feel a glimmer of excitement.
Not trepidation—fear was one of the emotions she never allowed herself
to experience. (She liked to say it was not in her vocabulary.) But as dark
gave way to dawn and she realized she might as well just get up, she felt a
spark of glee. Time and again, she'd been counted out, insulted, dismissed.
But she was still here, and she was back on top.

For years, pundits, the press and even some members of her own
party had treated her as little more than an inconvenience. They fret-
ted about her age and her polarizing public persona. They argued that,
however skilled her leadership, she was a liability for the Democrats,
and some called her selfish for clinging to her position in the party leadership rather than making way for a "fresher" face. When she pointed
out that she was good at her job—"I am a master legislator," she didn't
mind saying, because nobody else would—she only earned more ridicule: arrogant, delusional, tone-deaf, out of touch. Even after she helped
engineer a landslide victory in the November 2018 midterm elections,
the grumbling continued, and some Democrats tried to deny her the
speakership.

But what happened on December 11, 2018, changed everything. That
morning, Pelosi walked into the Oval Office to meet with President Donald Trump, along with Vice President Mike Pence and the leader of the
Senate Democrats, Chuck Schumer. She was expecting a routine, private
negotiation on government funding; as was often the case throughout her
career, she was the only woman in the talks. But Trump liked to humil-
iate people and keep them off balance. He invited the press to stay and
record the discussion, then began to harangue the two Democrats about
his desire for a border wall. As they spoke up to contradict him, the president, unaccustomed to being challenged, especially by a woman, became
infuriated. And then Trump insulted her, attempting to undermine her
very leadership position by implying she was hamstrung by her party's
divisions, saying, "Nancy is in a situation where it's not easy for her to
talk right now."

At that, Pelosi drew on the experience of a lifetime of refusing to let men speak for her, interrupting them if necessary. "Mr. President," she said icily, "please don't characterize the strength that I bring to this meeting as the leader of the House Democrats."

By the end of the meeting, Washington's balance of power had shifted. Pelosi and Schumer had gotten Trump to take sole responsibility, on camera, for the tremendously unpopular action of shutting down the government. ("I will take the mantle. I will be the one to shut it down," he said.) They had told the president to his face that he was a liar and that even his own party didn't want his stupid wall. Not for the first time, by asking the cameras to stay, Trump had humiliated no one but himself. When the meeting turned spectacle was over, Pelosi collected her coat, a knee-length rust-red overcoat with a funnel neck. She then strode out of the White House smiling and, smoothly, with both hands, affixed a pair of large, round tortoiseshell sunglasses to her face.

The image was indelible. "You come at the queen, you best not miss," one Twitter user captioned it. The internet immediately seized upon the moment, citing Pelosi as the epitome of a poised and competent woman who knew how to put men in their place. Another tweeter described her expression as "that look when you just got finished man-handling a man baby on the big stage." Others Photoshopped mushroom clouds or smoking rubble into the shot's background. Before long, Pelosi's coat had two parody Twitter accounts to speak for it—@NancyCoat touted its "Big Coat Energy"—and Pelosi's image was on T-shirts, cell phone cases and even greeting cards sold at a hip DC bar. The coat hadn't been on the market in years, but the designer, Max Mara, announced it would be reissued, citing demand. "This is diplomacy in motion, soft power wielded like a machete," the Oscar-winning director Barry Jenkins declared.

It wasn't just that Pelosi looked cool walking out of that meeting. After two years of Trump running roughshod over every institution, norm and cherished ideal in America, he had come to seem unstoppable, even almighty. In a single interaction, Pelosi had stopped him cold—and it wouldn't be the last time. All she needed was a little bit of leverage, her favorite word, and she would proceed to run rings around this amateur president as the political world watched in awe. Trump seemed positively flummoxed. She walked into the White House that day under a cloud of conflict and controversy, but she walked out an icon.

✧ ✧ ✧

When she first set foot in the Capitol's marble hallways, she was six-year-old Nancy D'Alesandro, a little girl from Baltimore, watching her father get sworn in for his fifth term as a member of Congress. She was never supposed to follow in Daddy's footsteps, no more than her mother had been allowed to fulfill her dream of going to law school in the 1930s. Nancy's father became the mayor, boss of the city, while her mother had to settle for being her husband's unseen, uncredited political brain. Nancy, too, was expected to one day fulfill her role as a behind-the-scenes helpmeet to the men who did the world's important work. Her five brothers were groomed to follow their father into the family vocation; she was groomed to be a nun. Women didn't have power. Women had responsibilities.

She didn't become a nun, but nor did she join the bra burners and dropouts and establishment smashers of her generation. Her rebellion was a quieter one. When she attended the March on Washington, she left before Dr. Martin Luther King Jr. delivered his "I Have a Dream" speech in order to prepare for her upcoming wedding. While some were burning their draft cards during Vietnam, she was pushing a stroller around her upscale New York City neighborhood, slipping Democratic leaflets under apartment doors, while her husband, a banker, put in long hours at the office. When violent riots broke out at the 1968 Democratic convention in Chicago, Pelosi was not with the protesters but inside the convention hall, watching her father and brother cast their delegate votes. Married straight out of college, she became a full-time housewife and mother, moving across the country to San Francisco to support her husband's career in finance and giving birth to five children in six years.

But her seeming conventionality was camouflage for a revolutionary soul, one that would defy stereotype and history to achieve something no woman ever had before. In fact, she never planned to follow her father into elected office. But when the opportunity came, she took it and made the most of it, trouncing a dozen other candidates in her first election to earn her seat in Congress in 1987. A decade later, when she decided to seek a spot in party leadership, the men who'd always been in charge grumbled, "Who told her she could run?" That only made her more determined. She spent three years lobbying her colleagues and finally defeated, by a handful of votes, the man who thought he was next in line for the job. In 2002, she became minority leader, the first woman ever to lead her party in Congress.

Four years later, in 2006, she powered Democrats to victory in the midterm elections based on voters' fatigue with George W. Bush and the Iraq War. That gave Pelosi's party the majority in the House, and made her the first woman Speaker. She soon established herself as a master of the game, using techniques she'd learned as a young Catholic mother. Nothing teaches you to deal with unreasonable egomaniacs like having five young children in the house. In Pelosi's home, the children formed an assembly line to make their own school lunches, and they set the table for breakfast as soon as dinner was cleared. Decades later, when congressional meetings grew contentious and lawmakers started talking over one another, Pelosi would silence them by barking, "Do I need to use my mother-of-five voice?" She rarely had to punish those who crossed her—the fear of her cold disapproval was enough to keep them in line. She led the charge to block Bush's attempted privatization of Social Security, and when the 2008 financial crisis was spiraling out of control, she worked with the unpopular president to pass a bank bailout and prevent further collapse, taking a major political risk to do what she thought was right.

After Barack Obama was elected in 2008, Speaker Pelosi became his essential legislative partner. She helped him rack up a generation's worth of long-sought liberal gains, from Wall Street reform to equal pay for women. When Obama's signature achievement, health care reform, was floundering, she was the one who convinced him to press on. "You go through the gate," she said at the time. "If the gate's closed, you go over the fence. If the fence is too high, we'll pole-vault in. If that doesn't work, we'll parachute in. But we're going to get health care reform passed for the American people."

Republicans spent years caricaturing Pelosi as the epitome of a "San Francisco liberal," to frighten heartland voters by conjuring images of hippies in Haight-Ashbury and gay pride marches in the streets. In 2010, they turned it into a campaign strategy, stoking the Obamacare backlash with a 117-city "Fire Pelosi" bus tour and ads depicting her as a rampaging fifty-foot-tall giantess. They succeeded in taking back the majority, and they proceeded to redraw the congressional maps in many states to make it nearly impossible for them to lose it. People expected Pelosi would quit, but that wasn't her style. She waited and worked, convinced that one day she'd win again.

The Republican men who succeeded Pelosi as Speaker didn't have her talents. Both John Boehner, the Speaker from 2011 to 2015, and Paul Ryan, the Speaker from 2015 to 2019, were unable to rein in the right-wingers swept in by the Tea Party wave. When she was Speaker, Pelosi had never lost a major vote on the floor of the House, because she wouldn't bring anything to the floor unless she could get the votes to pass it. She was so good at the job that she sometimes made it look easy. Boehner and Ryan, however, quickly discovered how hard it really was. Despite their large majorities, they repeatedly brought bills to the floor only to see them fail.

The Republican Speakers' failures were, in a way, the best illustration of Pelosi's mastery. The Republicans excused their defeats by pointing out how varied the members of their caucus were, from suburban moderates to Texas right-wingers, an inherently fractious bunch that was difficult to corral into agreement. But Pelosi's Democratic majority had been, if anything, even more diverse: male and female, black and white, liberal and centrist, urban and rural, and all animated by the freethinking, rebellious Democratic spirit. Still, she got them to do what she wanted nearly every time.

The Democrats spent eight grinding years in the minority as Pelosi tried and failed to get her gavel back. Even in that powerless position, she managed to be effective. The hapless Republicans couldn't keep the government open or get crucial bills passed without Democratic votes. They were forced to come to Pelosi and beg for her help. She used her leverage to negotiate deals that funded her party's priorities and protected liberal accomplishments, from the Affordable Care Act to family planning funds to labor and environmental regulations. In the two years Trump was president and Pelosi was House minority leader, Trump didn't get his health care bill and didn't get his border wall. Her techniques were a master class in the art of the deal—an art the rest of Washington seemed to have totally forgotten as it descended into chaos and gridlock.

Pelosi was determined to win again in 2018. She crisscrossed the country convincing potential candidates to run for Congress and appearing at event after event, from VIP receptions to rubber chicken dinners, to raise money to fund the campaigns. She drilled candidates on what to say, convincing them to run on health care and economic fairness rather than fixating on Trump, and she relentlessly pushed the idea that Trump's one legislative achievement, tax reform, benefited only the rich. Once again, the GOP's strategy was to put the supposedly scary "San Francisco liberal" in its ads—she appeared in more than a hundred thousand of them across the country. Nervous Democrats worried the blitz might be effective, and some called on Pelosi to step aside. "I think I'm worth the trouble," she responded. This time, the attacks didn't work, and the Democrats won an enormous, 40-seat victory.

But the years in the wilderness had left Democrats restless and frustrated. Even though Pelosi had masterminded and funded the winning campaign, even though 2018 was supposedly the Year of the Woman, she had to fight to overcome dissent in her own ranks in order to be elected Speaker once more. She called in the doubters one by one, and one by one, like a sniper, she picked them off. A congresswoman from Ohio agreed to support her in exchange for a subcommittee assignment. A congressman from upstate New York who had signed a letter pledging to oppose her announced he'd changed his mind. When the leader of the anti-Pelosi brigade, a young congressman from Massachusetts, decided he would negotiate with her instead, *Politico* dubbed the failed effort to oust her "the Pathetic Pelosi Putsch." The campaign to exploit her weakness ended up showcasing her strength instead—giving her an opportunity to demonstrate the very wheeling-and-dealing skills that qualified her for the speakership.

✦ ✦ ✦

Now, on that January morning when she would ascend once again to her rightful position, she put on a bright fuchsia sheath dress with three-quarter sleeves, which she'd ordered online for the occasion. It was formal, feminine, bold—exactly right. She hated shopping and usually threw on whatever was back from the dry cleaner; her husband of fifty-five years, Paul, would sometimes point out that she needed new clothes. She filed away each outfit in her systematic mind—this dress with these shoes; this pantsuit with this blouse and necklace—the same way she filed away which project a Democratic member of Congress was trying to fund in his district, or which member nursed a grudge against another, or the fine print in a budget deal that spanned hundreds of pages. Properly armored, Pelosi stepped into the black SUV that would take her across town to the U.S.

Capitol, where, with 220 votes, she would be elected Speaker of the House for the second time, doubters be damned.

The past decade's journey had changed her, steeling her will and bolstering her confidence but also rendering her, with her 1950s sensibility, ever more of an anachronism. At her first swearing-in as Speaker, she'd worn a sensible plum-colored pantsuit with a string of pearls. Twelve years later, the Speaker in the hot-pink dress was bolder and more knowledgeable, but also, perhaps, more rigid and out of touch. In the months to come, she would have to walk a tightrope, trying to harness the energy of charismatic young members like Alexandria Ocasio-Cortez while keeping them in line with the mainstream. She would have to negotiate budgets with an increasingly recalcitrant and lawless president. She would have to rein in the impeachment-hungry Democrats until the time was right. And then it would be up to her to lead the third presidential impeachment in American history, in a country that had rarely been so anxious, angry, or divided.

At 2:50 p.m. on January 3, the seventy-eight-year-old Italian American grandmother in four-inch heels who hadn't slept in a day and a half grinned and hoisted the gavel she'd earned, surrounded by a flock of children—her own grandchildren and the children of many of her colleagues. Outside the Capitol, all was not well. The government had been shut down for nearly two weeks. Trash was piling up in national parks, recipients of federal housing assistance faced eviction and government workers were taking out payday loans to keep their families fed. Even more serious, it seemed possible that American democracy itself was on the precipice. A president with authoritarian impulses shutting down the government and declaring a national emergency could well be the first step toward dictatorship—would he next declare martial law, dismiss Congress, cancel the next elections and begin rounding up dissenters? If he tried to do any of those things, would anyone be able to stop him? With Donald Trump in the White House anything seemed possible.

People had taken to calling it "Trump's Washington," shorthand for the surrealism of the situation in the capital—as if he owned the place, this indelicate newcomer, this monster, this buffoon. Trump offended Pelosi's sense of propriety as much as he threatened her values. But if his election represented the antithesis of everything she held dear, it was also an indictment of the politics she practiced. In 2016, the American electorate had risen up against the kumbaya ethos, cosmopolitan perspective and technocratic style she epitomized. When, during the campaign, Trump boasted that he knew how politicians get bought by donors because he'd done it himself, Pelosi was one of the politicians he was talking about: long before she became Speaker, she had gone to Trump Tower seeking his checks, and he'd given twenty thousand dollars. Later, he wrote her a congratulatory note, scribbled in Sharpie on a copy of the *New York Times*: "Nancy—you're the best."

Now she was the primary obstacle standing between Trump and total domination—standing, perhaps, between democracy and its greatest enemy. And for all her skill at leadership, for all her experience in governing, nothing had quite prepared her for this battle.

The story of Nancy Pelosi is the story of an extraordinary person who shattered the "marble ceiling" and blazed a new trail for women. It's the story of a career that stamped American history and helped enact policies that affected millions of lives. It's a story about politics and perception and women in public life. It's a story that will shape American politics in the Trump era and beyond.

Because, as Pelosi would proceed to demonstrate, it wasn't Trump's Washington. It was hers.

PELOSI

1

From an early age, Nancy D'Alesandro realized her mother never had much chance to be a person.

Annunciata Lombardi had always wanted more out of life. After high school, she found work as an auctioneer, but she gave it up to get married at nineteen. As a young mother, she started law school, but her three young sons all got whooping cough at the same time and she had to drop out. That was fine with her husband, Thomas D'Alesandro Jr., a traditional man who wanted his wife at home.

D'Alesandro was already in politics when she met him. A twenty-five-year-old member of the Maryland House of Delegates, he was a strapping and ambitious glad-hander who wooed her by asking her grandmother's permission to take her on a date. Baltimore at the time was a thriving industrial city, its air thick with smoke from the factories, its streets teeming with dockworkers and immigrants. Tommy was the picture of an old-school urban pol, with a pencil-thin mustache and an eighth-grade education. He wore bow ties and three-piece suits and straw boater hats, and not one but two gold pinky rings—one monogrammed, one with diamonds.

Urban politics was a game of tribes and factions. The Jews, the blacks, the Poles, the Irish—all had their own tightly segregated neighborhoods, with political bosses who could deliver their votes. The Italians had their own political machine. But after helping Tommy get elected to the State House, the machine's leaders began to see him as a threat to their dominance. In 1938, when he set his sights on a seat in Congress, he ran against an Italian American neighbor. Campaigning on helping President Franklin Roosevelt enact the New Deal, which his rival opposed, Tommy won by a narrow margin.

The family eventually became well off enough to leave Baltimore's Little Italy for more upscale digs if they wanted to, but they never did. Their cultural home and political base was one of the oldest parts of the city—the only neighborhood spared by a 1904 fire that ravaged the rest of downtown Baltimore—a cramped and densely populated twelve-block corridor. "I'm a *paisano*," Tommy said. "These are my people. This is where I belong." While he was climbing the political ladder, Annunciata bore three sons, only to see the middle one die of pneumonia at age three. The grief nearly tore her apart. She prayed, ceaselessly, for solace. Then she bore three more boys, and her husband began commuting to Washington, an hour away by train. And then, in 1940, her last child and only daughter was born. Annunciata named her Nancy, the Anglicized version of her own name.

Tommy might have run against the city machine, but he quickly built a machine of his own. Once, according to family lore, a candidate he supported won Little Italy by 450 votes to 1. "We're going to find out who that one is," Tommy said. While in his fifth term in Congress, when Nancy was seven, he sought and won the mayoralty—the first Italian-American to do so. During his three terms as mayor, he built schools and firehouses, converted the city from gas to electric streetlights and paved hundreds of miles of cobblestone roads. He brought professional baseball and football teams to the city and opened a new airport—although he himself was deathly afraid of flying—while presiding over a patronage system that allowed him to reward political allies with government jobs. He was the king of Baltimore, and he grew, quite literally, into the role, gaining more than a hundred pounds.

Annunciata dutifully kept the house while her husband pursued his political career, but she kept trying to do her own thing. She thought she might get into business, but again she was thwarted. She had ideas for investments, but women weren't allowed to invest without a man's signature, and Tommy wouldn't give his to her. She invented a beauty product, the first-ever device for applying steam to the face, and patented it. She called it Velvex: Beauty by Vapor. Customers around the country clamored to buy it, but Tommy wouldn't let her expand her business.

Instead, he entrusted her with much of his political operation. They lived in a three-story brick row house on Albemarle Street, on the same block where both of them had grown up. She organized campaign rallies, managed fund-raising and ran the Baltimore Democratic Women's Club out of the family's basement. At election time the women were crucial to turning out the vote, house by house, street by street, precinct by precinct. This was politics at the most fundamental, ground level—"human nature in the raw," as her oldest child, Thomas III, used to call it. Annunciata, or "Big Nancy," as she was later called, was the mayor's chief strategist and political enforcer. She knew where all the bodies were buried, and she never forgot anyone who crossed her.

She was also a sort of one-woman social service agency. In the family's downstairs parlor, decorated with large portraits of Presidents Roosevelt and Truman, people were constantly coming and going, seeking the D'Alesandros' help. It was Big Nancy who sat at the parlor desk and maintained Tommy's "favor file," writing on a piece of yellow paper the services people sought and keeping it in a folder. Her husband's name was the one on the campaign signs, but she knew whom to call at the Housing Authority, the public hospital, or the city courthouse. During the Depression, she kept a giant pot of stew always simmering on the stove, and if someone looked hungry she'd invite them to stay for dinner.

Big Nancy had a fiery temper. Once, when a precinct worker tried to push her around, she punched him. She wasn't intimidated by high office, either. When then-President Lyndon Johnson referred to her husband by the nickname he customarily gave Italian men, "Tony," she fixed LBJ with her coldest glare and informed him, "My husband's name is Thomas John D'Alesandro." Years later, when then-President Ronald Reagan planned to visit Baltimore, his staff telephoned the D'Alesandro house to see if the former mayor would join him for a ceremonial event. But it was Big Nancy who answered the phone, and she made clear her feelings about the Republican president: "After what he has done to poor people," she said, "he should not come near our house." She proceeded to put up campaign signs for Reagan's Democratic opponent, Walter Mondale, in every window of the house.

D'Alesandro's reign as mayor was not untarnished by scandal. In 1953, his twenty-year-old son Franklin D. Roosevelt D'Alesandro, known as "Roosie," was one of fourteen young men arrested for allegedly molesting two young girls, ages eleven and thirteen. Roosie was charged with statutory rape but acquitted of that charge as well as a subsequent perjury charge. The following year, Tommy's friend Dominic Piracci was convicted of fraud and obstruction of justice for his activities in the construction business. Piracci's daughter was married to D'Alesandro's son Tommy III—and Big Nancy's was one of the names he'd tried to erase from his business records. While testifying at his trial, she admitted he'd written her six checks for a total of about eleven thousand dollars but insisted it was not a bribe: the money, she said, was a wedding gift for her children and a loan to pay off her business debts.

D'Alesandro was running for governor of Maryland when the double whammy of these scandals hit, forcing him to pull out of the race. Failure hit the ambitious politician hard. He had a nervous breakdown, lost sixty pounds and was briefly hospitalized. But he soon recovered and sought a third term as mayor, which he won. In 1958, he decided to try for statewide office again, this time U.S. senator. His wife advised him against it: he'd be taking on the Republican incumbent, and he had no base outside the city. D'Alesandro dismissed her qualms; he had won twenty-three elections straight, and he was sure the Democratic machine would deliver for him. But she was right, and he lost. In 1959, he lost the mayoralty, too, and left politics for good. Later, when President John F. Kennedy appointed him to a federal board, investigators looked into long-standing rumors that D'Alesandro was tied to various Mafia figures, but they didn't find anything significant enough to stop his appointment.

As Nancy grew up, watching her mother clash with her father as she struggled to make a life of her own, she decided that Big Nancy had been born fifty years too soon. Behind every great man, people always said, was a great woman, and that was Big Nancy's place: behind. For the rest of her life, whenever Big Nancy heard about a young woman getting married, she'd say, "I don't know why she's rushing into this. She has all this talent, all this spirit and intelligence. Why does anyone have to get married so young?"

✧ ✧ ✧

"It's a Girl for the D'Alesandros," proclaimed the *Baltimore News-Post* the day after Nancy was born. That day, March 26, 1940, her father was supposed to be on the floor of the House of Representatives, whipping (i.e., rounding up) votes for a job-training bill being pushed by President Roosevelt. The congressman made a deal to swap votes with a colleague so he could skip the vote and be with his wife in labor. The black-and-white newspaper photo showed Big Nancy lying in bed holding baby Nancy, swaddled in white, as the infant's father and five brothers looked on.

Nancy was the princess of the family—endlessly indulged and endlessly scrutinized. Her room was on the second floor of the row house, where her mother and youngest brother slept, while D'Alesandro and the other four boys slept upstairs on the top level. During the years he spent in Congress, D'Alesandro stored copies of the *Congressional Record* under her bed.

When her father was elected mayor of Baltimore, seven-year-old Nancy held the Bible to swear him in—she would always remember the image of him in his dark suit, the flashbulbs popping in her face, the lectern ringed with microphones. It was there that Nancy, her dark hair parted in the middle and topped with a white hat, gave what she considered her first public speech, which the nuns at her school had helped her write. "Dear Daddy," she said, "I hope this holy book will guide you to be a good man."

Nancy's parents were indeed raising her to be holy—they thought she might become a nun—but she kept telling people something different: "I'm going to be a priest," she'd say. After hearing this a few times, her embarrassed mother finally corrected her and told her girls couldn't be priests. Very well, then—Nancy announced that she planned to go into politics instead.

In the 1950s, the chances that she would fulfill this ambition seemed scarcely more likely than the priesthood. If there were signs of political greatness in the youngest D'Alesandro child, no one was conditioned to perceive them in a girl. At the same inauguration where she swore in her father, she and two brothers were sent to color in a side room when a friendly man entered and tried to talk to her. Heeding her mother's rule against talking to strangers, she ignored him, not realizing the man was the outgoing mayor, Theodore McKeldin. Her brother Joey, who was nine, made fun of her and said he'd tell their mother she had been rude to the mayor. "If you do," she replied, "I will tell Mommy that you talked to a stranger." As Pelosi recalled it later, she didn't squeal on him, earning his respect and ensuring that he wouldn't squeal on her. She had just built her first strategic alliance.

By the time Nancy was eleven, her parents trusted her to staff the living room constituent services organization and administer the favor file. Even as a little girl, she later recalled, she knew whom to call to get a needy person on welfare, or into City Hospital, or a place in a housing project. While her brothers all went to the neighborhood Catholic school, Nancy went across town to the Institute of Notre Dame, the same all-girls school her mother had once attended. A plaque in the school's foyer summarized its ethos: "School Is Not a Prison, It Is Not a Playground, It Is Time, It Is Opportunity." Her father the mayor had his city-employed driver ferry her back and forth. She found this embarrassing and would have the driver stop a few blocks away from the school, so she could walk up like everyone else.

The family spent summers in Ocean City, Maryland, a sleepy village with arcades and hotels along a boardwalk. Nancy had an early curfew that kept her from her friends' beach parties; she was forbidden to ride her bike in the street or water-ski. She observed the curfew but ignored the other rules: out of her mother's sight, she rode in the street, water-skied and joined her friends going out on the waves on "surf mats." As a teenager in the 1950s, Nancy was less interested in her mother's holy ambitions than dancing to Elvis and hanging out with her girlfriends, wearing charm bracelets and Peter Pan collars and cinch belts. In high school, she joined the debate team. At a tournament she attended her senior year, Nancy's teammate drew the debate topic out of a fishbowl full of slips of paper. The topic to be debated was "Do women think?"

All she really wanted was to be in control of her life. She wasn't rebellious or difficult, but she hated having anyone tell her what to do. Her brothers were staunchly protective, her mother held her close and her father didn't even want to let her cut her hair. As much as Nancy loved her parents, she was different. Big Nancy was big and loud and rough around the edges, an immigrant who spoke with a Baltimore accent and suffered no fools. Nancy's friends from school had a more refined sensibility, and she modeled herself on them—a proper American lady. Like so many second-generation immigrants, she yearned to transcend her parents' ethnic enclave and be as American as everyone else.

She yearned, too, for a more elegant politics than the grubby, tribal favor-trading practiced by her father. Like so many American Catholics, she worshipped then-Senator John F. Kennedy. In 1957, when Kennedy came to Baltimore to speak at a dinner, Big Nancy pretended to be ill so her daughter could take her place at the head table. Kennedy's appeal was lofty and ideological, rooted in patriotism and faith. It would become the model for Nancy's evolving political orientation—Catholic social justice with a hint of noblesse oblige.

When Nancy finished high school, she decided she would finally break free. She set her sights on Trinity College, a Catholic women's school in Washington, DC, just forty miles down the road. Her father, who was at the time in the middle of the Senate campaign he would eventually lose, opposed it: he wanted her to stay in Baltimore, where she'd be safe. But her mother took her side. "Nancy's going to Trinity," she said.

"Over my dead body," her father said.

"That could be arranged," her mother replied. So she went.

❖ ❖ ❖

Her brother Nicky drove her down to DC, where she made her way to a dorm on the urban campus. She'd never been away from her big, tight-knit family before, and for two weeks she cried from homesickness. But she also looked around and thought of her mother, who'd never finished college. How much Big Nancy would have loved to be on her own like this.

Nancy made a group of girlfriends who would remain close for the rest of their lives. She majored in history, because a political science major wasn't offered, and prepared to fulfill her mother's dream—now her own—of attending law school. In 1960, she joined her father at the Democratic National Convention in Los Angeles—the first time either of them had ever been to California. Because of his fear of flying, her father took the train all the way across the country. Because he was an early Kennedy backer, they had front-row seats. Six months later, when JFK became president, Nancy attended his inauguration. "Ask not what your country can do for you," Kennedy famously declared. "Ask what you can do for your country." But it was the next line, far less famous, that moved her most deeply: "My fellow citizens of the world," he said, "ask not what America will do for you, but what together we can do for the freedom of man."

Nancy stayed in DC that summer of 1961 and took a class on African culture and languages at Georgetown's School of Foreign Service. After class, she would sit in the living room of one of her friends' houses, having heady college kid discussions of history and current events. It was on one of those days when a handsome Georgetown senior named Paul Pelosi happened to walk by the open windows and hear her discussing the Korean War with her friend Rita and Rita's fiancé, Denny.

Just as Nancy was leaving to pick up her clothes from the cleaner's, Paul invited himself in. He said, "While you're there, will you pick up my shirts?" and handed her a laundry ticket. When she got back, he was still there, but she hadn't brought his shirts. She said she'd forgotten them, which was true—but also, she was not about to pick up a man's shirts for him. ("After we were married, he once asked me to iron a shirt," she recalled in telling this story later. "That didn't happen, either.")

Paul began sitting in on her Africa course, and after class one day he asked her out for a beer, which she refused because she didn't drink. He asked her out for dessert instead, and their relationship, not yet a romance, began. Tall and ruggedly handsome, Paul, like Nancy, was a child of Italian immigrants striving to assimilate more fully into white-bread American culture. After his childhood in San Francisco, he'd attended prep school in Philadelphia before heading to Georgetown.

Nancy stayed in DC after she graduated and worked for U.S. senator Daniel Brewster, Democrat of Maryland. Brewster was a progressive and a civil rights advocate. He was also a drunk. It was Nancy's job to answer the phones in the front office. Everyone knew who she was—the D'Alesandro name was political royalty—but she never acted as if she thought she was better than anybody else. In the next room, separated from her by only a thin wall, sat another earnest young staffer, a working-class kid from the Baltimore suburbs named Steny Hoyer, who was going to law school and had previously worked nights at the CIA. Whether because he had nominal seniority or because of the gender norms of the time, Hoyer got to work on policy while Nancy was a receptionist. Nobody in that office could ever have imagined that, four decades down the road, Nancy and Steny would be the number one and two Democrats in the House of Representatives.

Paul Pelosi wasn't Nancy's only suitor, and she didn't really understand that he was in love with her until one day, after Mass, they were walking through a Jesuit cemetery talking about philosophy. "What are you going to do when you grow up?" she asked teasingly. He turned to her, deadly serious, and said, "I'm going to come looking for you." When Paul came to Baltimore to ask Nancy's parents for her hand, this time it was her mother who didn't want to let her go. "Oh my," she said, through tears. "I thought you'd always be with us." *You also thought I was going to be a nun*, Nancy thought to herself.

It was 1963, the publication year of *The Feminine Mystique*, Betty Friedan's culture-shattering depiction of the dissatisfactions of the educated American housewife. The book captured and stoked a wave of discontent among the women of America, who were realizing that their colleges were glorified finishing schools—they filled the women up with worldly knowledge and then sent them off to be little more than household pets, demure and domesticated and utterly limited and subordinate. What good would be their knowledge of Kant and Milton, or the languages and culture of sub-Saharan Africa, when they were stuck keeping house for the men who got to do the real work of the world? Friedan quoted Adlai Stevenson's advice to the 1955 graduates of Smith College: "This assignment for you, as wives and mothers, has great advantages," he insisted. "If you're really clever, maybe you can even practice your saving arts on that unsuspecting man while he's watching television!" To more and more American women, these expectations were no longer enough.

But Nancy D'Alesandro had missed the revolution. Shortly after she took the LSAT, she was Nancy Pelosi, she was pregnant with the first of five children she would bear in the space of six years, and she had moved to New York City to accommodate her husband's career in finance. For all her determination not to end up like her mother—dreams thwarted, relegated to the role of invisible caretaker of her husband's public career—she had fallen into exactly the same trap.

2

SHE HATED TO COOK AND HARDLY KNEW ANYONE WHEN THEY MOVED to New York, but Nancy Pelosi always insisted she loved being a housewife. The babies, the laundry, the meals, the house; playtime in the park, running errands with the stroller in tow—it was all very new and exciting. Any thought of restlessness she pushed out of her highly disciplined mind, so as not to feel an inkling of discontent.

As any parent knows, having even one baby, much less five in quick succession, rewires your metabolism completely. You might have thought you knew what it meant to be busy, or stressed, or tired. But once you are tethered to a helpless living thing that must be fed every couple of hours around the clock, you look back on your old life and realize how much slack there was in it, because it is all gone. You spend whole days thinking you must wash your face and then realize, as you go to bed, that you never got around to it. You find inner reserves of energy and endurance that you didn't know you had, and you make it through, one day at a time. You sometimes feel like a sort of superwoman—but you don't really have any choice.

The year after Nancy and Paul were married, their first child, Nancy Corinne, was born. Eighteen months after that came Christine. A year later, Jacqueline, then Paul Jr., then Alexandra. Alexandra was born the week Nancy Corinne turned six.

Pelosi had a habit, when she needed to focus, of keeping a single word in her mind. In these years, it was *survival*. Once, when she was pushing Nancy Corinne and Christine in the stroller while very pregnant with Jacqueline, a neighbor approached and whispered urgently, "Get help!" But even with money, it was nearly impossible to hire help for so many babies, or at least help that met Pelosi's standards. For everything to be done right, she had to do it herself. She lived for the fleeting, golden time each day when all the babies were napping at once. Before starting the laundry, she would do the *New York Times* crossword puzzle and eat a scoop of chocolate ice cream, savoring the rare feeling, the illusion, of adult autonomy.

"Did you ever imagine," her mother said, "that little bundle would be so much work?" Still, since becoming a mother, Pelosi felt that her capacity for doing things had expanded. She looked back with astonishment at her former life and all the free time she'd taken for granted. A memory flashed in her mind of the time, before she was married, when someone asked her to do something and she'd said, "Nah, I'm too tired." In retrospect, it seemed laughable. Before motherhood, she'd had no idea what "tired" meant.

Her oldest brother, Tommy D'Alesandro III, had embarked on a political career, and she lived vicariously through him. Though his father's name was his entree into Maryland politics, he styled himself more after JFK. Pelosi approved: Tommy Jr. seemed to her cooler, more modern, more measured than their father's vulgar, ethnic persona. Big Tommy had been a delegate for Hubert Humphrey at the 1968 convention; his son was a delegate for Bobby Kennedy. Throughout Pelosi's life and career, she would describe Tommy, nearly eleven years her senior, as her mental model of a "perfect politician."

In 1967, thirty-eight-year-old Tommy was elected mayor of Baltimore. The following year, Martin Luther King Jr.'s assassination sparked a wave of urban riots across the country. The rioting in Baltimore was among the worst, and Tommy was unable to bring it under control. By the time the National Guard was called in to restore order, six people had died, seven hundred were injured and tens of millions of dollars' worth of property had been destroyed in more than a thousand fires. Tommy was a progressive who believed in racial equality and integration and had good relations with the black community. But the riots were, in part, a rebellion against the well-intentioned paternalism of white urban Democratic machine politicians like him and his father, who had failed to end the disenfranchisement and segregation black residents faced.

Tommy became deeply unpopular and left politics after a single term as mayor, though he would later insist that he quit for his own reasons, not because of the riots. Later, when the wounds were healed and he could joke about it, he would say he had been so unpopular in some parts of the city that when he rode in a parade, the booing would start before he came around the corner. His adoring little sister would forever describe him as a sort of martyr to the ideal of racial equality who pushed for the right thing even when it upset the status quo.

❖ ❖ ❖

At the Pelosis' apartment in Midtown Manhattan, Paul was homesick for the West Coast. His father had just died, and he'd been offered an exciting job as an investment manager in his hometown of San Francisco. Their fourth child, Paul Jr., had just been born. Pelosi agreed to move on two conditions: that she could continue to get the *New York Times* every day and that she would never have to stay in someone else's house. As Paul knew, she prized having her own space.

It was on the plane west, Pelosi holding four-week-old Paul Jr., that her husband informed her that there had been a change of plans. They would not be staying in a hotel when they got to California. They would be staying with his newly widowed mother. Surely, Pelosi did not want to hurt her mother-in-law's feelings, he said; besides, it was just for one night. She had no choice but to go along.

One night turned into four months. Pelosi tried to make the best of things while frantically house hunting, but it was impossible to find a suitable rental in San Francisco with four young children. Finally, she found it: a big, elegant house, already childproofed, with a swing set and a sandbox in the spacious backyard. As Pelosi's heart soared, she asked, out of idle curiosity, why the house was on the rental market. It turned out the owners were moving to Washington. "My husband has been appointed deputy secretary of the Department of Health, Education and Welfare," the owner said proudly, "so we'll be going back east to join the Nixon administration."

Pelosi told the stunned real estate agent that the deal was off. As unhappy as she was at her mother-in-law's house, she refused to live in any place that had been, as she put it, "made available by the election of Richard Nixon."

The Pelosis finally bought a house instead, a grand fixer-upper on an exclusive private cul-de-sac called Presidio Terrace. Their fifth child, Alexandra, was born in California. Just when the last of the children emerged from diapers and Pelosi finally saw a light at the end of the tunnel, the next, even more grueling phase began: homework. Some days, she drove the school carpool with her nightgown still on under her coat.

She ran the household with precision. The children made their beds and straightened their rooms before coming downstairs, where she had breakfast waiting. Paul, who did most of the kids' clothes shopping, would help comb the children's hair and inspect their shoes, uniforms and teeth. (The girls could choose to put their hair in braids or ponytails; one day, Jacqueline went to school with one of each.) After school, it was a snack and homework and outside to play. Pelosi would ring a big brass cowbell from the steps to call them in for dinner. Then the children would make their lunches for the next day in assembly-line fashion and set the table for breakfast. A friend once remarked that she knew Pelosi was destined for political success when she saw the five young children all folding their own laundry.

Tattling and gossip were prohibited. Pelosi often dressed all five children in the same outfit—even Paul Jr.—to make them easier to spot in public. In classic Catholic mother fashion, if a child misbehaved, Pelosi didn't get mad, just disappointed. She rarely yelled, but she'd look at some mess or other evidence of misbehavior and say, "You children wouldn't have done that," and their hearts would sink. "Let's have some cooperation," she'd say. "I'm not taking any complaints," she'd say. "Proper preparation prevents poor performance" was another favorite aphorism.

She was the picture-perfect mother, chaperoning field trips, sewing Halloween costumes and bringing cupcakes to school. But she was also the leader of a fractious team of rivals, responsible for managing shifting coalitions and mediating constant disputes. They all had different personalities: Nancy Corinne was a natural hostess and nurturer; Christine was driven and bookish; Jacqueline was curious and kindhearted; Paul Jr. had his father's athleticism and gregariousness, and Alexandra was artsy and rebellious. Being fair to all of them meant making sure each got what they needed—not treating them all the same, but making them feel equally understood. Pelosi was the un-helicopter mom who knew it was more important to create responsible, independent adults than to be her kids' best friend. Unity was essential: it didn't mean conformity, but it did mean sticking together when it counted.

Paul's career had taken off, making the family comfortably well off. He ran a company that rented equipment to businesses, including computers for some of the earliest Silicon Valley start-ups, and also invested in real estate. (The Pelosis today are rich, but not Donald Trump rich or even Mitt Romney rich, with an estimated net worth of about sixty million dollars in 2016, according to the Center for Responsive Politics. She was the tenth-wealthiest member of the House.) Despite the family's money, they never had full-time help. Pelosi tried from time to time to hire a nanny, but prospective employees tended to take one look at the size of the family and run in the other direction. She could hardly blame them: she figured there were probably families with one or two children they could go work for instead. She gave up and resigned herself to doing it all on her own.

Pelosi's wellspring of inner energy felt potent, even if no one else could see it. Congress had recently passed the Equal Rights Amendment, sending it to the states for ratification and sparking a heated national debate about women's roles and rights. Following Betty Friedan's logic, some feminists were calling attention to the unrecognized labor of housewives. When Pelosi read that someone had proposed describing homemakers as "domestic engineers," she thought, *Well, maybe then they'll recognize our true value.*

When the kids were young and she had to spend hours at a time sitting in the park, watching them play, she thought to herself, *One day, I'll have time to really do something—like feed all the hungry people in the world.*

❖ ❖ ❖

Once the children were all in school, Pelosi suddenly found that she could breathe. After the intense, sleepless marathon of babyhood, caring for five young children who didn't need their diapers changed and who spent the day out of the house was a relative cakewalk. She could wash her face. She could make a cup of tea. Still, as hard as raising young children had been, once it was over she missed it. She and Paul would sometimes joke about putting the kids out in the rain so they'd shrink back into babies. For years afterward, she'd get a knot in her stomach every day at a quarter to noon, the time she used to have to pick them up from preschool.

Yet Pelosi was not the kind of person who was going to let her new-found minutes go to waste. Because they had the biggest house of all their friends, the Pelosis began hosting Democratic fund-raisers. It was, Pelosi reasoned, the one thing she could still contribute to her beloved party while raising five children. (Guests would sometimes look around at their spartan furnishings and remark that it was smart of her to have taken all the furniture out to make room for the party, and she would smile and nod, while thinking, *But this* is *the furniture.*) The children were pressed into service as coat takers, servers and nametag distributors. Driving around the city in her red Jeep Wagoneer, Pelosi kept campaign mailings on the passenger seat and stuffed envelopes whenever she stopped at a red light.

She had a natural talent for fund-raising, and the house became a well-known stop on the local campaign circuit. Precisely because it involves so much hostessing, political fund-raising had traditionally been women's work, only later professionalized after decades of being run by volunteers—that is, unpaid wives. But fund-raising also involves many skills that come in handy for a legislator: the ability to seek and return favors; the ability to flatter the egos of large numbers of people who believe themselves very important, making them feel doted upon and cared for, until they give you what you want.

Pelosi took on more volunteer work: she was an adviser to the U.S. Conference of Mayors, a trustee of the Leakey Foundation, a member of the Bicentennial Committee and co-chair of the San Francisco Film Festival. Sometimes she still thought she might go to law school one day. But as her children grew older, her fate seemed settled. She was destined to become a San Francisco grande dame, serving on PTAs and museum boards and attending galas as her husband kept getting richer.

But then, one day, the phone rang, and she got her first taste of her own power.

3

THE MAYOR OF SAN FRANCISCO WAS CALLING. YET THE FIRST THING HE said, when Pelosi picked up the phone, was something obnoxious.

The mayor, Joe Alioto, lived just a few doors down on Presidio Terrace. As fellow Italian American Democrats, the Pelosis knew the mayor well. Paul had coached the mayor's children in basketball. Alioto was a close friend and fellow mayor of Pelosi's brother Tommy. He was also a bit old-fashioned.

It was four o'clock on a weekday. The children had had their afternoon snack and were playing outside, and the previous day's *Times* had just been delivered—the newspaper was printed in New York, flown on a plane to the West Coast and delivered to subscribers from the airport late in the afternoon. Pelosi still devoured it every day, starting with the crossword puzzle.

"Nancy," the mayor said, "what are you doing? Making a big pot of *pasta e fagioli?*"

Pelosi bristled at the assumption that she was a little Italian house-wife slaving over a hot stove. But she swallowed her annoyance and simply replied, "No. I'm reading the newspaper."

Alioto, it turned out, wanted to appoint her to the San Francisco Pub-lic Library Commission, the policymaking body that oversaw the city's system of public libraries. Pelosi had spent a lot of time at the library with her kids; she'd also seen the institution through a political lens, as a vital resource for families that, unlike hers, couldn't afford books of their own. The library, to her, was nothing less than a pillar of democracy.

But her first response to the mayor's offer was to demur. She enjoyed volunteering for the library, she told Alioto, but she didn't need any kind of official position to do that.

"You shouldn't say that," he said sternly, surprising her. "You're doing the work. You should get official recognition for it." It was, she realized later, a feminist gesture, albeit from an unlikely source. Since time immemorial, in many institutions, women had been working for free while men made all the decisions and held all the power. Alioto was telling her that if she was going to provide the labor, she should get to make the decisions, too. Pelosi would come to see this exchange as a seminal one in putting her on the path to political power.

There was a political angle to it for Alioto, too. He'd recently appointed a new city librarian whose attempts to modernize and democratize the system were rubbing some longtime commissioners the wrong way. Putting Pelosi on the board would give the mayor and his librarian a crucial ally. Even at the library, everything came down to counting votes.

The commission, Alioto told Pelosi, would look good on her résumé if she ever decided to run for office. This struck her as ridiculous. "Mr. Mayor," she huffed, "I have absolutely no intention of running for office." But she thought about his argument that her labor entitled her to a voice. *I think it's time for you to get official recognition for your work.* She thought about how much she loved books. And with her youngest child, Alexandra, starting kindergarten, she reasoned, she'd have a bit of free time.

On June 6, 1975, the name "Nancy Pelosi" appeared in the *San Francisco Chronicle* for the first time. The brief item noting her appointment to the library commission described her as "Nancy Pelosi, neighborhood leader and sister-in-law of supervisor Ronald Pelosi."

As a political office, it was the smallest of small-time gigs. But to the thirty-five-year-old housewife it was a revelation. Having authority changed everything for Pelosi. Volunteers did what they were told, but commission members made policy. People treated her differently. They couldn't dismiss or ignore her just because she was a woman. They called and asked her opinion; they listened when she had ideas. For the first time, she felt that people actually cared what she thought. And it was all because she had a vote.

The commission also gave her a deeper view of her adopted town. San Francisco in 1975 was a city in transition, transformed by demographic shifts and wracked by political turmoil. In the '60s, the corner of Haight and Ashbury Streets had given birth to the hippie movement, while a newly visible gay activism had risen from the Castro District, and the Black Panthers had been founded in Oakland. Watergate and the Vietnam War had supercharged the younger generation's determination to over-throw the dominant culture. Shortly after appointing Pelosi to the library commission, Alioto would preside over a police and fire department strike that paralyzed the city for days and led to his house being bombed. A few years later, his successor as mayor, George Moscone, would be assassinated in a shooting that also claimed the life of the city supervisor and gay rights pioneer Harvey Milk.

Pelosi's cosseted life might have kept her far from these disruptions. But one of the library board's modernization initiatives was to attempt to make its deliberations more accessible to the public. Instead of holding all their meetings at the main library, the commissioners decided to hold them at smaller branches in the city's neighborhoods. The pampered, rich Pelosi with her elite friends was exposed to the rough-and-tumble San Francisco that existed outside Presidio Terrace.

◇ ◇ ◇

California was in transition, too. The state that had elevated Republicans such as Richard Nixon and Ronald Reagan had become a political battle-ground. Its Democrats were divided into rival political machines, both of them based in San Francisco. One was run by Leo McCarthy, Speaker of the State Assembly. The other belonged to Phillip Burton, dean of the state's congressional delegation. Throughout the 1960s, the factions battled over everything from State Assembly seats to control of the state Demo-cratic Party.

Pelosi's brother-in-law, Ronald Pelosi, was a member of the city Board of Supervisors and a McCarthy acolyte, so she was drawn into McCarthy's political orbit. A gentlemanly, idealistic son of Irish immigrants, McCar-thy commuted nearly ninety miles each way from San Francisco to the legislature in Sacramento so that he could be home with his wife and four children every night. In 1974, McCarthy decided to run for Speaker of the

State Assembly against Willie Brown, a Burton ally who was thought to have the post locked up. McCarthy called Pelosi, with her many connections in state politics, for help. She sprang into action, calling contacts in the Assembly who had attended her fund-raisers over the years and urging them to vote for McCarthy. In a surprise upset, McCarthy won, with 26 votes to Brown's 22. Asked later how he'd counted the votes, McCarthy replied, "One at a time."

The friendship with McCarthy was valuable to Pelosi, too. When the library needed to ask for more money in the state budget, her fellow commission members wondered how they could possibly appeal to the Speaker of the Assembly. Pelosi responded that it would be easy: Leo McCarthy, her personal friend, owed her a favor for helping him line up the votes to be Speaker. The library soon had the funding it needed, and Pelosi had seen her power in action. Without being elected to anything, she had been able to influence the course of political events. It was intoxicating.

Pelosi's alliance with McCarthy didn't keep her from forming a friendship with Burton, his rival. Though she didn't know it at the time, it was this friendship that would eventually alter the direction of her life.

Leo McCarthy and Phil Burton were similar in their politics, but vastly different in temperament. Where McCarthy was earnest and formal, Burton, hard-drinking and prone to fits of rage, was a passionate, volcanic street fighter who crusaded relentlessly for welfare, workers' rights and the environment. In 1965, he was one of only three to vote against funding President Lyndon Johnson's war in Vietnam. Later, he worked to abolish the House Un-American Activities Committee, which had bullied people believed to have Communist sympathies. "The only way to deal with exploiters," he once said, "is to terrorize the bastards."

Nancy Pelosi, wealthy housewife and fund-raiser, did not seem like a natural Burton ally. He regarded her warily, as a member of both the exploiter class and the Leo McCarthy faction. She viewed him as overbearing and arrogant. Their first conversation was a short one: "You have a big house," he informed her gruffly. "We'll be using it for Democratic Party events."

Pelosi wasn't intimidated. She'd grown up surrounded by men like Burton, and they didn't scare her. The next time he asked her for something, she refused. He started to yell. She didn't back down, but calmly explained why she was right and he was wrong. Burton stopped yelling; he grabbed her chin with one of his big hands, shook it affectionately and smiled. Accustomed to bullying people into submission, he'd found in Pelosi someone who wouldn't be cowed, and he respected her from then on.

Pelosi soon became a link between the McCarthy and Burton factions in California Democratic politics, helping mend the prideful men's longtime rift.

◆ ◆ ◆

At a fund-raising dinner in early 1976, McCarthy introduced Pelosi to another member of California's Democratic vanguard: the state's new governor, Jerry Brown. Brown, whose father had been governor before him, had gone to high school with Paul Pelosi's brother. Just thirty-six when he was elected, Brown was quirky and idealistic. A former seminarian, he brought an ascetic style to his post, eschewing the grand governor's mansion and a limousine in favor of a small apartment and a no-frills Plymouth Satellite. Brown was a social liberal, but a fiscal conservative, a believer in frugal budgets and modest government. He also had a touch of glamour: the young governor was unmarried, and his girlfriend was the singer Linda Ronstadt. Pelosi was enthralled by Brown's visionary zeal.

In early 1976, Brown decided to run for president. The Republican incumbent, Gerald Ford, had never been elected to the post, stepping into office after Watergate brought down Richard Nixon. He had issued a controversial pardon and looked weak amid a crippling recession and energy shortage. By the time Brown decided to enter the race in March 1976, the Democratic field was already crowded, and some of the other candidates had been campaigning for nearly a year. Crucial contests in Iowa, New Hampshire, Massachusetts and other states had already occurred, and it was mathematically impossible for him to win enough delegates in the remaining primaries to secure the nomination.

After unrest at the 1968 convention, the Democratic National Committee had opened up the candidate selection process to lessen the influence of party bosses and follow the desires of rank-and-file party members as expressed in state primaries and caucuses. These changes set in motion the nomination system that is familiar today, but at the time the convention was still where the nomination had historically been decided.

When Pelosi heard that Jerry Brown wanted to run for president, she was enthusiastic, but she thought his strategy needed work. California had one of the last primaries on the calendar, in June, and Brown figured he would win it as a favorite son and take that momentum into the convention. Pelosi believed it would be too late by then for him to make a splash. She took it upon herself to draft a memo proposing an alternative strategy and gave the memo to Leo McCarthy to pass along.

The memo proposed that Brown contest the Maryland primary, to be held in mid-May. Pelosi argued that the state's Democratic voters would be receptive to Brown's message and that the D'Alesandro family would work their connections on his behalf. Members of Pelosi's own family, including her brother Tommy, were skeptical. But Brown liked the idea.

Jerry Brown flew to Maryland and stayed with the D'Alesandros for the two weeks leading up to the primary. Tommy and his friend Ted Venetoulis (Pelosi's high school boyfriend, who was by now the Baltimore county executive, with a formidable political machine of his own) showed the young governor around, despite their misgivings. "My professional judgment is that it is impossible for a thirty-eight-year-old bachelor from California to come into this state and run for president," Venetoulis warned Brown. "It's ridiculous." To their surprise, Brown's candidacy caught fire. Thousands of young people flocked to his rallies, where Ronstadt accompanied him as he gave soaring speeches.

To the political world's amazement, Brown came out of nowhere and won Maryland. In his victory speech, he paid tribute to Pelosi, calling her the "architect" of his Maryland campaign. She found herself both abashed and energized by the attention. Her success was testament to an important part of her skill set: the ability to see opportunities where others might not, and the brazenness to seize them.

Pelosi was more than a housewife, more than a pocketbook, more than a hostess—she was a strategist. Attending the Democratic convention in New York City, she said to herself with private satisfaction, *Looks like I've got at least one foot outside the kitchen now, doesn't it, Mayor Alioto?*

The out-of-nowhere victory sent Brown's political stock soaring, and he went on to win the Nevada and California primaries. But it was too late for him to catch up to Jimmy Carter, and he came in third at the convention. Pelosi absorbed another valuable lesson: if you want something, start laying the groundwork early.

❖ ❖ ❖

Brown and Pelosi became friends. When he wasn't in Sacramento, the governor sometimes hung around the Pelosi house, lying on the couch talking about affairs of state while she got dinner ready. He urged her to run for state Democratic Party chair, but having never run for anything, and having never even been to a party central committee meeting, she told him, "Please find someone else." At his urging, she agreed to run for a lower-tier party post, Northern California chair, which she won easily. The first campaign flyer of her career read, "Nancy Pelosi—Volunteer."

Four years later, having learned the ropes of state party politics, she felt ready to run for chair of the California Democratic Party, the largest state Democratic Party in the country. With the backing of Brown, who'd been easily elected to a second term as governor, she won overwhelmingly. The party had to change its bylaws to refer to its first woman leader as "chair" rather than "chairman," a construction some of the old men found clumsy. No other large state had a woman chair, and some didn't have a single woman on their central committees. On a regular basis, people would walk into the party office, see the attractive young woman at the desk and say something like "Oh, do you work for the committee?" Pelosi took immense pleasure in responding, "I am the chair."

The country seemed to be on fire. California was wracked by political violence: a member of the Manson Family attempted to assassinate President Ford in Sacramento in 1975, and in November 1978, a Northern California congressman, Leo Ryan, was one of the 918 victims of the Jonestown cult massacre in Guyana. Just nine days later, Harvey Milk and Mayor Moscone were killed at San Francisco's City Hall. The economy was dismal, and Carter's approval rating sank below 30 percent. "A recession is when your neighbor loses his job," Carter's opponent Ronald Reagan said during the campaign. "A depression is when you lose yours. And a recovery is when Jimmy Carter loses his."

Democrats were also internally divided. Carter had multiple primary challengers, including Senator Ted Kennedy, who won twelve primaries and didn't concede the race until the convention. Jerry Brown also ran for president for the second time in the 1980 primary, with Pelosi's backing, but not the Pelosi children's: the four daughters all backed Kennedy, while eleven-year-old Paul Jr. was for Carter. But Brown's attraction to big, futuristic ideas and his dabbling in Buddhism had gotten him tagged as a New Ager—"Governor Moonbeam"—and he was dismissed as a fringe candidate. The 1980 election saw a Republican sweep, with Reagan winning forty-four states and the GOP taking the Senate for the first time since 1955.

Pelosi viewed Carter as weak and politically obtuse. She thought he'd made a series of mistakes that had hurt his reelection campaign. "We have been delinquent, or lazy, or not hungry enough," she said as she took the reins of the California Democratic Party three days before Reagan was sworn in. Her first act was to call a press conference to blast his proposed cuts to social spending and accuse Republicans of caring only about the rich.

The party chair job was all-consuming, and she loved it. There seemed to be ten crises every morning—it reminded her of the intensity and action of a campaign. From the start, she made it clear that hers would not be a ceremonial post. State parties vary widely in quality, from barely functioning volunteer operations to large paid staffs. In California, Pelosi took what had been a loose collection of activists and professionalized it. She got the party a full-time headquarters for the first time and hired an executive director. She tried to bring its operations into the nascent digital age, creating a database of the party's thousands of committee members and activists and computerizing its voter registration data. For the first time in the state party's history, she commissioned polling. She pledged to register a million new Democratic voters, but fell short and got only seven hundred thousand—still a record. She found that if she got up before 6 a.m., she could start making calls to the East Coast before her children woke.

Partisan warfare came naturally to her. When California Republicans complained about the gerrymandering of the Democrats' redistricting plan, she quipped that the GOP's complaints were "the squeals of sore losers." "If the Republicans wanted to draw the redistricting plan," she said, "they should have won the last election." One district, which Phil Burton carved out for his younger brother, John, was such an odd shape that some questioned whether it was really contiguous. "It is at low tide," Phil said.

Pelosi thought the party should hold its 1984 convention in San Francisco. She headed up the city's host committee to make its case to the Democratic

National Committee (as well as to local officials, such as Mayor Dianne Feinstein, who worried that a convention there would cost the city too much money). After Pelosi succeeded in landing the convention, the national party chairman, Charles Manatt, put her in charge of overseeing the thousands of convention delegates. This job consisted mainly of managing VIPs' disappointment, as locally prominent people from all over the country complained to her about their hotel or seat assignments. She had little sympathy, telling them about the faraway hotel and awful seats her father had had at past conventions. "Mrs. Pelosi, who oversees 10,000 volunteers, is a volunteer herself," the *New York Times* reported, "as are her eight honorary co-chairmen, the 300 members of the committee and most of her staff of 21."

Pelosi worried she was taking on too many responsibilities: the state party, the host committee, the delegate selection committee, all on top of her family and volunteer work. She asked her friend Lindy Boggs, a member of Congress from Louisiana, if she should give some of them up. (Boggs had gotten to Congress the way many women did in those days: she took over her husband's seat after he died.) "Darlin'," Boggs said, in her Southern drawl, "no man would ever, ever have that thought." Boggs said something else that Pelosi would never forget. It would eventually inspire the title of her memoir: "Nancy, know thy power." If someone gives you power, don't be bashful—*use it.*

Pelosi knew how to stick up for herself and her city. When a local TV journalist did a segment about the convention, she asked a male guest a series of political questions, then turned to Pelosi with a series of questions about parties. Pelosi waited until the commercial break, then turned to the reporter, eyes blazing. "Don't you ever do that to me again," she raged.

She also had no sympathy for fellow partisans who worried that the San Francisco counterculture, particularly the gay population, would make the party appear outside the mainstream. "Who are these gays? They're somebody's child, brother, sister, friend, that's who," she said. "This is a city of equal rights and all God's children." The city is the way it is, she said, "because other places out there don't practice what they preach."

At the convention, the Democrats nominated Walter Mondale, a liberal Minnesotan who'd served as Carter's vice president. As his running mate, Mondale picked New York congresswoman Geraldine Ferraro, the first woman ever to be named to a major-party ticket. To see her party choose an Italian American woman filled Pelosi with pride. But America didn't necessarily share her positive view. Republicans used the convention she'd organized to ridicule the "San Francisco Democrats," pinning the country's destabilization and turmoil on the city's roiling counterculture. They juxtaposed Reagan's sunny conservative vision with the rabble-rousing radicals whose calls for social and economic justice had led to out-of-control crime and high taxes. The Democrats were soundly drubbed in the 1984 election. Mondale and Ferraro won only thirteen electoral votes.

Pelosi was frustrated with her party. On the national level, she saw a complacent establishment that lacked the urgency to bring the party into the modern era, heal its internal divisions and make it competitive. Politics was changing, but the party's "databases" were still index cards kept in file cabinets. As she looked around, she didn't see anyone who seemed up to the task of pulling the party together and equipping it for the times.

She decided to run for chair of the Democratic National Committee. There were six other candidates, many of them longtime party players, five of them men—save for a few months in 1972, the national party had never had a woman chair. Pelosi believed she had the contacts, the strategy and the record she needed. She'd been officially involved in party politics for less than a decade, but she believed she had what it took to play at the highest level. She figured she could count on all the friends she'd made over the years—all the people she'd helped, all the favors she was owed, all the politicians for whom she'd raised money and made introductions. But it wasn't going to be that easy.

Pelosi attacked the campaign for party chair with her characteristic zeal. She rented an office in DC, hired a PR firm and budgeted $100,000 for the race. At a November 1984 meeting of the DNC, held in the U.S. Virgin Islands, she made her pitch to party insiders. She pointed to her record in California, a big state with a large and complicated Democratic Party. She touted her fund-raising ability, her modernizing vision and her technological savvy. As a westerner, she contended, she brought an individualistic, future-oriented outlook. She portrayed herself as the "outsider" up against the Washington establishment. The party's problem, she believed, wasn't that it was too liberal, but that it was too set in its ways.

"Can a 44-year-old mother of five with an Italian name from ultraliberal San Francisco persuade the good ol' boys in the South and Midwest that she can and should run their Democratic Party for the next four crucial years?" asked the *San Francisco Examiner*. Pelosi could sense that people didn't take her seriously. Delegates would say things like "We need firm leadership to take on the Republicans," and she knew they were really saying, "We need a man." People she considered allies, including some women, would ask her to her face who was going to take care of her children, or speculate that, as a liberal woman with an Italian name, she had a "Geraldine Ferraro problem."

The attacks stung. Paul urged her not to take them personally. (Her husband gamely supported her rising profile as a political player. When a reporter asked him about her DNC run, he explained, "I want to help her all I can because this is the first thing she has wanted to do for herself." The line surprised her—she didn't see it that way at all.) Then, one day, she got a call from her friend and supporter Mario Cuomo, the governor of New York and a fellow Italian Catholic liberal. One of Cuomo's aides had been talking to a top official at the AFL-CIO, which supported Pelosi's main opponent, a former Ted Kennedy aide named Paul Kirk. The official had supposedly referred to Pelosi as an "airhead."

She was apoplectic. At a breakfast with reporters in Washington (almost all of them men), she couldn't help herself. "Everywhere I go, they tell me, 'If you were a man this would have been over a long time ago—slam dunk,'" she vented. "I have all the credentials." She called out the AFL-CIO official, who denied the "airhead" remark, and she accused Kirk and his labor allies of engaging in a sexist smear campaign to discredit and tear her down. A few days later, recognizing that she didn't have the votes to win, she dropped out of the race. She couldn't resist a parting shot at her supposedly progressive party. "It is clear to me," she said, "many of you did not think the right message would go out if a woman was elected chairman of this party."

In later years, she would call the DNC race the most brutal, and educational, of her career. It taught her about the rough-and-tumble nature of politics, especially for a woman. The lesson would come in handy much sooner than she anticipated.

As a sort of consolation prize, Senator George Mitchell of Maine asked her to serve as finance chair of the Democratic Senatorial Campaign Committee, putting her in charge of national fund-raising for the party's Senate candidates in the 1986 midterm elections. Mitchell, who would go on to serve as Senate majority leader, had met Pelosi on fund-raising trips to California and was impressed with her intelligence and contacts. She excelled in the role and was, according to Mitchell, a key reason for the Democrats' banner year: they picked up eight Senate seats and regained the chamber's majority.

Mitchell was so impressed with Pelosi that, after the 1986 election, he urged her to run for governor of California. "You'd be a terrific candidate," he told her. He wasn't the first to make such a suggestion. Over the years, many of her professional politician friends, from Joe Alioto to Mario Cuomo, had encouraged her to get into the game. Mayor of San Francisco? Member of Congress? Over and over, she refused. She didn't consider herself a public person. She preferred being the strategist pulling the strings from backstage rather than the performer in the spotlight. For all her courage and confidence, she still saw herself, fundamentally, as a wife, a subordinate player, a helpmeet, an organizer. Sometimes she told people she could see herself being married to a politician but never being one herself.

Nothing, she was sure, could change her mind.

4

IN THE WEE HOURS OF SUNDAY, APRIL 10, 1983, FIFTY-SIX-YEAR-OLD
Phil Burton turned to his wife and said, "Jesus, Sala, I don't feel good."
Then he collapsed.

Burton's sudden death was untimely but not entirely unexpected. The
House's hard-charging liberal lion was known almost as much for his vices
as for his vision. He was a chain-smoker and a heavy drinker whose staff
knew not to bother him after a certain hour, when he would hole up in his
office downing Stolichnaya vodka. He was a glutton who ate every meal
as if it were his last, bits of food flying from his mouth and showering his
companions. He was a womanizer who, while he would never consider
leaving his wife of thirty years, had been seen on congressional trips with
a prostitute on each arm.

Friends had implored him to get in shape. Dolores Huerta, the farmworkers' advocate who invented the slogan "Sí, se puede," begged him to
see a doctor: "Phil," she pleaded, "you are the only person we have that
poor people can depend on." He ignored them all. He knew what the doctors would tell him, and he didn't want to hear it. And then it was too late.

People used to call Phil Burton the "fighting liberal." He was a savvy
and relentless legislative tactician with a passion for justice. His bullying
sometimes alienated colleagues—the drunken rages, the harangues, the
way he would get up close to people and jab his finger in their chest and
pepper them with spittle. Still, his antics tended to be portrayed as forceful and

masculine. "I like people whose balls roar when they see justice," he told one interviewer. Burton could slip an environmental provision so deep in a bill that no one noticed it, or bury a worker protection measure in an uncontroversial budget resolution. He was walking, talking proof that one determined person can make a difference in the House of Representatives and that knowing the process was the way to get things done.

Pelosi never served alongside Burton in Congress; he wasn't her mentor, though many would later call him that. (Observers were always assigning male influences to Pelosi, ignoring her when she protested that she'd actually learned more from her mother than her father, or more from motherhood than from Phil Burton.) But for anyone who believed government could be a force for good, no matter how imperfect its officeholders, Phil Burton was a totemic role model, and Pelosi counted both Phil and Sala as close friends. When it was campaign season, she could be found in their campaign office nearly every day, often with her children. Phil used to call her from Washington every Sunday night, and Sala also kept her counsel.

In 1976, with Democrats holding a longtime majority in the House, Burton, then in his sixth term, set his sights on becoming majority leader. It was the next step down from Speaker of the House, and whoever won it would likely be the next Speaker. Burton spent months gathering commitments from his colleagues and thought he had all he needed. He even spurned some potential supporters, telling them he already had the votes. But when the vote was held in December 1976, a secret ballot of the House Democratic Caucus, Burton fell short by a single vote. He was never the same after that near miss. Some colleagues whispered that he spent the rest of his years on Capitol Hill furiously trying to figure out who that one vote was. It haunted him to the day he died.

"DEATH OF A TITAN," blared the front page of the *Examiner*. Burton's death sent shock waves through California politics. For decades, he and his allies had exercised ruthless—critics would say authoritarian— control over the state Democratic Party, handpicking candidates for offices up and down the ballot and squashing dissent. At his San Francisco memorial service, attended by 117 members of Congress, one speaker quipped, "Half of you are here to pay your respects; the other half, to make sure he's really dead."

Sala, who had been at his side throughout his career, soon announced that she would run to fill the seat, which she won easily. (Phil's younger brother, John, had followed him into politics, but in January 1983, John resigned after five terms to seek treatment for his cocaine addiction. Before he died, Phil had tried to get Pelosi to run for the seat, but she declined.) Sala shared Phil's intense devotion to liberal causes—they had met at a Young Democrats meeting—but her personality was entirely different. She was as warm as Phil was prickly, as caring as he was callous, as discreet as he was expansive. A Polish-born Jew whose family had fled the Nazi occupation of Poland, Sala still spoke English with an accent, and she never learned to drive. When Sala was in DC, the oldest Pelosi daughter, Nancy Corinne, who was attending the now-defunct local women's college Mount Vernon, often drove her around in one of the family's old Jeeps. Pelosi saw how others sometimes underestimated Sala, but she knew that Sala's apparent shyness masked an inner strength.

Sala had been in DC only a few years when tragedy struck again. In early 1986, she was diagnosed with colon cancer, a lethal and fast-moving disease. For months, she managed to conceal her illness. In order to be reelected that November, she convinced her constituents that she was on the mend. But it wasn't true: doctors had given her no more than a year to live, and she was declining rapidly. By Christmas, Sala was so weak she could barely walk. Still, because another member of Congress who lived in a neighboring DC apartment might see her, she refused to call an ambulance. To get her to the hospital, her chief of staff, Judy Lemons, had to drape Sala's body over her shoulders and creep down the back stairs.

Sala was too weak to attend her own inauguration in January 1987, so the House passed a resolution allowing her to be sworn in at home. Shortly after, she called Pelosi and told her she wasn't going to run for reelection and wanted Pelosi to take her seat instead.

Pelosi's first instinct, once again, was to demur. "Come on," she told her friend, "you'll get better."

"You must promise me you will run," Sala insisted. "It's the only thing that will make me feel better."

"Fine, I'll run," Pelosi said, "but you're going to get better."

Pelosi asked Paul what he thought about her running for Congress. He told her she should do it only if she really wanted to, not because other people wanted her to. He also said he was sure that, if she ran, she could win.

Four of the five Pelosi children had left for college, and the fifth, Alexandra, was about to start her senior year of high school in San Francisco. Alexandra was the rebel of the family, mouthy and free-spirited, often dressing in thrift store clothes and ratty high-top sneakers.

"Alexandra," Pelosi said one day, "Mommy has an opportunity to run for Congress. But if you don't want me to do it, I won't."

Alexandra gave her mother a classic teenage girl's sneer. "Mother," she sighed, "get a life."

The colloquialism, which was new to Pelosi, touched on a harsh truth: for all Pelosi's trials, for all her hard work, she had not really had her own life up to this point. The power she wielded within the household was limited; her labor was invisible, her legacy minimal. Even her political work had been essentially just a rich housewife's dabbling. At the age of forty-seven, she found that it was, indeed, time for her to get a life. Little did anyone, least of all her, know how consequential her second life would be.

❖ ❖ ❖

In December 1986, Judy Lemons drove Sala Burton to the George Washington University Hospital for the last time, checking her in under a pseudonym. She called John Burton, Sala's brother-in-law, from a pay phone to tell him the end was near. Burton gathered Pelosi and a couple of other close confidants, and in January they flew to Washington through a raging snowstorm.

They gathered around Sala's hospital bed as she made her dramatic decree. "Nancy is smart, she's tough, she's operational, she's good on the issues," Sala told them. Then she asked everyone but Pelosi to leave the room. "You've got to be ready," she told her friend. "Are you ready?"

Pelosi said she was.

When they landed back in San Francisco, John read a statement to the press from Sala endorsing Pelosi to replace her. Sala died five days later. She was sixty-one.

Operational—that was also the word Phil Burton had always used for Pelosi. It was his highest compliment. It meant you were committed to getting things done above all, and had the ingenuity to figure out a way to do it. Everything was about results. Phil would sometimes go up to people after 5 p.m. and ask, "What did you do to pay the rent today?" He saw in Pelosi someone who understood the game and kept her eyes on the prize. To this day, there is probably no better word for Nancy Pelosi, and no better way to understand her, than Phil Burton's one-word description.

But when John Burton walked out of Sala's hospital room, he wasn't so sure. When Sala first told him she wanted "Nancy" to replace her, he thought she meant a different Nancy. When he found out it was Nancy *Pelosi*, he thought: *Really? Her?* But Sala insisted, so he went along. And when Pelosi started her campaign he agreed to help.

A special election was scheduled for June, with a primary to be held in April. The deathbed endorsement had created some goodwill for Pelosi, but it didn't clear the field. (Someone once compared California Democratic politics to a crowded parking lot, where cars circle and circle in the hope a spot will open up.) There were thirteen other candidates, including not only several Democrats and Republicans but also candidates from the Humanist Party, the Peace and Freedom Party and the Socialist Workers Party. (Welcome to San Francisco!) Under the rules of the special election, all fourteen candidates would be on the same primary ballot, and if none got more than 50 percent, the top vote-getter from each party would advance to a general election. Given the district's strong Democratic leanings, whichever Democrat came in first in the primary was almost guaranteed to win the seat.

But the primary field was formidable. Four of her opponents were members of the Board of Supervisors, well known to their constituents. The biggest names in labor, the environmental community and the gay community were all committed to other candidates. The once-robust Burton political machine had gone fallow from disuse. She would have to be creative and build her own coalition.

Pelosi launched her campaign with an anodyne speech at a union hall. "I believe the number one issue in the upcoming campaign will be who can accomplish the most for San Francisco," she declared. She dove into the six-week campaign with her customary intensity. She was up at 5 a.m. to canvass commuters at bus stops; she was up late at night conferring with her consultants. Her fund-raising prowess and personal wealth enabled her to spend one million dollars on the campaign (a quarter of that out of her own pocket), which was more than the rest of the field combined. John Burton soon became a believer. "Sala was brilliant," he remarked. "She endorsed someone who could raise a million dollars in six weeks!"

There was one complication: though the district covered four-fifths of the city of San Francisco, the Pelosis' house wasn't in it. Congressional candidates aren't legally required to live within the shifting boundaries of their districts, but the idea of an outsider seeking to represent them, even from just a few blocks over the line, tends to rankle voters. So Paul Pelosi went shopping for a new house. He soon found one, a stately brick mansion in the wealthy enclave of Pacific Heights, only about a mile from Presidio Terrace. One day, Pelosi came home to Presidio Terrace from a long day of campaigning only to be greeted by a surprise party in an empty house: everything but the piano had been moved. The party, naturally, doubled as a fund-raiser.

True to his warm, loyal and generally nonpolitical nature, Paul vowed to do everything possible to support his wife—he figured, after her years of domestic labor, it was her turn to shine in the world. He was also conscious that any involvement on his part was likely to be misinterpreted by people who would reflexively assume the man was in charge. "I've made a conscious effort to not give the appearance of being involved in her political career," he told a reporter later. "People should realize that she's the one." Indeed, Pelosi would spend much of her career trying to convince people that she and no one else owned her accomplishments, that they weren't attributable to her father or her husband or a male colleague or staffer. For better or worse, it was all her—her decisions, her ideas, her executing her own plan.

Pelosi's most formidable rival would be Harry Britt, a gay socialist former aide to Harvey Milk who had succeeded Milk on the Board of Supervisors. Britt campaigned as a historic candidate for the increasingly vocal gay community. The AIDS crisis was at its height, ravaging the community— San Francisco was seeing hundreds of deaths from the disease every year. Britt had a chance to be the first openly gay man elected to Congress in history, at a time when President Reagan refused even to acknowledge the disease. It was time, Britt contended, for gay men and women to be represented by one of their own, not merely a sympathetic outsider. "We need a leader, not just a friend," Britt's mailers to the gay community exhorted. "Harvey Milk taught us not to depend on others."

Clint Reilly, a well-known local consultant, initially turned down an offer to be Pelosi's lead strategist, because Britt had also offered Reilly a job, and Reilly thought Britt had a better chance to win. But Pelosi worked her connections, and soon Leo McCarthy and Jerry Brown leaned on Reilly to work for Pelosi instead. Soon after that, Reilly was on a plane when the inspiration for Pelosi's campaign slogan struck: "A Voice that Will Be Heard."

The campaign's adman was incredulous. "You want to run a woman who never held elective office as a candidate with connections and stature and effectiveness?" he asked.

"That's exactly right," Reilly told him.

Before long, the word *HEARD*, in giant letters, loomed over the city skyline on so many billboards that people joked about it. Pelosi's superior funding even allowed her to run a television ad, rare for a congressional campaign in those days. Over a soundtrack of the "Hallelujah Chorus" and scenes of the Golden Gate Bridge, the Capitol, and missiles being fired, a narrator intoned, "Nancy Pelosi: A voice that will be heard."

Britt countered with mailers calling Pelosi a "party girl" and "dilettante." The implication, that she was an unserious, entitled rich lady only playing at politics, would dog her throughout her career. A whisper campaign suggested that Sala's endorsement had been exaggerated or even manufactured. One brochure read, "Nancy Pelosi has spent her lifetime doing favors for the rich and powerful. Now they're returning the favor." Another accused "oil companies, highrise developers, Washington lobbyists and other special interests" of "pouring a million dollars into San Francisco to elect their candidate to Congress."

When Pelosi's friends called her, outraged, to tell her about nasty things they'd seen and heard, she lashed out at them: *Don't waste my time weighing me down with this negativity! If you want me to win, why don't you go out and recruit more volunteers, or raise more money for the campaign?* Once, when a group of activists was shockingly rude to Pelosi's face, John Burton was outraged on her behalf, but she was unruffled. Turning to Burton, she said calmly, "Someday they will realize just how insignificant they are."

In public appearances, Pelosi was attractive but stiff. Her impeccable style and striking looks led some to compare her to Audrey Hepburn, but she was still uneasy speaking in public. Her speeches tended to be halting and mechanical. But she knew that just showing up was half the battle—in six weeks, she made more than two hundred campaign appearances. Her mother-in-law instructed her on how to behave at bingo games in Catholic churches: introduce yourself, don't talk too long, make sure to say the date of the election, and "sweeten the pot" by dropping some cash in the prize pool on your way out.

Pelosi chafed at the constant attention to her hair and clothes, the questions (even from devoted women's libbers) about who was taking care of her children. But she didn't let her irritation show. "My children are grown and taking care of me," she'd reply, with a gleaming smile. She could be appealingly playful, and self-aware. One Saturday morning at her campaign headquarters, she gave a pep talk to the volunteers who were preparing to go out canvassing, carrying ironing boards to use as makeshift tables. "I have to admit, I didn't really know what an ironing board was," Pelosi told the volunteers, sounding every bit the clueless rich lady who'd never done a lick of housework. She paused for a beat, then added: "I'm a mother of five. All I do is take the clothes out of the dryer, shake them off and put them on the kids!" One source of strength the other candidates didn't see coming was the volunteers Pelosi had recruited for the 1984 Democratic National Convention. There were hundreds of them, they were fanatically loyal to her and she'd kept track of them all.

Despite her opponents' portrayal of her as an aloof, imperious elitist, Pelosi had an amazing ability to seem at home wherever she was. At one point, her daughter Jacqueline happened upon Pelosi working a room of advocates for the transgendered and homeless, treating each one with the same solicitous engagement she might have given a high-dollar donor at a fund-raiser. *What is Mom doing here?* Jacqueline thought. Pelosi had been raised to listen to people from every walk of life. Her father's "favor file" taught her that a politician's job is to help anyone who asks. Her faith had instilled in her a deep belief in the humanity of all people—and her Baltimore political family had taught her that every vote counted the same.

The candidates, all fourteen of them, met for a single debate, which devolved into a free-for-all. A Republican called for bombing Nicaragua "out of existence." The Peace and Freedom Party candidate interrupted the proceedings to yell, "This show is a fraud!" and to demand that the candidates discuss impeaching President Reagan. After he was ejected by security, one of the other Democrats attacked Pelosi for using her wealth to fund her campaign. Pelosi fired back: "I don't think you have to be sick to be a doctor, or poor to understand the problems of the poor."

Her campaign knew she would lose the gay vote to Britt. But by how much? If she could get one-fourth or one-fifth of the gay vote, they figured, she could win. Two of the city's prominent lesbian activists stood with her at her campaign announcement, while Jim Hormel, a major figure in the gay activist community and cofounder of the Human Rights Campaign, agreed to serve as a co-chair of the campaign. It was a difficult choice, but he'd worked with her on party matters and been impressed by her effectiveness. Nevertheless, some of Hormel's fellow gay activists didn't speak to him for years afterward. (An heir to the Hormel Foods fortune, Hormel would go on to serve briefly as President Clinton's ambassador to Luxembourg, making him America's first openly gay ambassador. In 2014, Pelosi officiated at his wedding to his longtime partner.)

The campaign targeted different messages to different demographics in the diverse city. John Burton used his union connections to court labor leaders, cutting into another Britt advantage. Pelosi's mother-in-law recruited her Italian American friends to a "Nana brigade" that sent postcards to the district's eight thousand Italian American voters. Mailers touting Pelosi's support for gay rights were sent to any home where two unrelated men of similar age lived together. Brochures sent to the city's wealthier, more conservative West Side featured a very different message: "The individual tax burden is too high," they proclaimed. "We need a representative who will fight all efforts to raise the personal income tax." These flyers, targeted at Republicans, were Paul's idea. Many of her brochures showed Pelosi surrounded by her big, gleaming, unmistakably heterosexual family, an image some Britt supporters saw as a subtle shot at his sexual orientation, though her campaign never openly attacked him for it.

Pelosi believed the campaign wasn't going to be won or lost in a televised debate or with a clever ad. It was going to be won in the streets, just like her father's mayoral campaigns had been. She remembered her father and brother going up to the roof of their house at 5 a.m. on Election Day, watching the headlights from every direction converge on the nearby campaign headquarters, where precinct workers were going to pick up their get-out-the-vote packets. Just like he had, Pelosi broke down the district into wards, precincts and blocks, with a volunteer captain in charge of every piece of territory. They canvassed relentlessly, constantly updating their lists of supporters. One week before the election, the campaign calculated that Pelosi was likely to win, but if Britt maximized his supporters' turnout and hers failed to meet expectations she could lose by 1,000 votes. So she set out to find 5,000 more Pelosi voters in the last week.

In the final days of Pelosi's first run, her father sent her brother Tommy out to San Francisco from Baltimore to check on her. Tommy took careful stock of the campaign's precinct maps, lists of volunteers and databases of voters. He called their father and reported, "She's better organized than we ever were."

In the end, Pelosi got 36 percent of the vote to Britt's 32 percent—a lead of 3,990 votes out of 105,000 cast. Her father, though obviously proud, was astonished she'd pulled it off. She'd managed to win an election thousands of miles from Baltimore, without using the D'Alesandro name, in a place where her pedigree wouldn't have meant anything anyway. She became the first daughter in history to succeed her father in Congress. In the ensuing decades, observers would reflexively attribute Pelosi's electoral success to her father's influence.

But she knew she had done it herself.

5

HAVING GONE STRAIGHT FROM COLLEGE TO RAISING A FAMILY, PELOSI had never lived by herself before she moved to Washington to serve in Congress in June 1987. For eighteen years in San Francisco, she'd presided over a big, lively household: children, guests, parties—it was rarely quiet and never empty. Now she was on her own. John Burton was worried about her: he thought she would be lonely. But she wasn't worried. She relished the chance to be independent at long last. She thought of herself as a bird. While her brothers had all stayed in Baltimore, she'd always been fated to fly away to fulfill her destiny.

Besides, it wasn't as if she'd really be alone. Her mother and father and brothers were an hour up the road, in Baltimore. Three of her children—Christine, Jacqueline and Paul Jr.—were in DC, attending college at Georgetown University. She suggested that they could rent a big house and all live together, an idea that appealed to them about as much as it would to most college students faced with having their mother as a roommate—that is, not at all. Instead, the kids said they would prefer to forget they were in the same city. So Pelosi rented an apartment a couple of miles from the Capitol. She would fly back to California nearly every weekend, to see Paul and Alexandra and her constituents. Sometimes it was hard to leave and go back to DC. But then she would remind herself that she might see her three children there.

She landed in Washington a few days after her election victory. Her office, befitting her bottom rank in seniority, was a small one inconveniently located on the fifth floor of the Longworth House Office Building, with a view of the highway and no reception area. On June 9, 1987, Pelosi held up her hand on the floor of the House and swore to uphold the Constitution.

Her husband, children and mother watched from the Visitors' Gallery, while her wheelchair-bound eighty-three-year-old father joined her on the floor—a privilege afforded all former members of Congress. (Numerous times during the campaign, he'd reminded her that because of that privilege he wouldn't need a ticket to her swearing-in.) Old Tommy wore a dark jacket and a white pocket handkerchief and beamed as his baby girl raised her hand before Speaker Jim Wright. Wheeling himself away, he beckoned to the Speaker and whispered in his ear the highest recommendation a congressman can make: *She ought to be on Appropriations.* The Appropriations Committee was the powerful and coveted assignment that dictated how the federal government's money would be distributed. Old Tommy had been an appropriator during his days in Congress. But he would never see his daughter rise to that position. Just a couple of months after she was sworn in, he was dead at eighty-four.

Pelosi had run as "A Voice that Will Be Heard," but the first thing everyone told her to do was keep quiet. George Miller, a congressman from a neighboring Northern California district who quickly became a close friend, said, "There's a free hedge-clipping service in Washington"— meaning the more you stuck your head up, the more likely you were to get cut down. Pelosi vowed to keep her head down. After being sworn in, she obediently took her seat. But then, to her surprise, the presiding officer called on her to speak.

She hurried to the dais, nervous and unprepared. She paid tribute to San Francisco and the Burtons, to her family and constituents, to "making government work for people." Her district, she said, prided itself on "its leadership for peace, for environmental protection, for equal rights, for rights of individual freedom." And she added: "Now we must take the leadership, of course, in the crisis of AIDS."

In later mythmaking, this maiden speech would be condensed into a brazen declaration: "My name is Nancy Pelosi, and I'm here to fight AIDS!"

But in its real, extended form, the speech was bold enough. Pleased with herself, she went to take her seat, only to be greeted by fellow members' horrified stares. Had she really just said that out loud? Didn't she know how it would look? Did she really want to associate the Democratic Party, and her own political brand, with *those people*?

But Pelosi had spent her campaign insisting she could advocate for San Francisco's gay community, and she was determined to prove it. It was a matter of politics, of course—both the crass matter of getting reelected and the democratic duty to speak for one's district. (One of her favorite aphorisms, repeated to newer colleagues to this day: "Representative is not just your title. It's your job description.") But her commitment to the issue was also a function of the firm and unvarying moral clarity that had always been part of her makeup. The Catholic Church's leadership might not share her view of gay rights, but she believed she knew better. "I was brought up to believe that all people are God's children, and the last time I checked, that included gay people," she told an interviewer.

◇ ◇ ◇

Pelosi had inherited most of Sala Burton's congressional staff, and they weren't sure what to expect from this well-dressed, middle-aged woman. Pelosi wore her brown hair down past her shoulders in those days, with a hank of bangs parted to the side, and always wore stockings and heels. She dressed in Armani suits, the power uniform of the 1980s—shoulder pads and all. She seemed so elegant, so glamorous, the staffers whispered to one another. But did she have any business being in Congress?

With her expensive clothes, frozen smile and tentative public manner, it was easy to write her off as a lightweight. But anyone tempted to patronize her would be quickly corrected. One of her campaign staffers had been Fred Ross Jr., a former farmworkers' organizer who went on to lead a group called Neighbor to Neighbor, which was calling for a human rights boycott of Salvadoran coffee. One day, an invitation came across Pelosi's desk to a reception on Capitol Hill hosted by the megacorporation Procter & Gamble, owner of Folgers, which was still sourcing its coffee from El Salvador. She decided to go, and invited Ross to join her.

The CEO of Procter & Gamble bounded up to her. "Miss Pelosi!" he gushed. The company had just put out a new perfume, he said, and she would want to be the first to try it.

Pelosi turned to him coolly, wearing a devastating smile. "I want you to meet my good friend and the leader of Neighbor to Neighbor—you've probably heard of him—Fred Ross," she replied.

The CEO blanched. He knew exactly who Ross was. "I must say," he stammered to Ross, "I find some of your tactics reprehensible."

As he marched away, Pelosi turned to Ross. "*Reprehensible,*" she said innocently. "I wonder if that's the name of the fragrance he was talking about?"

It was typical Pelosi: ballsy, confrontational, even bitchy. But the story has a coda that's even more characteristic: her office followed up with the CEO afterward and brokered a meeting between Folgers reps and Ross, which eventually led the company to agree to stop buying Salvadoran coffee. She followed through. She got it done.

Pelosi's staff soon realized she was anything but an airhead. She barely slept and hardly ever seemed to eat, except for chocolate. Liberated from the family responsibilities that had consumed her for so long, she seemed to do nothing but work, with a maniacal level of energy. Behind her back, they called her "the Energizer Bunny." Her curiosity about every policy issue was intense and earnest. She was determined to know everything about everything, to always be the most prepared, so that no one would ever be able to say she was in over her head. Pelosi would get up at 5:30 a.m., check the stoop for newspapers and then get frustrated when they weren't there yet.

Still, some worldly matters weren't her strong suit. She was always losing things—a purse, a wallet, a piece of expensive jewelry. Determined to respond personally to all her mail from constituents, she would stuff it in her carry-on bag to work on during one of her cross-country flights, but she never seemed to get through it all; some letters traveled with her for thousands and thousands of miles. In Washington, many of her colleagues didn't have a car, so she would give them rides, but they quickly learned they were taking their lives in their hands. Pelosi would be talking in the car, engaged in conversation, looking back at her passengers, as they yelled, "Keep your eyes on the road!" "But we always managed to get there," recalled then-Congressman Leon Panetta, "sometimes at great risk."

❖ ❖ ❖

Nationally, conservatism was on the march. Ronald Reagan was in his second term as president. The country had turned its back on the big-government visions of FDR and LBJ, fueled by a backlash to the excesses of '70s counterculture and President Carter's ineffectiveness. Yet Democrats still controlled the House. At the time Pelosi entered, Democrats had held it for thirty-two consecutive years, and fifty of the last fifty-four years; Republicans had held it for just two terms since 1933. It was a majority so large and durable that Washington insiders regarded it as unchangeable, like the law of gravity. Presidents came and went, but in the House the Democrats reigned.

Literally from birth, Pelosi's life had revolved around the Democratic Party. Her family, she often said, had three unswerving allegiances: to their Church, to their country, and to the Democratic Party. It was the party, more than any cause or movement, that was the vehicle for her youthful activism, and it was through the party that she found her second career as a fund-raiser, party official and, finally, politician. And it was to the party that she would devote the storied legislative career that was to come: understanding its nuances and factions, guiding its philosophy and direction, leading it into a new era in which it would, more and more, echo her personal politics.

But the Democratic Party that held the House in those years was far from homogenous and not necessarily liberal. Pelosi arrived right in the middle of the great partisan realignment that would define twentieth-century American politics, as the party that had once fought for slavery transformed into the party of civil rights and the welfare state. It didn't happen overnight. An oft-repeated quote has LBJ, upon signing the Civil Rights Act, muttering prophetically to an aide that the Democrats had just signed away the South for a generation or more. But the evidence he actually said that is slim, and in fact the process was much more gradual. It would be many decades after LBJ left office before the GOP succeeded in wiping out Democrats' dominance in the South. Nixon in the 1970s and Reagan in the '80s succeeded in using racial provocation to swing some Deep South states, but the majority of white southerners were still Democrats.

The Democratic Party, then, was an odd, disjointed mix of conservative southern Democrats and liberal northerners, along with, thanks to the Voting Rights Act, an increasing number of African American representatives from majority-minority districts. In Pelosi's father's day, liberal urban Catholics like Thomas D'Alesandro served alongside conservative southerners like Edward Hébert of New Orleans, who opposed desegregation and signed the Southern Manifesto. (In an infamous 1973 incident, Hébert, the powerful chairman of the House Armed Services Committee, forced two House freshmen appointed to the committee, Patricia Schroeder of Colorado and Ron Dellums of California, a black man, to share a single chair. He said he didn't appreciate having "a girl and a black" forced upon him. Hébert subsequently lost his chairmanship in a revolt of the liberal "Watergate babies" elected in 1974, led by none other than Phillip Burton.) Progressive accomplishments such as civil rights drew support from a cross-partisan group of Republican and Democratic racial liberals, even as many in LBJ's own party opposed his signature legislation. The "bipartisanship" so many Americans now pine for wasn't a function of politicians of different ideologies working together so much as it was politicians of similar ideologies belonging to different political parties. Indeed, in the 1960s, some reformers complained that there wasn't *enough* partisanship in Congress, depriving voters of clear policy choices.

So, in 1987, the congressional party that Pelosi joined was a feuding family that sometimes held together and sometimes didn't. The legendary Tip O'Neill had recently retired as Speaker, handing the gavel to Jim Wright, the congressman who had defeated Phil Burton for majority leader in 1976. An affable, energetic Texan, Wright saw his power attenuated by his deference to the House's influential committees, whose chairmen, the Old Bulls, had the clout to decide whose bills lived and whose died. They carved out deals, sometimes in literal smoke-filled rooms, and they padded bills with pork barrel spending and mischievous fine print. (Smoking, in fact, was allowed in the Capitol until Speaker Pelosi banned it in 2007.) The Speaker had only as much power as the chairmen allowed.

But Congress was changing. In 1979, C-SPAN was founded, broadcasting the previously little-seen proceedings on the floor to whoever wanted to tune in—and creating an opening for grandstanding by backbenchers like Newt Gingrich, who could give passionate orations to an otherwise empty chamber and have them broadcast nationwide as if he were a great and important statesman. Shortly thereafter, in 1980, CNN was founded, the country's first twenty-four-hour all-news cable channel, beginning the evolution of the news cycle and media environment to more minute-by-minute, incremental coverage. The louche and rowdy boys' club of Congress, where the nation's business was conducted by an insular, largely anonymous cabal, was beginning to open up—to women, to minorities and to the public eye.

✧ ✧ ✧

Pelosi had been in the House for only a few months when, one day, while sitting in her office with the floor action playing on a television tuned to C-SPAN, she heard something that caught her attention. A Republican member of Congress—from California, no less!—was ranting on the floor about the "gay lifestyle," calling HIV God's punishment for sin. Pelosi called her friend Barney Frank, who had become one of two openly gay congressmen when he came out earlier that year. Wasn't it awful? she said. Couldn't anything be done?

"Welcome to Congress, Nancy," the gruff, curmudgeonly Frank replied. "Don't complain to me about it. Go out on the floor and respond to him."

By 1987, AIDS had killed more than twenty thousand people, nearly 10 percent of them in San Francisco alone. The city had closed all its bathhouses in 1984, but the plague raged on. Pelosi had gone to innumerable funerals and memorial services for friends—many of them men in the prime of life. AIDS had even hit closer to home. In 1986, the younger sister of her sister-in-law Margie, Tommy's wife, had died of the disease in Maryland.

Yet President Reagan's attitude toward the deadly epidemic seemed to be one of indifference. The first time the White House press secretary was asked about AIDS, in 1982, he turned it into a joke and mocked the reporter who had brought it up. Reagan hadn't uttered the name of the virus until 1985, years after the first cases were widely reported, and didn't propose any measures to address it until a speech in April 1987 in which he called it "public enemy number one." Prejudice and paranoia were rampant, and there was little help for victims. Gay men were losing their jobs, health insurance and homes. But Congress wasn't necessarily focused on their plight. One Republican bill, introduced by Senator Jesse Helms of North Carolina, sought to prevent the Centers for Disease Control from funding any programs that "promote, encourage or condone homosexual activities."

The fight against AIDS would be Pelosi's first major crusade in Congress. It was a battle that would presage many of her skills as a lawmaker, while teaching her key lessons about how to be effective. She wasn't alone in the fight—other liberal lawmakers, notably her California colleague Henry Waxman, were already vocal on the issue before she arrived. But Pelosi attacked the crisis with a singular mix of moral urgency, doggedness, creativity and drive. It was, she realized, both a health issue and a civil rights issue. She couldn't cure the virus or end prejudice, but she wasn't given to thinking about what couldn't be done. The Nancy Pelosi way, when she was confronted with a problem, was to figure out something that could be done about it, however seemingly trivial or impossible, and then figure out a way to do it.

And so she started with the AIDS Quilt. Formally known as the NAMES Project AIDS Memorial Quilt, it was the brainchild of one of her constituents, a leader in the San Francisco gay community. The idea was that people all over the country would sew individual quilt squares to pay tribute to loved ones who had died of the disease, and then all the squares would be stitched together. The sheer size of the quilt, and the variety of styles and stories represented by its squares, would be a powerful symbol of the plague's scale. It would command attention and memorialize the victims, many of whom had been denied proper funerals, because either their families were ashamed or funeral homes refused to handle their remains.

When the organizers first approached her congressional office, Pelosi was skeptical; few people, including her, knew how to sew anymore, she reasoned. But once she made up her mind to help, she was all in. The first version of the quilt had 1,920 squares and was the size of a football field. Organizers wanted to display it on the National Mall, so Pelosi put in a request to the National Park Service. The government came back with a barrage of logistical objections that she suspected were disingenuous, meant to throw up bureaucratic obstacles to something the agency didn't want to allow, out of small-mindedness or whatever else. Among other things, the agency insisted that the quilt would kill the grass.

Pelosi was not going to take no for an answer. The Park Service had suggested, almost facetiously, a ridiculous-sounding potential solution: lifting up the quilt every twenty minutes, for the entire weekend. She set about calling their bluff. The activists, some two hundred thousand from around the country who marched on Washington, dutifully surrounded the quilt and raised it off the ground every twenty minutes on the dot. Pelosi joined a group of politicians and celebrities who read every name out loud, to tears from the audience. The quilt quickly became an emotional touchstone of the movement.

But Pelosi knew that the quilt, however moving, was just a symbol. To really help people, you needed money. She might not have had any previous political experience, but thanks to her fund-raising, activism and party work, she had some unusual resources at her disposal. She estimated that by the time she arrived in Washington, she knew two hundred representatives and senators personally, a bigger network than many members who'd been there for years. And, in many cases, they owed her a favor. Right away, this network of contacts came in handy: some AIDS-related legislation was stalled because, even though it had broad support, it was up to the powerful committee chairmen to decide whether to bring it to the floor to a vote. In a move that would be unthinkable for any other freshman, Pelosi called the eighty-eight-year-old chairman of the Rules Committee, Claude Pepper, who'd served alongside her father in the 1930s. He did as she asked and put two AIDS bills on the floor.

Despite her father's exhortation, Pelosi had not immediately gotten a seat on the Appropriations Committee—freshmen almost never did— and the first time she sought one, in a caucus election in 1990, she was defeated. The second time, a few months later, she won, and immediately set to work finding little pieces of the federal budget she could carve out for the purpose of helping AIDS victims. In her first major legislative victory, she created a program to provide housing assistance to victims of AIDS. She helped fund research into an AIDS vaccine and worked to extend Medicaid to AIDS victims; she introduced provisions to make existing federal programs available, such as an amendment to the 1985 Consolidated Omnibus Budget Reconciliation Act (COBRA) that would let AIDS patients maintain insurance coverage and an adjustment to Social Security disability and survivor benefits. She buried herself deep in health care regulations, seeking out minor tweaks that could have a major impact, even if her contribution went unnoticed. She spoke out in favor of antidiscrimination legislation and needle exchange programs, bashing Republicans as anti-science—the "Flat Earth Society," she called them—when they disagreed.

Pelosi intuitively grasped that a representative's job is about more than writing and passing legislation. It's also about calling attention to issues and changing public perception. Misinformation and fearmongering about the epidemic were pervasive, and many in Washington saw the disease as someone else's problem. She invited colleagues to her district for "field hearings" to force them to confront the ravages of the epidemic. In 1986, the U.S. Surgeon General had issued a thirty-six-page report setting out the facts, including what did and did not constitute safe sex, and that people could not contract the virus by sitting on toilets, hugging or being sneezed on. Pelosi had the report, in its entirety, sent to every resident of her district. The following year, the Reagan administration took a page from her playbook and ordered the report be mailed to more than one hundred million households.

Pelosi and her congressional allies' biggest legislative effort on AIDS was a bill named for Ryan White, a teenager in Indiana who had been expelled from his public high school after being diagnosed with the disease. A hemophiliac, Ryan was just thirteen when he fell ill after a blood transfusion. He was diagnosed with AIDS and given six months to live. Pelosi coauthored the Ryan White Act to create a federal fund specifically dedicated to the medical care of AIDS patients, which was bankrupting families and governments. The administration of George H. W. Bush resisted on fiscal grounds. Pelosi proposed that instead of granting an entitlement directly to victims, the bill could make grants to states and cities dealing with the epidemic. Remarkably, after years of dogged effort, the legislation passed and was signed into law by the Republican president. Ryan surprised his doctors and lived for five years, dying just a few months before the law with his name on it was signed. To date, the law has distributed more than twenty billion dollars and provided services to more than half a million people.

In January 1988, just a few months into Pelosi's tenure, the *San Francisco Chronicle* suggested that the new congresswoman who'd campaigned on her "voice" wasn't making much noise in Washington, describing her as a "backbencher" whose caution was holding her back. "I want to get a job done," she snapped back. "I'm not here to grandstand."

6

THERE WAS ONE OBVIOUS DIFFERENCE BETWEEN REPRESENTATIVE Pelosi, D-CA, and the typical member of Congress: she was a woman. There were just 23 other women in the 435-member House, 12 Democrats and 11 Republicans. It had been only a few months since Barbara Mikulski, a fellow Baltimorean who had attended the same high school as Pelosi, became the first Democratic woman ever elected to the Senate without being preceded in Congress by her husband. No prominent committees were chaired by women. There was not even a women's bathroom near the floor of the House, and it would be several years before women were allowed to wear pants on the floor. To the men who ran the place, the few female members were a rounding error, an anomaly—a curiosity.

The women in Congress had to be tough by definition to have gotten there. They were accustomed to fighting for respect. A couple of years prior to Pelosi's arrival, they'd waged a prolonged and vocal campaign to get women allowed into the House gym, singing, "Can't Everybody Use Your Gym?" to the tune of "Has Anybody Seen My Gal?" until their male colleagues reluctantly relented. Pat Schroeder, the pioneering Coloradan, authored the Family and Medical Leave Act that forced employers to grant unpaid leave to new parents and family caregivers—but when Bill Clinton signed her bill into law in 1993, it was with an all-male group of congressmen. (Quippy and indomitable, Schroeder once told the Pentagon officials testifying before her in a committee hearing that if they were women, they'd always be pregnant, because they never said no. Annoyed at Tip O'Neill's persistent habit of introducing her by recounting her husband's accomplishments, she once introduced the Speaker at a DC event as "Millie O'Neill's husband"—he got the picture.)

The humiliations were constant. Once, when Pelosi's friend Barbara Boxer, who represented a neighboring district—they were constantly being mistaken for each other—was speaking at a committee hearing, a colleague spoke next: "I want to associate myself with the remarks of the gentlelady from California," he said, following the protocol for amplifying statements. Then he added, "As a matter of fact, I'd like to *associate* with the gentlelady." Another member echoed the suggestive remark, and the two men chortled as Boxer, sitting right there, silently fumed.

The men were always winking, cracking cross jokes, laughing at them. Many cheated on their wives back home with an everybody-does-it, what's-the-problem-sweetheart brazenness. A prominent woman lobbyist recalls being asked, in the mid-1980s, to deliver a message to a couple of senators who were lunching at a restaurant, and being directed to a private room—where the two men were screwing their mistresses right out in the open. Behavior that would today be considered sexual harassment was rampant and unremarkable—the concept itself was a new one. It was the women's job to know which of the men surrounding them were the grabbers, the gropers, the ones you didn't get into an elevator with. In newspaper comics, the image of the boss chasing his secretary around the desk was still reliably good for a laugh.

Women had tried to get into leadership positions, but they never succeeded in winning any post but caucus secretary. Since caucus elections are conducted by secret ballot, the women who ran and lost never knew which of their colleagues had voted against them. When Pelosi's friend Barbara Kennelly ran for chair of the House Democratic Caucus in 1989, she thought she had secured enough commitments from her colleagues to win. But in the privacy of the secret ballot, they abandoned her and elected Steny Hoyer instead. "The boys don't really want us there," Schroeder told an interviewer. "They just didn't want to tell you that." The women were a curiosity, until they became a threat.

In 1985, Mary Rose Oakar of Ohio managed to get elected vice chair of the caucus, but she noticed that O'Neill never invited her to congressional meetings at the White House. When she demanded that he include her, he gave her a seat at the back of the room. She promptly walked out, refusing to return until she got a seat at the table. Vice chair of the caucus would be the highest leadership position any woman would occupy until Pelosi was elected whip in 2001.

Pelosi soon found her people: a group of Democratic lawmakers who met for dinner on Tuesday nights. At first, like most things in Washington, it was all men. Then Boxer insisted on joining, and by the time Pelosi arrived, the Tuesday night dinner gang was coed. Often they met at the "Animal House," the squalid Capitol Hill row house owned by George Miller, a congressman from a Northern California district who would become one of Pelosi's closest confidants. Other times they'd go to a restaurant—the greasy spoon Chinese joint Hunan Dynasty was a go-to. Sometimes a lobbyist would be invited along as a "hitter," to foot the bill, something that was common in those days but is illegal now, thanks to lobbying reforms Pelosi spearheaded decades later.

Enjoyable as they were, these evenings weren't altogether frivolous. The members built alliances and strategized. In between swapping stories and engaging in good-natured ribbing, they would seek one another's ideas about legislation and tactics. Boxer's contacts in the dinner group, for example, were key to her effort to reform the procurement process at the Pentagon. But Pelosi noticed that while the women were included in the group, their opinions were rarely sought. Once she noticed it, it nagged at her. Wouldn't the men ever turn to her or her female colleagues and ask, "What do you think?" But they never did.

The omission became particularly galling one day when the men began discussing their experiences with childbirth. Apparently, it had been quite traumatic for some of them. Representative Marty Russo of Illinois recalled that he had had a camera and was supposed to photograph the blessed event, but all he could think was "Oh God, get me out of here!" Another congressman jumped in: "Shit, I thought I was going to faint!" The women, disbelieving, shot one another significant looks. Was this really happening? Would it ever occur to these men to ask the input of the three women at the table who, between them, had given birth eleven times? It would not.

Finally, one day, it happened. Representative Don Edwards was new to the group. He had been the floor leader of the Equal Rights Amendment. During a conversation about the constitutional amendment, he turned to Pelosi and said, "What do you think?"

"Don, thank you so much for asking me what I think!" Pelosi replied, perhaps a little too gleefully. "How refreshing!" What do you mean? he asked. Pelosi told the story about the childbirth conversation. But all the men who'd been a part of it denied that it had ever occurred. *They don't even have a clue that they don't have a clue*, Pelosi thought.

Pelosi decided that she hadn't come to Congress to change the attitudes of men; she'd come to change policies. But seeing power up close tends to have a demystifying effect. The men, Pelosi saw, didn't have any kind of "special sauce" that qualified them for their positions. She could see she was just as capable as they were.

So she put up with indignities such as being introduced at a dinner by a Democratic colleague as the "pretty girl from California." But she grew tired of being treated like she didn't belong. She grew tired of the Capitol Police officers who frequently stopped her as she made her way around the Capitol, saying, "Sorry, lady, that's for members only."

One day, when she was stopped as she attempted to follow a colleague through the Speaker's Lobby, she decided she'd had enough. Rather than patiently explain herself yet again, she snapped at the guard, "I can go anywhere I want! I am a member of Congress!"

Sheepishly, he replied, "Congresswoman, that's the men's room."

◆ ◆ ◆

If the AIDS fight was a national crusade, a more parochial fight would prove just as educational for Pelosi. Right next door to her former home on Presidio Terrace, in the shadow of the Golden Gate Bridge, stood the Presidio, a beautiful old Spanish fort situated on acres of rolling green waterfront property. The oldest continually operating military installation in the United States, it had been an active army post since its acquisition from Mexico in 1846, serving as a military hospital and staging ground for the invasion of the Philippines and America's Pacific operations in World War II. It was at the Presidio that the orders were issued to round up Japanese Americans and send them to internment camps after FDR directed the military to do so in 1942.

San Franciscans regarded the fort as a local treasure and assumed it would always belong to the army. But in 1988, a commission looking to cut Pentagon spending recommended it for closure. It was costing the Defense Department seventy-four million dollars a year to maintain, and with the

Cold War coming to a close, there were few threats to justify the expense. The federal government proposed selling the land for development, which would surely fetch a pretty penny—if the people of San Francisco ever allowed it. By one estimate, the real estate was worth four billion dollars, the equivalent of more than eight billion in today's dollars. Local environmentalists said they'd never stand for seeing their beloved jewel auctioned off, and wanted to turn it into a national park. But Democrats in Congress worried that it would be so expensive to operate that there wouldn't be enough room in the budget for the rest of the National Park Service. And as pretty as it might be, was it really national park material? As one Republican congressman noted drily, "It's not Yosemite."

Pelosi and her colleague Barbara Boxer assigned their staffs to research the issue, and they made a stunning discovery. After he lost his bid for majority leader, Phil Burton had taken as a kind of consolation prize the chairmanship of the Interior and Insular Affairs Committee, and threw himself into its work creating and overseeing national parks. One of them was the Golden Gate National Recreation Area. And true to Burton's modus operandi of passing baroquely complex bills studded with sneaky hidden provisions to benefit progressive causes, he had tucked a clause into the bill mandating that if the Pentagon ever relinquished control of the Presidio, it would become part of the Golden Gate National Recreation Area.

The two women considered their discovery a legislative coup. Now, they thought, there would be no choice but to turn the installation into a park. They rushed over to see John "Jack" Murtha, the chairman of the Appropriations subcommittee that doled out funds to the Pentagon.

Murtha and Pelosi had already become unlikely friends. They could hardly have been more different: he was a tough, bearlike former marine from rural Pennsylvania, a conservative Democrat—pro-coal, pro-gun, pro-military—who presided over the knot of surly old white men whose section of the House floor was known as the Pennsylvania Corner. An unapologetic pork barreler, Murtha directed so much federal spending to his hometown of Johnstown, Pennsylvania, that seemingly every building and facility in the city bore his name. In the waning years of his career, he would be engulfed by a wide-ranging pay-to-play corruption scandal before dying in office in 2010.

Murtha was no feminist. He was exactly the type of old-school congressman who might have been expected to write Pelosi off as a ditzy rich lady from flaky, nutty California. But she caught his eye when, as a freshman, she voted against leveling ethics charges against a Murtha ally, a congressman from Pittsburgh who'd been accused of misusing funds. Pelosi thought the man deserved the benefit of the doubt and refused to join the overwhelming majority of her colleagues in censuring him. Murtha was impressed that she refused to take the easy, politically expedient vote. "You've got a hell of a lot of guts for a freshman," he told her gruffly. Once Murtha started to take Pelosi seriously, he became impressed with her tenacity, savvy and work ethic. She cultivated him, too, sensing the utility of having allies in different ideological quarters of the party. When Murtha would come to her office, she'd put on her desk a little doll made of coal that her father had saved from his work with the coal miners' union.

When Pelosi and Boxer told Murtha about the Presidio, he taught them a lesson in practical politics. Sure, he knew about the Burton provision. But using it to convert the site into a park immediately was "completely amateurish," he said, and would only put it at risk. The Park Service would then be on the hook for cleaning up the former military site and making it suitable for civilian use, which Murtha knew from experience could be exceedingly pricey. Make the Pentagon keep it, he told the women, and the cash-rich Defense Department would have to pay for the cleanup instead of the National Park Service. So, instead of fighting to turn the base over, Pelosi and Boxer began campaigning against closing it. They mounted a full-court press, and for several years they succeeded. By the time Congress voted to go ahead with the closure, the Pentagon had already committed more than $65 million to cleaning up the Presidio.

Once the base was ordered closed, Pelosi had another fight on her hands. Selling off the Presidio was intolerable, but it would be a tall order to ask the Park Service to shoulder its full maintenance cost, estimated at $45 million per year—an order of magnitude more than any other park, and more than the combined operating costs of Yellowstone, Yosemite and the Grand Canyon. Pelosi embraced an idea to split the difference. The Presidio, she proposed, could be turned into a public-private partnership. Some parts, such as buildings and a golf course, could be leased to private operators, generating revenue that would help the Park Service run the rest as a public facility.

It was a complicated plan that pleased no one: not the environmentalists, outraged that their own congresswoman seemed to be selling out their
precious local treasure; not conservatives, who saw an unworkable scheme
that would leave taxpayers on the hook if, as they thought likely, things
didn't go as planned. Pelosi worked on the bill for five years before it finally
passed the House in 1994 with mostly Democratic votes. But the Senate put
off considering it, and then, in the 1994 midterm elections, Republicans
won control of Congress. To keep the Presidio alive, Pelosi would have to
get the bill through the House again in the new session. It had been hard
enough to get it through a Democratic House; it was hard to imagine that
Newt Gingrich's conservative revolutionaries were ever going to go along.
Many of Pelosi's colleagues assumed she would give up.

Instead, she set about finding Republican allies. She enlisted California's GOP governor Pete Wilson and Republicans in the California delegation to lobby other Republican lawmakers. Wealthy San Francisco
Republicans who wanted to protect the site were assigned to call their well-
placed friends in Washington. Pelosi made a spreadsheet and scoured her
network for potential avenues. Noticing that Senator Frank Murkowski of
Alaska had been a banker before entering politics, she got a banker friend
to call a banker he knew in Alaska to call Murkowski. She invited every
Republican on the House committee overseeing parks to come to San
Francisco and personally led them on tours of the site, appealing to
their skepticism of big government by arguing that San Francisco's cum-
bersome regulatory process would make it impossible to sell off the site,
and that what she was proposing was really the free-market alternative to
liberals' desire for government to manage the whole thing. This did not go
unnoticed by the liberals in her district: community activists, as well as the
mayor and board of supervisors, pushed her to designate the Presidio for
public housing rather than private profit and accused her of working to
"privatize" a civic landmark. The *Bay Guardian*, the city's liberal alt-weekly,
denounced her for it and refused to endorse her ever again. To this day, the
paper endorses Pelosi's opponent in every election. (And indeed, the housing
crisis now plaguing San Francisco might not be so intense if the Presidio
was affordable housing, instead of a pretty place that is mostly enjoyed by
rich people.)

Pelosi, however, believed her solution was the most workable compromise. She offered concessions to the GOP, such as giving business more of

a voice on the Presidio board. In another clever move that would become a signature tactic, she offered what seemed like a major concession to get the bill over the line: if the Presidio didn't pay for itself within fifteen years, it would be designated as "surplus" and revert to the possession of the General Services Administration. Pelosi and her staff acted as if this were a truly painful provision for them. But in fact the "concession" was a phony one. Pelosi's chief of staff had traced the Presidio's provenance all the way back to the 1848 Treaty of Guadalupe Hidalgo, which had deeded the land to the United States from Mexico. According to the treaty, the land belonged to the Department of the Interior, not the GSA—leaving it to the government to administer at taxpayer expense, the very outcome the Republicans wanted to avoid. But they didn't tell the Republicans that, and they got a counter-concession in return.

All the wheeling and dealing finally bore fruit. The bill passed the Republican House in late 1995 and the Senate a year later. President Clinton signed it into law. As one writer marveled, Pelosi "had managed to get a Republican Congress to create the nation's most expensive national park in, of all places, Democratic San Francisco."

As for the Treaty of Guadalupe Hidalgo, the discovery was never put to the test: the Presidio Trust was self-sufficient ahead of the deadline.

7

THE TANKS ROLLED INTO TIANANMEN SQUARE ON A SUNDAY NIGHT. FOR weeks, hundreds of thousands of protesters had been massing across China. On June 4, 1989, they gathered in the vast plaza at the center of Beijing, demanding reforms. But the People's Liberation Army crushed them. The tanks ground civilians beneath their treads as soldiers fired machine guns indiscriminately into the crowd. Hundreds, perhaps thousands, were killed.

Pelosi reacted viscerally to the sight of a state brutally slaughtering its own people. She had long been passionate about international human rights, protesting outside the Soviet consulate in San Francisco during the Cold War and outside City Hall when the Philippines dictator Ferdinand Marcos visited. The demonstrators in Tiananmen Square reminded her of her own college-age children.

Now she summoned her staff into her office. Something had to be done.

Pelosi had just been elected to her first full term with a resounding 76 percent of the vote—after her close call versus Britt, she would never face more than token opposition and rarely received less than 80 percent of her district's support. The same election elevated a Republican president, George H. W. Bush, to succeed Reagan, while preserving the Democrats' majorities in the House and Senate. With foreign policy generally the domain of the White House, it wasn't clear what Congress could do about the outrage unfolding overseas. Pelosi's chief of staff, Judy Lemons, an old congressional hand, was flummoxed, but she locked the staff in a room and told them they wouldn't be getting out until they came up with something—anything.

Tens of thousands of Chinese students, they discovered, were living and studying in the United States on visas that were set to expire when they finished their studies, forcing them to return to China, where they could be persecuted. Many of the students had attended pro-democracy demonstrations in the United States, where Chinese spies had photographed them in order to send threatening letters to their families back home. There were thousands of such students in San Francisco alone; Pelosi's district had one of the largest concentrations of Asian Americans in the country. Pelosi, her staff suggested, could propose legislation to waive the visa requirements, which would allow the students to stay.

It wasn't much, but it was something. Pelosi started working on her colleagues. Many were skeptical. Then she heard that a colleague had an intern who had a friend who had been in Tiananmen with a camera hidden in the basket of his bicycle and had smuggled the film out in an empty tear gas canister. The photos were wrenching and bloody. Pelosi marched down the hall with them to the office of the chairman of the Judiciary Committee. "This is why I want to do something," she said. He agreed to help, and by the end of June, her bill to waive student visa requirements had more than one hundred cosponsors.

The fight for human rights in China would establish the new congresswoman as a force to be reckoned with, rather than just another voice in the crowd. In the course of her crusade, she would put herself in physical danger and take on two presidents, including one from her own party, as well as Big Business interests, including some of her own donors and constituents. She was tactically creative and publicly outspoken, raising her own profile in the process. It was also a window into her motivations. Why did she fight so vigorously for the rights of people half a world away? It couldn't be explained simply as working on behalf of her constituents. Although many people in her district were Chinese Americans who sympathized with the dissidents, she also had a large constituency that wanted unconditional economic relations with China, a growing powerhouse, which she vocally opposed. With unstinting moralism—critics would say self-righteousness—Pelosi disdained as sellouts the colleagues who differed with her on the issue, many of them fellow Democrats who were more focused on the economic opportunities China presented than the rights of a faraway people. She fought for Chinese democracy because it was, to her, simply the right thing to do.

President Bush disagreed. A former diplomatic liaison to Beijing, as president he seemed to view her visa crusade as well-intentioned but naïve, the work of a San Francisco bleeding heart who didn't understand the harsh realities of international relations. After her bill passed the House overwhelmingly in November, Bush threatened to veto it. The Senate passed it anyway, and veto it he did.

Pelosi called Bush's veto a "slap in the face to the forces of democracy," and claimed Congress was ready and willing to override him. But this was mere bluster. It takes a two-thirds vote of the House and Senate to override a presidential veto, a rebuke to the executive branch that is difficult to achieve and rare.

She didn't yet have the votes, but she set about getting them. Every day on the floor, she buttonholed colleagues (Republicans and Democrats, northerners and southerners, liberals and conservatives), pleading for their support. She called thirty colleagues a day and planned to keep doing so during a holiday recess until her staff warned her that interrupting fellow members' vacations might lose her votes rather than winning them. (Instead, she spent her vacation in Mexico with Paul, furiously plowing through books on U.S.-China relations.) As the day of the override vote neared, she orchestrated a full-court press, with television interviews, news conferences and floor speeches blasting "the butchers of Beijing." On January 24, 1990, the House overrode the president's veto by an overwhelming bipartisan vote of 390–25.

Bush proposed a compromise: instead of Pelosi's bill, he would issue an executive order that would have much the same effect without tying his hands. The president also did his own lobbying, calling senators privately and assuring them that the override wasn't necessary. He sent handwritten notes to some senators' wives, pleading with them to tell their husbands to vote against the override. It worked: the override got just 62 of the 67 votes necessary in the Senate.

Several months passed. No executive order was forthcoming. Pelosi suspected that this had been Bush's plan all along, and she was furious that he seemed to think he could put her off. And so, one day, the *Washington Post* came into possession of one those notes the president had written to a senator's wife, promising to issue the executive order—a promise he had apparently abandoned.

The story embarrassed Bush into acting. He issued the executive order.

✧ ✧ ✧

The following year, 1991, Pelosi set out to see China for herself. She arranged to lead a bipartisan congressional delegation, or CODEL, to Asia, accompanied by two fellow lawmakers: John Miller, a Republican from Washington State, and Ben Jones of Georgia, a Democrat who, before entering politics, had played Cooter on TV's *The Dukes of Hazzard*. Pelosi's husband, Paul, came along.

They stopped first in Hong Kong, where many of the Chinese dissidents who hadn't been killed or imprisoned had fled. An activist gave the Americans a banner made of black cloth. In silver letters in English and Chinese, it read, "To Those Who Died for Democracy in China."

The group went on to Beijing, where the government refused to allow them to visit imprisoned dissidents. The Chinese officials insisted, in fact, that there were no political prisoners in China, where free speech, they claimed, was rampant. Pelosi gave a news conference calling for the prisoners' release anyway, which the regime did not appreciate.

On the last day of the trip, Chinese officials had scheduled a visit by the members of Congress to the Great Wall—an all-day trip several hours' drive away. The Americans, however, told their handlers they were too tired and would prefer to spend the day resting before their scheduled dinner with the Chinese foreign minister. Then they sneaked out the back of the hotel and hailed a cab to Tiananmen Square. Jones tipped off a local CNN crew to where they were headed.

When they got there, a small group of cameras was waiting. Jones then unfurled the banner, which he had smuggled into China in his underwear, and the three members of Congress held it in front of them. Pelosi, clad in an oversize tan blazer, her hair gathered in a ponytail at the nape of her neck, stood between the two men in their dark suits. Each of the three carried a white cloth rose.

"There is a memory which still burns bright," Jones, a bespectacled bear of a man with a mop of gray hair, intoned in his gentle Southern drawl. "And it is a cause which will never die."

As the trio turned to lay their flowers at a makeshift memorial to the protesters in a corner of the enormous plaza, the police moved in. Pointing and shouting, Chinese officers in khaki uniforms, as well as plainclothes "tourists" who suddenly turned out to have walkie-talkies, surrounded the lawmakers, ordering them to cease and the press to stop filming. One grabbed and slapped Miller, the Republican congressman. Another was about to do the same to Jones before the big man stared him down.

Pelosi addressed the cameras, appearing far more unfazed than she felt: "We've been told for two days now that there's freedom of speech in China," she said.

The lawmakers hurried away and got back in their car as police roughed up the journalists, detaining seven of them. But the footage made it out. Pelosi's sound bite was on the *CBS Evening News*.

Pelosi and the others still showed up for their dinner with the foreign minister, where the Chinese officials in attendance shifted in their seats and avoided eye contact. After she returned to Washington, she kept the picture of the three of them, holding the unfurled banner, on her desk, next to a quotation from Mother Teresa: "God does not always expect us to be successful, but He does always expect us to be faithful."

❖ ❖ ❖

The Chinese human rights issue connected an odd group of activists. Pelosi helped assemble a loose coalition that included conservative anti-Communists and evangelical Christians alongside liberal activists and Bush critics. At one point, she held a press conference with the "family values" activist Gary Bauer, a prominent opponent of abortion rights and gay rights. She worked to bring new voices into the mix, knowing that the broader the group, the more influential it would be.

At a human rights conference she attended at Harvard, she got the idea to go after China's "most favored nation" trade status with the United States. The status, which guarantees advantageous trade terms, came up for presidential review every year—an annual opportunity for leverage, Pelosi thought. As the Chinese economy opened to the world, it became more dependent on U.S. consumers, and stood to lose more if tariffs were reimposed. If the regime were forced to, Pelosi believed, it would agree to human rights concessions to stop that from happening.

She drafted an amendment that would require China, if it wanted to keep its trade status, to release political prisoners and demonstrate progress on human rights. The Bush administration, which wanted warmer relations with Beijing, strongly opposed the idea. Bush's State Department argued that its strategy of dialogue and trade was working better than coercion to improve the Communist dictatorship's human rights practices. In a hearing, Pelosi retorted that any human rights gains were due to China's fear of a congressional trade crackdown, not Bush's work. Many of Pelosi's fellow Democrats disagreed with her approach, believing that opening the Chinese economy would inevitably pave the way to political liberalization. She had little patience with this argument, which she dubbed "trickle-down liberty." To one colleague who made this argument, she retorted, "I hope you can live with your conscience." Pelosi's amendment passed the House but died in the Senate.

By this point, the 1992 presidential election was under way. In 1991, Bush nominated Clarence Thomas to the Supreme Court. Thomas seemed set to glide to an easy confirmation despite accusations he'd sexually harassed underlings—the Senate's all-male Judiciary Committee, chaired by Senator Joe Biden of Delaware, didn't even plan to hear testimony on the issue. Seven of Pelosi's female House colleagues marched over to the office of Senate Majority Leader George Mitchell, on the other side of the Capitol, to demand that the Senate hear from Anita Hill, one of Thomas's accusers. For House members to pressure the Senate in this manner was considered a breach of decorum. One Republican senator mistook the women for staff and ordered them to get against the wall, out of the lawmakers' path. "They are men," Pelosi told a reporter. "They can't possibly know what it's like to receive verbal harassment, harassment that is fleeting to a man and lasting and demeaning to a woman." The women got their hearing, but Thomas was confirmed nonetheless—triggering a wave of women's activism across the country that would lead to a historic election for women in 1992.

In the 1992 presidential race, few big-name Democrats wanted to take on Bush, whose popularity had soared following the 1991 Gulf War. (Pelosi opposed the war, which was widely regarded as a success.) Jerry Brown, who had dropped out of politics for a few years to study Buddhism in Japan and work with Mother Teresa in India, made his third run for president but got little traction. Pelosi hoped to back her friend Mario Cuomo, the governor of New York, who became known as "Hamlet on the Hudson" for his dithering about whether to get in the race. At one point, a jet was gassed up and ready to take him to New Hampshire. Pelosi sat at her desk in San Francisco waiting for him to call and green-light the campaign. But at the last minute he declined.

The nomination went instead to a charismatic, little-known Arkansas governor named William Jefferson Clinton. His entry came at a crossroads for the Democratic Party. Despite their success in Congress, Democrats hadn't held the White House since Carter's one uninspiring term. Reagan had captivated the nation, even winning the youth vote, potentially minting a whole generation of conservative voters. Many voters viewed Democrats' positions as outside the mainstream. The party was associated with far-left ideas such as handgun bans, racial quotas and welfare rights; it was viewed as soft on crime, weak on communism and antagonistic toward family values. Some Democrats believed the path back to the electorate's good graces was to double down on liberal positions, excite the party's base, and work to get more poor people and minorities to the polls. There was no point, this faction said, in trying to appeal to Reagan voters, whom they viewed as fundamentally backward. But another bloc believed moderation was the answer. This group called themselves the New Democrats. They founded an organization called the Democratic Leadership Council and produced a manifesto arguing that the liberals were in denial. Even if minorities and low-income voters had voted at historically high rates in 1988, its analysis showed, Michael Dukakis would have lost the election. This group joined forces with Clinton for what appeared at first to be a long-shot presidential campaign.

As Bush's popularity dropped in 1992, Clinton made use of the China issue to accuse the incumbent of "coddling tyrants." Pelosi, by this point, was being written up in the papers as "one of the Democrats' rising national stars." She oversaw the party platform at the '92 convention in New York City, using the opportunity to insert a strong statement on AIDS. She was even mentioned as a potential vice presidential nominee, though she let it be known that she wasn't interested. Clinton promised Pelosi that if he won, he would attach human rights conditions to China's trade status, and after he won he followed through. Pelosi stood behind him, beaming, as he signed the order at the White House.

American businesses, which were profiting handsomely from Chinese trade, began a furious and well-funded lobbying campaign to pressure the administration to renew China's trade status. It was up to the Clinton administration to determine whether the Chinese were making the "progress" the executive order demanded. Some forty billion dollars in annual commerce was at stake. Many of the biggest import-export businesspeople were based in or near Pelosi's district. The San Francisco Chinese Chamber of Commerce, ordinarily supportive of Pelosi, criticized her stance.

The idea that money might come before human lives and democratic values offended Pelosi's sense of justice. The business groups' lobbying weakened the United States' leverage over the regime, she said, by signaling to the Chinese that powerful American interests were desperate to keep the trade relationship alive. Instead of pressuring the American government, why didn't the businesses pressure China to improve its human rights policies instead? "What a laugh for the Chinese government to see these businesspeople groveling for favor among the Chinese," she said, calling the debate one of "ideals versus deals."

But Clinton was waffling. He and his brain trust worried about the economic and foreign policy debacle a trade war could cause. It was clear that China hadn't done much of anything to improve human rights, but did it really deserve to be in the same category as North Korea and Cuba? Maybe, Clinton thought, Bush's strategy of economic engagement wasn't such a bad idea. Pelosi's friend Leon Panetta had joined the administration to serve as Clinton's chief of staff. The president asked Panetta if Pelosi would be a problem. "A big problem," Panetta replied.

Shortly before the deadline for most-favored-nation-status renewal, Clinton called Pelosi. They talked for nearly an hour as he broke the bad news: not only was he going to renew the status this time, but he was going to stop making it conditional on human rights altogether. He hoped she could find a way to swallow her objections and support her party's president.

If Clinton thought Pelosi would take this defeat quietly, he was mistaken. More than betrayed, she felt humiliated for having trusted him. Not long after hanging up the phone, she publicly accused Clinton of "coddling dictators," just as Clinton had once accused Bush of doing. The president, she told a reporter for the *San Francisco Chronicle*, was selling out human rights for lucre. "I cannot say one thing about George Bush's policy and another about Bill Clinton's when they are the same policy," she said.

Though she continued to support Clinton, Pelosi never trusted him after that. The incident created a longtime rift between Pelosi and both Bill and Hillary Clinton. She called on the administration to boycott the Fourth

World Conference on Women, to be held in Beijing in September 1995, but the First Lady went anyway, famously proclaiming, "Women's rights are human rights"—a rather discordant declaration to make, Pelosi thought, against the backdrop of the Chinese government's state-sanctioned torture.

Pelosi also earned the lasting enmity of some in the business community for her China crusade. For all her fund-raising prowess and personal wealth, she had not hesitated to take on monied interests. When Clinton, during his reelection campaign, was caught up in campaign finance scandals over illegal contributions from Chinese nationals, and for trading access to events (such as coffees at the White House) for donations, it only reaffirmed Pelosi's view of him as a corporate sellout. And she did not mince words. When Clinton hosted the Chinese premier Jiang Zemin at a state dinner in 1997, she called it "the ultimate coffee." Rather than attend the dinner, she joined the protesters outside the White House.

"There is nothing more dangerous than a leader whose policy has failed and now he has to justify it," Pelosi said. "Clinton is very good at it. He can do it without blinking."

The issue made her internationally known. A columnist in Singapore wrote that Pelosi's name was enough to "give an American businessman trading with China heartburn," while an American columnist described her and her allies as the "congressional freedom squad fighting for the rights of dissidents all over the world." For years, Pelosi commemorated the June 4 anniversary of Tiananmen by reading aloud the names of China's political prisoners on the floor of the House.

She lost the fight, but she never stopped believing she was right. Clinton granted China permanent trade status in 2000, paving the way for its ascension to the World Trade Organization in 2001. "I predict," Pelosi said at the time, "that the trade deficit will soar, the human rights violations will intensify, the proliferation of weapons of mass destruction will continue uncurbed. The only lever we had was free trade."

China's entry into the WTO triggered a period that economists dubbed "China shock." Millions of American manufacturing jobs disappeared as American companies outsourced their operations abroad to take advantage of cheap Chinese labor. Economists mostly believe that the American economy benefited overall in the long run. But decades later, the massive Chinese trade deficit, China's unfair trade practices and a Rust Belt landscape dotted with hollowed-out towns and empty former factory buildings would be a major engine of Donald Trump's political rise. And the Chinese people continued to suffer under the thumb of their repressive government.

Pelosi never gave up the fight. In 2019, she repeatedly spoke out against Beijing's brutal repression of pro-democracy protesters in Hong Kong, even as the National Basketball Association and other multinational corporations were cowed into silence. She personally whipped support for the Hong Kong Human Rights and Democracy Act imposing sanctions on the regime. The bill put many members of Congress in an uncomfortable position, but she insisted that every member's vote be recorded rather than letting it through on a voice vote. It passed, 417 votes to 1.

8

THE WAY NEWT GINGRICH SAW IT, REPUBLICANS IN WASHINGTON WERE a bunch of lily-livered dopes. Gingrich was nobody, an untenured academic at an obscure Georgia college who won a seat in Congress on his third attempt in 1978. But that did nothing to temper his belief in his own vision.

Most Republicans in Congress seemed to accept their status as a permanent minority. They were content to temper the Democrats' liberal impulses in minor ways. If Democrats proposed a hundred billion dollars in new spending, Republicans would meekly object to a frivolous program here and there (or, worse, put their hand out for some of the spoils for their own districts), get the Democrats to agree to "only" ninety billion dollars and call it victory. The idea that the Democrats were dangerous and needed to be stopped, that the *fundamental direction* of American policy was wrong—this did not seem to have occurred to the lily-livered dopes.

Gingrich the visionary—sarcastic, grandiose and inveterately competitive—dared to dream. He rejected the establishment's genteel fatalism and insisted that winning must be the only goal. In the 1980s, as Democrats continued to rule the House despite Reagan's popularity, Gingrich recruited some fellow junior members to form a club they called the Conservative Opportunity Society. The constructive name belied its intentions. The dozen or so society members weren't interested in putting their heads down and making the most of their committee assignments or seeking win-win compromises with the Democrats. They were interested in war. "One of the great problems we have in the Republican Party is that we don't encourage you to be nasty," Gingrich told a group of College Republicans. "We encourage you to be neat, obedient, and loyal, and faithful, and all those Boy Scout words, which would be great around the campfire but are lousy in politics."

Instead of legislative successes, Gingrich and his acolytes sought publicity. They positioned themselves in front of the C-SPAN cameras when there was no business being conducted on the House floor, giving diatribes against liberalism to a live audience that consisted of a few teenage congressional pages. In one speech, Gingrich called on Democrats to defend their love of country and then gloated because, not being present, they did not do so. This so incensed the Democrats that they instituted a new protocol: the C-SPAN cameras would periodically pan around the House floor to show the audience (or lack thereof). The controversy, "Camscam," played into Gingrich's hands by elevating his profile. "I am now a famous person," he boasted to the *Washington Post*.

The attacks on Democrats were not only rhetorical. In 1988, Gingrich and his gang asked the Ethics Committee to investigate charges that the Speaker, Jim Wright of Texas, was guilty of financial improprieties related both to a memoir he had written and to his wife's job at an investment company. Wright was never found guilty of anything, but the investigation and other unsubstantiated rumors Gingrich helped spread so undermined Wright's effectiveness that he resigned—the first Speaker of the House in history to resign as a result of scandal (though not, as it turned out, the last). In his final speech on the House floor, Wright decried the "mindless cannibalism" of Gingrich's brand of politics, proclaiming, "When members of each party become self-appointed vigilantes carrying out personal vendettas against members of the other party . . . harsh personal attacks upon one another's motives and one another's character drown out the quiet logic of serious debate on important issues."

Gingrich had claimed a powerful scalp. His colleagues elected him minority whip, the second-most-powerful position in the caucus. But he would not rest until his enemies, the Democrats, were vanquished. Working with the pollster Frank Luntz, he drafted a memo entitled "Language: A Key Mechanism of Control," which recommended that Republicans use words like "sick, pathetic, lie, anti-flag, traitors, radical, corrupt" to describe the Democrats. Taking the helm of a national organization called GOPAC, Gingrich traveled across the country recruiting young, aggressive partisan warriors to run for Congress, arming them with his memos and instructional cassette tapes.

In Washington, Gingrich and the GOP weaponized the legislative process. The Republican minority blocked every bill they could, even bipartisan or nonpartisan measures, then went around criticizing the party in power for the resulting "gridlock." Commentators and some Republicans cried foul, but voters hardly noticed. To appeal to the public, Gingrich devised a document he called the Contract with America, a ten-point agenda of poll-tested proposals such as welfare reform, term limits and a balanced budget. It was unfurled with maximum fanfare: on the steps of the Capitol in September 1994, three hundred Republican candidates signed the Contract as Gingrich declared it "a first step towards renewing American civilization."

By that year, the second of Bill Clinton's presidency, voters were starting to sour on the onetime boy wonder president. His attempt to reform the health care system had failed, but Clinton and the Democratic Congress had racked up some major accomplishments, including the 1993 Family and Medical Leave Act, the 1994 crime bill and the Brady bill mandating background checks for gun purchases. The Cold War was over, and the economy was expanding. But Clinton's administration was chaotic and crude; it seemed permanently mired in one penny-ante scandal or another, from the president's "bimbo eruptions" to conspiracy theories about the 1993 suicide of Clinton's lawyer and confidant Vince Foster—theories Gingrich irresponsibly stoked.

Midterm House elections often register a backlash against the president's party. But 1994 was unprecedented. Republicans won 54 House seats and took control of both the House and Senate for the first time in forty years. When the triumphant GOP took over the House in January 1995, Newt Gingrich was made Speaker.

✧ ✧ ✧

This should never have happened, Pelosi thought. She had not come to Congress to waste away in the minority. To say the Democrats were demoralized by the Republican Revolution, as Gingrich's takeover was dubbed, would be an understatement. They were in shock. So total was the red wave that the Democratic Speaker of the House who had replaced Wright, Thomas Foley of Washington State, was defeated for reelection after thirty years in the House—the first time in 130 years that a Speaker lost his seat. It felt like more than merely a changing of the guard. It felt like an inversion of the natural order, a rip in the space-time continuum. Democrats moped and mourned. Many saw the election as an aberration. The voters, they thought, would soon recover from their temporary insanity and put the Democrats back in power.

Speaker Gingrich was determined to prevent this from happening, and he set about using the powers at his disposal to help Republicans' political prospects, even if it meant changing or corrupting the House's traditional practices. More and more of the schedule was devoted to phony votes, stunt bills not designed to pass but only to put the other party on the record on unpopular issues or "gotcha" amendments that could be taken out of context in inflammatory campaign ads. Gingrich slashed the House's budgets for staff and other resources, a little-noticed change that gutted lawmakers' ability to do their own analysis of important issues and put more bill-drafting power in the hands of outside actors such as think tanks and lobbyists. He shortened the House's legislative schedule to just three working days a week so that members could spend more time campaigning and fund-raising—a change that reduced what the body could accomplish while giving members less time to form collaborative, bipartisan friendships. Further undermining collegiality, he urged Republican members to keep their homes and families in their districts rather than in Washington—closer to their constituents, but farther from one another. Under Gingrich, collegiality was discouraged.

In 1995, budget talks between the congressional Republicans and Clinton came to a standstill. Republicans believed that the 1994 elections had given them a mandate to slash government spending, but Clinton believed the cuts Republicans proposed to Medicare, education and the environment were unacceptable, so he vetoed the budgets Congress sent to his desk. Further negotiations went nowhere as each side accused the other of being unreasonable. It was perhaps the natural result of Gingrich's polarity-driven politics: two equal and opposite forces, pulling in opposite directions, had created a standstill. In mid-November, the government shut down, then reopened, then shut down again, staying closed for a total of twenty-six days. Voters blamed Republicans, and Gingrich in particular: a New York *Daily News* cover cartoon depicted the House Speaker as a baby in a diaper throwing a tantrum and alleged that Gingrich had triggered the shutdown out of spite when Clinton made him sit at the back of Air Force One.

Eventually, Clinton and Gingrich reached an agreement to balance the budget, and both sides would later take credit for the federal budget surpluses that followed. But many also blame Gingrich's tactics for unsavory features of Congress that persist to this day. The House and Senate almost never come to agreement with the White House on a budget without the threat of shutdown; brinkmanship is constant. (Shutdowns aren't just a harmless pause in the administration of government: they delay federal workers' paychecks and the checks that beneficiaries of many federal programs depend on, disrupting families and costing the overall economy billions.) Many analysts fault Gingrich for the GOP's devolution into a party devoted more to blocking Democrats at every turn than to advancing any positive agenda of its own.

Gingrich's base argument—that Republicans had helped enable Democrats' long-term dominance of the House—wasn't wrong. The government kept getting bigger, and liberal policies kept passing no matter who was in the White House. A nation that did not have a national income tax as recently as 1913 was, by 1994, spending $1.5 trillion per year on all sorts of programs, from parks to welfare to fighter planes in peacetime. Reagan, despite his rhetoric, had failed to shrink the government—he eliminated a single, small workforce-training program while overall spending continued to grow. He campaigned on eliminating the Department of Education, but at the end of his two terms the department had not only survived but grown by 14 percent. This arrangement—Republican presidents and Democratic congressional majorities—had seemed to suit the American public fine, perhaps because while many voters agreed with conservative sentiments in the abstract, in practice they did not want to see any curtailment of government largesse that benefited them.

After 1994, the truce was over. Republicans were playing to win, by any means necessary. If that made Gingrich powerful in the process, so much the better.

✧ ✧ ✧

As many Democrats sat paralyzed or in denial after 1994, Pelosi fell back on her old maxim: don't agonize, organize. Even before the Republican takeover, some of her colleagues had tried to get her to run against Foley for Speaker. The effort was serious enough to earn her a rebuke from some allies of the usually affable Foley, who warned her, "You're not doing your-self any good around here by putting out the idea that you might run for Speaker." Pelosi assured them that the insurgency was not her idea, that the Speaker had her loyalty and that she was not interested in any leadership position.

Instead, she plunged into policy, apprenticing herself to more experienced members of the Appropriations Committee and then earning a coveted spot on the Intelligence Committee, which over-sees the CIA and other top-secret agencies and has access to classified information. Colleagues were impressed with her range of knowledge. She devoured briefing books and could rattle off numbers from the federal budget, a document that runs to thousands of pages. She had an enviable mastery of the House's procedures and rules. Her brother Tommy, a close confidant who could be brutally frank with his lit-tle sister, had advised: know your facts, know your figures, know the procedure. If you know your stuff, he said, it's very hard for them to diminish you.

Extreme preparation is common in women seeking power, who tend to arm themselves with knowledge in order to ensure they're taken seri-ously. They know that, unlike men, they will rarely be granted the assump-tion of legitimacy or be able to coast on glib ignorance; rather, they will constantly have to prove they're qualified. Pelosi frequently had things she already knew explained to her by men who assumed they knew more than she did. She sat through meetings where her suggestions were ignored, but where a man would later make the same suggestion and everyone would think it was a great idea. On a trip to Guatemala to investigate the killing of an activist Catholic bishop, the country's defense minister started to feed her the government line when she stopped him: "I've been on the Intel-ligence Committee for five years," she said. "I have this pain in my back from sitting up reading thousands of pages of transcripts about what's happened down here. So, don't even say that."

But with colleagues it was trickier: men don't like to be put in their place, and Pelosi couldn't afford to alienate them. She tempered her assertive attitude with an abundance of traditional feminine graces. Especially in those days, many female politicians avoided talking about their families for fear of being considered soft or relegated to work on "women's issues." Pelosi, however, did not take this advice; she referred frequently to her family and to her concern for the world's children, which to this day she cites as her driving political motivation. At the same time, in her legislative career she gravitated toward the "hard" committees, the ones that did work traditionally seen as masculine: dollars and cents, war and peace. Meanwhile, she continued to fundraise with superlative skill. After just two years in Congress, she was the House's leading fund-raiser.

In April 1995, Pelosi's mother died of a heart attack. Her obituary in the *Baltimore Sun* was headlined, "Nancy D'Alesandro, 86, Matriarch," and noted, "Mrs. D'Alesandro was a traditional Italian wife from the Old Country who nevertheless raised a namesake daughter who now represents California's 5th Congressional District." Her son Tommy was quoted saying, "She was really the true politician of the family."

◇ ◇ ◇

Pelosi also served stints on the Banking Committee and the Government Operations Committee, and in 1991 she took a seat on the Committee on Standards of Official Conduct, which would later be renamed the Committee on Ethics. The Ethics Committee was a different assignment from typical committee work. Where other committees had more majority members than members from the minority, the Ethics Committee's party lineup was balanced, with seven Democrats and seven Republicans. Empowered to investigate their colleagues' personal and political conduct, they carried out their work in total secrecy. It was a job that had the potential to make its members unpopular with their peers. Serving on it was viewed as an unpleasant duty, but one that earned brownie points with leadership.

After falling victim to Gingrich's smear campaign, Speaker Wright had urged his fellow Democrats not to retaliate in kind by abusing the ethics process to go after Republicans. But the target was too tempting to pass up: Gingrich, who had criticized Wright for hiding profits from his book royalties, himself had a book deal that appeared to be structured to circumvent campaign finance laws. He had also set up a maze of interlocking nonprofits for his political activities, which Democrats believed were being used to avoid taxes, and he used tax-exempt contributions to subsidize his teaching of a college course called Renewing American Civilization, which Democrats charged was more about political propaganda than educating students.

The Democrats' minority whip, David Bonior of Michigan, thought it was essential to expose Gingrich as a liar and hypocrite. Some other Democrats worried they would be viewed as vengeful or overzealous. But Pelosi agreed with Bonior. She pursued the dozens of ethics complaints against Gingrich zealously. Over the two years of the investigation, she spent hundreds of hours reviewing the evidence. Because the committee's members pledge total secrecy, she once kicked her husband out of the bedroom at three in the morning to take a phone call related to the ethics work.

By late 1996, the committee had concluded that Gingrich was guilty of violating House rules and lying to investigators. They made a deal with him: he would accept a reprimand and a $300,000 fine, the first such penalties ever levied against a Speaker, in exchange for the committee not recommending he be censured.

The deal was still secret when the new Congress convened in January 1997. Clinton had been reelected, and the Republicans' majority had shrunk to just 19 seats. Some Republicans wondered whether they should make Gingrich Speaker again, considering the ethical cloud still hanging over his head. Under House rules, an official censure would make him ineligible to serve as Speaker again. But two Republicans on the Ethics Committee released a letter to their colleagues assuring them that they "knew of no reason" that he would not be eligible. Pelosi was incensed. Gingrich was reelected Speaker, and her term on the Ethics Committee ended, whereupon she was free to finally speak her mind and blasted him for not resigning. "Most of us have more respect for the job of Speaker than the Speaker himself," she said.

In the ensuing years, many in her party would continue to pine for the comity of the old Congress. But because of experiences like these, Pelosi saw the new partisan reality for what it was and chose to adapt to it. Romanticizing the good old days was not going to win the next election, get a policy vote onto the floor or feed a hungry child. Like Phil and Sala Burton had said, Pelosi was *operational*. Her clear-eyed estimation of the Republicans' motives and trustworthiness would serve her well in the years to come. Other Democrats might bring a knife to a gunfight. Pelosi would always come fully armed, and if it got her labeled a strident partisan, so be it.

Her determination to relieve Democrats of their minority status only increased after their failure to win back the House in 1996. As she saw it, the men in charge weren't getting the job done. The retirement in late 1997 of a colleague who had served as caucus chair meant there were no longer any Californians in the Democrats' leadership positions, causing the delegation to buzz about whether one of them should try to move up. Some of Pelosi's donors asked when she would be rewarded for her party spadework. (As John Burton memorably put it, "She raised the fucking dough, she ought to be able to get something for it.") The minority leader, Dick Gephardt, repeatedly asked her to chair the Democratic Congressional Campaign Committee and steer the party's campaign to regain the majority.

But she didn't want to be pigeonholed as a fund-raiser. Nor did she want to be caucus secretary, the leadership position to which women in the caucus had traditionally been consigned. She didn't want what she thought of as "derivative power," executing someone else's decisions. She wanted to lead her party in the House, doing the nation's business, and she believed she was qualified.

The top position in the majority party is the Speaker, who is named in the Constitution, elected by the entire House (not just her party) and second in the line of succession for the presidency. After that come a series of posts decided by the party caucus: the leader, responsible for managing the action on the House floor; the whip, responsible for rounding up votes; caucus chair, vice chair, deputy leaders and whips, and others. (Beyond whip, the posts are not static, and the structure can be changed by the Speaker or leader.) Thus, the minority party has one fewer leadership position than the majority, and if control of the House changes, an extra spot in the top leadership ranks opens up.

In July 1998, Pelosi convened her closest friends for dinner at an upscale Italian restaurant on Capitol Hill and let them know she was considering running for party whip if and when the post became available. She wasn't looking to topple the incumbent whip, her friend Bonior. But if the Democrats managed to capture the House in 1998, Leader Gephardt would become Speaker Gephardt, Whip Bonior would become Leader Bonior and there would be a vacancy for whip.

"It is my assumption that we will win," she wrote in a letter to her colleagues at the time, "that Dick Gephardt will become Speaker and that Dave Bonior will become Majority Leader, leaving the Whip position as the highest opening for new leadership."

Based on her own informal count, Pelosi figured she could get enough votes to win. But several other members believed they were in line for the post. Chief among them was Steny Hoyer of Maryland—the same Steny Hoyer who'd worked alongside her in Senator Brewster's office back in 1963. While Pelosi was raising children and fund-raising on the West Coast, Hoyer had remained in Maryland. He finished law school, got elected to the Maryland State Senate, and in a special primary election in 1981 (another odd parallel with Pelosi's career) was elected to Congress from a strongly Democratic district in the Baltimore suburbs.

Hoyer was a politician straight out of central casting, with a swoosh of shiny hair across his forehead and a toothy smile. Descended on his mother's side from a signer of the Declaration of Independence, he was a moderate Democrat with an affable manner and a firm handshake. Everybody in the House seemed to like Hoyer. He had already served as caucus chair and deputy whip, and in 1991 he had run—with Pelosi's support—for whip and lost. Hoyer assumed that if there was an opening in leadership, it was his for the asking, and a lot of his colleagues did, too.

So when Pelosi called Hoyer in August 1998 and informed him that she planned to run for whip, the same post he wanted, he was stung. He noticed that she didn't ask him what he thought of her running; she just told him. Others among the Democratic establishment also noticed this. Word got back to Pelosi that, behind her back, men in particular were grumbling: "Who said *she* could run?" If she hadn't been determined before, that did it. *Light my fire, why don't you?* she thought. She didn't need anyone's permission.

❖ ❖ ❖

As the Democrats jostled, the partisan warfare intensified. In 1994, former solicitor general Kenneth Starr was appointed under Watergate-era rules to serve as an independent counsel and investigate allegations related to the Clintons' investments in the Whitewater real estate development company in Arkansas. Starr found no wrongdoing by the Clintons in that case. He also concluded that Vince Foster had indeed committed suicide, contra the conspiracy theorists. But Starr's investigation dragged on for years, expanding into a wide-ranging watchdogging of the president's administration and personal life.

In September 1998, Starr released his famous report detailing Clinton's dalliance with White House intern Monica Lewinsky and his perjury when he lied to the grand jury about it. Unlike previous and subsequent special counsels, Starr's report was sharply prosecutorial and opinionated, asserting definitively that Clinton had committed a crime that merited impeachment. It was also shockingly explicit; parents across America struggled to explain to their children the descriptions of sex acts that were splashed across the front pages of newspapers.

Clinton's recklessness split his Cabinet, Democrats in Congress and party supporters. Some called on him to resign, while others, including feminists such as Gloria Steinem, defended him. (Another woman's accusation that Clinton had raped her, buried in a Starr Report footnote, was virtually ignored.) Pelosi, though never a major fan of the president, echoed most in her party when she said, "The president's actions are cause for embarrassment but not impeachment." Clinton remained popular with the public throughout the scandal, and polls showed majorities opposing impeachment.

Some Republicans worried that impeaching the president for fibbing to cover up an affair would strike the public as partisan overreach and trigger a political backlash. But others, including Gingrich and his band of partisan warriors, wanted to throw the book at Clinton. Under the Constitution, a majority of the House must vote to impeach, after which the Senate holds a trial, requiring a two-thirds vote for conviction and removal. The House voted to open an impeachment investigation in October 1998, on the eve of the midterm elections. And the public soon delivered its verdict on the gambit: rather than picking up seats as the party out of the White House almost always did in midterms, the Republicans gained zero seats in the Senate and lost 5 in the House. It was the worst midterm performance by a nonpresidential party in more than sixty years.

The vote to impeach Clinton in December 1998 was the last one Newt Gingrich would ever cast as a congressman. His colleagues blamed him for the dismal election result and worried that his own extramarital affair with a young congressional staffer might make them come across as hypocrites, given the party's moralistic crusade against Clinton. Gingrich stepped down as Speaker and resigned from Congress, huffing to his colleagues, "I'm willing to lead, but I'm not willing to preside over people who are cannibals." It was the very epithet Jim Wright had used to describe his own persecution at the hands of Gingrich.

Despite losing 5 seats, the GOP held on to the House majority in 1998, rendering Pelosi's campaign for whip moot. But Pelosi was on her way up the ladder, and she wasn't going to stop. She announced that she would continue campaigning for whip—for two years down the road. At the same time, her friend Rosa DeLauro of Connecticut narrowly lost her bid for caucus chair, meaning there was, yet again, not a single woman in Democratic leadership.

9

WHEN PELOSI RESUMED HER WHIP CAMPAIGN RIGHT AFTER THE 1998 election, her opponents—John Lewis of Georgia was running as well as Hoyer—complained that if she was campaigning, they would have to start their campaigns, too. Even her friend Jack Murtha thought it was too soon. "I can't believe we're getting into this now," he muttered. But Pelosi believed in starting early, and she insisted they keep going, so Murtha, the manager of her whip campaign, went along. Lewis soon dropped out, citing the ridiculous intensity of the race.

Pelosi believed that when men objected to her machinations, what they were really saying was that they didn't want her to get ahead. She was, she reminded Murtha, trying to reverse two hundred years of history—two hundred years of men following men following men in every leadership position. Power would not be given to her; she would have to take it.

"Dear Colleague," she wrote in August 1999, the standard salutation for formal congressional letters. "The response to my interest in becoming a candidate for Majority Whip in the Democratic-led House has been excellent and my endeavor to unseat Tom DeLay"—the GOP majority whip— "is going exceedingly well."

A Democratic victory was so close she could practically taste it. Clinton was still popular, the economy was roaring and the failed impeachment had tarnished Republicans and shrunk their majority. Democrats needed to pick up only 7 seats in the 2000 election to take the House.

Pelosi was prepared to do her part. In addition to her usual fund-raising, there were 5 Republican-held seats in California that she thought the Democrats had a shot at flipping. Leave it to me, she told the national party. She went to work, helping recruit five solid candidates, three of them women, and teaching them about campaigns. ("Money, message, mobilization" was her alliterative mnemonic for the key to winning elections.) If her California plan worked and the party could find just 2 seats to flip across the rest of the country, Democrats would have their majority.

In the summer of 2000, Pelosi's daughter Alexandra, who had become a journalist, was working for NBC and covering George W. Bush's campaign for president. When Bush had a rally in Oakland, Alexandra covered it, then went out to lunch with her parents at the hotel where the campaign was staying. A Bush campaign aide noticed them and offered to introduce Pelosi to Bush, then the governor of Texas. Pelosi didn't want special treatment and didn't want to embarrass her daughter, so she declined. But the aide insisted: "If anybody else's parents were here, he'd want to say hello to them." So Nancy and Paul Pelosi went up to the candidate's suite to see George and Laura Bush.

"Well, here I am in California," Bush said with a big, confident grin. He seemed like someone who could take a joke, Pelosi thought.

"And welcome to you, Governor," Pelosi said evenly. "But please understand we're doing everything possible to make sure you don't win."

Bush guffawed and winked at his wife. "Isn't this a great country?" he said.

On Election Night, November 7, 2000, everything initially appeared to be going according to plan. All five of Pelosi's California candidates ousted their Republican opponents. Things were looking good for Al Gore as well as for the Democrats' chances in the House. Pelosi went out to a late dinner at a fancy restaurant in downtown San Francisco with her old friend Leo McCarthy.

It was around midnight on the West Coast when things started to take a turn for the worse. First, the presidential election was too close to call. Then, rather than picking up the 2 House seats Democrats needed outside California, the party somehow managed to *lose* 3 seats. This meant that, combined with the California wins, the party's net gain for the House was just 2 seats—5 short of what it needed. Democrats would spend at least two more years in the minority.

On the afternoon of November 8, Pelosi, trying not to sound defeated, announced, "Today is the beginning of the election for 2002."

A few weeks after the election, she hosted the dozen newly elected Democrats. She had recently moved into a million-dollar penthouse in Georgetown, a chic, high-windowed corner unit with views across the Potomac River. The event was a get-to-know-you cocktail party, but it was not a purely social occasion. Midway through the evening, Pelosi addressed the crowd. She led a case-by-case review of the campaign commercials each new representative-elect had aired, and talked about the Democratic campaign committee's handling of their respective races. She told them how tired she was of being in the minority and how she believed it was necessary to move past stale campaigns based on television ads. Candidates, she said, needed to learn how to organize from the ground up, as she had. The new members who'd showed up for pigs in a blanket had instead gotten a heady dose of Pelosi's determination to, as she put it, "operationalize victory."

The presidential recount wore on, ending on December 12 in yet another disappointment, as the Supreme Court decided the election in favor of George W. Bush. Pelosi had an idea. The fact that Democrats were winning in California but losing in other states suggested that the Californians knew something that could benefit the rest of the party. She offered to host a presentation at the next caucus retreat with the California party's consultants, about using modern communications methods and marketing insights to reach voters.

But the arrogant establishment was not particularly interested in new ideas that might threaten their time-honored methods for losing the congressional majority. When, after much pestering, they finally agreed to put Pelosi's presentation on the schedule, none of the members of leadership and few other Democrats showed up to hear it. As Pelosi left the presentation room, George Miller could see she was seething and trying not to show it. "You know what?" she said to him as they walked out. "I don't think these boys know how to win."

◇ ◇ ◇

The whip race extended into its third year. For three years, Pelosi and Hoyer had been shadowboxing, fighting fiercely for a job opening that did not exist. They campaigned with candidates who hadn't yet been elected, showering them with donations in the hope that they'd get to Congress and return the favor. In the 2000 cycle, Hoyer gave $1.5 million to House candidates—a staggering sum at the time, five times what Bonior had given to candidates in the past decade. Pelosi gave $3.9 million.

When a Virginia congressman died suddenly, and a special election was scheduled to replace him, Hoyer and Pelosi both immediately sent $10,000 checks to their preferred candidates in the primary. They both chipped in wherever there was a competitive race, but Pelosi also sent checks to members whose seats were safe, symbolic donations to let them know she was paying attention to them, too.

Pelosi was accused of playing dirty. The one woman in the California delegation who was supporting Hoyer alleged that Pelosi had threatened to draw her out of her district in the next redistricting. Pelosi denied this, but it was utterly plausible that her allies in Burton World might have made such a threat, with or without her knowledge. Pelosi's partisans, meanwhile, believed it was Hoyer who was playing dirty, feeding negative stories about her to the press and echoing the Republican narrative that she was an out-of-touch "San Francisco liberal."

In May 2001, the shadowboxing ended. Bonior, the whip since 1991, said he would step down from the position in January 2002 to run for governor. The whip job was finally going to be open, and the race for Democratic whip was officially under way.

Pelosi and Hoyer had different constituencies. She had the automatic support of most of the women and Californians in the caucus and of politically sympathetic liberals. But she also had allies, such as Murtha, who came from the right side of the caucus and supported her because they respected her abilities. Other moderate Pelosi fans included Mike Thompson, a moderate California Democrat whom she'd helped win a primary against a more liberal candidate, and Collin Peterson, one of the most conservative House Democrats, who represented an agricultural district in rural Minnesota. They set to work convincing their like-minded colleagues that she was a pragmatist, not an ideologue.

Pelosi talked about the importance of a fresh perspective and a voice from the West. Above all, her pitch was about taking on the Republicans and knowing how to win. Where Hoyer, like Gephardt, preferred to blur partisan differences and emphasize consensus, Pelosi sought to sharpen party lines. She thought Democrats needed to know what they stood for, be resolute about it and offer a clear alternative. Which vision prevailed would have lasting consequences for the party's trajectory.

Pelosi also talked about the symbolic significance of putting a woman in a top leadership post. But Murtha cautioned her against leaning too far into gender: "There are a hell of a lot more men in this goddamn Congress than women," he said, "so let's be a little careful about what you're pushing here." Unlike in a public election, the number of total votes was fixed: 215 House Democrats, with 108 needed to win.

Murtha was a crucial validator for Pelosi with older male members of the caucus who might not have been inclined to take her seriously. He told them: *This woman has a vision. She has political skills that nobody else in Congress has. Don't think she's from San Francisco. She's from Baltimore.* Murtha was also close to Gephardt and urged the leader to stay neutral in the race rather than endorsing his friend Hoyer. As awful as the 2000 defeat had been, it had given Pelosi a convincing new talking point: she knew how to win, and the establishment she was running against did not.

Pelosi had learned to be thorough. Years earlier, when she was new to Congress and seeking a seat on Appropriations for the first time, she approached a more senior member to seek his support. "Without even knowing who else is in the race, I'm for you!" he told her. She marked him down as a "yes." But then he voted for someone else. She reproached the elder: I thought you said you were for me! No, he explained, I said I was for you without knowing who else was running. Once I found out who else was running, I wasn't for you anymore.

Pelosi learned to listen to what people were actually saying, not what she wanted to hear—and to get it in writing if possible. "You'd be a great whip!" was not a "yes." Only a commitment to vote was a "yes," and even then, people could always betray you on the secret ballot—best to get some extra commitments for insurance. This ability to hear what people were actually saying would, in the years to come, be a crucial component of Pelosi's vote-counting skills.

Every Wednesday, Pelosi met with her campaign team for a catered lunch in her office. To make sure people came, she ordered the best sandwiches in Washington. Each member would get assigned three colleagues whose votes were up for grabs, and at the next week's lunch they'd report back on whether they'd nailed them down, or how they might be gettable. By September, Pelosi claimed 120 commitments out of the 108 necessary. Some she named publicly, in a blizzard of letters she released from every possible constituency: the Blue Dogs, the black caucus, the Hispanic caucus, and so on. Others expressed private support. But Hoyer claimed 102 commitments. The total of their supposed pledges was more than the number of Democratic members, so someone was being lied to.

Hoyer believed it was Pelosi. "There are members who publicly said they are voting for Nancy Pelosi that have indicated privately that they are voting for Mr. Hoyer," a spokeswoman told reporters. Hoyer assumed when they said it to him, they were telling the truth. People, he insinuated, wanted to seem politically correct by publicly supporting the woman candidate. But on the secret ballot, he believed, they'd put down the candidate they preferred to lead them—him.

The vote was slated for shortly after Bonior planned to formally announce that he would resign as whip: September 11, 2001.

❖ ❖ ❖

It was a bright September morning. The East Coast was up and about and heading to work. Pelosi was at a meeting when she heard. The first plane struck the North Tower of the World Trade Center at 8:46 a.m. The second hit the South Tower at 9:03. Panic and confusion reigned. No one knew quite what was happening. Cell phone signals in Manhattan were jammed. Planes were still in the air. Two of them had been hijacked and were headed for DC.

When she first saw the footage, Pelosi thought it must be a simulation of some sort. Then the reality set in. She wasn't at the Capitol, but her staff was. They were sitting in a committee office watching the attacks on TV when she called, her voice calm but stern. "Get out of the Capitol," she said. The staffers didn't seem in any hurry to comply. She said it again: "The building you are in is not safe. You need to get out of there." When they hung up the phone, they realized that Capitol Police were marching through the halls ordering everyone to evacuate immediately.

The third plane hit the Pentagon, located just across the river from the Capitol.

Pelosi called her office in San Francisco, where it was not yet 7 a.m. Some staffers were already headed into work at a downtown government building. She told them not to go in.

A sort of numb shock descended. She did what she always did in a crisis, which was to detach her emotions and act. She couldn't reach Alexandra, who lived in Manhattan, and the worry gnawed at the back of her mind, but she focused on what she could do.

At 9:59 a.m., the South Tower, burning for nearly an hour, collapsed.

At 10:03, a fourth plane crash-landed in a field in Pennsylvania. It had been scheduled to fly to San Francisco, but its trajectory suggested it had been headed for DC—possibly the Capitol or the White House.

What was there to do? More than a hundred members huddled at the Capitol Police headquarters a couple of blocks from the Capitol. They watched the events unfold on television. Pelosi was the top Democrat on the Intelligence Committee. The administration convened a briefing at the end of the day. It was decided that one way to reassure the American people would be to send a message of bipartisan unity and resolve from Congress.

The next day, Pelosi joined Gephardt; the Speaker, Republican Dennis Hastert; and the Intelligence Committee chairman, Porter Goss, at a press conference. Stay calm, they said. The adults are in charge. We will handle this. Pelosi spoke up to insist that civil liberties would not be a casualty of the attacks.

She went back to San Francisco and attended a memorial service at a Baptist church in the Fillmore District. A man named Paul Holm, the partner of Mark Bingham, one of the Flight 93 victims, was in attendance. The church's pastor, echoing the views of many San Franciscans, intoned, "America, is there anything you did to set up this climate? America, America, what did you do?"

Many of the politicians who were there, such as Senator Dianne Feinstein and Governor Gray Davis, walked out in protest of the anti-American sentiment at an event that was supposed to be about memorializing victims. Pelosi didn't leave; she thought someone should stay and speak up. When it was her turn, she rebuked the pastor: "The act of terrorism on September 11 put those people outside the order of civilized behavior, and we will not take responsibility for that," she said. Afterward, she found

Holm and apologized for what the pastor had said. He noticed that her eyes were full of tears.

✧ ✧ ✧

The attack immediately changed the political climate, as Americans rallied around the White House and the flag. Everything before 9/11 seemed distant, frozen. The politicking on Capitol Hill was temporarily suspended, and the whip election was postponed. Gephardt scheduled the vote—a closed-door caucus meeting at which the candidates would have an opportunity to make their final pitch—for 9 a.m. on October 10.

Hoyer hinted to his colleagues that this might be a particularly awkward moment to elevate a leader from a far-left district like Pelosi's. He pointed out that Pelosi, like many antiwar liberals, had frequently voted against Pentagon budgets: "Nancy has simply not been as supportive as I have on national security," he told the *New York Times*.

Pelosi found this offensive, but having checked and rechecked her commitments, she was not worried. In a letter to colleagues, she pointed to her foreign affairs and intelligence committee work to argue that she was the one more qualified to lead the party "at this particularly difficult time."

When the day of the vote arrived, Team Pelosi had a plan. They made wake-up calls at 7:30, to ensure that none of their key supporters had slept in, and sent cars to anyone who needed a ride to the Capitol. Breakfast was served in Pelosi's office. Her aides roamed the halls with walkie-talkies. When they noticed that John Conyers of Michigan wasn't at the meeting, a staffer found him in his office and urged him to get to the Caucus Room. Another member chartered a plane from Tokyo to get back in time. Even though she was viewed as the front-runner going in, Pelosi remembered what had happened to Phil Burton—losing by one vote.

The Democratic members trooped into the Caucus Room in the Cannon House Office Building, next to the Capitol. It was a big, ornate room with Corinthian pilasters, crystal chandeliers and gilded friezes above the tall windows. Rows of folding chairs faced a lectern at the front.

Hoyer gave a soaring speech that invoked the Kennedys. Pelosi had Murtha speak for her. He talked about her track record of knowing how to win. Outside the room, Leo McCarthy, her old friend from California politics, joined Pelosi's daughters Alexandra and Christine, who were waiting anxiously for the result.

In the final tally, it was 118 votes for Pelosi, 95 for Hoyer. Her count was almost exactly right; it was his that fell short. It turned out that Hoyer was the one being lied to by members who promised their votes. He chalked the loss up to demographics. "If she hadn't been a woman or from California, I think we would have been okay," he said later. "C'est la guerre."

Pelosi emerged from the room beaming her clenched-teeth grin, and a cheer went up from behind her. Before the bank of TV cameras that had been set up, Bonior handed her the big, black leather whip that had hung in his office. It was thick and ugly, a gleaming, braided snake coiled into a lasso-like circle. Pelosi clutched it with both hands as she faced the assembled media. For the first time, she was a leader of her party in the House. For the first time, a woman had cracked the ranks of the top leadership of Congress.

"If it were not for the tragedy in this country, I would say this is a very happy day for me," she said, speaking quickly and forcefully. "But let me just say this. In the vote taken today, the Democratic Party not only has made history, I believe it has made progress as well."

Hoyer spoke next, congratulating her and trying to sound humble. "I'm Steny Hoyer, former aspirant for whip," he said. Standing to his left, Pelosi raised her right hand and clapped him on the shoulder, as if to say, "Very funny." She had won the first round. But the rivalry between them would continue.

10

THE MINORITY WHIP'S OFFICE WAS A STEP UP FROM PELOSI'S OLD QUAR-
ters. In January 2002, she moved in and hung the ugly black whip on the
wall. But she hung no pictures, and she told her staff not to get too comfortable, because they would not be staying long. Victory for the Democrats was just around the corner, she assured them, and with it would come
her promotion to majority leader.

That same month, she went to the White House for the first time as a
member of congressional leadership. Bush received them in the Cabinet
Room: Pelosi, Minority Leader Gephardt, Speaker Denny Hastert, Majority Leader Dick Armey, and their counterparts in the Senate. It was far
from the first time she'd been the only woman in the room. But it suddenly
hit her that she wasn't just the only woman in *this* room, at *this* moment.
She was the only woman *ever* to be part of a meeting between the president
of the United States and the leaders of the legislative branch. For two-
hundred-plus years of American history, from George Washington to Bill
Clinton, presidents had been meeting with Congress to plot the course of
the nation. Hundreds of combinations of lawmakers had participated in
those meetings, making the decisions that determined the country's fate—
whether its sons would be called up to fight in another war, how to save its
farmers from drought and depression, the healing of the nation's sick and
the education of its children.

And until she got there, every one of those decision makers had been a man.

The 2002 midterm election was only ten months away. Going on eight years in the wilderness, some Democrats were starting to lose hope. The double whammy of Bush's election, which many Democrats viewed as illegitimate, and 9/11, which had rallied the country behind the commander in chief, made them feel cursed. Pelosi told them to buck up. *Don't think of yourself as Congressman So-and-So,* she'd say. *Think of yourself as Mr. Chairman, Madam Chairman—the title you'll get when we win.*

There was already a meeting of the caucus whip team every Thursday, but Pelosi instituted a second one, on Tuesdays, so they could start the week on the same page. The Republicans' majority was so narrow that they needed Democratic votes to get many things through the House. This gave the minority leverage to advance its own priorities here and there. In February, Pelosi scored a big and unexpected win. The GOP was blocking the House's version of the landmark campaign finance legislation that would come to be known as McCain-Feingold. Although it had bipartisan support, Republican leaders refused to allow a vote in committee, leaving the bill effectively tabled. Democrats decided to employ a little-used House tactic called a "discharge petition," which forces a bill to the floor if it has the support of 218 members, a majority of the House. This is an extremely difficult feat to pull off, because it requires members of the majority party to go on the record against their own leadership and colleagues—inviting retaliation.

The Republicans' whip, Tom DeLay, was known as "the Hammer" for his skill at enforcing party discipline. A swaggering born-again Christian from Texas, DeLay had initially won his colleagues' loyalty not with strong-arm tactics but by bringing snacks to the House Republican Cloakroom. But he loved the "Hammer" nickname, and the implication that, while others avoided the fray, he was the one getting his hands dirty. When he served with Gingrich, of whom he was not terribly fond, DeLay liked to say that Newt was the visionary and he was the "ditch digger." It was DeLay who had whipped the impeachment of Bill Clinton through the House in 1998, and DeLay who would later be reprimanded by the Ethics Committee for bribing and bullying members to get bills passed. DeLay knew Pelosi and liked her; as a fellow practitioner of the same game, he respected her grit. Still, she was an amateur, only a few weeks into her job, and he thought he could teach her a thing or two.

The discharge petition came to the floor, and DeLay got an unpleasant surprise: all but 12 Democrats voted for the bill, along with 41 Republicans. The bill passed and went to the Senate, and Bush signed it into law. The Democrats, despite being in the minority, had managed to push through a major piece of legislation over the objections of GOP leaders. That was the moment DeLay realized that Pelosi was going to be a formidable opponent.

Still, with George W. Bush's approval rating hovering around 80 percent, many Democrats thought they should stand with the president when it came to foreign affairs, lest they be viewed as unpatriotic. The country felt under siege; people feared that the next 9/11 was just around the corner. It was supposed to be a time of national unity, not partisanship. Pelosi agreed with this—to a point. She supported the president's handling of terrorism, but she thought that people needed to know that the Democrats had a different vision for the economy. The tax cuts Bush had pushed through a few months before 9/11 were mostly benefiting the wealthy, she noted, and Democrats shouldn't let him get away with it by wrapping himself in the flag.

Patriotic unity, she believed, also shouldn't mean never questioning the president or holding the intelligence agencies accountable. Shortly after the attacks, she wrote and the House passed a bill authorizing Congress to investigate what had happened on September 11. During the hearings on the subject a year later, Pelosi said Democrats "stood shoulder to shoulder with President Bush to remove the threat of terrorism posed by al-Qaeda." But she sharply criticized the White House for withholding information Congress needed to complete its investigation. This helped lead to the formation of the 9/11 Commission, which had a broader mandate to trace the attacks' origins.

Her job as whip was to supply the votes while Gephardt led the Democrats' positioning and strategy. But Gephardt was something of an absentee leader. It was an open secret that he planned to run for president in 2004. When members came to him with a problem, often he wouldn't make a decision; he'd hear them out, tell them he'd take it under advisement, and then wait for things to work themselves out without his intervention. Democratic members started going to Pelosi instead when they needed the caucus to sign off on something or wanted help advancing a policy priority through the budget negotiations with the Republicans.

After months of rumblings, in September 2002, Bush announced that he planned to seek Congress's permission to wage a preemptive war on Iraq if the administration deemed it necessary to stop Saddam Hussein's regime from possessing weapons of mass destruction. Bush's political advisers saw an opportunity to box the Democrats in by holding the vote on the eve of the midterm elections. Would they dare vote against the resolution and risk being branded as soft on terrorism, perhaps in an ad that flashed their faces alongside pictures of Osama bin Laden and Saddam Hussein? The Republicans ran such an ad against Georgia senator Max Cleland, an army veteran who had lost three limbs (both legs and an arm) in a grenade accident in Vietnam. Cleland voted for the war, but the ad pointed to his votes on minor homeland security measures to imply he was letting the terrorists win.

For the sake of his party as well as his presidential aspirations, Gephardt thought the Democrats should back the war. If the public viewed the war as a bipartisan, nonpolitical endeavor, Bush's strength would be neutralized, he reasoned. Democrats would then be free to differentiate themselves on other issues. Most of the party's top brass agreed. Senators Hillary Clinton, John Edwards and John Kerry all favored the war resolution, as did the Democrats' Senate leader, Tom Daschle. When Bush presented his war authorization proposal to the public on October 2, 2002, Gephardt stood beside him in the White House Rose Garden, looking grave. "We have to do what is right for the security of our nation and the safety of all Americans," Gephardt said.

Pelosi agreed with that sentiment, as far as it went. But what did Iraq have to do with keeping America safe? Like many liberals, she suspected Bush's real motives had to do with the unfinished business of his father, who'd stopped short of taking out Saddam when the United States invaded Iraq in 1991. To many on the left, the push for the war seemed hasty, cavalier, ideological—the work of a cowboy president obsessed with proving his machismo on the world stage, backed by a band of neoconservative ideologues and war profiteers. The same day that Bush announced his war resolution, Pelosi made her own statement. "The case of using force in Iraq has not been made," she said.

"Are you calling the president a liar?" a reporter asked.

"I'm stating a fact," she replied.

It was a bold break with her own party's leadership. Behind the scenes, party elders cautioned her to be careful. Voices like hers, they worried, were making it too easy for the GOP to depict Democrats as a bunch of peaceniks who lacked the spine to defend the homeland and who, if given power, would put it at further risk.

As the top Democrat on the Intelligence Committee, Pelosi had access to the evidence most others didn't get to see, and she scrutinized it closely and skeptically. (She would eventually become the longest-serving member in the committee's history.) It wasn't that she didn't believe Saddam had or was working to get WMDs; she believed he was, and she had supported President Clinton's 1998 air strikes on Iraqi weapons facilities. But she wasn't convinced by the current administration's questionable attempts to draw a link between Iraq and 9/11; nor did she believe that Saddam, however brutal and dangerous he might be for his own people and for the Mideast at large, posed a threat to the United States.

Rather than advance the nation's effort to combat international terrorism, Pelosi believed that an invasion would set it back. And just as she had in 1991 with the Gulf War, she didn't think war was worth what it would cost—in American lives, in money, in the cost to the United States' alliances and stature in the world. Her district's strongly antiwar disposition surely played a role in determining her decision. Before the vote, Pelosi got twelve thousand calls in three weeks from her constituents, and only twenty of them supported the war. Partisanship—her dislike of the Republican president—was part of the equation as well. But in this case her partisan instinct led her to be wary of a manufactured consensus in the making. "When we go in, the occupation—which is now being called 'liberation'—could be interminable, and so could the amount of money, unlimited, that it will cost," she said in a floor speech that received almost no press coverage.

The Iraq issue divided the Democrats. The caucus meeting after Gephardt announced his support for the war resolution was a brutal one. Gephardt insisted that by participating in negotiations with the administration, he had succeeded in getting an authorization bill that had more avenues for diplomacy and additional conditions for military action. The president and CIA director had repeatedly assured him that the intelligence behind the case for war was strong, that diplomacy would come first and that simply taking out Saddam was not the main goal. But liberal members believed their leader was being used by the administration to give cover to its misbegotten goals.

Pelosi came up with an idea to offer an alternative to the president's resolution. She asked John Spratt, a hawkish, conservative Democrat from South Carolina, to craft an amendment that would make Bush come back to Congress for permission if the United Nations didn't authorize war. Spratt, a senior member of the Armed Services Committee, was no pacifist, but he opposed a unilateral rush to war. The caucus's liberals were grateful for the alternative the amendment represented to the president's all-or-nothing offer.

The administration-backed authorization for the war came to the House floor on October 10. Gephardt was not directing Democrats to vote one way or another—it was a "conscience vote," up to each individual member to decide his or her position based on principle or political interest. He had made up his own mind, he told the caucus, and it was up to them to make up theirs.

With the vote officially not being "whipped," the party whip would seem to have little to do besides cast her own vote. But that was not Pelosi's style. She buttonholed her colleagues on the fence and made her case in vehement, moralistic terms, appealing to their sense of principle. On the day of the vote, she could be seen darting here and there across the floor, personally lobbying members, as her staff trailed behind her, struggling to keep up. (Members understood that this was Pelosi's personal crusade and not an effort to undermine Gephardt; the resolution had enough Republican support that it was sure to pass no matter how the Democrats voted.) By the time the vote closed, Pelosi had been successful: 60 percent of House Democrats voted against the resolution. Seventy percent, 147 Democrats, voted for the Spratt Amendment, but with scant GOP support it did not come close to passing; still, it provided a symbolic outlet for Democrats' angst. It was a different story in the Senate, where only 21 of the 50 Democrats opposed the administration's war powers authorization.

Another midterm election came and went in 2002—another loss for the Democrats. They lost 6 seats in the House, terrible compared to the typical midterm presidential backlash, but not too bad considering the way the national pro-war mood had buoyed Bush and the Republicans. Pelosi thought the Democrats' divisions on the war had muddled their message and made it hard for voters to know what they were about. She also believed that the Republicans had used clever rhetoric to make it seem as if they were the ones who supported education and health care and fighting poverty, and that Democrats hadn't done enough to fight back.

The day after the election, Gephardt announced that he would step down as Democratic leader, in part to take responsibility for the midterm loss and in part to focus on his presidential campaign. He called to tell Pelosi, who said she was sad she wouldn't get to see him be Speaker. She meant it. But no sooner had she hung up the phone than she picked it up again to start calling her colleagues. For, without Gephardt, the Democrats were going to need a new minority leader.

◇ ◇ ◇

Pelosi had, as usual, done her part. She raised seven million dollars for the 2002 cycle, a pace so prodigious that a *Times* columnist criticized her for turning Congress into "a self-lubricating money machine." She created not one but two political action committees in order to siphon still more cash from her biggest donors—a move that the Federal Election Commission found to be illegal, forcing her to close one of the PACs. In a not atypical weekend that began the day after the vote on the war resolution, a reporter traveling with Pelosi recorded that "over a 72-hour span, Pelosi would fly 3,678 miles, ride 14 hours in rented vans, shake more than 600 hands, visit three grandchildren, speak to two dozen reporters, and raise money for eight House candidates," from Houston to Boulder to the outskirts of Scranton, Pennsylvania. And all of it in pantyhose and high heels, and without the benefit of a cup of coffee, a glass of wine or more than a few hours' sleep each night.

One moment, she would be doing a million things at once, such as dialing her cell phone, skimming a briefing book, checking in with her husband and children and fellow members of Congress, and scoping the electoral map—she once rebuked a staffer who tried to build some breathing room into her schedule, "I don't do downtime"—and the next, she would transition instantly into the picture of attentiveness, focused completely on the person in front of her and the conversation at hand. Scientists once thought that women's brains were better than men's at multitasking. But brain studies found that multitasking doesn't exist—the human brain can do only one thing at once; what we call "multitasking" is just the brain rapidly switching between tasks. Women, scientists concluded, aren't inherently better at switching than men. They just tend to have to do more things.

Redistricting after the 2000 Census made the electoral map more challenging for Democrats in many states. In Michigan, the new map forced two longtime Democratic colleagues, John Dingell and Lynn Rivers, into the same Detroit-area district, meaning they'd have to run against each other in a primary for a single seat in Congress. Dingell was something of a legend. The powerful chair of the Energy and Commerce Committee, a vast fiefdom that oversaw most environmental and economic legislation, he had been in Congress since the 1950s, succeeding his father, also named John Dingell. When Pelosi sent ten thousand dollars to Rivers, she was criticized for taking sides and potentially making a powerful enemy in Dingell. But in the whip race, Rivers had been with her, and Dingell had not. Pelosi knew the donation would be noticed, and her colleagues would see how loyal she was to the people who were loyal to her. "Mother-loyal," she called it. Rivers lost, and Dingell remained in the caucus as a thorn in Pelosi's side—but a few years later, Pelosi would have the last word.

Within twenty-four hours of Gephardt's stepping down, Pelosi had called 150 of her colleagues and personally asked for their vote. She started the day by calling the East Coast members in the morning, then moved westward across the time zones, making calls to the West Coast after Washington had gone to bed. She soon sent a letter announcing that she had secured 111 commitments out of the 104 she needed—and she listed all 111 names.

A rival, Martin Frost of Texas, who served as caucus chair, tried to mount a late coup against Pelosi, holding a press conference to criticize her for being too liberal and predicting that voters wouldn't support a party that opposed Bush's popular foreign policy. "I believe our party must occupy the center if we are to be successful," he said. Though the press called him a "centrist" and her a "liberal," Frost and Pelosi had voted the same way 85 percent of the time. But the more alike people are, the more they strain to differentiate themselves—"the narcissism of small differences," as a German saying puts it. Frost dropped out when he realized Pelosi had the votes to win. Another challenger, thirty-two-year-old Harold Ford Jr. of Tennessee, made a similar pitch for centrism, painting Pelosi, ironically, as one of the "party elders" who had led the party to a decade of defeat.

But it wasn't even close: on November 14, 2002, Pelosi won the caucus election for minority leader, 177–29. Hoyer, her former rival, won the whip job, making him her second-in-command.

The Democratic Party had made a momentous choice: for its first-ever woman caucus leader, but also for a political theory that said that you started with your principles and worked to the middle, rather than the other way around. It was Pelosi's party now, and she made clear her diagnosis of the Democrats' woes. "Never again," she told her colleagues, "will Democrats go into a campaign where we don't have a message as to who we are and what we stand for, how we are different from Republicans." With her at the helm, that wouldn't happen again.

11

WHAT WAS AMERICA TO MAKE OF THE DEMOCRATIC PARTY'S NEW leader in Congress? The day after Pelosi won the post of minority leader, a columnist in the *Wall Street Journal* described her leadership style as consisting of "den-motheresque whip letters—full of team spirit and kudos for individual members." The conservative talk radio host Rush Limbaugh affixed Pelosi's head on a beauty queen's body on his website and labeled her "Miss America." The editor of the right-leaning *Washington Times* called her the party's "new prom queen." It was all very diminishing: *Look at this perky little lady. How adorable!* At the same time, Limbaugh complained that Pelosi's aggressive nature was ruining her looks. Liberal women like her, he said, were "always whining and complaining about something, and it shows." If only they'd all just shut up and sit down and smile.

At age sixty-two, Pelosi was a national figure now, the leader of her party in the House. The GOP professed to be delighted. She made a perfect foil. When their base voters in rural America and the South thought of Democrats, Republicans wanted them to think of people like Pelosi: out-to-lunch "latte liberals" from the West Coast who, they charged, wanted to take away guns, turn children gay and disarm the military. Another conservative columnist warned readers that Pelosi came from "the Fidel Castro wing of the Democratic Party." Voters might not be wild about Republicans, but one look at *that* would be enough to keep them in the tent.

The weekend after her election, Pelosi made her maiden appearance as Democratic leader on the hallowed Sunday morning show *Meet the Press*. The moderator, Tim Russert, was a dean of the Washington punditocracy, that elite clique of Very Serious Men whose estimations of American leaders were taken as gospel by the DC power class. Russert grilled Pelosi on her liberal views and whether they would hurt her party's image. He surprised her with a taped interview with a party leader from the South who said, "Her face is one we don't want shown in South Carolina."

Pelosi brushed off the criticisms. "You know the story. It's like the Thanksgiving turkey," she said. "You bring it out, you get this great honor, everybody oohs and aahs ... and then they begin to carve you up."

The *Meet the Press* appearance was widely viewed as disastrous. Pelosi was wooden and unsteady, and seemed to be trying to have it both ways, insisting that Democrats supported the president's fight against terrorism and would even support an Iraq war that went through the proper channels at the same time as she defended her record of antiwar and anti-Bush votes. She had only just gotten the job, and already the conventional wisdom was coalescing around the conclusion that she would be a problem for her party.

In fact, as Pelosi understood, few ordinary Americans had any idea who she was—or, for that matter, who any congressional leader was. Two-thirds of Americans can't name a single Supreme Court justice, and nearly a third don't know the name of the sitting vice president, much less the brand-new leader of the minority party in the House of Representatives. When Gallup polled Pelosi's national ratings for the first time in early 2003, 23 percent of Americans viewed her favorably, 18 percent unfavorably— and nearly 60 percent didn't recognize her name. Despite the GOP's publicity campaign on her behalf, she was fundamentally an inside player, and not going to be a household name anytime soon. To Pelosi, what people thought about her in Peoria simply did not matter.

It was what she would do in the House, not how people might perceive her, that Pelosi was focused on. Her elevation to leader was a turning point. For the first time in her congressional career, there was no one above her, no man calling the shots. It would be up to her to absorb the cacophony of viewpoints of the House's 205 Democrats (plus one liberal Independent, Bernie Sanders of Vermont), take stock of the opposition and public sentiment and all the other considerations, and decide what to do. Fortunately, decisiveness had always been one of her strong suits. She wasn't a ditherer who wavered back and forth, tortured, unable to weigh the pros and cons; she might consult a few confidants, but she generally had her mind made up quickly. Decisive to a fault, perhaps—once she made up her mind, she hardly ever changed it. One of her favorite axioms—she deployed it, for example, when a colleague mounted a hopeless presidential campaign, failed utterly to make a mark, and quit the race to slink back to the lesser glories of the House—was "Decisions are liberating."

The two chambers of Congress make their own rules, constrained only by tradition and the Constitution, which offers precious little guidance. It's up to the leaders of the parties to work out what the committees will be, how large each will be and how many committee seats each party will get. Before the start of the 2003 session, Pelosi spoke with Speaker Dennis Hastert, a laconic born-again Christian from rural Illinois, to work out the committee structures. (Hastert, a former wrestling coach, would eventually earn two historical distinctions: the longest-serving Republican Speaker ever and, after his post-retirement conviction on charges related to child molestation, the highest-ranking elected official to go to prison.) The relatively small change wrought by the 2002 election, a 6-seat gain for the GOP, didn't substantially alter the partisan balance, so Hastert told her the committees would stay the same size. Ever the stickler, Pelosi asked him to put this in writing, and he dutifully sent her a letter to that effect.

Pelosi then convened the Democrats' steering committee for perhaps the leader's trickiest and most internally divisive task: the distribution of committee assignments. This would require taking into consideration all 205 members' seniority; the nature and competitiveness of their home districts; regional interests; political positions; pet issues; geographic, gender, racial, and ideological diversity; and relationships—with Pelosi and with one another. It's like drawing up the seating chart for a two-hundred-person dinner party at which everyone knows which tables are the best, but some people like certain tables more than others, and most people want to be able to sit at more than one table, and the tables have to be both heterogenous and capable of working together, and there are sub-tables that also have to be both diverse and harmonious, and the guests, who love to complain and will be stuck at their tables for two years, have the ability in some cases to go rogue and overrule the host. By the end of the hours-long meeting it was done. The committees were stocked, the members had their assignments, and the press releases announcing the rosters were being drafted.

While Pelosi was in the meeting, DeLay—whom many considered the real power behind the mild-mannered Hastert—called. Twice. When she called him back, he told her the Republicans planned to give the Democrats one fewer seat than before on the Ways and Means Committee, the powerful panel that writes the tax laws.

This was unacceptable to Pelosi. It would upset the whole balance of the committee assignments she'd just painstakingly distributed. She had already given away the two open Ways and Means slots, one to a Blue Dog from Texas, who could use it to show his swing district constituents he was building Washington clout; and another to an Ohioan who would make history as the first black woman on the committee. Plus, Pelosi had it in writing—from the Speaker—that the number of seats was not changing.

DeLay said he knew that, but was it really such a big deal? The new chairman wanted a slightly smaller committee, and both parties would be giving up a seat. With two fewer total seats on the panel, Democrats would actually have a slightly larger proportion. Couldn't she find a way not to be difficult about this one little thing?

Pelosi chose her words carefully and spoke them slowly into the phone. "Life on this planet as you know it will not be the same if you persist in this notion," she said.

The Congressional Black Caucus, she told DeLay, had a press conference later that day. Republicans would not want the black members to spend their press conference blasting away at the Speaker for going back on his word and taking a top committee spot away from a history-making African American woman, would they?

The phone call ended with no resolution. Later, Pelosi's staff told her the Republicans were threatening to go after her personally. "I'm shaking in my boots," she replied. "That is so pathetic. Tell them, 'C'mon.'"

DeLay backed off, and Pelosi got what she wanted. More important, she had laid down a marker: she was no lightweight and, unlike the easygoing Gephardt, she was no pushover. She would fight for every scrap, she would always stick up for her people and she was impervious to personal threats. As she liked to tell people, the only thing that could scare her was having her children taken away; anything else was trivial by comparison.

The Republicans used their rule-making power to shut the Democrats out as much as possible. They blocked the minority party from submitting amendments and kept them out of negotiations with the Senate. They drafted bills in secret and presented them without holding hearings. The Speaker announced that he would abide by his own "Hastert Rule" and bring to the floor only those bills that were supported by the majority of Republicans—sharply curtailing bipartisanship by ruling out many proposals that both Democrats and Republicans supported. Democrats couldn't hold hearings of their own to bring attention to issues. The Republican majority even pressured K Street firms to hire Republican lobbyists and curtail Democratic donations.

Hastert would not be the last Republican leader to find Pelosi's inflexibility and hyperattention to detail galling. He complained to colleagues that she was always so nice to him in person, but then she'd send him the nastiest, most demanding letters. Gone were the days when two guys could just get together and grease the wheels with a handshake, making everyone's lives easier—especially their own. Pelosi, by contrast, seemed determined to pick every nit, fight every battle, argue over every dime. "Republicans have come to the realization," Hastert told a reporter, "that she's not a foil. She's someone you have to deal with."

Pelosi could have told them that, but they wouldn't have listened. She had to show them instead.

✦ ✦ ✦

On March 19, 2003, Pelosi got a call from Condoleezza Rice, the national security adviser. "The president asked me to inform you that in one hour we will initiate an attack on Iraq," Rice said.

"Why now?" Pelosi asked. The administration, in her view, hadn't exhausted the potential diplomatic options. Rice insisted that now was the time, but she would say no more. Pelosi later learned that the administration thought they could take out Saddam Hussein that very night.

They were wrong about that, just as they were wrong about the presence of weapons of mass destruction they said would justify the invasion. They were wrong when they said the troops would be greeted by the Iraqis not as an invading army but as "liberators." They were wrong when they said that Iraq's own resources, not the American taxpayer, would fund the country's speedy reconstruction. And they were wrong when, less than two months later, Bush, after a photo op in an olive-green flight suit, declared,

"Major combat operations in Iraq have ended," under a banner that read, "MISSION ACCOMPLISHED."

The war, at first, was popular. In the beginning months, the networks were wall to wall with jingoistic coverage. The foreign policy and journalistic establishments were behind it, from Thomas Friedman at the *New York Times* to the centrist *Washington Post* editorial page to the liberals at the *New Republic*. The right pooh-poohed the war protesters who filled the streets—many of them women—as nutty and unserious, washed-up hippies not sophisticated enough to comprehend the mortal peril the nation faced. In polls, the public trusted Republicans over Democrats to handle national security by a two-to-one margin.

With her party in the minority, Pelosi had little of the coin of the legislative realm, leverage. What she had was her voice, along with that of the other opponents of the war. But it was difficult to articulate a clear message with her party divided and the nation in a bellicose mood. She tried to thread the needle by expressing support for the troops even as she continued to oppose the war. The distinction might have been clear in her mind, but it came off as contradictory when, having only recently questioned the president's judgment and trustworthiness, she declared, "I do not have any intention of second-guessing the strategy of the commander in chief." She avoided the antiwar protests, and voted in favor of a Republican resolution praising Bush's leadership as well as the troops—enraging the party's activist base, which was organizing with the help of the nascent blogosphere and flocking to antiwar movement leaders such as Howard Dean, the former governor of Vermont and a presidential candidate, and Barack Obama, a state senator in Illinois who had written a powerful memoir and was running for U.S. Senate.

Notwithstanding Bush's "MISSION ACCOMPLISHED" banner, the war wore on, devolving into just the kind of fiasco Pelosi had predicted. After more than a year, there was no end in sight. More than a thousand American service members had been killed. It was clear to Pelosi that Bush needed to be defeated for his mishandling of the war, but nobody in Washington was making the case in a way that made people sit up and take notice. So she decided to do it herself.

In a series of speeches, Pelosi abandoned her previously compliant tone. She slammed Bush's "go-it-alone foreign policy" and called him "divorced from reality." Then, in an explosive interview with the *San*

Francisco Chronicle, she went further, declaring that Bush was "in over his head," had "no judgment and no plan," and had "on his shoulders the deaths of many more troops." He had created, she said, "a hotbed of terrorism in Iraq," and he needed to be replaced with a new president. "As far as we can tell, the shallowness that he has brought to the office has not changed since he got there," she said.

Her communications director, who was sitting in on the interview, began to look like he'd swallowed something that didn't agree with him. What was she thinking? Why hadn't she warned him she was going to go so far? When he asked her, she replied, "I didn't want you to talk me out of it."

Just as Pelosi had hoped, Republicans promptly flew off the handle. From the White House press secretary to the Bush-Cheney reelection campaign to the Republican National Committee, they denounced Pelosi as a troop hater and a terrorist sympathizer. DeLay said she was "so caught up in the partisan hatred for President Bush that her words are putting American lives at risk."

But her press conference the next day was packed with reporters and cameramen, and every question was about Iraq. She had changed the debate.

◇ ◇ ◇

The war still dominated the news, but Bush was straining to accomplish a domestic agenda as well. The centerpiece, in 2003, was his plan to create a new add-on to Medicare, the enormously popular health system for Americans age sixty-five and older. During the campaign, Bush had promised to help seniors afford the rising cost of prescription drugs. His political strategist, Karl Rove, viewed it as one of three key initiatives to attract swing voters for Bush's reelection; the others were bipartisan education standards legislation (No Child Left Behind, enacted in 2002) and immigration reform (which never got done, despite bipartisan support, because Bush's own base rose up in protest).

The idea of a drug benefit for seniors was something Democrats, including Pelosi, had supported before. But Bush's proposal allowed private insurers to offer supplemental plans to Medicare beneficiaries, which Democrats believed was an attempt to open the program up to eventual privatization. And it didn't allow Medicare to negotiate with drug companies for lower prices. Democrats viewed Bush's proposal as a giveaway to the pharmaceutical and insurance industries—not that Bush was asking what they thought: they were frozen out of the bill-drafting process. "Republicans have offered up a Trojan horse, a deceptive gift intended to win their forty-year war against Medicare," Pelosi charged.

Some conservative Republicans also hated the bill, which they considered an expensive new government entitlement. Bush and the GOP leaders worked hard on their party's dissenters, making calls from Air Force One and sprinkling the bill with giveaways to members' pet projects. DeLay brought it to the floor just before Thanksgiving 2003. A previous version of the bill had attracted some Democratic supporters; Pelosi lectured them sternly on the importance of unanimous opposition. If Republicans wanted this so-called reform, she thought that they alone should have to answer for it.

By the time the bill came up for a vote, it was 3 a.m. on November 22, a Saturday. The initial tally was 216 in favor, 218 against—enough to send the bill down to defeat. Republican leaders refused to close the vote. It was supposed to last the standard fifteen minutes, but they kept it open for three hours as DeLay searched for members he could flip—an unprecedented abuse of normal procedure. (The last time a vote was held open, for fifteen extra minutes in 1987, then-Congressman Dick Cheney called it "the most arrogant, heavy-handed abuse of power I've ever seen in the ten years that I've been here.")

Members were falling asleep in their seats on the House floor as the GOP leaders literally chased down recalcitrant members. One Republican congresswoman physically hid on the Democratic side of the floor, crouching down and refusing to make eye contact. Another member was told the party wouldn't fund his run for Senate if he didn't change his vote. And one Republican held firm despite DeLay offering $100,000 for his son's congressional campaign if he switched—and threatening to defeat his son if he didn't.

At 6 a.m. the gavel finally came down. The bill passed, 220–215, including 16 Democrats. The Medicare expansion would wind up being popular and, as Rove had predicted, provide a boost to Bush's reelection. But it also began the gradual alienation of conservatives that would contribute to Bush's ultimate second-term unpopularity and the fissures in the GOP that would play out dramatically over the next decade and beyond.

Pelosi was furious about the GOP's procedural hijinks. This went beyond traditional arm-twisting and horse-trading. The Republicans, she said, had won "Florida style," a reference to their techniques during the 2000 recount. (DeLay would later be admonished by the Ethics Committee for his strong-arm tactics on the Medicare vote.) But Pelosi was just as annoyed with her own members for crossing party lines. Without those 16 Democrats, Bush would have lost the vote. Under Gephardt, moderate and conservative Democrats had freely strayed from the party line to protect their independent brand with voters back home. But Pelosi believed that disunity had sapped Democrats' leverage and given Republicans too much leeway in a narrowly divided House. And she did not like surprises. If members were going to break with the caucus, she thought they ought to have a good reason, and they ought to let her know their plans in advance. She defined "a good reason" as "conscience, constituents or the Constitution." Political branding was not a good reason. One member recalled telling her, "I can't be with you on this; it's really unpopular in my district," only to have her retort, "Then you should go back and educate your district."

In the wake of the Medicare vote, Pelosi began to sound out caucus members on a change to the party rules that would put the steering committee in charge of certain subcommittee chairs—a seemingly technical change that, in practice, would mean that members who didn't vote with the party could lose their positions. Some of the caucus's more conservative members strongly opposed the change, saying it would put too much pressure on members in tough districts to take politically toxic votes.

But the caucus passed the rule change overwhelmingly. Pelosi had used tactical creativity and a tough, unyielding stance to send a message to her troops that would reverberate in future battles. For the caucus, it was a wake-up call. No more would they stumble around in the confused, sleepwalking haze that the minority had existed in since the days of Gingrich. Pelosi believed that discipline, like decision making, is liberating. "If you feel that anybody can vote any way on a key vote, it's dispiriting," a senior staffer said at the time. "Breaking that psychology is really important."

Pelosi thought it was about time the Democrats showed a little spine. "If you're a loose conglomerate of people who have a commonality of interests but who can't tie it together, who wants to join that club?" she told a reporter for the liberal magazine *The American Prospect*. The magazine dubbed the move "Nancy Pelosi's school for hardball." So much for Miss America.

◇ ◇ ◇

Pelosi's foremost task was for the Democrats to win back the House in 2004, when the still-popular George W. Bush would be up for reelection. Democrats would have to claw back 13 GOP-held seats to regain the majority after a decade in the wilderness. If they did, she would become Speaker of the House. But she insisted that the lofty title mattered less to her than the prospect that Democrats would get to act on some of their policy ideas. She didn't want Democrats to win the House so she could be Speaker, she told people; she wanted to be Speaker because it would mean that the Democrats—ideally, working with a new Democratic president—were setting the legislative agenda.

Leaders always say things like this, pretending to be selfless and unambitious when their very political careers refute the notion. But Pelosi's friends believed it. Behind her pragmatism was an ironclad commitment to principle and a lofty sense—some considered it self-righteousness—of the moral urgency of her cause. The best way to make her truly angry, her staff had found, was to suggest that she compromise on something she considered a matter of principle.

Many of her friends from the Tuesday night dinner gang had gone on to bigger things, like the Senate or Cabinet. But Pelosi never wanted to leave the House, and everyone knew it. Unlike Gephardt, she had no interest in being on a presidential ticket or being a national political celebrity. She relentlessly insisted on sharing credit: at press conferences for legislation she'd pushed, she would always begin by introducing every other member in the room, showering them with gratitude, to the point where her events became famous for being mind-numbingly dull. It didn't matter what the audience thought; it mattered that every member she worked with felt good about what they'd achieved together. If she thought a press release drafted by her staff gave her too much credit, she would send it back insisting that they change "I" to "we" and pay tribute to others' contributions, no matter how minuscule.

It was the single biggest key to her success. After so many years spent managing the emotions of toddlers, teenagers and politicians, the three

neediest and most egotistical types of people in existence, she had honed
her instinctive grasp of human motivation to a very fine point. And if there
was one thing she had learned—the sort of thing that seems obvious, that
everyone knows in theory, but that the majority of people are too needy or
self-centered to put into practice with any consistency—it was that people
love to be praised and love to be thanked, and no one ever complained
about getting too much of either.

The 2004 election was scheduled for November 2, but a test of the
political climate came sooner. A congressional seat in Kentucky became
vacant when the Republican who held it was elected governor. Democrats
were not inclined to make a strong play for a district Bush had won by 13
points, and they were not expected to field a strong candidate in the February 2004 special election.

Pelosi had the campaign committee poll the district in December
anyway, and the result was surprising: some thirty thousand voters were
strongly anti-Bush and eager to cast a vote registering their disapproval.
One in eight of the district's voters was a veteran, and the Bush administration's plan to close the local veterans' hospital had not gone over well.

The Democratic state attorney general, Ben Chandler, had just lost the
gubernatorial race and wasn't interested in making another race so soon.
But Pelosi paid him a visit and appealed to his sense of duty. Democrats
needed him, she said. With his help, they could win—and begin the task
of retaking the House. "She is not easy to say no to," Chandler said later.
He said yes.

The Democrats spent $1.4 million on the race, nearly double the
Republicans' expenditure, and bused in five hundred volunteers to help
get out the vote. *Message, money, mobilization.* Turnout was triple that of a
normal special election, and Chandler won by a 12-point margin.

It seemed like the seeds of the anti-Bush wave. Soon, Pelosi believed, it
would make John Kerry president and her the Speaker of the House.

12

WHEN GEORGE W. BUSH DEFEATED JOHN KERRY IN 2004, THAT WAS when the Democrats truly freaked out.

Pelosi had been as sure as anyone that they had it this time. "I put my credibility on the line here," she said on national television on the eve of the election. "John Kerry will be the next president of the United States." She viewed it as part of her job always to project confidence, but this time she really did believe it.

The shock went deeper than just losing an election. Democrats felt as if they had woken up in a different country from the one they thought they knew, a country devoted not to progress and compassion but to fear and nostalgia. Bush had won by mobilizing religious Christians to an extraordinary degree. One of his campaign's tactics was to help get referendums banning same-sex marriage on the ballot in a dozen states, to drive evangelical voters to the polls to vote for "traditional marriage." In states such as Ohio, the Kerry campaign had gotten as many votes as it thought were needed to win the state—only to find that Bush had beaten them getting even more votes, more votes than the Democrats thought possible. *Who are these people?* Democratic campaigners wondered. *Where did they all come from? Is this really the country I live in?*

With Bush's reelection, Democrats could no longer tell themselves that 2000 was just a fluke. Given a do-over after what they viewed as a stolen election, given a chance to get rid of a president they viewed as a disaster,

America, it turned out, really did want Bush and his party in charge of
the presidency and Congress. Bush won 31 states and 286 electoral votes,
with 270 needed to win. The GOP increased its hold on both chambers of
Congress, gaining 3 seats in the House and 4 in the Senate. Tom Daschle of
South Dakota, the Senate Democratic leader and Pelosi's partner in leadership, lost his reelection bid, the first defeat of a Senate party leader in
more than fifty years. Some Democrats refused to accept Bush's triumph,
and concocted elaborate, unsubstantiated conspiracy theories to insist that
Republicans had stolen the election.

Bush did not hesitate to rub it in. "I earned capital in the campaign,
political capital," the president proclaimed two days after the election, with
his usual swagger, that quizzical smirk, the head that jutted forward like a
chicken's. "And now I intend to spend it." His strategist Karl Rove, whom
Democrats had come to see as a sort of dark wizard, began talking in historic terms, framing the victory as the beginning of a limitless new era
of Republican dominance. Conservative commentators crowed about a
"realignment." The nonpartisan analyst Charlie Cook, author of an influential Washington newsletter, posited that Democrats now ran "the risk of
becoming perpetual losers, with a self-defeating mentality to match."

Pelosi was not buying any of this. She believed Bush was popular only
because voters had not seen him and his policies for what they really were.
He had gotten away with portraying himself as a sort of warrior-statesman,
but she saw instead a combination of incompetence, arrogance, stupidity
and greed, an administration determined to pursue a tragically miscon-
ceived war no matter the cost and to unravel the social safety net domes-
tically. Pelosi even protested the GOP's attempt to take FDR's face off the
dime as an attack on the legacy of the New Deal. She did not see any kind
of philosophical defeat in the election result, only a failure of tactics—
not enough money, not the right message, insufficient mobilization. But
the issues? There was nothing wrong there. Political scientists, for what
it's worth, largely agree that fluctuations in political control in a closely
divided country don't signal tectonic sea changes in public loyalty.

The Democrats were in danger of settling into permanent minority
status the way Republicans once had. But Pelosi never accepted what others saw as inevitable. Winning, she told people, was a decision you made.
You decided to win, and then you did it.

A month after the election, she met with the Democrats' new Senate leader, Harry Reid, a pale, taciturn Nevadan who'd been unexpectedly thrust to the head of his caucus by Daschle's loss. Pelosi and Reid agreed that the analysts' diagnosis was unacceptable. If the environment for Democrats was bad, they decided, they would have to create their own environment.

Pelosi saw that two things needed to be done. First, Bush needed to be redefined to the public. And second, the Democrats needed to up their game. She had a plan for both.

✧ ✧ ✧

To win the House, Pelosi needed a general. And she had just the man for the job.

Rahm Emanuel had been in Congress for only one term, but he had a higher profile than the average freshman. He was a hyperaggressive fireplug of a man, a hard-charging Jew from Chicago known for his profanity-laced diction and his missing middle finger. The finger had been amputated at the joint when it became infected after a teenage run-in with an Arby's meat slicer. Emanuel's friend and future employer Barack Obama joked that the loss of his middle finger "rendered him practically mute."

Emanuel, then forty-five, had previously worked as a political operative and as a senior adviser to President Clinton. In the Clinton White House, he was viewed as partly responsible for some of the administration's policy successes—as well as its sometimes less-than-liberal bent. It was Emanuel who had muscled the North American Free Trade Agreement, or NAFTA, through Congress in 1993, over the objections of unions and liberals. Emanuel assured Democrats that the agreement wasn't like the corporate-friendly free-trade deals Republicans had pursued, and that it included safeguards to protect American workers. Pelosi was one of the Democrats who voted for NAFTA—the biggest stain on her otherwise pristine liberal record, and a choice she came to regret. Emanuel also worked the House for Clinton's 1994 crime bill, which banned assault weapons, funded local police departments, expanded the federal death penalty and dramatically increased criminal sentences. Emanuel got Republicans to support it by leading a campaign to depict the bill's opponents as anti-cop.

Unlike the stiff and stilted Pelosi, who guarded her privacy and took even accidental slights personally, Emanuel was the kind of freewheeling, colorful character whom journalists can't get enough of. Profiles depicted him as swaggering, charismatic and larger than life. Colleagues vouched for his aggressiveness in hypermasculine terms: an "alpha male," a "rooster" with a "big old pair of brass balls." He was nicknamed "Rahmbo." A role on the TV series *The West Wing* was based partly on him—in one episode, the character, Deputy Chief of Staff Josh Lyman, sends a dead fish to an enemy, just as Emanuel once did. Emanuel ordered the fish from a company called Creative Revenge, and had it sent to a pollster he blamed for losing an election he was working on.

They might have had different styles—Pelosi preferred the velvet glove to the spiked bat—but she appreciated Emanuel's drive. She needed someone who wasn't there to make friends, someone with an operative's win-at-all-costs mentality. Over the course of the next two years, Democratic members of Congress would sometimes complain to Pelosi that Emanuel was being mean to their Republican friends—Republicans they liked, Republicans they'd worked with for years. Pelosi rebuffed their complaints. These nice Republicans weren't going to vote for Democratic priorities. They weren't going to make Nancy Pelosi Speaker of the House. In fact, many of the "good Republicans" were the Democrats' top targets: moderates representing the swing districts that Democrats had best chance of flipping. Emanuel was also openly ambitious, and made no secret of his aspiration to be Speaker, but that, too, was fine with Pelosi. It meant he was hungry, and personally invested in victory.

Pelosi called Emanuel just a few weeks after the election, when most Democrats were still busy licking their wounds. There were others who wanted the job of chair of the Democratic Congressional Campaign Committee, a leadership position and potential stepping-stone to something higher, but the choice was the leader's prerogative, and she had made up her mind.

Emanuel was celebrating Thanksgiving with his wife and three children in Michigan when she called. He accepted on the spot. But even he didn't think the House could be retaken in the next election, in 2006. To take back the House, Democrats would have to pick up 15 seats, a monumental task given the political landscape. Analysts didn't believe that that many Republican-held seats could conceivably be in play. Almost all the sitting GOP members of Congress represented districts that had voted for Bush by healthy margins.

"We have to start realizing this is a two-cycle process," Emanuel told

Pelosi. If Democrats had a really good year in 2006, he said, they might pick up 9 or 10 seats. Then, he said, they could finish the job in 2008, when Bush was no longer a factor.

◇ ◇ ◇

Bush soon revealed how he intended to spend the political capital he'd earned in the campaign. In his February 2005 State of the Union address, he unveiled the centerpiece of his second-term domestic agenda: a major overhaul of Social Security. He would take the universal government-run pension plan and partially privatize it, giving people individual accounts that they could choose to invest. It was necessary, he argued, because without reform, the program was "headed toward bankruptcy."

Democrats were not sure how to respond. They didn't like Bush's proposal, but many thought they should have their own solution to the crisis the president described. If they didn't, voters might view them as irresponsible or obstructionist. Bush's approval rating was still high, at 57 percent, and large majorities of Americans agreed that the Social Security program was in trouble.

Pelosi sensed a trap. Despite what Bush was saying, she believed there was no crisis with Social Security; his "reform" was just another of Republicans' plans to undermine and eventually tear down the welfare state. "If we, as the Democratic Party, cannot defend Social Security, we belong in the dustbin of history," she told her colleagues.

If Democrats offered their own plan, they'd be tacitly conceding Bush's argument that Social Security needed to be saved. Plus, any responsible plan to improve the program's balance sheet would have to include such unpopular measures as benefit cuts or tax increases—which would make Bush's proposal look better by comparison. (Bush had not laid out a way to pay for his expensive idea, so in the absence of a Democratic alternative, Republicans would have to fight among themselves about how to fund it.)

In order to stop Bush, Pelosi told her colleagues, they had to keep the focus on his plan, not their alternative. So they wouldn't offer one. If people asked the Democrats what they proposed instead, their answer would be, "Social Security *is* our plan."

Commentators were aghast at Democrats' stubbornness. The *Washington Post*, in an editorial titled "Where Are the Democrats?," accused them of hypocritically blocking Bush merely to deprive him of a political win, and of ignoring "what's right for the country." Pelosi's members started to go wobbly: a Democrat from Florida floated a proposal to raise taxes, earning him a Pelosi tongue-lashing over the phone. To another member, who'd been pestering her for weeks about when the Democrats would unveil a proposal, she finally retorted, "Never. Is never good enough for you?"

Surprised by the Democrats' intransigence, Bush threatened to turn the public against them and embarked on a national tour to sell his Social Security proposal. But the more he talked about it, the less popular it got. Pelosi said that the next time Bush wanted to go on a campaign swing, she'd be happy to pay for it. She urged Democratic lawmakers to hold forums on the subject in their districts, and over the ensuing months they held more than a thousand events. The people who showed up weren't DC opinion makers demanding to know what Democrats planned to do about the deficit. They were worried seniors seeking assurances that their benefits would be protected. Within a few months, Bush's Social Security "reform" had plummeted in popularity.

By June, congressional Republicans had tabled the plan indefinitely. The failure of what Bush had hoped would be a major legacy proposal represented more than simply the defeat of a single policy initiative. It shattered the aura of political invincibility surrounding Bush. It began the redefinition of Bush in many people's minds from "compassionate conservative" to someone who wanted to take away people's benefits. And it gave Democrats a foundation for the campaign to come.

✧ ✧ ✧

By that time, Bush had other problems. Hurricane Katrina struck the Gulf Coast in late August 2005, breaching the levees that kept New Orleans dry and displacing hundreds of thousands of people. News reports were full of images of terrified residents standing on roofs as the water rose. The death toll would eventually be assessed at more than a thousand. Bush, who was on vacation when the storm hit, appeared not to comprehend the magnitude of the disaster. When he returned to Washington from his Texas ranch, the White House released a photo of him peering down at the storm from Air Force One—an image intended to demonstrate concern that seemed instead to capture his detachment.

The Federal Emergency Management Agency, which handles disaster relief, responded sluggishly. It was headed by a lawyer named Michael

Brown, who had no disaster-relief background—his previous job was heading the International Arabian Horse Association—but was friends with Bush's campaign manager. When Bush finally made it to the Gulf, he declared, "Brownie, you're doing a heck of a job."

By mid-September 2005, Bush's approval rating had dropped to 38 percent. Then things got worse for the Republicans. There were already minor scandals brewing around Congressman Randy "Duke" Cunningham's alleged acceptance of bribes, White House official David Safavian's arrest and a federal investigation of Senate leader Bill Frist's financial dealings. Then, in late September, Tom DeLay, Pelosi's onetime counterpart and longtime liberal bogeyman, was indicted on criminal campaign finance charges. The following month, an aide to Vice President Dick Cheney, Lewis "Scooter" Libby, was indicted for leaking a covert CIA operative's identity in an attempt to discredit her husband's criticism of the intelligence case for the Iraq War. (Libby would later be pardoned by President Donald Trump.)

A few months later, mega-lobbyist Jack Abramoff pleaded guilty in a wide-ranging influence peddling case that also implicated DeLay, prompting DeLay to announce he would resign from Congress. A little-known Ohio congressman named John Boehner was named majority leader in his stead. Deliciously for the Democrats, a Texas judge ruled that DeLay's name couldn't be taken off the ballot, so Democrats won his suburban Houston district by default. DeLay's conviction was later overturned, but his exit from the House meant Bush had lost one of his fiercest enforcers.

Democrats began an aggressive campaign against what they termed the "Republican culture of corruption." GOP candidates in swing districts distanced themselves from the president, driving Bush's support lower by splintering his base. Democrats had a scandal of their own when William Jefferson, a congressman from Louisiana, was caught hiding ninety thousand dollars in alleged bribe money in his freezer. But it was the Republicans' corruption that dominated the headlines. On the eve of the election, GOP congressman Mark Foley of Florida confessed to having sent sexually charged messages to underage male congressional pages, actions that Republican leaders had known about for months and had done nothing to stop.

Veteran Republican members of Congress, who had not gotten to be veteran congressmen by being unable to sense shifts in the political wind, began announcing their retirements, despite their leaders begging and even threatening them to stay—they were informed that if they retired and became lobbyists, their former colleagues would refuse to speak to them, depriving them of the access that lobbying requires. They sprinted for the exits nevertheless.

The retirements were a boon to the political efforts of the Democratic Congressional Campaign Committee and Rahm Emanuel, its chairman. Incumbents are much harder to beat than new candidates. With Pelosi's assistance, Emanuel undertook an aggressive drive to recruit strong candidates for the Democrats. She directed him to find candidates that fit their districts, regardless of ideology. The Democratic challengers in three Indiana districts, for example, were anti-abortion and pro-gun. The liberals of the burgeoning "Netroots" blogger community howled in protest, but the Democrats, Pelosi and Emanuel believed, would win only with a big-tent strategy. Emanuel was relentless. One local officeholder who'd never met him before picked up the phone to hear, by way of a greeting, "Are you tired of being fucking mayor yet?" "It's better than being a fucking congressman," replied the mayor, one of the few who resisted Emanuel's entreaties.

Another recruit, former Washington Redskins quarterback Heath Shuler, an evangelical Christian from rural North Carolina, worried about the toll a congressman's life would take on his family, so Emanuel made a habit of calling Shuler from his own kids' school plays and soccer games. Shuler said Emanuel's courtship was more intense than the experience of being a star recruit for college football and the NFL. In his case and many others, it worked.

To counter Republicans' portrayal of Democrats as wimpy bleeding hearts, Emanuel especially sought out candidates who seemed tough and macho: sheriffs, athletes, war heroes. It is a truism of politics that while voters hate Congress, they tend to like their own congressmen. Emanuel's campaign committee worked to change that dynamic by nationalizing the election, turning it into a referendum on Bush and his party. The Democrats pumped out statements to local newspapers demanding that such-and-such congressman denounce DeLay or stand up to Bush. And with the help of Pelosi's prodigious fund-raising—she raised more in a single cycle than Gephardt had raised in the previous decade—Emanuel kept the Democratic challengers supplied with staff and cash, and blitzed their districts with slashing TV ads.

Pelosi watched the campaigns closely. Emanuel quickly learned that though she kept a thick briefing binder with information on all the congressional races, most of the information was in her head. She seemed to have a mental picture of the electoral map and would go through districts geographically, moving from west to east, north to south. No detail escaped her notice.

Meanwhile, the war in Iraq seemed to be taking a turn for the worse, with no end in sight. Republicans' accusation that Democrats wanted to "cut and run" was wearing thin with war-weary voters, while Democrats' critique took hold: Bush, they charged, had no plan to extricate the beleaguered military from an expensive and deadly quagmire. Moderate voters, who'd stuck with Bush to that point out of fear of terrorism, were increasingly alienated by a GOP that Democrats depicted as being made up of far-right culture warriors. At the same time, Pelosi's insistence on party discipline made it more difficult for Bush to win his legislative battles. Without Democratic votes to rely on, GOP leaders could pass Bush's bills only with the support of moderate Republicans, who could then be attacked for "rubber-stamping" conservative legislation.

In May 2006, with six months to go until the election, Bush's popularity hit its lowest point, 29 percent—just 5 points higher than President Richard Nixon's approval rating right before he resigned over Watergate.

✧ ✧ ✧

But what did the Democrats stand for? While they railed against Bush's failures, they hadn't articulated a clear agenda of their own. As the election drew nearer, Democratic insiders quarreled over whether the party needed to present a more substantial case to voters.

Gingrich's Contract with America was always invoked as the gold standard of an out party's persuasive pledge to the electorate. (Never mind that, with a Democratic president in the White House, few of Gingrich's grand ideas ever made it into law.) Emanuel wanted the Democrats to have something like it, but Pelosi kept putting off his demands. In early 2006, he sent her a memo recommending that the party focus on stem cell research and reducing the national debt, but she ignored it. Shortly afterward, he sent her another missive with a four-point plan to go after Bush's Medicare prescription drug benefit, which had become unpopular for (just as Democrats had predicted) failing to keep up with the price of prescriptions. Again, she put him off. You focus on the political strategy, she told him, I'll take care of the legislative leadership.

By June, Democrats' internal fretting was spilling out into the open. At Emanuel's urging, a group of top Democratic strategists sent Pelosi a sharply worded memo that marshaled polling and focus groups to make the case that Democrats were falling flat. "The Party's image has weakened, not strengthened, producing a growing alienation with politics and the parties that could limit our gains to perhaps a net 10 seats," they wrote. The satirical newspaper the *Onion* got into the game with a headline reading, "Democrats Vow Not to Give Up Hopelessness." "Nancy Pelosi" was quoted in the article, as saying, "In times like these, when the American public is palpably dismayed with the political status quo, it is crucial that Democrats remain unfocused and defer to the larger, smarter and better equipped Republican machine."

What the strategists didn't know—what Pelosi hadn't even told her top political lieutenant, Emanuel, even though they talked multiple times every day, to the point where they began to communicate in a sort of short-hand code—was that Pelosi was holding back on a Democratic program by design. At the beginning of the election cycle, she had sought out experts on marketing and branding from the private sector, believing they would have fresher insights on selling a message to the public than the tired Beltway political consultants who seemed stuck on a losing strategy. The experts told her that timing was crucial. If the Democrats led with their proposals, they would get buried by the force of Bush's bully pulpit, and by the time the election came around their agenda would be old news. What the Democrats needed to do, they said, was first drag down Bush's image. Only then, with the president weakened and people hungry for an alternative, should they present their own plans. Elections happen on a predetermined calendar. Just because you did something in March does not mean anyone is going to remember it in October.

So Pelosi waited, resisting the many urgent pleas that something must be done *right now*. Patience is an exceedingly rare quality in politics. Moreover, it's almost impossible to keep your composure and not give anything away when you're being constantly attacked for not doing something you have every intention of doing when the time is right. You can't even signal that there's a plan in place, because the worriers will reflexively start spreading the word to quiet their fellow worriers, and the plan will leak out and be ruined. It's actually good to have a spate of news articles about people being frustrated by the thing you're not doing, making it all the more attention-worthy when you then start to do it. Pelosi withstood the pressure, until she decided the time was right.

In late June, it was time. The Democrats rolled out their agenda with great fanfare. As a manifesto for the nation, it was decidedly small-bore. It did not include instating universal health care, tackling global warming or pulling out of Iraq—ideas beloved by liberals that might alienate the swing voters Democratic candidates needed to win over. Instead, it called for such unobjectionable measures as implementing the recommendations of the 9/11 Commission, improving college student aid, enacting a minimum wage increase, legalizing stem cell research, investing in renewable energy, and allowing Medicare to negotiate prescription drug prices. The substance of the ideas was less important than the fact that they existed—an answer to the question "What difference does it make if Democrats win?" (Republicans responded with their own "American Values Agenda," but its contents were a clear signal that they were desperately trying to hold on to their base: it included allowing displays of the Ten Commandments, passing a constitutional amendment banning gay marriage, and requiring that women seeking abortions be told that their unborn child could feel pain.)

The Democrats' "Six for '06" plan fell short of many liberals' hopes. At a town hall in San Francisco, where Bush in 2004 had received just 15 percent of the vote, constituents demanded that Pelosi support impeaching the president. Republicans began claiming that impeaching Bush was the Democrats' real agenda. Tim Russert asked Pelosi about it on *Meet the Press.* "Democrats are not about impeachment," she insisted. "Democrats are about bringing the country together."

Pelosi herself was becoming an issue for some Democratic candidates. This was only fair: it was Democrats who had sought to nationalize the election, and the national consequence of a Democratic majority would be Speaker Pelosi. Conservative voters enamored of a folksy, charismatic local candidate might feel differently if they remembered that a vote for Heath Shuler was, in effect, a vote to put a San Francisco liberal in charge of Congress. Shuler's opponent ran ads that showed Pelosi alongside Hillary

Clinton and Howard Dean, with narration that said that "Heath Shuler and the liberals" favored "partial-birth abortion on demand," gay marriage and amnesty for illegal immigrants. A radio ad in Indiana declared that if the Democrat won, "Speaker Pelosi will then put in motion her radical plan to advance the homosexual agenda." Despite the best efforts of Rush Limbaugh and others on the right, Pelosi was still little-known nationally, but this campaign was the start of what would be a decade-long, multimillion-dollar GOP project to make her unpopular with voters and to use her as a weapon against Democratic candidates.

On Election Night, Pelosi holed up in an office at the Democratic campaign committee on Capitol Hill. At the front of the room, a gaunt, exhausted Emanuel and his frazzled staff were recording the local election returns one by one on a whiteboard. Focused as Pelosi was on the second-most-momentous election of her career to date, part of her mind was elsewhere. Alexandra, her youngest daughter, was pregnant with Pelosi's sixth grandchild, and her due date had already passed. For the campaign's final weekend, Pelosi traveled only to swing districts within one hundred miles of Manhattan, where Alexandra lived. Pelosi's press secretary sent reporters a reminder: "If grandchild number six arrives, Pelosi will cancel her schedule."

The polls began closing on the East Coast at 6 p.m. Right away, the Democrats notched an unexpected win: in Louisville, Kentucky, a left-wing candidate Emanuel had virtually written off, a quirky political newcomer who was the editor of the local alt-weekly, knocked off a longtime Republican incumbent. As more states reported, more wins went on the board. All three Democrats in Indiana won. In North Carolina, Heath Shuler won. For the first time since 1922, the party did not lose a single seat that it had previously held.

At 11:08 p.m., CNN's Wolf Blitzer announced that by the network's tally the Democrats were projected to take the House.

Never surprised, always poised, Pelosi was momentarily speechless. She stared at the television, hugged Paul, and said over and over, "I can't believe it. I can't believe it." Emanuel wrapped her in an effusive hug. "Madam Speaker!" he said. She looked shell-shocked. Her phone rang, and she picked it up: it was the junior senator from Illinois, who'd campaigned intensively for the Democrats. "Barack," she said. "Thank you, thank you, thank you." She hung up the phone and muttered, "I have to call my brother," as the staffers around her rose in a standing ovation.

In the final accounting, the Democrats won 31 seats, double what they needed and far more than anyone had thought was possible. There was plenty of luck involved—for two years, it seemed that the Republicans couldn't catch a break. But many of the Democrats' "lucky" breaks were rooted in GOP policy failures, whether it was the war in Iraq going badly, the bungled response to Katrina or the party's lax policing of its members' ethics. And the public perception of those failures was framed by the Democrats' effective messaging, which deflated Bush's invincible image and made voters see him as not a lovable, patriotic cowboy but a dangerous bungler, in over his head. Even the wave of Republican retirements came in response to Democrats making their lives unpleasant.

The Democrats' victory seemed inevitable in retrospect, and plenty of people would claim they'd seen it coming, or that it could have been predicted by some bloodless political science model. It would also be widely attributed to the publicity-hungry Emanuel and his captivating machismo, rather than to the woman who had hired him for the job. But it was Pelosi who had laid the groundwork. It was Pelosi who, from the beginning, believed that every little thing mattered and nothing was guaranteed—and that anything was possible if you had the right strategy and stuck to it.

She got home at 2 a.m. and went to bed, awakened by the phone ringing five hours later. She assumed it must be Alexandra. "Are we getting a baby this morning?" she said excitedly into the phone.

On the other end of the line, President George W. Bush said, "Is this Madam Speaker-to-be?"

13

It was February 2007. She had been Speaker for a month, and people would not shut up about the stupid plane.

Here she was, the first woman Speaker of the House, the most powerful woman in elected office in American political history. There were so many things to do—laws to pass, promises to keep, two wars spinning out of control half a world away—and all anyone seemed to want to talk about was whether Pelosi had "demanded" a "big fat jet" so that she and her fancy, self-important friends could swoop around the country on the taxpayer's dime, presumably looking down and laughing at the little people all the while.

What really happened was this. After 9/11, when the hijackers seemed to have come perilously close to wiping out the Capitol, the White House, or both, the federal government instituted new security protocols for leaders including the Speaker of the House. To get to and from his district, Speaker Hastert started taking a small air force plane, a twelve-seater modeled on the Gulfstream III, a common private jet. Sometimes his family or other lawmakers would catch rides with him. No one seemed to notice or care.

But Hastert only had to get to Illinois. Pelosi had to get back to her district in California. The House sergeant at arms, a congressional employee who had served since Gingrich's day, asked the air force if the new Speaker could use the same plane as Hastert to get to San Francisco. He asked about the protocol for bringing guests on the plane, such as who else could fly with her and whether they would have to repay the government, so that Pelosi's staff could understand the trappings of her new position. The air force responded that the jet Hastert used would probably not be able to get to San Francisco without stopping to refuel, but there were other, larger jets Pelosi could use to fly nonstop. Subject to availability, Pelosi's options included one military jet, which was the size of a 757, with business-class seats for forty-five, beds and a stateroom. Guests, the military said, were allowed, but they would have to reimburse the government for the price of an equivalent plane ticket.

A rumor circulated among the Republicans in the House that Pelosi had *demanded* to be ferried across the country in a *luxury jet*, and was planning to bring her *wealthy liberal donors* along with her in a pay-to-play scheme. The story entered the public bloodstream when the conservative *Washington Times* ran an article with the headline "Pelosi's Power Trip— Non-stop Nancy Seeks Flight of Fancy." The information was attributed to unnamed Pentagon sources. Pelosi's team suspected a deliberate leak by the administration to make her look bad and distract the public from the war.

The story caught fire on Fox News and conservative radio. Fox host Sean Hannity expressed indignation: "She thinks she's the president!" Then-CNN host Lou Dobbs informed viewers gravely that "Nancy Pelosi . . . can now fly in style at your expense." One Republican congressman accused her of "an arrogance of office that just defies common sense," while another railed against "Pelosi's abuse of power" and said she was "exploiting America's armed forces and taxpayers for her own personal convenience."

Republicans spent two full hours debating the "issue" on the floor of the House and attempted to amend an unrelated bill to prohibit such travel. Egged on by a blizzard of Republican news releases, mainstream reporters picked up the story. When Pelosi took questions at the end of an event with a group of Iraq War veterans meant to highlight health care for service members, every reporter's question was about the plane instead.

To Pelosi, it was a nothing story, ginned up by Republicans to trigger the most knee-jerk, retrograde feelings of resentment of a powerful woman. It was also the beginning of a cycle that would become familiar and confining: Republicans attacked her for something made up or innocuous, the press amplified the "scandal," and many Democrats were loath to defend her for fear of annoying their conservative constituents. If she defended herself, she only made it worse by seeming defensive or arrogant.

The attacks made her toxic, her toxicity made people distance themselves from her, and their distancing became fresh evidence of how toxic she was. And she was powerless to do anything about it.

The plane was not the only trapping of her new office to get accustomed to. Pelosi now had a security detail, a crew of plainclothes Capitol Police officers with bulletproof vests and earpieces who followed her everywhere she went. (She would always offer them a cup of coffee or a bite to eat, but they always declined.) When a bird flew in the window of her Washington condo and got trapped inside, the agents were waiting downstairs, but she didn't want to put them out (or be accused of treating them like hired help). She called the building superintendent instead, and while she was waiting for him, she chased the bird around the place. By the time the super arrived, she had caught the bird herself, and she presented it to him in a brown paper bag.

She couldn't travel inconspicuously anymore, and she couldn't go anywhere by herself. It was a difficult transition for someone who cherished her hard-won independence, whose staff was still trying to break her of the habit of scheduling her own appointments, taking her own suits to the dry cleaner and making trips to the salon to get her hair done. (Mindful of the privilege of not having to comb her own hair, she would say, "Thank you, Paul Pelosi," as she sat down to read the paper during her daily twenty-minute hair appointment.) When Alexandra drove down to Baltimore to see her mother honored with a street named after her on the block where Pelosi grew up, Pelosi's motorcade so shut down the surrounding streets that it took hours to get out of town and drive back up to New York. "Thanks a lot, you got us stuck in traffic," Alexandra told her mother. Pelosi replied, "At least you have your freedom."

The airplane scandal, which eventually died down, was a bracing lesson in what was to come for Pelosi and her staff. People who didn't think she deserved her power were eager for any hint that she seemed demanding, entitled, too big for her britches. It didn't really make sense—she was objectively one of the most powerful people in the country, entitled as a matter of law and custom to the powers that came with the high office to which she'd been elected. The powerful men who made the laws of the land weren't accused of being on a "power trip" or ridiculed for wanting to get from place to place. (Gingrich really did have delusions of grandeur, but when allies excused him by calling him a "visionary," that became his reputation instead.) Men never got called a "diva" or a "prima donna" when they asked for things. The idea of Pelosi believing she deserved respect as the Speaker of the House just seemed to drive certain men insane.

There would, in other words, be no honeymoon for Madam Speaker. Her staff had carefully orchestrated a four-day pomp-and-circumstance-filled "Pelosi-palooza" around her inauguration, hoping to define her image to a public that was mostly learning about her for the first time. There were ceremonies in San Francisco and Baltimore. There was a women's tea in Washington, where five hundred colleagues and supporters wore buttons featuring Pelosi's face on the iconic Rosie the Riveter image, with the words "A Woman's Place Is in the House…as Speaker." There were tote bags. Unlike many female politicians who have to work to toughen their image, lest they be trivialized as unserious or stereotyped as weak, Pelosi had the opposite problem: everyone wanted to see her as a battle-ax, and no one seemed to see the warm Italian Catholic grandmother underneath, the prim and proper lady who once bailed on a congressional trip to the Middle East at the last minute because another grandchild was about to be born.

The day Pelosi took the gavel, January 4, was full of unprecedented moments. She broke with tradition by bringing her grandchildren up to the Speaker's desk, holding Alexandra's six-week-old baby, swaddled in white, in her arms. Boehner, the Republican leader, gave a speech honoring her historic accomplishment. (Many Republicans, including Hastert, did not join the standing ovation that followed, and some refused even to applaud.) The image of Pelosi, in her plum-colored jacket and oversize pearls, raising the gavel aloft with a jubilant smile was beamed around the world; in the following days, fan mail flooded into the office.

But the image campaign didn't stick. It was drowned out by the protesters who held up "Pelosi Preys on Children" signs as she drove by. Her own Catholic alma mater had to close a Mass she attended to the public in the face of protests. Not a single American newsmagazine featured her on the cover—not *Time* (which had made Newt Gingrich the Man of the Year in 1995), not *Newsweek*, not *U.S. News*. Feminism was out of fashion, and the culture wasn't ready to appreciate the complexity of a woman who was both devoted to her family and a hard-charging, ruthless pol. "Badass" had not yet entered the American lexicon as a characteristic for women to aspire to. It was the caricature of Pelosi as a rigid, ditzy, castrating, loony tunes liberal that seemed to take hold in the public mind.

Pelosi resolved to ignore all this. Her district was safe, her members were with her, and they had important business to transact on behalf of the American people. But her staff could be hair-trigger defensive, seeing sexism everywhere, bridling at every description that mentioned Pelosi's clothes even though her style was undeniably an important part of her public persona. (Despite a popular perception that it's inherently sexist for journalists to describe what women politicians wear, perception and its management are an essential part of politics that shouldn't be off limits; in recent years, researchers have found that women pols' clothes are no more likely to be mentioned than men's in political coverage, and that non-derogatory portrayals of female candidates' appearance don't have a negative effect on voters' perceptions.) Was Bush diminishing her as a woman when he joked about sending her "some Republican interior decorators who can help her pick out the new drapes in her new offices," or just playing on a common, gender-neutral cliché? Was Vice President Dick Cheney belittling her like a little girl when he said her trip to Syria was an instance of "bad behavior," or was he just being a prick, as was his wont?

When people asked her how she put up with it all, she'd say, "I get up, eat nails for breakfast, put on a suit of armor and go into battle." The suit of armor she had created, an extreme and steely toughness that dismissed any hint of vulnerability, would keep her safe. It might also hide the parts of her that she wanted people to see.

◇ ◇ ◇

Pelosi never could have gotten where she was without Jack Murtha. It was Murtha who, since her earliest days in Congress, had vouched for her to the colleagues with whom she had the least in common, convincing the grumpy old men who might otherwise have dismissed her to take her seriously. Murtha had taught her the ins and outs of Appropriations, helped her build support for the Presidio and introduced her to the tricks and traps of the Pentagon budget (which, like many in the caucus's left flank, she hardly ever voted for). Murtha's 2005 turn against the Iraq War had given powerful ammunition to the Democrats' case against Bush in the midterms, helping win the election that made her Speaker.

But when Murtha decided to run for leadership, it was emphatically not the right time.

In the summer of 2006, in the thick of the intense midterm campaign season, Murtha surprised his Democratic colleagues with a letter announcing that if the Democrats took back the House, he planned to run for majority leader. That would mean running against Steny Hoyer for the number two post in the caucus, a position Hoyer believed he was in line to inherit after years of working, mostly amicably, as a team with Pelosi, his former rival. Murtha's announcement threatened to interrupt the drumbeat of negativity around Bush and his party that Democrats had labored for so many months to create—it had gotten so bad that ABC News joked that GOP stood for "Got Oversized Problems"—and replace it with a story line about divided, feuding Democrats.

Hoyer, for his part, felt betrayed by Murtha's announcement. Hoyer had promised he would never challenge Pelosi for the speakership, and he was under the impression that the nonaggression pact was mutual. But now one of Pelosi's closest allies was proposing to run against him for majority leader. Hoyer met with Pelosi and told her he thought such a race would be divisive to the caucus.

Pelosi told Hoyer she didn't understand why Murtha was running and hadn't encouraged him—but she also, with ruthless cool, said she did not plan to dissuade him. "You know," she told Hoyer, "I think competition is a good thing." But she prevailed on Murtha to suspend his campaign for leader until after the election.

The day after Democrats won back the House, the leadership race was officially on. There were a number of ways Pelosi could choose to handle it. No one would have been in a better position than she was to gently talk her friend Murtha out of his decision to run, convincing him that leadership wasn't his thing, that such a move would hurt her speakership, that he would be better off focusing on his defense work. She could have allowed Murtha to run but declined to take sides (the typical move for a party leader), in the name of staying above the fray and not playing favorites. She could have endorsed her friend in a nominal way, allowing him to say he had her support but declining to campaign on his behalf so as not to be perceived as trying to influence the result. She could have offered him some other position instead—that's what she did for Rahm Emanuel, successfully pressuring him to run for caucus chair rather than challenge Jim Clyburn for whip; Pelosi's intervention to protect Clyburn, a wily, experienced South Carolinian, earned her crucial political capital with the Congressional Black Caucus, whose members had a historically difficult relationship with the top House leadership.

Pelosi did none of those things. Two days after the election, after their first post-election meeting with Bush, as they stood in the White House driveway, she curtly informed Hoyer that she would be backing Murtha over him for leader, then walked away with no further explanation. Her decision, announced in a letter a few days later, shook the caucus. In the letter, addressed to Murtha and released to the media, she wrote, "I salute your courageous leadership that changed the national debate and helped make Iraq the central issue of this historic election." Pelosi's own staff was confused by what they viewed as an inevitably doomed crusade, and some of her allies tried to talk her out of it, to no avail.

It was not in her nature to choose the cautious course; nor was it in her nature to do anything halfway. She tackled Murtha's candidacy with her usual intensity. She brought it up with colleagues at social events and unrelated meetings. She raised the subject with members who came to her office to talk about committee assignments. Some lawmakers who'd previously committed to Hoyer complained that Pelosi's deputies were threatening them with demotions if they didn't switch their backing, accusing her of "strong-arm tactics." Many in the caucus viewed her interventions as an unbecoming violation of decorum. But to Pelosi, she was about to be Speaker of the House; shouldn't she be able to bring in her own leadership team? Wouldn't the same colleagues who were about to elect her to lead them want her to have around her the people she trusted, people who she felt would make the caucus maximally effective? And left unsaid: wouldn't the defenestration of Hoyer definitively establish her as the caucus's sole power center, and a leader no one wanted to mess with?

Pelosi's refusal to see the possibility of defeat had been an asset when it came to winning the election. But in the leadership race, that kind of blinkered confidence led her badly astray. For all Murtha's strengths, he was miscast as a leadership candidate. He was more lone wolf than team player, with views that were far more conservative than those of the majority of the caucus. And then there were the ethics problems. In the 1980 Abscam scandal, in which seven lawmakers were convicted for accepting bribes in an FBI sting operation, Murtha narrowly avoided arrest by agreeing to testify against his colleagues. He was notorious for, and unapologetic about, steering pork to his rural Pennsylvania district; his friends and family had stood up defense contracting empires just to sop up all the federal largesse Murtha controlled, and his small Rust Belt hometown of Johnstown had become an improbable hub of the military-industrial complex. An independent ethics watchdog group named him one of the fifteen most corrupt members of Congress, and it would later be revealed that he was under FBI investigation. Shortly after the 2006 election, Murtha disparaged the ethics reform legislation that was a centerpiece of the Democrats' proposal to clean up the Republicans' mess, calling it "total crap" in a private meeting of conservative Blue Dog Democrats—although, he added, he planned to support it because Pelosi wanted it.

Although Pelosi was loath to recognize it, Hoyer, who called himself a "member's member," was well-liked and had broad support in the caucus. Many Democrats thought the disparate styles of Pelosi and Hoyer complemented each other. Being forced to choose between the two of them had a "Mommy and Daddy are fighting" sort of feel. But choose they did, decisively: in the same caucus meeting that unanimously elected Pelosi Speaker, Hoyer won majority leader by a vote of 149 to 86.

The Murtha episode damaged Pelosi in the moment, creating the impression of a fractured caucus and a weakened Speaker on the eve of the crowning moment of her career. It raised questions about her judgment, and reinforced the image of Pelosi as grudge-holding and vindictive— some members even whispered that Murtha's run had been Pelosi's idea, an attempt to wound Hoyer, her old rival, and warn him he'd never be safe. "It was a terrible mistake, the only big mistake I think I've ever seen her make," Barney Frank, the congressman from Massachusetts, said later. "It was the one time people might have said she's putting her personal feelings ahead of the interests of the caucus."

Other Pelosi loyalists argued that, in the long run, it wasn't a mistake at all. In backing Murtha even when he couldn't win, she was sending a message about the intensity of her loyalty—one that bound members to her all the more tightly because they knew that when the time came she would go to bat for her friends. Some also contended that if a man had supported his longtime friend, it might have been seen as tough and impressive rather than petty and personal.

❖ ❖ ❖

Pelosi hated how the House smelled, the air thick with smoke, the marble hallways musty with the scent of cigarettes. It was her House now, and things were going to be different. By 2006, most big cities and an increasing number of states had banned smoking in public areas and restaurants. Pelosi issued a rule eliminating smoking in the House's halls and meeting rooms, though it was still up to members whether to allow it in their offices—John Boehner, the Republican minority leader, was a notorious chain-smoker. She also introduced paper cups, compostable corn-based plates and biodegradable utensils to replace the plastic implements in the Capitol's cafeterias, which prompted some grumbling when they proved frustratingly flimsy.

The smoking ban was a neat symbol of her rise to power: Pelosi had quite literally eliminated the smoke-filled rooms where men had been making decisions for so long. Her House would be neat, tidy, under control. She extended the workweek that Gingrich had truncated. She fine-tuned the committees, giving prime seats to freshmen, women and people of color, to ensure that they reflected the diversity of the caucus.

At first, Pelosi said she would not shut out the Republicans as they had done to the Democrats. She pledged that the House would return to "regular order," with opportunities for the minority party to introduce amendments and have a say in the process. As minority leader in 2004, she had tried without success to get Hastert to agree to a "Minority Bill of Rights," which would have guaranteed the right to offer relevant amendments, required that members be given at least a day to read new bills before they were put up for a vote, and included the minority party in House-Senate conferences. But Republicans immediately set about abusing the privileges Pelosi offered them, and indulged in shenanigans such as the amendment targeting her airplane travel.

She had set a target of passing the "Six for '06" agenda that Democrats had campaigned on in the new Congress's first one hundred hours, besting the one-hundred-day time line that Gingrich had set for passing the Contract with America. But that would never happen if Republicans were allowed to gum up the works with amendments, so the bills were introduced under a "closed rule," requiring an up-or-down vote with no alterations. All of them passed easily, most with numerous Republican votes as well as a nearly unanimous Democratic caucus.

❖ ❖ ❖

President Bush pronounced himself humbled by the midterm results, which he deemed a "thumpin'." In a departure from his preelection bluster, he struck a more conciliatory tone. The day after the election, Defense Secretary Donald Rumsfeld, viewed as the architect of the failed Iraq strategy, announced his resignation, something Democrats had been demanding for months. Bush made a statement in the East Room of the White House pledging a new commitment to "finding common ground." Out of the partisan glare, he and Pelosi had a teasing rapport. When Alexandra's baby, Paul Michael, was born, a week after the election, he called to congratulate Pelosi, and she joked that when his parents were picking out a name, Paul had just barely beaten out George.

For the next two years, Pelosi would be the Democratic House Speaker serving with a Republican president, a situation that would require her to perform a high-wire act. She'd put the Democrats in power by harshly attacking Bush at every turn, and she disagreed with almost all his proposed policies. But she also maintained that Democrats did not share Republicans' nihilistic approach to governing; they were willing to work with the president and compromise to reach common goals.

Not for the last time, Pelosi had to satiate a rabid liberal base that wanted the Democrats to investigate, harass and oppose the president they hated—up to and including impeachment. She had to convince the liberals that Democrats were serving as an adequate check on the administration while reassuring the rest of America that Democrats were responsible and would not go too far. She had to advance the liberal ideas that she believed in while protecting the moderate Democrats who would be seeking reelection in conservative districts.

Activists were furious at her for trying to work with Bush and taking impeachment "off the table." Liberal lawmakers such as Dennis Kucinich of Ohio drew up impeachment articles anyway. The antiwar activist Cindy Sheehan, who had become nationally famous when she camped out near Bush's ranch in Texas after her son was killed in Iraq in 2004, announced she was running against Pelosi for Congress because of Pelosi's failure to start impeachment proceedings. The radical women's antiwar group Code Pink, founded in 2002, set up a "Camp Pelosi" round-the-clock protest in Pelosi's front yard in Pacific Heights, putting on stunts like afternoon tea and an Easter egg hunt. Pelosi was unwavering: "We have to make responsible decisions in the Congress that are not driven by the dissatisfaction of anybody who wants the war to end tomorrow," she said. Unlike the GOP's leaders, Pelosi would not be cowed by pressure from her party's base.

Led by Pelosi, Democrats pursued bipartisan compromise, accepting half a loaf rather than digging in. They worked with the White House and congressional Republicans on an energy bill that increased vehicle fuel efficiency standards for the first time in three decades—but didn't include the renewable energy standard that environmentalists wanted. They found bipartisan agreement on a farm bill that made food stamps more generous—but did nothing to curtail the subsidies that propped up Big Ag. They worked to expand children's health insurance coverage, passing a bipartisan bill that covered four million kids—only to have Bush veto it on ideological grounds. They worked with Bush to pass budgets and fund the government, and when he refused to budge on some aspects, they conceded rather than allow a government shutdown.

As the economy started to show signs of strain, Pelosi's Democrats worked with the Bush administration to pass stimulus bills to try to stave off a recession. Democrats thought food stamps and unemployment benefits were the best way to do this, while Republicans favored tax cuts. In one negotiation, Boehner accused Pelosi of trying to use the stimulus bill to redistribute wealth; Pelosi retorted that what she was trying to do was prevent "your potential recession." The $168 billion stimulus that Bush signed in February 2008 included both Democratic and Republican priorities, and Bush expressed hope that it would see the economy through a "rough patch." That hope would turn out to be severely misplaced. And when, not long after, a Democratic president was trying to fix the economy, Republicans would not return the favor.

Despite their differences, Pelosi and Bush were committed to making divided government work. But in one area, they were fundamentally at odds, and neither planned to give in. That was the war in Iraq.

14

On November 17, 2005, Jack Murtha called a press conference. The seventy-three-year-old congressman was a big man, with a linebacker's shoulders, a jowly face, and blond-white hair parted sharply on the left. "The war in Iraq is not going as advertised," he said. "Our military is suffering. The future of our country is at risk. We cannot continue on the present course." The American troops had become targets, Murtha said, making the situation more rather than less dangerous by their continued presence. The case for war had been discredited. The military was under-resourced and stretched too thin.

It had been two and a half years since the start of the war. More than two thousand American troops had been killed, thousands more had been injured, and perhaps thirty thousand Iraqis had died. Despite reports of increasing chaos and violence, the Bush administration continued to insist that all that was needed was to "stay the course." Those who questioned the war's progress were condemned as unpatriotic. Presidential candidate John Kerry's heroic service in Vietnam was distorted and smeared by a group called Swift Boat Veterans for Truth. The Dixie Chicks were banned from country music radio after they came out against Bush. Vice President Cheney, in June 2005, insisted that the insurgency was in its "last throes," and that reports depicting a worsening quagmire were the product of a biased and overly negative media.

Years of war, waged by a too-small volunteer force, were straining the soldiers and their families, Murtha said. The Iraqi economy was in tatters; people lacked jobs and there was not enough clean water. American casualties had skyrocketed since the abuse and torture of detainees at the Abu Ghraib prison complex had been revealed. Yet the Bush administration refused to listen to critics. When Murtha, the top Democrat on the military funding subcommittee, sent a letter to the president seeking answers, he got no response for five months. And then all he got was a form letter from an assistant defense secretary.

After reciting all this, Murtha's tone became emotional. Almost every week since the beginning of the war, he said, he'd been visiting the wounded at the military hospitals near Washington, Bethesda Naval Hospital and the Walter Reed Army Medical Center. He had met young widows who still went to the hospital to visit their husbands' comrades, a blinded soldier hounded for medical payments by a collection agency, a triple amputee desperate for psychiatric care, a Vietnam veteran rubbing the hand of his comatose son, whose brother was still overseas.

"One other kid lost both of his hands," Murtha recounted. "Blinded. I was praising him, saying how proud we were of him, how much we appreciated his service to our country. 'Anything I can do for you?' His mother said, 'Get him a Purple Heart.'"

The soldier, he said, had been maimed trying to dismantle unexploded bomblets, but the military considered the incident friendly fire and thus ineligible for the medal that honors those wounded in combat. "I met with the commandant," Murtha said, his voice breaking. "I said, if you don't give him a Purple Heart, I'll give him one of mine." Murtha uttered a deep sigh and leaned forward, both hands on the lectern. "And they gave him a Purple Heart."

A reporter asked Murtha about the Republican charge that it was irresponsible for Democrats to criticize the war. "I like guys who have never been there to criticize us who've been there," he said.

Another reporter said, "I assume you have Ms. Pelosi's endorsement of this."

Murtha interrupted him. "No, no, you have to talk to her," he said. "I was very careful to say this is not a caucus position. A lot of people suggested it should be, but I was very careful. This is my own position, my own conclusion I've reached."

That afternoon, Pelosi had her own regularly scheduled press conference, and reporters asked her if she agreed with Murtha. "That was Mr. Murtha's statement," she said. Nine times, she refused to comment or take a position on his bill to pull American troops out of Iraq.

The impact was swift and forceful. Murtha's statement led all the newscasts. The sight of the grizzled veteran with tears in his eyes was profoundly moving. The White House accused Murtha of wanting to "surrender to the terrorists." On the floor of the House a few months later, Republican congressman Louie Gohmert sneered that it was a good thing Murtha wasn't in charge during World War II, "or we would be here speaking Japanese or German."

Murtha, incensed, rose and replied, "Were you there? Were you in Vietnam? Were you in Iraq?" Gohmert admitted he was not.

The debate now was between a president intolerant of criticism and a marine with his heart on his sleeve—not a bunch of antiwar activists or liberals from San Francisco. It would be hard to overstate the impact of Murtha's announcement. One analyst later dubbed it the "Murthquake," and antiwar activists credited Murtha with a seismic shift in the public debate. With his gravitas and conviction, he had taken something experts and liberals increasingly believed and given it the searing power of truth.

But where was Pelosi? She remained silent. In the days that followed, antiwar bloggers attacked her and other Democratic leaders for seemingly leaving the war hero out on a limb. The newly formed liberal Out of Iraq Caucus of congressional Democrats was furious with her; some of her major donors called Murtha to complain. They thought Pelosi was being timid, sandbagging him to disassociate the caucus from his controversial proposal. In San Francisco, activists staged a mock trial and "convicted" Pelosi. On *Saturday Night Live*, the comedian Darrell Hammond, playing MSNBC host Chris Matthews, interviewed Amy Poehler, playing Pelosi. "Miss Pelosi, the Bush administration is in turmoil, top Republican leaders are under indictment, and the vice president's top priority seems to be getting the go-ahead to attach a car battery to a man's nipples," Hammond said. "Yet, despite all this, the Democrats have stayed relatively quiet. What are the Democrats proposing to counteract all this corruption?"

Poehler answered, "That's easy, Chris. We're going to do nothing."

Pelosi let them criticize her even though she knew the truth: she and Murtha had orchestrated the whole thing, and agreed that it had to look like a one-man crusade. In fact, she had been in on the idea all along.

Pelosi and Murtha had been talking about the war from the beginning. He had voted to authorize the invasion, but almost immediately began to have doubts. Privately, he told Pelosi that he was increasingly convinced the war could not be won. So, in November 2005, she asked him to formulate an alternative for the party to rally around. He immediately agreed, and his plan for a six-month withdrawal went even further than she expected. It was the sort of thing many in the caucus's left flank had been pushing for but, Murtha told her, their views were discounted in the war debate. Coming from him, the proposal would carry different weight.

"This is going to be a huge deal," she told him. "People are going to come after you."

Murtha shrugged. "I can handle it," he told her.

When he unveiled the proposal in a closed-door meeting of the House Democratic Caucus, he got a standing ovation. Members of the Out of Iraq Caucus were eager to make Murtha one of their own. They wanted to sign on as cosponsors of his bill. They wanted to join his press conference to show their support. But Pelosi wouldn't let them do any of that. She insisted that Murtha make his announcement alone. Not until two weeks after Murtha's press conference did she announce, with little fanfare, that she supported his legislation. And not until years later did she acknowledge her role in the episode. In order for the plan to be effective, it could not be seen as primarily the brainchild of the caucus's antiwar left.

The Murtha episode was an illustration of Pelosi's theory of public opinion. There was a quotation from Abraham Lincoln that she repeated constantly: "Public sentiment is everything. With public sentiment, nothing can fail; without it nothing can succeed." But this quotation was frequently misunderstood. Most people who heard Pelosi say it assumed she meant that politicians should do only things that were popular, carefully reading polls and making sure not to antagonize the public consensus. That wasn't what she meant at all: she meant that if you want to get something done, you have to first get the public on your side. Leaders, she believed, should be shapers of public sentiment, not slaves to it. She had done it with Social Security, and she would do it with Iraq. The public could see that the war wasn't going well and the administration's excuses were not believable. But the argument had to be articulated by a messenger whom people would find believable, and framed in a way that convincingly laid the blame at Bush's doorstep.

A month after Murtha's speech, Bush for the first time expressed regret about the war, giving a speech in which he acknowledged the flawed intelligence the administration had relied on, though he still defended the invasion. By early 2006, polls showed that two-thirds of the public disapproved of Bush's handling of Iraq, and a majority thought the war was a mistake.

But with Republicans still in charge of the House, Murtha's proposal went nowhere. And some Democrats still worried opposing the war would be bad politics for the party. Hoyer, Pelosi's deputy, issued a statement opposing Murtha's legislation and arguing that "a precipitous withdrawal of American forces in Iraq could lead to disaster." In caucus meetings, Democrats argued with one another and could not reach agreement.

As the 2006 elections drew near, Emanuel, too, urged Pelosi to ease up on the antiwar message, worried that it would alienate the conservative-leaning voters the party was trying to court. But when the election was over, the public's verdict on the war was clear. How to translate that verdict into policy would be the central challenge of Pelosi's first two years as Speaker—a challenge at which she would arguably fail.

✧ ✧ ✧

When Pelosi took the Speaker's gavel in 2007, the war was her top priority. Analysts had concluded that public backlash against the war was primarily responsible for the midterm results. When Defense Secretary Rumsfeld announced his resignation, it seemed to be a sign that the administration, chastened, wanted to show it was changing course. Pelosi, who had gone against so many top Democrats to oppose the war, suddenly had lots of allies. All the Democrats who'd voted with Bush, from Gephardt to Hillary Clinton, were apologizing and eating their words.

But as Republicans never tired of pointing out, the same Democrats who loved to criticize Bush's war didn't have a plan of their own to offer. Instead, there was a wide range of opinions, from liberals who wanted an immediate pullout to hawks who sided with Bush—a range that had grown wider with the election of so many Emanuel-approved moderate Democrats from conservative districts. The big tent that had created the Democrats' majority now threatened to be the thing that unraveled it.

To Pelosi and, by that point, most Americans, it seemed devastatingly obvious that the war had been a tragic misadventure, a bad idea executed with shocking incompetence, leading to untold human misery at home and abroad. The cowboy in the White House had dismissed the experts who warned that an invasion of Iraq would be complex and dangerous. He and his advisers had thought they could rout Saddam with a skeleton force and get out quickly. They didn't want to hear about war crimes laws and counterinsurgency doctrine; all that stuff was for pointy-headed weaklings. They wanted to wage war the old-fashioned way, by blowing away the enemy. And this was the result. The Army War College's Strategic Studies Institute published an analysis calling Iraq "an unnecessary preventive war of choice" that had "stressed the U.S. Army to the breaking point" and "created a new front in the Middle East for Islamic terrorism and diverted attention and resources away from securing the American homeland."

Pelosi assumed that with the election behind them, Bush would come to the negotiating table. She thought he would work with the Democrats on a compromise proposal to begin winding down the American troop presence. But that was not what happened. To Pelosi's shock and dismay, Bush steadfastly refused second-guessing. He would change personnel and strategy, but he would not back away from the war.

Bush and his allies had come around to the idea that the war hadn't been executed right—hence Rumsfeld's departure—but they refused to concede that pulling out was the solution. In fact, they believed that would make things worse. Iraq had become a tinderbox and a hotbed of anti-American terrorism; left to its own devices, it might spiral into civil war or a larger regional conflict. In his January 2007 State of the Union address, Bush declared that rather than agree to a pullout, he planned a "surge" of tens of thousands of additional troops to bring the security situation under control. If the problem with the initial effort had been not enough troops, this time they would put in enough resources to get it right—effectively a do-over to clean up the mess the Americans had made. (The war in Afghanistan was also continuing, less controversially but with a similar lack of apparent success.)

On the other end of the spectrum were the liberals, for some of whom Murtha's six-month pullout plan didn't go far enough. They called for an immediate withdrawal, and believed that congressional Democrats should refuse to vote for military funding as long as the war continued. The liberals also believed that Bush was a criminal who needed to be held immediately accountable—piecemeal investigations and slow-paced congressional oversight hearings were not, to them, nearly enough. In Pelosi's careful deliberations and incremental chess moves, they saw cowardice and a lack of urgency about an intolerable problem. Code Pink protesters roamed the halls of Congress and disrupted committee hearings in flamboyant hot-pink outfits.

Liberal columnists denounced Pelosi for weakness. "Motivated by partisan concerns over the 2008 elections, the new speaker is following President Bush around like a sheep while he solidifies an imperial presidency and diminishes the Congress into irrelevancy," Bruce Fein wrote in *Slate*. Fein depicted Pelosi as callow and inexperienced, and called on the Democratic caucus to remove her. "Checks and balances and protections against government abuses are too important to be left to an imperious amateur with a Bush-like mental worldview."

Caught in the middle of all this, Pelosi wanted results. Impeachment, she believed, would achieve nothing, causing a national frenzy and discrediting Democrats' claims to constructive bipartisanship. Investigations and oversight might be less emotionally satisfying, but they would expose the administration's wrongdoing and rein in its lawlessness, however slowly. Yanking Pentagon funding would be abandoning the troops in the field, which the public (and moderate members of the caucus) would not tolerate; presenting alternatives to Bush's strategy, and demonstrating that these had widespread support, was the best way to pressure the administration to change course and negotiate a responsible compromise.

At first, Pelosi and Harry Reid, the Senate majority leader, hoped to work in tandem, mobilizing both houses of Congress to express the people's will for the war to end. But Reid's caucus had just 51 senators, and Senate bills require 60 votes to move forward. Some Senate Republicans were starting to express qualms about Bush, but most still stood behind the president's war strategy. Senate Republicans blocked Reid from even putting an anti-surge resolution to a vote. It would be up to Pelosi alone to chart the way forward.

The first step was to put the administration on notice. With the surge, Bush was behaving like a president who believed he was accountable to no one. (Given that Pelosi, right after the election, had declared impeachment "off the table," Bush was right to believe this, liberals contended.) Pelosi needed to show that the new Congress, empowered by the public backlash to the war, was serious, and could not be cowed by phony attacks on their patriotism. She needed to show Bush that he was no longer viewed as a strong, decisive leader and would have to accept some limits. The Congress he had bossed and bullied for six years was not afraid of him anymore. She would show her power.

To do all that, she needed a proposal that members could rally around—all the Democrats, from the Blue Dogs to the progressives, and hopefully some Republicans as well. It would have to be simple, straightforward and largely symbolic. Pelosi threw her weight behind a nonbinding, ninety-four-word resolution that expressed support for the troops at the same time as it denounced the surge. On Tuesday, February 13, 2007, the resolution came to the floor of the House, and four days of emotional debate followed.

Everyone was given a chance to speak, and 392 of the House's 434 members took it. Pelosi kicked things off with a speech declaring that the soldiers deserved "a course of action that is worthy of their sacrifice." One after another, Democrats—including three newly elected Iraq War veterans—argued that the war was a costly distraction from the real war on terror, while Republicans accused them of defeatism. Boehner, the Republican leader, said the resolution would put the war on "a very treacherous path." Don Young of Alaska called his colleagues "saboteurs" whose action would damage morale and undermine the military.

The resolution passed, with 17 Republicans joining all but two Democrats. The 64-vote margin for passage marked the strongest rebuke of a war president since Vietnam. "Let us hope," Hoyer said after the vote, "the commander in chief hears this counsel."

But if the resolution was intended to send a message, Bush didn't seem to get it. Shortly thereafter, he submitted a request to Congress for $100 billion in additional war funding.

The next step in Pelosi's plan, a legislative alternative to Bush's war strategy, would be more difficult than a symbolic statement of disapproval. Murtha wanted to impose conditions on the bill to fund the Pentagon, including stating that troops must receive special training before they could be deployed and must have a rest between deployments. These requirements were too much for Republicans and moderate Democrats, who accused Murtha of wanting to tie the hands of the commander in chief.

Pelosi met with Murtha and a few others to come up with a plan. In early March, she announced that Democrats planned to propose a withdrawal time line that would bring U.S. troops home in a little over a year, by September 2008. It was a risky gambit: she hadn't yet unified the Democrats around such a proposal, but she was betting that this was the compromise that she would eventually be able to get everyone to agree to.

The liberals were deeply skeptical. They filed into Pelosi's office in the Capitol for a contentious meeting. She shared their views, she told them, but if they wanted to get anything done, they had to come up with something that the whole of the caucus could support. Wasn't something better than nothing? The meeting-cum-therapy-session went on for nearly three hours. Members raided the candy basket Pelosi kept on her conference table, piling up wrappers as the discussion wore on. While Pelosi was still talking to the group, three of the liberals walked out of the meeting and held their own press conference, demanding a speedier withdrawal. "No more chances. No more waivers," declared Jan Schakowsky of Illinois. "No phony certifications. No more spending billions of dollars to send our children into the meat grinder that is Iraq. It is time to spend the money to keep them safe and bring them home."

The moderates, too, were skeptical—for the opposite reason. To them, the proposal went too far. As soon as Pelosi's meeting with the liberals was over, she went down one floor to Hoyer's office, where he was meeting with the moderates, trying to convince them that the troop requirements in the bill were not as onerous as the conditions Murtha had sought.

In the weeks that followed, Pelosi deployed all the vote-wrangling skills she'd learned over the years, from the Presidio fight to the whip race. She met personally with colleague after colleague, listening for as long as they wanted to talk and talking for as long as they wanted to listen. She and her team loaded up the bill with "sweeteners"—funding for Katrina recovery, children's health insurance and veterans' rehabilitation and treatment—with the result that the price tag came to $120 billion. Antiwar bloggers protested that rather than hold Bush in check, the Democratic Congress was actually giving him more money than he had asked for to fund the war. "With the Democrats back in power, Congress will provide 'oversight' to this war while tens of thousands of Iraqis and hundreds of U.S. soldiers continue to be killed," one blogger wrote.

Pelosi had originally planned for a vote on her proposal after only a week, but the votes weren't there yet, so she reluctantly postponed it—knowing that legislation, like fish, tends to smell worse the longer it's left in the sun. The party's liberal base was adamant that the Democrats must not pass the funding. Activists flooded Congress, staging an "occupation" to demand they defund the war completely. A marine mom confronted Congressman David Obey, chairman of Appropriations, as her fellow activists filmed the encounter. Obey was a staunch liberal who'd voted against the war, but now his frustration with the left boiled over. "We're using the supplemental to end the war, and it's time these liberal idiots understand that," he shouted at her. "Do you see a magic wand in my pocket? How the hell are we going to get the votes? We ain't got the votes for it. We do have the votes—if you guys quit screwing it up—we do have the votes to end the legal authority for the war."

Little by little, Pelosi won the liberals over. Schakowsky flipped after being convinced, over several conversations, that Pelosi really did want to end the war—that the legislation wasn't mere public relations kabuki. Lloyd Doggett of Texas came around after Murtha promised that the withdrawal time line would not be dropped from the bill in negotiations with the Senate. That left Pelosi 4 votes short. She postponed the vote another day, to Friday, March 23. On Thursday, she met with the remaining liberal holdouts and begged them for 4 more votes. Finally, enough of them agreed to come on board. Raul Grijalva, a die-hard progressive from Arizona with a signature walrus mustache, told reporters afterward, "My head tells me it's a step, a flawed step. My heart tells me I'm still voting to escalate the war."

The caucus met Friday at 8:30 a.m. Pelosi made a final pitch for support and unity; she praised Murtha for his military efforts, and Obey for his work on the funding. As the caucus applauded, Obey yelled, "I don't want your applause—I want your damn votes!"

When the bill came to the floor, Pelosi left nothing to chance. She posted sentinels by the doors leading off the floor to make sure no one tried to sneak out without voting. The debate was raucous, punctuated by cheers, boos and interruptions from protesters in the gallery. Fourteen Democrats—7 liberals and 7 moderates—voted against it, while 2 Republicans voted for it. Every freshman Democrat voted in favor. The bill got exactly as many votes as it needed to pass, 218 and no more.

She had done it: for the first time, Congress had taken a real step to rein in the war and mandate a change in course. It was a high-stakes test of Pelosi's abilities as Speaker, and she had shown she could move mountains. "Pelosi Wins on House War Vote," proclaimed a headline in *Politico*. The

Los Angeles Times called it "the most difficult trial of her speakership," and declared that "the 218–212 vote vindicated the risk she took in championing the controversial withdrawal plan before she had the votes."

Exhausted but relieved, Pelosi ended the debate with a bang of her gavel. "I stand here on this historic day for the Congress," she said. "This Congress voted to end the war in Iraq."

A few weeks later, Bush vetoed the bill.

❖ ❖ ❖

Pelosi thought that getting the bill through the House would create momentum, forcing the Senate to act and making it hard for Bush to veto. She was right except for the last part. Bush said he wouldn't support any kind of deadline attached to funding; Pelosi and the Democrats said there would be no funding without one. Finally, with time running out to keep the government funded, the Democrats caved and allowed the war funding to pass without a time line. Pelosi herself voted against the war-funding bill she'd had no choice but to put forward.

Overall, her strategy had failed: she didn't end the war, and she didn't get Bush to back down from the "surge," which most observers judged a military success; it stanched the chaos and prevented Iraq from descending into full-fledged civil war.

But analysts credited Pelosi and the congressional Democrats with changing the debate from one about the war's effectiveness to one about an "exit strategy." Just as important, she managed to unify her party on the issue that had threatened to blow it apart. As Republicans would later learn with Obamacare, it's one thing to promise your base voters you'll undo a presidential policy they loathe; it's another to make it happen. And it's another thing still to find an alternative that the party can rally around. Unlike Gingrich before her and Boehner after her, Pelosi kept her party's most extreme members from splitting or paralyzing the caucus—and from throwing her overboard.

In the years to come, even a Democratic president would prove incapable of solving the problem Bush had created. The war dragged on and on. A generation grew up in the shadow of never-ending military conflict. Finally, in 2011, the last U.S. troops came home from Iraq—only to return in 2014 as ISIS arose. As of 2019, about six thousand soldiers were stationed there.

15

The crash happened slowly, and then all at once. On Thursday, September 18, 2008, Hank Paulson, the treasury secretary, called Pelosi with panic in his voice. "A very serious situation is developing," he said.

It had been clear for more than a year that the economy was in trouble. As unease mounted and the signs of economic weakness piled up, Wall Street and Washington frantically worked behind the scenes to prevent the country's biggest banks from imploding. But now it was happening. Earlier that week, the nation's fourth-largest investment bank, Lehman Brothers, had declared bankruptcy, the largest bankruptcy filing in U.S. history. Now Paulson was telling Pelosi that the Fed and the administration had done all they could on their own. They needed help from Congress—fast.

Pelosi called the chairman of the Federal Reserve, Ben Bernanke. "If things are this bad," she said, "why aren't you calling me?" She offered to arrange a meeting of the Democratic and Republican congressional leaders the following day. But Bernanke said it had to be sooner. If they waited until tomorrow, he told her, there might not be an American economy to save.

They gathered in Pelosi's conference room that evening: the leaders of both parties in the House and Senate, plus Paulson, Bernanke and a representative from the White House. Bush himself purposely stayed away. Paulson outlined what the administration was asking for: congressional authorization for the Fed to buy up banks' "toxic assets," stabilizing their massive debt loads so they wouldn't go broke. The plan, Paulson said, would cost hundreds of billions of dollars. And even then, many more people would still likely lose their homes.

The proposal could hardly have been more odious to both political parties. Republicans hated the idea of government meddling so drastically in the economy (and spending so much taxpayer money to do it); it sounded like nationalizing private enterprise, a slippery slope to socialism. Meanwhile, to Democrats, it sounded like Bush was trying to protect his Wall Street buddies from the consequences of their own bad decisions, while turning a blind eye to the policy failures that had triggered the crisis and doing nothing to help the ordinary Americans who were losing jobs and homes. What was needed was the kind of bipartisan compromise in which both parties agreed to do something necessary but unpopular— holding hands and jumping off the cliff together, so neither could blame the other for the result.

The Senate Republican leader, Mitch McConnell, a quiet, jowly Kentuckian, said his caucus was committed. "If it means saving the country's financial system, we can do it." Both parties came away convinced they had to act, but it was not at all clear they'd be able to rise to the occasion.

✧ ✧ ✧

In the years leading up to 2008, just about anybody could get a loan to buy a house, even people with bad credit histories, people who couldn't prove they could afford a mortgage and people who lied about their income. With little oversight, banks doled out "subprime" mortgages, often using deceptive and predatory practices to trap borrowers in bad or unnecessarily expensive loans. The banks issuing the mortgages sold them to Wall Street, where they were bundled into investment vehicles called mortgage-backed securities.

In August 2006, the number of people delinquent on their mortgages began to rise for the first time in a decade. Housing prices fell as the bubble deflated, decreasing the value of the securities and causing the banks that owned them to lose money. By the time defaults and foreclosures began to climb, the banks had leveraged themselves so extensively that they couldn't cover their losses. Markets seized up, and credit became scarce. A chain reaction began to unfold in slow motion as businesses that couldn't borrow money began laying off workers or failing.

The housing boom had created a construction boom, and the housing bust cut that economic engine off at the knees. In growing cities like Las Vegas, where new housing developments continually sprouted at the outer edges of the city, the effect was stark: the money ran out, the bulldozers stopped and the workers left mid-project. Half-finished neighborhoods— foundations laid, cul-de-sacs paved, partial frames reaching skeletally toward the sky—suddenly became ghost towns, the subdivisions' cheerful, made-up names memorialized on highway billboards like tombstones.

The Bush administration at first insisted it was only a temporary slowdown. In February 2008, Pelosi helped Bush pass a $150 billion stimulus package consisting mostly of middle-class tax rebates. But the failure of Bear Stearns soon followed, setting off a wider panic. In July, the administration and Congress passed another bill aimed at stemming the subprime crisis by allowing borrowers to refinance. Officials still insisted that what was happening was merely a "correction," that the subprime problem could be contained, and that only a few bad apples on Wall Street were responsible.

Liberals, however, saw a systemic problem: an out-of-control financial sector born of conservative ideology and driven by greed. President Reagan had argued that markets should be free to work their will without the government's pesky intervention, only to see his loosening of mortgage and banking restrictions lead to the savings and loan crisis of the late 1980s. But it wasn't only Republican administrations that pushed for freer markets. Bill Clinton had styled himself a fiscal conservative and proclaimed that "the era of big government is over," a slogan Pelosi publicly criticized and privately loathed. Clinton stocked his administration with Wall Street–friendly officials and presided over the repeal of Depression-era restrictions on bank consolidation. He also, in one of his last acts as president, signed a bill the financial industry had ardently sought, banning regulation of the financial products called derivatives that the mega-investor Warren Buffett had called "financial weapons of mass destruction."

Under Bush, these deregulatory trends accelerated. Restrictions on banks' debt loads were relaxed, and investment banks were largely left to regulate themselves. Regulators who took a dim view of government action turned a blind eye to investment banks' increasingly exotic accounting and investment strategies. Meanwhile, Bush's massive tax cuts for the rich, combined with the unfunded wars in Afghanistan and Iraq, wiped out the budget surpluses Clinton and Gingrich had created. Federal agencies ignored fraud and other problems, and when the head of the Securities and Exchange Commission called for more regulation of mutual and hedge funds, he was blocked and eventually quit. Pelosi called it "cowboy capitalism": Republicans, she charged, saw the market as a wide-open frontier where anything goes.

✧ ✧ ✧

All this was unfolding against the backdrop of a high-stakes presidential election. With Bush's second term almost up, the fight was on to replace the now historically unpopular president. Senator Hillary Clinton, elected to represent New York as her husband's presidency was coming to an end in 2000, was the odds-on front-runner for the Democratic nomination. But Clinton, who had voted for the Iraq War, faced an unexpectedly stiff challenge from a first-term senator, Barack Obama, elected to represent Illinois in 2004 on an antiwar platform.

Pelosi didn't publicly take sides, but she admired Obama's political instincts and inspirational campaign. Two of her closest congressional allies, George Miller and Anna Eshoo, both endorsed Obama. Besides, Pelosi's relations with the Clintons had been chilly dating back to Bill Clinton's presidency. The Clintons' network of supporters took note when, at a party fund-raiser held in DC when Hillary was already in the Senate, Pelosi thanked "President Clinton and the First Lady," an unintentional slip that Hillary's inner circle took as a slight.

Obama's surprise win in the January 2008 Iowa caucuses catapulted him to front-runner status, and while Clinton continued to win primaries here and there, Obama began to amass a near-insurmountable delegate lead. Clinton, however, refused to drop out, insisting she was more electable. An ugly whisper campaign on her behalf, implying that Obama's name and background would strike voters as "un-American," is sometimes cited as the origin of the false and racist "birther" theory that Obama was hiding his true past as a Kenyan-born Muslim.

Clinton argued that she was still viable in part because she was supported by a large number of the party insiders automatically awarded votes at the convention, known as "superdelegates." Obama's campaign argued that this represented an undemocratic establishment plot, and they urged superdelegates to follow the will of the voters. In a March 2008 interview on ABC News, Pelosi was asked about this intraparty controversy and replied, "If the votes of the superdelegates overturn what happens in the elections, it would be harmful to the Democratic Party"—essentially echoing Obama's line. Clinton's supporters, including some of Pelosi's top donors, went ballistic and sent Pelosi a letter that seemed to threaten to pull their contributions to the Democrats' House campaigns if she didn't back off. Pelosi also got a call from Harvey Weinstein, the still-powerful movie mogul and Clinton backer, who tried to get her to support the campaign's last-ditch primary gambits. The attempts to pressure her only strengthened Pelosi's resolve to hold off the Clinton machine, and the Obama-supporting progressive grass roots hailed her for it. In an interview with the *Wall Street Journal*, she maintained her neutrality but observed, of Obama's policy platform, "Some might say he's advocating what I've been advocating for a long time."

The Republicans realized the election would be an uphill climb thanks to Bush's dismal ratings. They nominated John McCain, the war hero and Arizona senator who had lost the presidential primary to Bush in 2000. Now the Republicans hoped that McCain's reputation as a "maverick" capable of crossing party lines would represent a break from the unpopular president. Bush was so unpopular that he wasn't even invited to speak in person at the Republicans' 2008 convention, in St. Paul, Minnesota. But the star of the convention, it turned out, was not McCain but Sarah Palin, the GOP vice presidential nominee. Hoping for a surprise that would give the faltering McCain a much-needed boost, his campaign had selected the little-known governor of Alaska, a fellow "maverick" from outside the Beltway with a bipartisan track record, youthful energy and social-conservative cred.

Palin introduced herself to the nation with a searing convention speech in which, calling herself a "hockey mom," she bashed the Washington elites—a role in which she cast Obama. "Before I became the governor of the great state of Alaska, I was mayor of my hometown," she said. "And since our opponents in this presidential election seem to look down on that experience, let me explain to them what the job involved. I guess a small-town mayor is sort of like a community organizer, except that you have actual responsibilities." Conventiongoers were rapturous. They wore pins with slogans like "The Hottest Governor from the Coldest State" and chanted, "Drill, baby, drill!"

Unlike McCain, Palin had no qualms about going after Obama with personally and racially tinged attacks, accusing him of "palling around with terrorists" and raising the issue of his former pastor, the radical reverend Jeremiah Wright. McCain had banned his campaign from bringing up Wright in speeches or ads. But the campaign's attempts to rein in Palin failed. And in a telling and premonitory glimpse of the GOP's soul, it was Palin, not McCain, who drew enormous crowds of enraptured supporters. Republicans wanted Palin's angry, anti-elitist cultural resentment, not McCain's polite forbearance.

❖ ❖ ❖

The Lehman Brothers bankruptcy and Pelosi's emergency meeting came just two weeks after Palin's explosive convention speech. Pelosi had been persuaded by Paulson and Bernanke that there was a crisis that demanded action. But if the Democratic Congress was going to help the unpopular Republican president take an action bound to be controversial—on the eve of an election, no less—the solution could not be one-sided. Pelosi herself faced attacks as one of the wealthy elites who seemed to be fiddling while America burned. The day after the meeting, she called President Bush to confer.

The call was the first time Pelosi and the president had spoken in months. Bush said he wanted a solution that was quick and targeted and that wouldn't get bogged down in a negotiation over partisan policy priorities. "Let's get it done," he told her. "Simple and lean."

Later that day, Bush announced the administration's rescue plan in a Rose Garden speech that was broadcast live to an anxious nation. He emphasized the severity of the crisis and the need to act. "There will be ample opportunity to debate the origins of this problem," he said. "Now is the time to solve it."

But when the administration's actual legislative proposal reached the Hill, lawmakers were none too pleased. The bill was a bare-bones, three-page document that was exceedingly vague on details. The proposed Troubled Asset Relief Program, or TARP, gave Treasury wide-ranging authority to purchase "troubled assets," the suddenly near-worthless mortgage-backed securities and related products, so that banks could stabilize their balance sheets and keep from going under. The idea was that Treasury could hold on to these assets until the market recovered and their value rebounded. But the administration's proposal included no oversight of the program, no reforms to corporate governance, no restrictions on executive compensation—not even a requirement that banks repay the government.

Congressional leaders and the administration set to work coming up with legislation that would be able to pass the House and Senate. Among other things, they added a requirement that companies receiving TARP funds would pay the money back with interest. But what if there were a shortfall? In one drafting session, the Republicans suggested that domestic spending be cut to make up the difference. Pelosi's chief of staff, John Lawrence, knew that this was a nonstarter and said so. He and the Republican negotiator, Senator Judd Gregg, began to argue, and Gregg finally shouted, "You're not listening to me!'

"Well, Senator, you're not listening to me," Lawrence replied. "Why don't you go down the hall to the Speaker's office and see what she thinks of your idea?"

Gregg stormed off to Pelosi's office. He returned, cowed, just a few minutes later—their conversation had been a brief one. "Okay, that isn't going to work," he growled.

Days passed, and still there was no bill. The Republicans said they wanted to do something, but they were maddeningly disengaged with the details. Some in the GOP said they didn't think the crisis was that bad, while others thought the banks should be left to fail. Boehner was evasive about what House Republicans wanted in the bill. McCain, on the campaign trail, was bad-mouthing the legislation, and Bush seemed to be in hiding. Pelosi was exasperated. "Tell the president to lead!" she urged Paulson. If the president wasn't going to push for his own administration's proposal, all this negotiation would be for naught. "It is an insult to you," Pelosi told Paulson, who replied glumly, "I'm beyond that point."

McCain was a veteran senator known for his foreign policy and military expertise. Over the course of his career, he'd worked on campaign finance, immigration and gun control. But when it came to economic policy, he was out of his depth. Now, as he fell behind in the presidential race, he needed to prove he had the leadership qualities to deal with an economic crisis. On September 24, he called Pelosi and demanded to know why it was taking so long for Congress to come up with a bill. "We are making progress," she said. "It is not accurate to say otherwise."

McCain saw an opportunity to exert leadership and, perhaps, gain a political advantage. He publicly announced that he was suspending his campaign to focus on the crisis, and called for both candidates to meet with congressional leaders at the White House. Democrats and many in the White House viewed this as a political stunt, and Pelosi worried it would delay the process rather than help it. But they agreed to the meeting.

The group gathered in the Cabinet Room on September 25. Obama and McCain sat at opposite ends of the table. Bush opened the proceedings, urging quick action and warning against clogging up the bill with unrelated provisions. He urged both parties to support whatever Paulson and Bernanke signed off on. "You damn sure don't want to be the people who see it crater," he said.

The Democrats designated Obama to speak first, and he made a detailed and eloquent opening statement. House Republicans suggested alternative ideas to the TARP proposal; Democrats protested that it was too late for that. As the two sides bickered, McCain sat silent. Obama interjected: it was McCain's idea to have this meeting; shouldn't he have something to say?

But McCain had no ideas or firm position of his own, and little knowledge of or preparation about the technical details of TARP. Shocking even the Republicans present, he stumbled through a bland nonstatement, saying he shared the other Republicans' concerns.

Bush leaned over to Pelosi, who was sitting beside him, and whispered in her ear. "I told you you'd miss me when I'm gone!" he said.

Pelosi replied, "No, I won't." (She was mistaken: after Trump became president, she would frequently express nostalgia for Bush.)

After the meeting ended, the Democrats clustered in the adjacent Roosevelt Room, chattering about what had just happened. Suddenly, Paulson burst in. Exhausted and anxious, he feared the whole plan was about to unravel. He walked up to Pelosi and got down on one knee. Bowing his head, he implored her: "I beg you, don't blow this thing up."

The Democrats were incensed. They weren't the ones threatening to blow up the deal—the Republicans were! Pelosi looked down at the kneeling Paulson with amusement. "Why, Hank," she said, "I didn't know you were Catholic!"

✧ ✧ ✧

It was time, Pelosi decided, to call a vote. She and Boehner made a deal: he would come up with 100 Republican votes, and the Democrats would make up the rest—at least 118. Lawmakers' phones were jammed with angry calls from Americans enraged by the proposed bailout, and it was only going to get worse. The Republicans begged for more time. Boehner said he couldn't promise more than 75 votes, while Bush and Paulson frantically implored members to support their own party's president.

The Democrats were also rebelling. Jim Clyburn of South Carolina, the Democratic whip, told Pelosi he expected no more than half the caucus to vote in favor. The black and Hispanic caucuses were especially angry on behalf of their poverty-stricken communities, while moderates in tough districts were worried about reelection. Pelosi dispatched Barney Frank, the cantankerous chairman of the Financial Services Committee, to talk to the black caucus, Hispanic caucus and Blue Dogs. "When is the asshole caucus," Frank shot back, "and do I have to address them?"

The caucus's liberals did not believe their party should put its credibility and electoral prospects on the line to clean up the mess caused by a Republican president they didn't trust. "President Bush tells us that we face unparalleled financial doom if this $700 billion bailout is not approved today," declared California congressman Pete Stark. "He and his treasury secretary, a former Wall Street fat cat, tell us that we have reached the point of 'crisis.' That is a familiar line from this president. It sounds like the disastrous rush to war in Iraq and the subsequent stampede to enact the Patriot Act. As I opposed the Iraq War and the Patriot Act, I stand in opposition to his latest rush to judgment."

It was against this backdrop that Pelosi prepared to make perhaps the most consequential floor speech of her career. She had to convince her own members that she had no intention of letting Bush and the Republicans off the hook. She had to give the world's most persuasive sales pitch for a bill she hated and convince members of both parties that they had no choice but to suck it up and support the plan that Boehner had dubbed a "crap sandwich."

Pelosi took the lectern in a collarless beige jacket and large beaded necklace, her short hair parted severely on the side. "Seven hundred billion dollars—a staggering number, but only a part of the cost of the failed Bush economic policies to our country," she began. She railed against the president's fiscal irresponsibility and "anything goes" economic policy. "No regulation, no supervision, no discipline. And if you fail, you will have a golden parachute and the taxpayer will bail you out. Those days are over. The party is over," she said, one hand slashing the air as she spoke.

She described the warnings from Paulson and Bernanke and the shortcomings of their original "arrogant and insulting" proposal. And she lacerated the administration for ignoring the crisis as long as it affected only ordinary Americans and leaping into action only when Big Business was in trouble. "When they describe the magnitude of the challenge and the precipice that we were on, and how we had to act quickly and we had to act boldly and we had to act now, it never occurred to them that the consequences of this market were being felt well in advance by the American people," she said.

Democrats, she said, would not rest until regular people were taken care of. But for now, they had to do the hard thing. "We are on the brink of doing something that might pull us back from that precipice," she said. "I think we have a responsibility. . . . This is a bipartisan initiative that we are bringing to the floor. We have to have a bipartisan vote on this. That is the only message that will send a message of confidence to the markets. I know that we will be able to live up to our side of the bargain. I hope the Republicans will, too."

When Boehner, who was famously emotional, addressed the floor, tears welled up in his eyes and threatened to trickle down his suntanned face. "I didn't come here to vote for bills like this," he said. "But let me tell you this, I believe Congress has to act."

The Republicans didn't listen to their own leaders. When the vote was called after hours of speeches, there were 205 votes in favor, 228 against. Pelosi had done her part: 140 of the 235 Democrats voted yes. But on the Republican side, just 65 of 198 were in favor. The ayes included only 4 of the 19 Republicans from Texas, even though Bush had phoned every one of them.

As the votes came in the market began to plunge. A Republican congressman narrated the collapse from a corner of the floor, his phone pressed to his ear: "Two hundred points . . . five hundred points . . . seven hundred points . . ."

"That's it," Pelosi muttered. "We're finished."

The Dow's 778-point fall was the biggest one-day loss in history, wiping out $1.2 trillion in wealth. And then, after this failure, the Republicans had the nerve to blame Pelosi. Her floor speech, they claimed, had been so partisan that they could not bring themselves to vote for the bill.

Pelosi knew that this was just an excuse to paper over the truth: with or without her, they didn't have the votes.

✦ ✦ ✦

The market drop put the fear of God into the Republicans. ("Anarchy Reigns Over GOP," a typical headline blared.) In the Senate, Harry Reid sprang into action. He and Mitch McConnell loaded up their version of TARP with corporate giveaways, such as tax credits for oil companies, to buy Republican votes. Pelosi told Reid she thought this was disgraceful, but he told her, "You can't be a virgin if—"

She cut him off before he could finish.

But Reid's plan worked. The bill passed the Senate by a wide bipartisan margin. Annoyed but out of other options, Pelosi told Boehner she had done all she could. On October 3, she put the Senate bill on the floor, and it passed, 263–71, with 172 Democrats and 91 Republicans in favor. Working with the Republicans, she concluded, had been a waste of time: they never did come up with 100 votes. She would have been better off writing the bill Democrats had wanted from the very beginning.

The public detested the bailouts, which helped spur the rise of the Tea Party movement as well as, years later, Occupy Wall Street. In the final months of his term, Bush never got around to helping out Main Street as he had promised. TARP might not be popular, but it worked, and it didn't end up costing taxpayers a dime: five years later, analysts concluded, the government had taken in $31 billion in profit from the program.

Pelosi played a pivotal role in saving the U.S. economy from near-certain catastrophe. She bailed a Republican president out of a mess of his own making, for the good of the country, at enormous political risk. John Lawrence, her chief of staff, later wondered: if the president had been Obama, would Republicans have done the same?

16

WHAT STRUCK PELOSI MORE THAN ANYTHING, AS THE NEW PRESIDENT took his oath of office on a freezing, crystal-clear day, was the silence.

Nearly two million people flocked to the National Mall to see Obama's inauguration. Pelosi, clad in a periwinkle-blue coat with an elegant scalloped collar, led the new president's procession through the Capitol, then sat on the dais behind him as he gave his inaugural address. A vast human sea stretched westward, from the majestic Capitol Building to the Washington Monument more than a mile away. And yet, when Obama spoke, nobody moved. Everybody just listened.

Obama had won twenty-eight states and 53 percent of the vote—the most resounding Democratic victory since Johnson in 1964. Voter turnout was the highest in four decades, and for the first time in history more than a quarter of the electorate was nonwhite. Obama won seemingly red states such as Indiana and North Carolina; he flipped nine states Kerry had lost in 2004. His inspirational, transpartisan message unified Democrats, despite the bruising primary, and even won over one in ten Republican voters. On his coattails, Democrats gained 7 seats in the Senate, with another race, in Minnesota, headed to a recount. In the House, the Democrats' majority increased by 21 seats, to 257 out of 435.

For Pelosi and other liberals, Obama's election was as gratifying as Kerry's defeat had been crushing. They savored the feeling that theirs was the "real America": not Sarah Palin's closed-minded vision of the traditional heartland lifestyle, but a nation of multiculturalism and tolerance, progress and fellow feeling. Obama had galvanized a coalition that was young and diverse—the future of America—as he promised to erase the old divisions and heal the wounds of not just the nation but the planet. It was time to put away the old hatreds and culture wars: America had elected a black man named Barack Hussein Obama. All over the world, crowds cheered, and across the country African American neighborhoods rejoiced.

As Republicans nursed their wounds, analysts talked about a generational realignment. Democrats had forged a new coalition that brought white liberals and moderates together with black voters, Hispanics, Asians and other minorities. Two-thirds of voters said the economy was their top issue, and with the GOP's historical reputation as the party of fiscal soundness having gone up in smoke, Obama won those voters by nearly 10 points. Obama erased Republicans' onetime advantage with women and suburbanites; he won both the poorest and the richest groups of voters, and was the first Democrat ever to win a majority of college graduates. Based on demographic trends, all the groups in the Democratic tent were growing while the Republicans' base shrank. One columnist called the GOP "the party of the aging white man" and predicted "doom" for it. Another proclaimed that Obama could remake the American political landscape as FDR had done. The new president-elect had campaigned on "Change You Can Believe In," and the nation had given him a mandate for progress. *Time* magazine's cover pictured the GOP elephant under the heading "Endangered Species."

For Pelosi, it was the opportunity of her political lifetime. Up to that point, her entire tenure as a Democratic leader was against the backdrop of Republican rule—a member of the opposition party charged with trying to stop the party in power from winning its agenda while hammering out advantageous compromises. She'd steered her party in a progressive direction while reining in the extreme left. But with a Democrat in the White House, she could do more than stop bad things from happening. "We're going to do it," she told the House Democrats in a caucus meeting, "not just talk about it and posture."

She thought of it in terms of paleoanthropology, a hobby of hers since her days on the board of the Leakey Foundation. The early humans were hunter-gatherers who spent their lives simply struggling to survive. It was only when they established agriculture and put down roots that they could aspire to more. "We have been on a long trek to get where we are today," she told her colleagues, some of whom seemed mystified by the obscure analogy. "Now we're not in survival mode. This is our time to invent and create."

Thanks to Obama, Democrats could actually pursue some of the new policies they'd been incubating for a decade. They could not just fix the economy but take it out of the hands of the bankers and exploiters and put it in the hands of working people. They could expand health care, tackle climate change, liberalize immigration. The new president had big plans. In his powerful inaugural address, he talked about summoning the American spirit to take on crisis. He pledged to make the economy stronger and stabler, to build new infrastructure, invest in science and technology, expand renewable energy and modernize education. "There are some who question the scale of our ambitions—who suggest that our system cannot tolerate too many big plans," he said. "They have forgotten what this country has already done; what free men and women can achieve when imagination is joined to common purpose, and necessity to courage."

Pelosi and Obama didn't know each other well, though they had become acquainted over the course of the campaign. Like her, he considered himself a practical idealist, a progressive willing to compromise to get things done. Unlike her, he'd styled himself a Washington outsider, a bridge builder allergic to partisanship and rigid ideology. Where her lodestar was results, his was consensus.

As Pelosi looked forward to a productive partnership, she was also appropriately wary. She wanted to help the new president, but she was determined not to be a rubber stamp the way the Republicans had been for Bush. She had to protect the role of the House and its voice in the debate. Even before the inauguration, she and Obama publicly disagreed on how to bail out the auto industry. Obama was Pelosi's ticket to a raft of accomplishments, but his election also pushed her aside as the most powerful Democrat, the face and voice of the party. She would now have to strike a balance between pursuing her own vision and executing the White House's agenda.

Even as the Democrats celebrated, the national mood remained bleak. The economy was still in free fall. "The challenges we face are real," Obama said in his inaugural speech. "They are serious and they are many. They will not be met easily or in a short span of time." It would be up to the

Democrats to stop the bleeding and clean up the many messes of a decade of Republican rule. As the *Onion* put it, "Black Man Given Nation's Worst Job."

❖ ❖ ❖

After the election, the House Democrats reelected Pelosi as Speaker by a unanimous vote. Over the course of her first two years as Speaker, her caucus had come to trust her implicitly.

The reasons started with personal relationships. Not only did she know every one of her members by name—a difficult enough feat in a 435-member body that turns over every two years—but she knew their history, their district, their ideology, their spouse and kids and parents. If she found out your wife was having surgery or you were going through a divorce, she'd call repeatedly to check in. Orchids from her favorite DC florist would appear, for thanks or congratulations or sympathy, before you thought you'd even told anyone what was happening. The most powerful woman in America somehow had time to show up for a child's school play or a parent's memorial service. If your mother died, you got a handwritten condolence note along with a poem written long ago by Pelosi's own mother.

Pelosi's first term as Speaker showed her caucus what she was capable of. She had held the party's wide ideological spectrum together, enforcing a record level of party unity. Despite her liberal bona fides, she'd worked to defuse cultural wedge issues, keeping abortion and gun control off the House agenda and even watering down gay rights legislation: the anti-discrimination bill the House passed in 2007 did not protect transgender people, to the chagrin of many advocates. (It died in the Senate.) Centrists who'd feared she would rule as a San Francisco liberal had come to respect her pragmatism. Pelosi wasn't afraid to antagonize the left, whether it was by refusing to impeach Bush or defund the war, or by overruling liberals and her own preferences to reauthorize Bush's warrantless wiretapping.

She also always had time to listen. Members referred to the endless meetings with Pelosi as therapy or prayer sessions: she knew that sometimes all people needed to work through a decision was to feel that they'd been heard, and she would take as long as it took to make that happen. Sometimes caucus meetings dragged on for hours as she insisted everyone get a turn to speak. Others were free to leave, but she stayed until the end. Previous Speakers were often remote figures: some members worked under Tip O'Neill for years without ever getting a private audience with him. But Pelosi held meeting after meeting after meeting. She never went into a discussion without a plan for how she hoped it would end, but she was open to persuasion and better ideas and would sometimes change course as a result.

She would hear people out, but she wouldn't give them false hope, and members valued her straightforwardness. They always knew where she stood, even if they didn't like it. One new member told Pelosi he'd like to be on the Appropriations Committee. "That's not going to happen," she told him matter-of-factly. "What other committees are you interested in?" In return, she expected them not to surprise her. Refusing to vote with the party was forgivable, but only if they warned her first.

And then there was her energy, which, though she was now sixty-eight, seemed not to have flagged in the slightest. Overworked members could hardly complain when their leader seemed to work at least twice as hard as they did. She continued to be a formidable fund-raiser, criss-crossing the country nonstop to raise money whenever she didn't have to be in Washington. Just as she didn't seem to need sleep or caffeine, she seemed immune to jet lag. Her trips abroad were packed with meetings from the minute the plane landed—no downtime and no time for sight-seeing. (Once, in Berlin, her chief of staff sprinted from their hotel to see the Brandenburg Gate in the only downtime available to him: Pelosi's twenty-minute morning hair appointment.) Members who traveled with her learned to pack a suit in their carry-on to change into on the plane, because even after a long overseas flight they wouldn't be stopping at their hotel before their first meetings. They also learned they'd need to set aside some time to catch up on sleep when they returned.

The press respected Pelosi but tended to find her boring. She didn't have a big, colorful personality like Rahm Emanuel, nor did she share his self-mythologizing instincts. She wasn't loose or chummy, and her quirks weren't relatable to the overwhelmingly male Capitol Hill press corps; she reminded them of a strict teacher or a demanding mother-in-law. Her sense of humor was prim verging on childish, and she never swore. In interviews, she revealed little, tending to repeat the same talking points; her speeches were salted with the same worn-out slogans, touchstone quo-tations and alliterative mnemonics. She disdained gossip and distrusted most reporters, sometimes freezing them out in retaliation for a story or column she didn't like. Tightly wound and officious, Pelosi's persona was the opposite of the folksiness fetishized by political media.

Aides had brought in speaking coaches, and Pelosi had improved since the early days, but she still struggled as a public speaker and sometimes made embarrassing gaffes. Once, a press aide, trying to give constructive feedback, informed her that a certain speech had been a bit meandering; for weeks afterward, every time she came offstage, she would snap at him, "How was that? Did I *meander*?" Her habit of repeating talking points was actually an improvement over her tendency to wander off message.

She could be hard to work for—not abusive, but demanding; unlike many pols who rely on a trusted adviser or panel of consultants, Pelosi largely kept her own counsel, made her own decisions and did her own floor work. (George Miller joked that the *click-click-click* of her approaching heels reminded members of the theme from *Jaws*.) Her staff didn't have the feel of a family like some leaders' did. But many stayed with her for years nonetheless, attracted by her sense of mission.

Her determination to do everything herself could become controlling. There was a fine line between being detail-oriented and micromanaging, and members sometimes felt Pelosi crossed it. She had an extreme need for control and a tendency to hold grudges, using her power to settle personal scores if necessary. In 2007, she passed over the next person in line for chair of the Intelligence Committee, Jane Harman, a fellow Californian with more hawkish national security views, for a more junior member. A rumor even circulated that it all started when both women wore the same dress to a function, a sexist "catfight" story line with no basis in fact. Harman found out about Pelosi's decision to deny her the post from the papers and never did figure out what, if anything, it was payback for.

But few in the caucus could imagine any other leader doing what Pelosi had done. For two years, she had been the principal face of the Democrats as they sought to return to power—and in 2008, the public agreed to put them in charge of everything.

✧ ✧ ✧

Despite Pelosi's clashes with Hoyer, she and her deputy had developed a good working relationship, though he maintained an independent power base and would never be under her control. She trusted Clyburn, who made up in relationships and wisdom what he sometimes lacked in vote-counting skill. Obama had hired Emanuel to be his White House chief of staff, which opened up the position of caucus chair and raised the possibility of an internal battle. John Larson of Connecticut was next in line, but Chris Van Hollen, a rising star from Maryland who'd run the 2008 House campaign, had his eye on a promotion. To defuse the conflict, Pelosi created a new position for Van Hollen, "assistant to the Speaker," allowing Larson to take the caucus chair slot uncontested. She leaned on Van Hollen to stay at the Democratic campaign committee, even though he wanted out of that thankless job. Pelosi was grooming him as a possible successor, and he knew it. He did what she asked.

But while she headed off some conflicts, there were others she notably did not. John Dingell, the chairman of the Energy and Commerce Committee, had long been a thorn in Pelosi's side. The veteran lawmaker from Detroit had been in Congress since the 1950s, in a seat previously held by his father. Tall and ornery, he was a close ally of Hoyer's who had managed Hoyer's leadership campaigns, and he ran his committee like a kingdom. Dingell was a relic of the days when chairmen could be more powerful than Speakers. His base of support, organized labor and the auto industry, was one whose clout was fading in the Democratic Party that Pelosi had helped forge, where coastal and ideological liberals reigned—and, critics charged, where heartland voters felt overlooked. Dingell was an ally of the National Rifle Association and opposed many environmental measures on behalf of his friends in the auto industry. In the 1990s, he fought against clean air and water legislation, finally allowing it to be pushed through in watered-down form.

Pelosi's disagreements with Dingell were well known and long-standing. She had supported Dingell's primary opponent in 2002. When she first became Speaker in 2007, she created a special committee on climate change, brazenly undercutting Dingell—who she worried would obstruct climate legislation or make it too industry-friendly—by taking the issue out of his jurisdiction. As Democrats prepared for life under Obama, many of the big-ticket issues they planned to tackle, from climate change to health care, were destined to move through Dingell's powerful committee.

The day after the 2008 election, Pelosi's California colleague and liberal ally Henry Waxman announced that he would challenge Dingell for the Energy and Commerce gavel. Dingell immediately called Pelosi and reminded her of a conversation they'd had on the House floor over the summer. "You told me you had my back," Dingell complained.

"That's not what I said," she replied. What she'd told him was that he was doing a good job, which, she contended, was not the same thing.

Pelosi and Hoyer both announced they would not take sides in the Waxman-Dingell fight, but their colleagues knew where they stood and regarded it as a proxy fight between the two top leaders. It was a close and bruising contest, and when Waxman won on the secret ballot, 137–122, it sent a message. It bolstered Pelosi's control, both by installing an ally rather than a rival and showing other potential troublemakers what fate might befall them. And it made a statement about where the caucus's mainstream lay when it came to top priorities.

Some influential commentators were urging the Democrats to move slowly and carefully, not to alienate the American public by "overreaching." They pointed out that Democrats had won in many traditionally conservative areas that would react badly to too much change, too liberal an agenda. But Pelosi was not interested in timid, Clinton-style triangulation. The point of power was to do something with it. The breadth of the Democrats' victory was a license to expand the party's ambitions, not rein them in.

Obama and his team seemed to agree. Emanuel, speaking to a group of business leaders a week after the election, said the dire state of the economy was an opening to do big things rather than papering over problems. "You never want a serious crisis to go to waste," he said. "Things that we had postponed for too long, that were long term, are now immediate and must be dealt with. This crisis provides the opportunity for us to do things that you could not do before."

17

THERE WAS MUCH TO BE DONE AND NO TIME TO SPARE. WITHIN DAYS OF Obama's inauguration, he had signed two major Democratic bills into law: the extension of the Children's Health Insurance Program that Bush had resisted and the Lilly Ledbetter Act mandating fair pay for women.

But the highest priority was the economy. Even before he took office, Obama had to expend political capital getting the second tranche of TARP funds through the Senate. It took a round of frantic phone calls from the president-elect to his erstwhile colleagues, five days before his inauguration, to muscle it through by a 52–42 margin.

Obama's first major piece of legislation would be a massive economic stimulus package. Right after the election, Democrats huddled with experts for what they would later describe as the scariest briefings they'd ever experienced. Moody's chief economist, Mark Zandi, who had served as an adviser to McCain's presidential campaign and was regarded as one of the soberest market analysts, told a group of congressional leaders that the American economy, still shedding seven hundred thousand jobs per month, was in the process of "shutting down." Christina Romer, a Depression scholar Obama had tapped to head the Council of Economic Advisers, said a similar fate awaited the country if cash weren't injected into the economy quickly. Obama told Pelosi he wanted the House to put together a stimulus bill he could sign on his very first day in office.

The idea of the stimulus was to pump money into the economy, boosting demand and reversing the vicious circle the recession had created. With people losing their jobs and homes and banks tightening up credit, there was no money available to spend on products and services. Without demand for products and services, businesses that couldn't sell their wares had to lay off workers or go under, putting more people out of work, making more people unable to afford their mortgages, and on and on. But the federal government could borrow money and inject it into the economy, where it would circulate through the system like lifeblood.

By this theory, which originated during the Depression with the British economist John Maynard Keynes, it didn't really matter what the money was spent on, as long as it was spent right away. The government could simply give people money, in the form of welfare programs or by cutting taxes; it could give grants and loans to businesses to keep them running and spur them to hire more people; it could fund projects and create programs to give people jobs, reducing unemployment and injecting cash into the system at the same time. These programs might be beneficial and lasting, like the parks and roads and bridges and schools built by FDR's New Deal. But that wasn't really the point: Keynes supposedly said the government "should pay people to dig holes in the ground and then fill them up." The point was to give people work and get money circulating until the economy was healthy enough to stand on its own.

Most mainstream economists accepted Keynesian theory, but it could be a hard sell with the public. If your family was broke, you'd tighten your belt, not go take out a new mortgage. But that counterintuitive idea was what the government was proposing. Republicans, many of whom still denied the scientific consensus on climate change, didn't necessarily buy the economists' consensus, either. Some had latched on to a faddish new book, Amity Shlaes's *The Forgotten Man*, which argued that FDR's stimulus had made the Depression worse, not better, even though most historians disagreed. One elderly Republican congressman, Roscoe Bartlett of Maryland, told Obama to his face that he'd been six years old when FDR took office, and "I don't remember that Roosevelt's spending had anything to do with bringing us out of the Depression."

While Bush was still president, Pelosi pleaded with him to do more for struggling Americans. She urged a White House aide to show some compassion at a time when families were lining up at soup kitchens—helping them, she said, shouldn't be a partisan proposition. But the aide disagreed. "Madam Speaker," he informed her, "Republicans have a different view on stimulating the economy." Their solution was to make permanent the Bush tax cuts for the wealthy, which were scheduled to expire in 2011. She couldn't believe what she was hearing—it was as if the White House lived in another universe. "That's what got us into this mess!" she said.

In October, before the election, Obama campaigned on a $175 billion stimulus plan. But the economy kept nose-diving, increasing the need—and the price tag. Half a million jobs were lost in October, and a staggering eight hundred thousand in November. Unemployment was up to 6.5 percent. The *Washington Post* reported, "The economy is unraveling so fast as to defy analysis through the usual statistical methods." Obama's team of economic experts kept revising upward the amount of money they planned to ask Congress for. Three hundred billion dollars, $500 billion, $700 billion—every time they came up with a number, it started to seem too small.

Pelosi told Emanuel she didn't think the House would go for anything over $600 billion. But Obama's adviser Larry Summers thought that even then, unemployment would remain at around 8 percent after two years. Christina Romer calculated that the "output gap," the gulf between the American economy's actual production and its potential, was a staggering $1.8 trillion. At a December meeting with the Obama team in Chicago, Romer said starkly, "Mr. President-elect, this is your holy-shit moment." The White House decided to ask for about $800 billion in stimulus—bigger than TARP. As a share of GDP, it would be the largest public investment in U.S. history.

It was a "holy shit" moment in more ways than one. After the meeting, Obama's campaign manager and political adviser David Axelrod took Obama aside and informed the president-elect, who hadn't even moved into the White House yet, that in two years' time, no matter what he did, the midterm elections were going to be brutal.

◆ ◆ ◆

Had it been up to the House Democrats, the stimulus would have been a pretty straightforward matter. If there's anything Congress knows how to do, it's spend large amounts of money. Pelosi wanted to immediately repeal the Bush tax cuts—hiking taxes was hardly Keynesian, but raising marginal income tax rates on those in the upper brackets would, by definition, hit people who were still making good money, and it would bring in revenue that would lower the bill's price tag. The Democrats would prefer to put money into traditional liberal spending programs like food stamps and public works, providing immediate relief to the needy while pumping cash and jobs into the economy. They would let individual members add pet projects, called earmarks, to the bill, ensuring they'd not just vote for it but talk it up in their districts. Even Republicans would likely be swayed by this type of "peanut butter politics"—spreading money around—and if they weren't, Democrats might let them win some tax cuts in negotiations.

The White House had other ideas. Obama and his economists, who were largely centrist technocrats, had already ruled out eliminating the Bush tax cuts. Having campaigned against business as usual in Washington, Obama wanted the bill to contain no earmarks, which conservatives decried as wasteful pork. In keeping with his political brand, he didn't want to put more money into the same tired programs. He wanted a down payment on the future, a bill that didn't just prop the economy back up but shaped it in a progressive direction. And as an olive branch to Republicans, a sign that he planned to incorporate the best ideas of both parties, his proposal would include a healthy proportion of new middle-class tax cuts to put money in people's pockets.

Obama had chosen Pelosi's old electoral lieutenant Rahm Emanuel as his chief of staff in part for his perceived effectiveness as a House whisperer. Being a "Washington outsider" was essential to Obama's political brand, but he knew he was going to need some inside juice to get his ambitious plans through Congress. Emanuel, uniquely, had both high-level White House experience in the Clinton administration and high-level congressional experience as a member of House leadership. He had relationships with congresspeople and senators, if not unanimously positive ones, and he knew the system's pressure points. It hadn't been easy for Obama to convince Emanuel to leave the House, where he harbored dreams of being the first Jewish Speaker. But his decision to join the administration was a promising sign to Pelosi and her fellow House Democrats. A relentless schmoozer, Emanuel still worked out (and buttonholed lawmakers) every morning at the House gym, and he took lawmakers and other legislative players to dinner at fancy restaurants nearly every night.

The Obama White House didn't want to write the stimulus bill. They wanted to dictate what was in it, but they thought the House would give it more favorable consideration if the lawmakers were the ones who wrote it. In fact, while every new president is subject to some amount of congressional hazing, House Democrats were generally as gaga for the new president as the rest of the Democratic Party, and eager to be part of a team effort. What they didn't like was the rapidly developing feeling that Obama thought he was too good for them. It was true enough: the president complained privately about how much he hated schmoozing members, with their "petty egos" that perpetually needed to be stroked. But had things gone a little differently, he would have been one of them: before setting his sights on the U.S. Senate, Obama had run for a Chicago House seat but failed to topple the incumbent in the primary.

When it came time to draft the bill, the White House's nonsensical posture led to a bizarre scene. Rob Nabors, the incoming deputy director of the Office of Management and Budget, sketched out the White House's vision for the legislation and took it to David Obey, the chairman of the Appropriations Committee. Nabors and Obey knew each other well: Nabors had just left his job as Obey's staff director to join the Obama administration. In the office they'd once shared, Nabors read Obama's wish list off a sheet of paper, but he refused to let Obey see the paper itself. Nabors ticked off White House priorities such as electric cars, electronic medical records and education reform—a far cry from the traditional pork-laden infrastructure bill House Democrats had in mind. The irascible Obey let his former staffer know he was not pleased. "If my staff director was still here," he grumbled, "he'd tell you to go to hell!"

The White House seemed to want to get its way on policy without taking any responsibility for the legislation itself. House Democrats were also skeptical about Obama's confidence that Republicans would go along. Shortly after the meeting with Nabors, Obey met with Jerry Lewis, the top Republican on Appropriations. Obey told Lewis the $800 billion price tag and asked what Republicans wanted to get in the bill. "I'm sorry," Lewis said, "but leadership tells us we can't play."

Pelosi also met with the Republican leader Boehner to try to convince him that spending was better than tax cuts for stimulating growth because it had a "multiplier effect": a dollar spent on food stamps or unemployment benefits, according to experts, will produce about $1.75 in economic activity as the money spent on food or necessities is used to hire more workers and produce more goods, which in turn generates more activity. Boehner was skeptical. "Let me get this straight," he said. "We're going to take a dollar and turn it into a dollar seventy-five?" Democrats and Republicans, Pelosi argued, ought to be able to agree on the need to create jobs. But Boehner said, "Why would we want to help you on that?"

❖ ❖ ❖

In fact, shortly after Obama's election, the Republicans had decided that their path back to power was to oppose him at every turn. Boehner, a fifty-nine-year-old congressman from the Cincinnati suburbs, had been inspired to run for office by the effect of government regulations on his plastics business. A Catholic with working-class roots, Boehner had made himself the picture of an old-school country club Republican. He loved golf and cigarettes, nice suits and a good Merlot; though he was a staunch fiscal conservative, back in 2001 he'd teamed up with Ted Kennedy on the No Child Left Behind education bill. Boehner and Pelosi were cordial, but that was about it.

Their huge electoral defeat and Obama's popularity spooked Republicans. After their first meeting with Obama in January 2009, Boehner's deputy Eric Cantor muttered, "Phew, we may be in this minority for a while." But they quickly decided that compromise was not the path back to victory. Republicans calculated that if they went along with Obama's plans, they'd deprive the public of the alternative argument, and make it look like the president was indeed a bipartisan healer. Obama's election was a product of circumstance, they maintained, not a rejection of Republican principles. The problem, some conservatives maintained, was that Republicans had nominated a moderate, McCain, and failed to articulate their vision boldly enough.

Obama's inaugural address, in which he proclaimed "an end to the petty grievances and false promises, the recriminations and worn-out dogmas that for far too long have strangled our politics," was practically still echoing when the GOP went on the attack at what they dubbed the "porkulus." Republicans ridiculed programs in the stimulus such as renovating the National Mall, increasing family planning assistance, upgrading Amtrak and funding arts programs. They took a line item for disaster aid for farmers and claimed it constituted "honeybee insurance." Pelosi had kept earmarks in the bill but held them to a minimum. Republicans invented imaginary pork instead: in speeches and press releases, they cited a $300,000 grant to a sculpture garden in Miami and $30 million for an endangered mouse, neither of which was in the bill.

The Republican attacks worked: the public turned against the bill, and the media narrative turned sharply negative. Obama, surprised by the attacks and convinced that Republicans could be reasoned with, called Pelosi and asked her to take out the objectionable items, while Emanuel, who had assured the president the bill would get lots of Republican votes, went around her and urged some conservative Democrats to put pressure on her. This back-channeling earned Emanuel a stern lecture from Pelosi, who demanded to be notified from then on of any White House contacts with her members. Reluctantly, she agreed to take out the family planning grants and Mall renovation funds. She tried to warn the president that making concessions to the Republicans wouldn't do any good: they would just find something else to pick apart. Concessions would only make them smell blood and would contribute to the perception that the bill was an unholy mess.

But Pelosi was also a team player who wanted her president to succeed. When Democratic divisions threatened to become the dominant narrative about the stimulus, she kept her members in line. The chairman of the Transportation Committee, Jim Oberstar of Minnesota, complained publicly that the bill needed more infrastructure spending. In a Democratic caucus meeting, he started in again about the desirability of public works over tax cuts, but Pelosi stopped him. "The only reason we're talking about stimulus is that Barack Obama won the election," she said. "He promised tax cuts, so that's going to be in the package."

Obama was still too popular for the Republicans to attack, but by distancing himself from the congressional process, he'd given them an opening. Rather than go after the president for the "porkulus," they went after Pelosi—using Obama's words as ammunition. Obama, they'd say, had campaigned on fiscal discipline, but the "Washington Democrats" wouldn't go for it. Obama wanted to reach across the aisle, but Washington Democrats didn't want to play ball. At a press conference, an irritated Pelosi, tired of being asked to bend over backward for a minority that had no intention of cooperating, said, "Yes, we wrote the bill. Yes, we won the election." It was a factual statement. But Republicans howled in indignation, and rallied around the idea that she was trying to steamroll them. To the president, Pelosi privately said, "Stop throwing me under the bus."

Obama tried to reach out to Republicans even though Pelosi and others warned he was being naïve. Charlie Dent, a moderate from Pennsylvania, was one of a group of Republican lawmakers invited to watch the Super Bowl at the White House, where his wife chatted with Michelle and his kids played with Sasha and Malia Obama. In the end, Dent voted against the bill—and blamed Pelosi. "I believe the president was absolutely sincere in looking for a bipartisan outcome," he told *Newsweek*. "But the White House lost control of the process when the bill was outsourced to Pelosi." Democrats joked that if they wanted to see Obama, the best way was to join the Republican Party.

Every single House Republican voted against the bill. So did 11 Democrats, mostly conservative Blue Dogs concerned about spending. Pelosi's majority was large enough that she could afford to lose some votes, and the bill still passed by a healthy margin. After the House vote, Obama hosted congressional leaders at a White House cocktail party—which Boehner and the Republicans had the gall to attend.

Pelosi hoped the neophyte president had learned a lesson. "At the end of the day, this was going to be a tutorial for the Obama folks," a House staffer close to Pelosi told *Politico*. "They're all going to vote against you and then come to your cocktail party that night." The key to Obama's triumph had been not his ability to reach across the aisle, but Pelosi's skill at holding her caucus together.

She also hoped Republicans would pay a price for their opposition. After all, these lawmakers had voted against money for projects in their districts and jobs for the American people. (With remarkable shamelessness, more than 100 Republicans would return to their districts and tout local stimulus spending—despite having voted against the bill.) The day after it passed, Pelosi's office sent out a memo titled "The Republican Problem," which contended, "The House Republican leadership put its members in another politically untenable position yesterday." Just like in 1993, when Gingrich demagogued Clinton's budget and it passed without a single Republican vote, they were relying on Democrats to clean up their messes.

But that's not how the public saw it. Obama had lost control of the narrative, the stimulus had become unpopular, and there was a steady drumbeat of press stories about its inadequacies. At Pelosi's press conference after the House passage, a reporter asked, "Is it your fault in some ways that Barack Obama's first vote was so partisan and not bipartisan?" She replied, "I didn't come here to be partisan. I didn't come here to be bipartisan. I came here, as did my colleagues, to be nonpartisan, to work for the American people."

The stimulus went through a similar meat grinder in the Senate, where the White House had hoped for a big bipartisan vote but instead managed just enough votes to squeak through. But it got done—not on Inauguration Day, but before the February 16 President's Day holiday that Pelosi had deemed a more realistic deadline. To pass such a mammoth bill within a few weeks of a new president's inauguration was a major achievement, even if few saw it that way at the time. The economy didn't soar, but it didn't slide into a depression, either, and over the next several years it gradually stabilized.

◇ ◇ ◇

For both Obama and Pelosi, still getting the feel for their working relationship, the stimulus was a learning experience. During the campaign, Obama's opponents, both Hillary Clinton and John McCain, had derided him as glib and inexperienced, a giver of lovely speeches with nothing to back it up. Pundits predicted he would excel at persuasion while struggling with the nitty-gritty of legislation. But in his first presidential test, the opposite had happened: he had accomplished something real and substantial with remarkable speed, but failed to win over the public.

Liberals learned from the stimulus that the president and his advisers were surprisingly economically conservative. In particular, Treasury Secretary Timothy Geithner and OMB director Peter Orszag had teamed up to kill progressives' desires, from a provision to help home owners to restrictions on Wall Street bonuses. They referred to such populist priorities as "pitchfork fever," and prided themselves on being too sophisticated for such things. Within a year, the administration would fail to enact any large-scale jobs or housing programs, and unemployment would reach double digits, while at the same time, Geithner and Orszag advocated not for further stimulus but for deficit reduction. With no countervailing lefty voice on the economic team, progressives such as Elizabeth Warren would maintain that Obama's economic timidity had prolonged the recession and stoked public anger.

For Pelosi and House Democrats, the stimulus battle left them feeling scapegoated and taken for granted. It was clear that Obama and his political advisers didn't like getting their hands dirty or being perceived as entangled in the gritty business of legislating, even though he was the president of the United States trying to enact an ambitious policy agenda into law. How else, exactly, did he expect to do that? they wondered. But what the White House took away from the battle was that the House *could* be taken for granted; it was the Senate that might require some spade-work. Rather than concluding that they should work more closely with their allies in Congress, Obama's team decided they needed to dispel the perception that he had become part of the Washington machine. After all, Republicans wouldn't blame him—they'd blame that awful Nancy Pelosi. This framing was good for keeping Obama's political brand pure, but it wasn't necessarily good for his agenda or his party.

The campaign had earned Obama a reputation as a canny and strategic poker player, but on the stimulus he had proven to be a lousy negotiator. Later, Obama himself would wonder how much support he could have got-ten if he hadn't offered the GOP tax cuts up front, if he'd put more pressure on Republican governors whose states needed the money, if he'd called the bluff of GOP senators threatening to kill the bill if it didn't cut a few bil-lion in school funding, if he'd allowed it to be loaded up with pet projects. Republicans would wonder the same thing. It had taken a mighty effort by GOP leaders to keep their members from voting for the bill; at one point, Boehner thought half his caucus might vote with the Democrats, perma-nently weakening his control and changing the tenor of the years to come. But the White House's ineptitude helped ensure that this wouldn't happen. Pelosi knew that making people feel heard, making them think they were getting something, was at least as important as meeting them halfway on policy, but Obama didn't seem capable of absorbing this lesson. Again and again, he would offer Republicans what he thought they were supposed to want, then be shocked when they wouldn't take it. Some Senate Democrats took to referring to Obama as "Mr. Fifty Yard Line," for the way he seemed to give up half the game before it started.

You get only one chance to make a first impression, and the stimulus created perceptions that Obama couldn't undo. Republicans had seen that resistance was power. They had seen that they could roll over Obama and blame him for the problems he'd inherited that they hadn't done anything to help him solve. They realized that Obama had promised something—

PAPA'S OFF TO VOTE

Six-week-old Nancy D'Alesandro in the arms of her mother as her father, Rep. Thomas D'Alesandro, departs to vote in his 1940 Democratic primary for reelection. Her five brothers—Thomas III, Franklin Roosevelt, Nicholas, Hector and Joseph—look on.

Seven-year-old Nancy swears her father in to begin his first term as mayor of Baltimore, 1947.

Young Nancy does homework with her mother in the 1940s.

Nancy, then in high school, meets then-senator John F. Kennedy at a Democratic Party dinner in Baltimore, 1957.

Nancy's yearbook photo from Trinity College, 1962.

Nancy at her 1963 wedding to Paul Pelosi.

Pelosi at the 1984 Democratic National Convention, which she helped bring to San Francisco.

Campaigning for Congress in 1987.

Declaring victory with John Burton on Election Night, 1987.

Pelosi being sworn in as her father looks on, 1987.

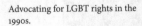

Advocating for LGBT rights in the 1990s.

With President Bill
Clinton, 1993.

With Steny Hoyer, 1997.

Pelosi emerging victorious from
the Democratic caucus whip
election, 2001.

Pelosi at Farmfest in rural Minnesota, 2006. Not visible here: the jeans and cowboy boots she wore to the event.

With Rahm Emanuel and Harry Reid on Election Night, 2006, when Democrats took the House and Senate.

Hoisting the gavel surrounded by grandchildren as she's elected Speaker in 2007.

With President Obama at the Capitol, 2010.

Signing the Affordable Care Act, 2010.

Watching President Obama sign the ACA.

Handing the Speaker's gavel to John Boehner, 2011.

Applauding President Trump's call for unity at the State of the Union, 2019.

Confronting Trump at a national security briefing, 2019.

bipartisanship—that he needed their help to deliver, and by withholding it, they could prevent him from fulfilling his central promise.

It was a strategy that would haunt and cripple Obama's tenure. In the stimulus fight, Pelosi tried to warn him that he wasn't going to be able to win over the GOP. But he would keep trying.

18

THE TIME LINE BORDERED ON PREPOSTEROUS: NOT ONE BUT TWO GIANT pieces of liberal legislation in the space of a single year. But Pelosi liked big plans.

Obama's team had drawn up a schedule for its main priorities once the stimulus was out of the way. (The stimulus, they wrongly thought, would be easy.) The House would spend March through June getting an energy and climate bill passed, while the Senate spent that same period working on a health care bill. Both would finish their work by the July 4 holiday, and then they would switch. By fall, the House would be passing health care and the Senate would be picking up the climate bill.

In the wake of the brutal stimulus fight, this time line began to look about as realistic as the idea that the American Recovery and Reinvestment Act would glide through Congress with bipartisan support, immediately get the economy chugging away and be admired by a grateful public. Long-time Washington observers were skeptical. The Congress, they said, could focus on only one big thing at a time. And with the economy still cratering, shouldn't that one thing be jobs, not pie-in-the-sky liberal wish lists? Republicans started throwing Emanuel's "never waste a crisis" line back at him, accusing the White House of using the recession as cover to smuggle in its big-government agenda.

The president's more politically minded advisers Emanuel and Axelrod were starting to think the pundits might be right. Maybe they needed to pick one big priority at a time and focus on that. Health care and climate reform were both massive endeavors. Both would be big, complex, thousand-page pieces of legislation. Both would entail massive structural changes to the U.S. economy, which was still circling the drain at an alarming rate.

But the "Yes We Can" president didn't want to be told to trim his sails. He saw health care and climate change as challenges that couldn't wait. And he knew that according to historians and political scientists, presidents tend to notch the most accomplishments at the beginning of their terms, when their momentum and political capital are highest. In interviews, Obama had taken to repeating a line from FDR's 1933 Inaugural Address: "Action and action now."

Obama's bold ambition impressed Pelosi. She believed in pushing hard and gambling big. She found Obama's hopeful message and grand vision genuinely inspiring. "Let's not try this, it will never work" was about as persuasive an argument to Pelosi as "I can't vote for this, it's unpopular in my district." And she was tired of notching "accomplishments" that consisted mostly of snatching concessions here and there from the GOP without ever being able to set the agenda. Her members had been waiting since 1994, fourteen years, for a Democratic Congress and Democratic president to be able to enact some of the policies they held dear. For more than a decade, they'd campaigned on the solutions they thought would solve America's problems, only to have to settle for little or nothing after they got done bargaining with a Republican Speaker or Republican president. Under Bush, they could do little but pass bills that went nowhere or hold hearings to expose wrongdoing. Now it was finally time for Democrats to govern, and they had lots of pent-up ideas. "It's a new day in the capital," Pelosi declared.

Both climate and health care legislation would have to move through the same House committee, Energy and Commerce, now chaired by Henry Waxman. A stubby Californian with a bald pate and a bottle-brush mustache, Waxman was a renowned liberal policy maven, a true believer in the power of government. Since his arrival in Washington with the "Watergate babies" of 1974, his accomplishments had included the Clean Air Act, food labeling, pesticide regulation, and bringing Big Tobacco to heel. Under Bush, he'd chaired the Oversight and Government Reform Committee, in which capacity he'd mercilessly showcased the administration's scandals—

including, in October 2008, the first hearings on the financial crisis, in which former Federal Reserve chairman Alan Greenspan was forced to admit that his ideology of self-regulating markets had turned out to be wrong. Alan Simpson, a Republican senator from Wyoming, once described Waxman as "tougher than a boiled owl." (Waxman, whose Los Angeles district included Hollywood, was also valuable to Pelosi as a fundraiser.) After the election, Waxman's longtime chief of staff, Phil Schiliro, had been hired as the Obama White House's chief congressional liaison.

Waxman's maneuver to become chairman of Energy and Commerce by toppling the longtime chair John Dingell was a divisive move. But Waxman had done it because he believed he was better suited to the task of moving big, liberal bills through the crucial committee. His partner on the climate bill would be Ed Markey, a liberal congressman from Massachusetts who had been in charge of the special climate committee Pelosi had created to undercut Dingell two years prior.

After the bruising fight on the stimulus, Obama summoned Waxman to the White House. Did he really think they could handle both big bills? Waxman told him it would be difficult, but he thought it could be done. He was ready to get started on the climate bill, he said. Obama said he supported both proposals, but he worried that getting started on energy would make it harder to then jump to health care. Waxman didn't think that would be a problem—in fact, he told Obama, it could even be the opposite: if climate was a success, it might create momentum for health care.

Momentum seemed to be on their side as Waxman and Markey began drafting the climate bill. The ever-increasing threat of global warming was no longer in any doubt among scientists, the public increasingly favored action and many business leaders had decided they needed to get on board. Before he ran against Obama, John McCain had pushed for climate legislation in partnership with Democrat Joe Lieberman, and other Republicans such as Senator Lindsey Graham were talking about the issue. A group of CEOs and environmentalists had formed an organization called the U.S. Climate Action Partnership, to push for their preferred solution, a "cap-and-trade" system that would limit total carbon emissions (the cap) but allow polluters such as utilities to buy and sell emission permits (the trade). The business community preferred this market-based approach to more government-centric solutions such as a carbon tax. Obama, too, liked the cross-partisan appeal of it: a conservative solution to a liberal issue.

Waxman hoped for Republican support. He even attended a retreat of the committee's Republican members—the first Democrat ever to address such a gathering—where he made the case that they could all agree on the goals of energy independence, clean-energy jobs and lowering emissions. But when Waxman approached the committee's top Republican, Joe Barton, a Texan and former oil industry consultant, Barton scoffed. "I don't believe in the science of global warming," he said. "I don't think it exists. And I don't see why we should take such extraordinary efforts to combat a problem that's fictitious."

Waxman still thought the Republicans might crack. He paraded CEOs before the committee—usual GOP allies like DuPont Chemical, Alcoa Aluminum and Duke Energy. These were some of the same Big Business interests that had battled Waxman on the Clean Air Act in the 1990s, but now they were saying they wanted to be part of the solution, not part of the problem. "This bill will make our economy stronger over time," the Duke CEO said. As their erstwhile friends in industry spoke about their support for cap and trade, Barton and the other Republicans on the fifty-nine-person committee shook their heads.

Democrats pointed out that the Environmental Protection Agency had just announced it planned to regulate carbon dioxide, which it could do without congressional input and in a far more heavy-handed way than Waxman's bill would. The oldest trick in the legislative book is to persuade your opponents that something is happening with or without them, so they might as well get on board and make it more to their liking. As the saying goes, if you're not at the table, you're on the menu. But the GOP, in what was becoming a familiar dynamic, didn't seem interested. In a Sunday show interview, Boehner mocked the very premise of the legislation. "The idea that carbon dioxide is a carcinogen that is harmful to our environment is almost comical," he said. "Every time we exhale, we exhale carbon dioxide." The appearance was widely ridiculed, but it was an apt summation of the Republican leaders' stance.

At the outset, the bill's main obstacle was expected to be not partisan but geographical, as members from coal-producing regions—a large swath of the country, particularly in the heartland—could be counted on to oppose it. But with partisan opposition added to the mix, many experts doubted the bill would ever pass. That would have been fine with many of the more conservative Democrats who viewed cap and trade as political poison. The old-timers recalled Bill Clinton's 1993 energy bill, which included a tax on BTUs, the unit that measures the heat content of fuel used in heating and air-conditioning. The BTU tax passed the House but died in the Senate, and the Democrats who voted for it out of loyalty to their party's president were hung out to dry. Many considered the energy tax to have been more significant in the brutal 1994 election than the Contract with America. Early in the legislative process for cap and trade, a House Democrat told Markey, "We are not going to get BTU-ed!"

Another senior Blue Dog, John Tanner of Tennessee, flagged down Hoyer on the House floor to register a complaint on behalf of the new members from tough districts. "Steny! You are *killing* these freshmen!" Tanner cried. "They're not going to come back after this!" Hoyer privately agreed, but he had learned from experience not to stand in Pelosi's way.

It was clear Pelosi was determined. A committed environmentalist, she sometimes told people that climate was her "signature issue." She approached a longtime ally, Collin Peterson, an affable rural Minnesotan who was one of the most conservative Democrats in the House.

Despite their ideological differences, Peterson had supported Pelosi all the way back to her race for whip. She might not know a lot about farming, but she was willing to listen. In 2006, she visited his district and attended its annual "Farm Fest," in what is likely the only documented instance of Nancy Pelosi wearing jeans in public, and ate not one but two pork chops on a stick. Pelosi had made Peterson chairman of the Agriculture Committee and helped him pass the panel's signature legislation, the farm bill, in 2008. Now she wanted a favor in return.

Peterson told Pelosi he was not in favor of cap and trade. It was toxic in his district and with the agricultural interests he worked with. "The farmers hate this," he said.

Pelosi, undaunted, told him, "Tell Henry what you need."

So Peterson huddled with his interest group allies—the Farm Bureau, the corn growers, the cattlemen's association. They got together in his office and went through the bill, pointing out every provision they found odious. When they were done, Peterson had a list of forty-nine things that would have to be taken out or changed to get his vote. He figured he was off the hook—there was no way the environmentalists would allow all those changes.

A few days before the vote on the bill, Waxman handed Peterson a piece of paper. "You're getting all forty-nine of your requests," he said. Peterson was trapped; he felt duty bound to keep his word. Afterward, he would have to explain his vote to an angry seven-hundred-person town meeting back home.

Even with Peterson's vote, however, the whip count was not looking good. Waxman was having no luck flipping Zack Space, a second-termer from Ohio. Then, one day, Space, whose ancestors were Greek, started getting calls from national Greek American donors. Pelosi had put them up to it. Space flipped.

The full-court press continued. Obama made calls. Al Gore made calls. At the Hawaiian-themed congressional picnic on the White House Lawn, the president pulled members aside individually to beg for their votes. At this point, the bill was so watered down that environmental groups like Greenpeace refused to support it. This is the eternal dilemma of the legislator: at what point do the trade-offs outweigh the merits of a step in the right direction? The Republicans had dubbed it "cap-and-tax" and were claiming that the bill would cost the average American family $3,000 per year. (The Congressional Budget Office's analysis put the number at $175.) As July loomed, the Democrats still didn't have the votes.

Jim Clyburn, the Democratic whip, was sitting in the House Democratic Cloakroom when Pelosi approached, *click-click-click*. (Each party has a "cloakroom" off the House floor, which resembles a lounge more than a closet—a narrow, frumpy den lined with overstuffed leather couches, it's a place to retreat, strategize and grab a snack when legislative action is under way.) "How do we look?" she asked.

"We're not there, and I don't think we can get there," Clyburn said. "Not this week, at least. I think we ought to go home and work on it over the weekend."

"Let me see your sheet," she said. Clyburn was an able vote-counter, but he knew that the price of serving as Pelosi's whip was that she would always think she knew the job better than he did, and she would often be right. Clyburn's sheet listed the caucus members with columns for "yes," "leaning yes," "undecided," "no response," "leaning no," and "no."

As Clyburn watched, Pelosi scanned the columns. She even seemed to be looking at the ones he'd marked down as definite nos. Then she handed the sheet back to him and said, "Call the vote."

On Friday, June 26, 2009, the vote went to the floor. To the amazement of Clyburn and everyone else, Pelosi had a trick up her sleeve: she and Obama had secretly met with a group of moderate Republicans and somehow come away with 8 GOP votes. In the Obama-era House of Representatives, that constituted a veritable groundswell of bipartisanship. The bill passed by a tally of 219–212, with 8 Republicans in favor and 44 Democrats against. To this day, Clyburn says, he doesn't know how Pelosi pulled that off. (One of the Democratic nays, Ciro Rodriguez of Texas, had broken a promise to Pelosi to vote for the bill, and he knew he would be in trouble as a result. After casting his vote, he ran off the floor at full speed—pursued by Congressman Anthony Weiner, who was whipping the bill for Pelosi, yelling, "Ciro! Ciro!" as he tried to chase him down.)

"We are at an extraordinary moment, with a historic opportunity to confront one of the world's most serious challenges," Gore, the vice president turned environmental advocate, proclaimed. "Our actions now will be remembered by this generation and all those to follow." As of 2019, the bill remains the only climate legislation ever to clear a house of Congress.

But it was the Republicans who seemed to be doing the most rejoicing, convinced that the bill would be political poison for the Democrats. Boehner went over his allotted speaking time to give a passionate speech against the bill that became known as the "Boehner-buster." On the floor of the House when the bill passed, Republican members broke into a chant of "BTU! BTU!"

Pelosi was still in the process of educating Obama, and cap and trade was a powerful lesson. If he hadn't before, he was starting to appreciate her formidable reputation. She had gotten a massive bill through the unruly House against all odds—with Republican votes—and on schedule. But that was not the case in the Senate. Far from being finished with health care legislation, they had barely started. Cap and trade would have to wait.

19

As she pleaded with her Democratic sisters, Pelosi had tears in her eyes. She knew they hated what they were being asked to do. She hated it, too. But if they didn't relent, the whole thing, the thing they'd worked so hard for, for so long, could fall apart. They had a once-in-a-lifetime chance to accomplish something truly monumental, a goal that had eluded Democratic presidents for nearly a century: the creation of a universal health care program. But the only way to get there, she was telling them, was to compromise one of their most cherished principles: a woman's right to choose abortion.

It was Friday, November 6, 2009. The House was scheduled to vote on its health care bill the following day. For months, Pelosi had been immersed in negotiations on the massive, complicated legislation. Now it had come down to the final sticking point, one that could not have been more personal or painful for Pelosi, who had long been caught between her party and her Church. The U.S. Conference of Catholic Bishops had announced that while it supported expanding health care, it would not endorse the health care bill unless it sharply restricted women's access to abortion, and a small group of pro-life members said they would not commit to vote for the bill unless the bishops signed off.

All day, Pelosi had been in meetings and on the phone, trying to get the bishops to compromise, the women to relent. But neither group was budging. Now it was evening, and she had run out of tactics. The only thing left was to lay all her cards on the table with the members who most counted on her to speak for them and protect their interests—the liberal women. "I don't know what to do," she told them—a rare, or perhaps strategic, admission of weakness by Pelosi, who always seemed to know what to do.

The women were irate. Louise Slaughter, the eighty-year-old chair of the House Rules Committee, had grown up in Kentucky keeping the secret of a friend's illegal abortion. She marched in abortion rights protests in her youth, pushed for reproductive rights in Congress and was a founding member of the Pro-Choice Caucus. She arrived in Washington in 1987, just a few months before Pelosi, and cheered Pelosi's rise through the ranks as a victory for women everywhere. For Slaughter and the other liberal women, the abortion issue was about a woman's inviolable right to determine what happened to her body out of the purview of the state and the patriarchy. It was nonnegotiable—at the core of the feminism that had animated their careers.

Now, in a bitter irony, the first woman Speaker of the House was asking them to cave.

Pelosi listened patiently as the women vented about how unfair it was. The vast majority of House Democrats were among the 190 members of the Pro-Choice Caucus, and yet they were being told that they were the ones who had to give in to a stubborn, unreasonable minority. This, Slaughter said, was a betrayal—of not just the women in Congress, but the women of America.

Pelosi pushed some papers across the table: her tally sheets. The story they told was more powerful than any argument she could make. Without the bishops' amendment, she said, "I don't have the votes."

❖ ❖ ❖

Ever since the New Deal, Democratic presidents had been trying to create a national health care program. FDR twice proposed universal health insurance, but both times he stopped short of putting it to Congress, fearing it would torpedo the rest of his expansive economic agenda. His successor, Harry Truman, also favored universal coverage, but never made it a priority. John F. Kennedy pushed for a program to insure the elderly, Medicare, but fell short, leaving it to Lyndon B. Johnson to get the job done in 1965. Johnson also created Medicaid, which partially funds state programs to provide health care to the poor.

Bill Clinton thought he would be the one to finally get it done. After taking office in 1993, he assigned health care policy to his wife, Hillary, who became the first First Lady to have a space in the West Wing, the part of the White House that's used for offices rather than living quarters. She worked on the legislation in near secrecy with her health care adviser, Ira Magaziner, then presented the giant bill to Congress as a fait accompli. Hillarycare, as it became known, was market-based, but would have eliminated the system of employer-based health insurance entirely, replacing it with nationwide networks of health maintenance organizations.

Republicans argued that the plan would give the government too much control, driving up already-skyrocketing costs and giving people fewer choices. Some argued that the government shouldn't be involved in health care at all. Other Republicans said they shared the goal of universal coverage, but wanted it done in a less disruptive, more fiscally responsible way. The conservative think tank the Heritage Foundation proposed a system whereby people who weren't covered by their employers would be mandated to buy health insurance on the private market, with help from the government if they couldn't afford it. This would keep the insurance companies in business while forcing people to take responsibility for their health care decisions.

The health care industry, seeing Hillarycare as an existential threat, reacted by flooding the airwaves with frightening television ads. In one, "Harry and Louise," a middle-aged white couple, are sitting at their kitchen table sorting through a pile of bills. "But this was covered under our old plan!" Louise says.

"Oh yeah," says Harry, "that was a good one, wasn't it?"

"Having choices we don't like is no choice at all," Louise says, looking despairingly into the distance.

The Democrats in Congress didn't think much of Hillarycare, either. They were disinclined to take up the controversial legislation whose composition they'd been cut out of, while the White House didn't want its carefully constructed policy changed. Then-Speaker Tom Foley let multiple committee chairmen fight it out, producing several competing proposals. Pelosi was part of a group of progressives who, frustrated with both the policy and the process from the White House, introduced legislation to create a British-style, wholly government-run "single-payer" system. The Clinton plan was never voted on in the House or Senate, and what followed was the 1994 Republican landslide, killing health care reform's prospects for more than a decade as Democrats decided the issue was politically radioactive. (In his second term, Bill Clinton did manage to pass a program to provide health insurance to children from low-income families.)

But the problem, a messy and cruel patchwork of private insurance and charity care, increasingly unaffordable and arbitrary, only got worse. Most people got health insurance through their employers, but if they lost their job, they were at the mercy of the lightly regulated private market. Insurers were free to pick and choose their customers, which meant they would refuse to cover anyone who was already sick, and charge women more than men for the same coverage. Insurance companies hunted for excuses to deny claims, drowning doctors in paperwork and making sick people fight for the care they needed. And as unregulated costs spiraled ever upward, premiums and deductibles ate up more and more of businesses' budgets and families' paychecks. Many Americans were just one accident or diagnosis away from bankruptcy.

In the absence of federal action, some states tried to build their own systems. In Massachusetts, a reform-minded Republican governor named Mitt Romney signed legislation in 2006 that was modeled on the Heritage Foundation proposal from the 1990s: a mandate for all people to have coverage, with state subsidies for those who couldn't afford to buy insurance on the private market. Within just a few years, 97 percent of Massachusetts residents were covered, the highest rate in the nation.

Health care hadn't been a priority for Obama during his brief time in the Senate, but when he started running for president, polls showed it was voters' top issue. By the time he accepted the Democratic nomination, reforming health care had become a central promise of his campaign. In ads and speeches, he spoke emotionally of his mother, Ann Dunham, who had died of ovarian cancer at age fifty-two in 1995. Her final months, Obama said, were consumed not by reflecting on her life and family but by fighting with medical billers and worrying about her insurance.

The Obama administration had studied Clinton's experience and was determined to learn lessons from it. In particular, it wanted Congress to craft the legislation rather than having the president hand it down on "stone tablets," as Obama's political adviser David Axelrod put it. And they wanted the health care industry brought in as well, to avoid a "Harry and Louise"–type campaign.

Romney's program appealed to Obama as a blueprint for the approach he would take. Like cap and trade, it was a conservative, market-based solution to a liberal problem. Obama proposed leaving the employer-based system intact, so that most people who already had insurance wouldn't see any change. New regulations would stop insurers from engaging in abusive practices, require them to cover more procedures, and rein in profits. People without employer-based insurance would be able to shop for a plan on state marketplaces modeled on the one in Massachusetts, and companies would compete to offer the best deal. To prevent people from waiting until they got sick to buy insurance, an "individual mandate" would require that everyone get covered. Those who couldn't afford to would get subsidies. Or, if they were poor, they would get insurance directly from the government through an expansion of LBJ's Medicaid program, which the federal government would fund by increasing its state grants.

A proposal to remake the health care system, which constituted about one-sixth of the American economy, would have been a heavy lift for any president under the best of circumstances. But it was being put forward by a congressional neophyte in the middle of an economic collapse. Axelrod understood the issue's importance—his daughter's chronic epilepsy had nearly bankrupted his family—but he warned Obama as the new president took office that perhaps the time wasn't right. Obama disagreed. If they didn't do it now, he argued, it might not get done for another decade or more, as the problem continued to worsen. "What are we supposed to do," he said, "put my approval rating on the shelf and admire it for eight years?" He calculated that health care reform might cost him 10 or 15 points in public approval, but it would be worth it to prove that America was capable of solving big problems.

This was the Obama that Pelosi liked: the gambler, the dreamer, the president who believed, in the words he often quoted from Martin Luther King Jr., in "the fierce urgency of now."

✧ ✧ ✧

Rahm Emanuel, like Axelrod, worried about the politics of health care. He tried to get Obama to scale back, perhaps by merely expanding the Children's Health Insurance Program that Clinton had created. (Pelosi called this idea, dismissively, "kiddie care.") The 2008 election had left the Senate with 58 Democrats (counting two liberal-leaning independents, Bernie

Sanders and Joe Lieberman). But then one Republican senator switched parties, and Democrat Al Franken was declared the winner of his election after a long recount. By July 2009, there were 60 Democrats in the Senate, the largest majority for either party since the 1980s.

But while the House finished its work on cap and trade on schedule, the Senate was barely out of the gate on the health care bill. It was bottled up in the Finance Committee, chaired by Max Baucus, a Montana Democrat who had good relations with his Republican colleagues and hoped he could get some of their support. The White House was engaged in a furious courtship of moderate Republicans who Obama and his aides thought they could win over.

Pelosi, as she had with the stimulus, thought wooing Republicans was a fool's errand. She thought Baucus's GOP friends were playing him in order to drag out the legislative process, sapping it of momentum in order to kill the bill. When other Democrats would bring up the idea of getting Republicans on board, Pelosi had a stock line. "They love their families. They love our country," she would say, sometimes waggling a finger in her interlocutor's face. "But they do not share our values." From the beginning, she predicted the legislation would get zero GOP votes. "Does the president not understand the way this game works?" she asked Emanuel. "He wants to get it done and be beloved, and you can't have both—which does he want?"

Rather than waiting for the Senate, the House got started on its own health care bill. Waxman's committee started working with two others who had jurisdiction, an unusually cooperative effort. More commonly, committees fought over turf and produced competing approaches to the same problem. But time was short, and Pelosi ordered them to work together, forming a "Tri-Com" that had its own logo and tote bags.

Single-payer wasn't on the table, but House liberals sought to include a "public option," a government-run health insurance plan that would sell policies to the public and compete with the insurance companies. Without a profit motive, they reasoned, the government could offer cheaper plans than industry—perhaps even driving health insurance companies out of business and creating a single-payer system by default. Insurance companies naturally saw the public option as a mortal threat.

While the Senate continued to dither with no end in sight, the House bill was out of committee by the end of July. Pelosi was furious with the Senate—and with the White House for not pushing the Senate harder. But Senator Baucus said he just needed a little more time.

✧ ✧ ✧

By August, everyone was ready for a break. Congress traditionally takes the month of August off, giving members a chance to relax, recharge and reconnect with their constituents back home. But August 2009 was not shaping up to be much of a vacation for congressional Democrats.

At town hall meetings in their districts, Democratic lawmakers faced a furnace blast of anger. Hundreds of activists stormed the meetings, even in Democratic districts. The target of their rage was the health care law they had dubbed "Obamacare," and the August push was calculated to bring down the bill—and the president. "If we're able to stop Obama on this," one Republican senator told a group of right-wing organizers, "it will be his Waterloo. It will break him."

Sarah Palin, the defeated vice presidential candidate, led the charge. She seized on a provision—actually proposed by a Republican—that would fund optional end-of-life counseling sessions for seniors, and twisted it into a sinister Big Brother plot to euthanize the elderly via "death panels." Chuck Grassley was the main Republican senator who'd been negotiating with Baucus, stringing him along for months. But back home in Iowa, Grassley told an audience, "You have every right to fear. We should not have a government program that determines if you're going to pull the plug on Grandma." So much for bipartisanship.

Then, at the end of August, Senator Ted Kennedy died after a long illness. This was another psychic blow to Democrats. Kennedy had called universal health care "the cause of my life." In 1980, he challenged his own party's president, Jimmy Carter, for reelection, citing in part their dispute over how to pursue health care reform. Before Kennedy became too sick to serve in the Senate, he had worked with Baucus and others to lay the groundwork for health care reform in 2008. Kennedy was also an early and influential endorser of Obama during the presidential primary against Hillary Clinton.

The Democrats needed a boost. Obama scheduled a prime-time address in the House chamber. The television networks carried it live, but it was aimed as much at the lawmakers in the room as the public. The health care debate had become mired in technicalities and misinformation. Obama needed to remind Congress what they were there to do.

In his speech, Obama read from a letter Kennedy had written before his death. In it, Kennedy wrote that health care was "above all, a moral issue." As Obama made an impassioned case for urgency, Democratic lawmakers' hearts stirred—here was that old Barack Obama magic that they'd missed in all the haggling over public options and cost curves. Obama confronted the myths being spread about the bill, promising that it contained no death panels, would not pay for abortion coverage and would not cover illegal immigrants.

Suddenly the president was interrupted by a shout from the audience: "You lie!" It was Joe Wilson, a Republican congressman from South Carolina. To Pelosi, who sat behind the president and seemed to glare at the assembled Republicans as he spoke, the tableau was a perfect illustration: the eloquent, high-minded African American president, his lofty ideals crashing headlong into the irrational anger of a white southerner who preferred his emotions to the facts. (After the speech, Wilson's cell phone rang. It was his wife. Who, she wanted to know, was "that nut" who had shouted at the president?)

Right-wing talk radio, of course, hailed Wilson as a hero.

✧ ✧ ✧

And then there were the bishops. Pelosi's Catholic faith was real and devout, a core part of her identity since childhood. But her politics didn't always track with the positions taken by the Church. The Church strongly opposed abortion, but Pelosi took the hairsplitting position that she supported women's right to make the decision for themselves even though she personally believed abortion to be wrong. "A woman," as she put it, "has free will given to her by God." It was a stance that put her at odds with her own family back in Baltimore. Early in her career, as she prepared to give a floor speech in favor of reproductive rights, she confided to a colleague that she hoped her mother wouldn't see it.

Pelosi's clashes with the Church became bitter and public as she rose in prominence. On the eve of her swearing-in as Speaker in 2007, when protesters gathered as she attended Mass at Trinity, her alma mater, the service was closed to the public to prevent chaos, and Pelosi sneaked in and out through a back door. A Catholic magazine decried her "faith in the culture of death." Some archbishops said she should be denied Communion, and she lived in fear that she might be refused the sacrament. For a time, she attended a different church in San Francisco every Sunday to avoid being singled out. When she traveled to the Vatican in February 2009 and met Pope Benedict, he lectured her sharply on abortion and euthanasia, then put out a public statement boasting about having done so.

And so, when the Church's position on abortion became the final sticking point in the House's 2009 health care talks, it was acutely personal for Pelosi. She tried everything she could to get around the bishops' opposition. She put language in the bill banning abortion funding. She personally phoned a cardinal she knew in Rome. She won over groups of nuns. But none of it was enough. The bishops sent an urgent bulletin to every American parish calling for the bill to be defeated if they didn't get their way. They printed leaflets that showed a pregnant woman with the words "Abortion is not health care, because killing is not healing." They sent a phalanx of bishops to the Capitol to lobby. The archbishop of Boston personally pressed Obama on the issue as they shook hands at Ted Kennedy's funeral.

Pelosi had done everything she knew how in order to collect the votes she needed. She promised two California members that she'd take up their water issues. She persuaded a liberal congressman who was planning to retire to stay until health care was finished. She got a former president of the University of Notre Dame to lean on a moderate Democrat from Indiana. She attended the annual football game between members of Congress and Capitol Police, wearing a jersey that read, "MEAN MACHINE 1," and cheering for Heath Shuler, the Redskins quarterback turned congressman, who was undecided on the bill. She added a provision for transplant patients, a tax on medical devices and a tax break for paper companies, each giveaway picking off a vote or two. On a single day in November, she called fifty members. At one point she was so exhausted she drank half a cup of coffee on purpose—a fearful situation for her staff, who knew that the slightest bit of caffeine would increase her usual level of intensity to a frightening degree.

And still, with the bishops opposed, she didn't have the votes.

And so, on that Friday, after a long day of negotiations, she summoned her liberal female colleagues in and laid out the situation. As the therapy session wore on, she ordered cheeseburgers for everyone and continued to listen.

It was 11 p.m. by the time the women stormed out of the meeting, furious at the reality Pelosi had forced them to acknowledge: the bill wasn't happening without the bishops' amendment, and they weren't going to let the bill go down after they'd come this far. She knew it, and they knew it. She sat with them until they realized there was no other way.

Louise Slaughter was so angry that she refused to attend the late-night meeting of the committee she chaired. She holed up in her office with two other pro-choice women. They watched on C-SPAN as, at the hearing they'd boycotted, their committee approved the bill. The next day, by a vote of 220–215, health care reform passed the House.

◇ ◇ ◇

The Senate finally began hearings in mid-September, and in October the bill was approved by Baucus's committee with a single Republican vote. Senate leaders had given up on getting more Republican support, but they still needed the votes of every single Democrat, including moderates from the South. The public option was dropped from the bill to secure the vote of Senator Joseph Lieberman of Connecticut. Pelosi worried that the bill might be too weak to be effective. But at last, on Christmas Eve, the Senate bill passed.

The House and Senate had passed different bills, and now they needed to hammer out a compromise they could agree on. Obama told the lawmakers to go home, get some rest and come back after New Year's Day. Pelosi went on vacation to Hawaii, which had become a post-Christmas tradition for her and Paul.

Back in Washington in January, Obama presided over three days of contentious White House negotiations between House and Senate Democrats. Pelosi thought the House had already compromised enough, drafting a bill conservative enough that it ought to be palatable to the Senate. But the House bill's price tag was over a trillion dollars, while the Senate's cost eight hundred billion, and Obama wanted them to meet in the middle. On the second night, they took a dinner break, and Obama asked them to come back afterward with what they were willing to give. The senators ordered pizza, combed through the bill and came back with seventy billion dollars in concessions. Then it was the House's turn.

"The House," Pelosi announced, "will give you nothing."

Talks continued, and with prodding from Obama, the gap between the House and Senate was reduced to just twenty billion dollars—pocket change in budget terms. Obama proposed a way to close the gap, and Waxman piped up. "You've put forward a number that seems reasonable," he said. "I can't speak for the House, but it seems like something we can work toward."

Pelosi shot out a hand to cut him off. "Henry is right about two things," she said. "One, you've put forward a number. And two, Henry doesn't speak for the House."

To the other negotiators, Pelosi seemed unreasonably stubborn. Obama grew weary of what he viewed as childish bickering. Everyone in the room agreed that they wanted to reform health care. Their basic approaches were nearly identical. Yet they were tearing each other apart over relative pennies. "Stop this bullshit," the president said. "I'm going upstairs and going to bed."

Pelosi and the others began gathering their things to leave. But Emanuel stopped them. It was nearing midnight, but he would not let them leave until he'd gotten them to come together on a number. So, at last, in the wee hours of the morning, Pelosi relented.

❖ ❖ ❖

The negotiations were nearly finished when a thunderbolt struck. On January 19, Massachusetts held a special election to fill Kennedy's Senate seat. And despite the beloved Kennedy legacy, despite the fact that it was one of the most liberal states in the country, Massachusetts elected a Republican named Scott Brown.

It was a body blow to the Democrats' health care hopes, made crueler by the irony of its being Kennedy's seat. Without 60 votes in the Senate, with the Republicans now clearly unified in opposition, it didn't matter what compromise the House and Senate came up with, because the Senate wouldn't pass it.

Health care reform was over. "It's dead," Barney Frank told reporters. Other Democrats voiced similar views on cable TV. Emanuel and Axelrod advocated falling back on the "kiddie care" option. Pelosi told the White House to rein in Emanuel and get him to stop pestering her members about his "eentsy weentsy bill."

There was one other avenue. If the House passed the bill the Senate had already passed, Obama could sign it into law. But Pelosi had already declared the Senate bill "a nonstarter." She had barely gotten the House bill over the line, with its delicate balance of liberal and conservative concessions. If that had been a Herculean feat, to get the House to pass the Senate bill seemed downright impossible. Even the senators didn't love the Senate bill—they had passed it with the understanding that they could work out the kinks in negotiations with the House.

The president seemed to be wavering. In an ABC interview the day after Scott Brown's win, he said he would support a bill that could pass quickly even if it contained only "the core elements" of reform. At a meeting in the Oval Office, Pelosi confronted the subject directly. "Mr. President, I know there are some on your staff who want to take the namby-pamby approach," she said. "That's unacceptable." Obama took her side. They were going to go for it.

Pelosi estimated she had no more than 180 members who would vote to pass the Senate bill at the outset, meaning she needed about 40 more. Failure was not an option. The United States had never been so close to achieving national health insurance. At one of Pelosi's press conferences, reporters asked how she planned to proceed. "You go through the gate," she said. "If the gate's closed, you go over the fence. If the fence is too high, we'll pole-vault in. If that doesn't work, we'll parachute in. But we're going to get health care reform passed for the American people."

At the first meeting of the House Democratic caucus after the Massachusetts election, Pelosi just listened. The meeting went on for hours, as member after member lamented the demise of the legislation they'd worked so hard on. All that effort, the tearful negotiations with the bishops, their two-thousand-page behemoth of a bill to give health insurance to more than thirty million people—all for nothing. Members filed out of the room convinced that it was over.

At the next caucus meeting, Pelosi got up to speak. Here, she said, is how we're going to pass health care reform.

The members couldn't believe what they were hearing. But at this point, they knew better than to doubt her.

❖ ❖ ❖

The White House had come up with a plan. A procedural maneuver called "reconciliation" would allow budget-related aspects of health care legislation to go through the Senate with just 50 votes. But reconciliation couldn't be used for the main parts of the bill that entailed structural changes to the health care system. So, the White House proposed, the House could pass the Senate bill it loathed, and then, under reconciliation, both houses could pass a companion bill with a set of budgetary tweaks to the massive overhaul of American health care they'd enacted.

The Senate bill was more conservative than the House bill, with no public option and a smaller price tag. Its prohibition on abortion funding was weaker than the House's. The Senate bill also included a number of conspicuous giveaways to states represented in the Senate by moderate Democrats, who'd demanded the provisions as the price of their vote. In the old days, this pork barreling was the kind of thing a senator touted proudly. But in a sign of how much more ideological politics had become, these deals were seized upon as corrupt, and the senators who'd proposed them now disavowed them. Under the White House's two-step plan, the reconciliation bill would remove these provisions and rejigger other financing aspects, notably regional rates for Medicare reimbursement, which were highly contentious. It was left to Pelosi to convince her caucus to pass the Senate bill combined with the reconciliation "sidecar."

After a few weeks' mourning, the House Democrats were coming to terms with the reality: they'd come tantalizingly close to their one-hundred-year goal. They had passed health care reform legislation out of both the House and Senate. Were they going to abandon the effort now, over what amounted to a few technicalities? Programs like Social Security had started small and been expanded and improved as the years went on; national health insurance, once the basic structure was enacted, could also be incrementally improved.

The health care bill was unpopular, and members from swing districts worried they'd lose their seats over it. But the damage was likely already done—they could be attacked for trying and failing, or they could be attacked for trying and succeeding. Pelosi even told colleagues she believed health care reform was an accomplishment so monumental it would be worth losing the majority over. The point of power, to her, couldn't be just to hold on to it—it had to be to achieve things with it that would benefit people.

In late February, Obama convened a televised bipartisan health care summit, where he made the case for reform to a small group of lawmakers from both parties, including some moderate Republicans the president still—after all they'd been through—thought he might be able to win over. More important, the summit stiffened Democrats' spines, reminding them of their purpose and convincing them that the president still believed. Meanwhile, California's Anthem Blue Cross announced it was raising its rates by as much as 39 percent, sparking public outrage and reminding Democrats of the gravity of the problems they were trying to solve.

Pelosi began another furious round of vote-wrangling. To get the pro-lifers, the White House promised an executive order that would restrict abortion funds as sharply as the House bill had. To get the skeptical Blue Dogs, Pelosi and Harry Reid worked out funding compromises in the reconciliation bill. To bring along wavering liberals, Pelosi and Obama played on their consciences, reminding them of the moral significance of a bill that, while imperfect, would make health care accessible to an estimated thirty-one million Americans. Pelosi demanded that Reid get every Democratic senator to sign a letter promising to vote for the reconciliation bill, so that her members wouldn't get hung out to dry yet again.

On March 12, Pelosi sent a memo to her caucus. "We have to just rip the Band-Aid off and have a vote," she wrote. Obama barnstormed the country, drumming up public support at a series of rallies and glad-handing members in meeting after meeting. (For some, the thrill of a private meeting with the president was all the persuasion they needed.) Pelosi also worked the members relentlessly. At one point, after presenting her with a list of more than sixty members who needed a phone call, John Lawrence, her chief of staff, expected she'd divvy up the list among the leadership team. "Give me the list," she told him, and proceeded to call each of them herself.

The talks went down to the wire yet again. On the eve of the vote, a group of moderates walked out of a midnight negotiating session over reimbursements. But on March 21, with the bill on the floor, Pelosi rose to make her closing speech. The members who voted for this bill, she said, would go down in history: "We will be joining those who established Social Security, Medicare, and now, tonight, health care for all Americans."

Boehner, the Republican leader, took the floor to excoriate the process. "Look at how this bill was written. Can you say it was done openly? With transparency and accountability?" he shouted. "Hell no, you can't!" The viral rant made him a hero to the Tea Party—an effect that would prove decidedly temporary.

The vote was called, and as the tally crept upward, Democrats on the floor of the House began chanting, "Yes, we can!" After the bill passed, 219–212, with no Republican votes, the floor exploded in cheering and hugging.

Many of the books and articles subsequently written about the Patient Protection and Affordable Care Act would emphasize the president's achievement—which of course it was—and the protracted drama in the Senate, more than Pelosi's work in the House. Senate leaders always think their job is harder because they have to get to 60 votes, while House partisans argue that the House, with its hundreds of personalities and layers of overlapping interests and blocs, is infinitely more complex. But it's impossible to say whether the Senate struggled because Reid's job was inherently harder than Pelosi's or because Pelosi was better at the job of getting controversial legislation through the chamber her party controlled.

To Pelosi's allies, the Senate was like the misbehaving child who gets all the attention, and is praised lavishly for minor progress, while the gifted, well-behaved sibling has to meet higher expectations. This was the case with many of her accomplishments: she defied the odds and the naysayers with such regularity that people took her for granted. Because she made it look easy, people assumed it was. She compared herself to the swan that seems to glide regally across the water, but actually is paddling its big, black, ungraceful webbed feet furiously underneath. At a caucus meeting, a liberal congressman, Steve Cohen, passed out buttons that read, "PelosiCare: I was there."

The bill was still unpopular—just 39 percent of Americans approved of it, according to one poll taken shortly after passage—but Democrats believed that would change now that it was the law of the land. Speaking to a conference in early March, Pelosi had said, "We have to pass the bill so that you can find out what is in it, away from the fog of the controversy." Republicans pilloried her for the statement, arguing that it proved that Democrats had drafted their legislation in secret and jammed it through sight unseen, which wasn't true. What she meant was that once the bill was implemented, people would see that it didn't contain death panels, abortion funding, government coercion or any of the other bogeymen opponents conjured.

Obama might not be the greatest legislative tactician, but if there was one thing he was thought to be good at, it was giving inspiring speeches. Now, Democrats believed, he could go out and convince the American public that this legislation was a good thing. It was Republicans who would look unreasonable, for standing in the way of an epochal accomplishment. "What was striking was the mood," a top Democratic staffer wrote in his diary the night Obama signed the bill. "A bill that has been so pilloried, so vilified, so hated, so disparaged was seen today as the right thing to do."

As Obama signed the bill, Pelosi stood behind him. A hot microphone caught Vice President Joe Biden summing up the legislation's import: "This is a big fucking deal."

20

THE DAY AFTER THE HOUSE PASSED THE HEALTH CARE BILL, THE
Republican National Committee's chairman, Michael Steele, appeared on
Fox News with a major announcement. The party, he said, was rallying
around a new initiative, which could be found at its very own website:
FireNancyPelosi.com.

It was a fund-raising gambit born of desperation. The GOP was deep
in debt and deeply discouraged. Republicans' wall-of-opposition strategy
hadn't been enough to stop Democrats from getting the Affordable Care
Act through Congress: a massive new entitlement program that got the
government involved in every American's health care. To conservatives,
it seemed likely that, as with Social Security and Medicare, voters would
become attached to the new benefit, making it virtually impossible to get
rid of down the line. Pelosi's effectiveness had been crucial to getting the bill
passed, and so Pelosi had to be taken out for the Republicans to rise again.

The Fire Nancy Pelosi website featured an image of Pelosi with her
fists raised in the air, superimposed on a background of enormous, licking
flames. It urged visitors to donate to ensure "No More Madam Speaker." A
thermometer showed progress toward the goal, which the party had set,
ambitiously, at $400,000, the high end of what could be expected from a
successful fund-raising gimmick.

But the goal proved not ambitious enough. Inside the committee's
Capitol Hill headquarters the next morning, staffers watched, astonished,

as the donations flooded in. By noon, the thermometer had to be extended and recalibrated. Within a week, it had topped $1.5 million.

Before long, there were Fire Pelosi ball caps and Fire Pelosi yard signs for sale on the RNC's website. A Fire Pelosi banner hung above the door of the party's DC headquarters. Steele announced that he would embark on a Fire Pelosi bus tour, which would make 117 stops in cities across the country.

It wasn't the first time they'd gone after Pelosi. As far back as 2006, Republicans had mentioned her in ads attacking Democrats in districts far from San Francisco. There was nothing new or out of bounds about an opposition party going after the other party's congressional leaders; Democrats had previously done it with Newt Gingrich, while Republicans had galvanized their base by invoking Ted Kennedy and others. One 1981 GOP ad compared the federal budget to then-Speaker Tip O'Neill: "fat, bloated and out of control." And it wasn't only Pelosi they were attacking in 2010. Obama, too, came in for plenty of hostile fire; with the honeymoon over, his popularity was now middling. White Southern Democrats, in particular, found themselves depicted in ads alongside the black president, even if they'd never met him or didn't support him—a tactic that proved disturbingly effective.

But the Republican base clearly nurtured a special, visceral ire for Pelosi. A Republican candidate in Texas told the *Washington Post* he'd taken to mentioning Pelosi more than Obama in his speeches: "If you go to almost any grassroots event and you mention the Speaker's name," the candidate, Bill Flores, said, "you will get a huge response from the audience." It was a gut feeling more than anything; according to a top RNC staffer at the time, the party didn't test the Pelosi attacks with focus groups or polling. They just went with what felt right.

Soon Pelosi was the star of the GOP's advertising effort for the upcoming midterm elections. A candidate in North Carolina said in his campaign announcement video, "If you're a small-business owner, you get up every morning and you put your helmet on, because you think that Nancy Pelosi is going to come into your bedroom and hit you over the head with a baseball bat." A conservative group depicted Pelosi as a cartoon giantess with lightning bolts coming out of her eyes and fingers: the spot was titled "Attack of the 50-Foot Pelosi." By the time the election cycle was over,

Republicans had aired 161,203 anti-Pelosi spots at a cost of seventy million dollars.

If anyone mentioned the ads to Pelosi, she insisted she didn't care, or even took them as a compliment. She could absorb the incoming fire; she wasn't in any electoral danger back home. Outside San Francisco, the only constituents she cared about were her members. "You know what, I'm in the arena," she said. "We have big issues. I can't be bothered about what they say about me. All I'm interested in is getting the job done."

❖ ❖ ❖

Outside Washington, a rebellion was brewing. The grassroots groundswell called itself the Tea Party, after the famous antitax Boston protest that helped spark the Revolutionary War.

The first spark was the stimulus. In February 2009, shortly after Obama signed the American Recovery and Reinvestment Act into law, a commentator on CNBC let loose with a rant over all the bailouts and spending, as well as a newly announced executive action to help underwater home owners. "How many of you people want to pay for your neighbor's mortgage that has an extra bathroom and can't pay their bills? Raise your hand!" the commentator, Rick Santelli, shouted. "President Obama, are you listening?" What was needed, he said, was a new "tea party" to rise up in protest.

Just eight days after Santelli's viral tantrum, coordinated protests unfolded in forty cities. (The small-bore executive action on housing went ahead, but largely because of the episode, the Obama administration did little else to address the foreclosure crisis—an instance of political timidity that likely stymied the recovery.) Tea Party protests started springing up regularly all over the country. Some protesters wore tricorne hats and other Revolutionary War garb. They waved yellow Gadsden flags, with a coiled rattlesnake and the words "Don't Tread on Me." Others hurled racial slurs or compared Obama to Hitler.

There was no one leader of the Tea Party—the movement sprouted spontaneously from coast to coast, organized by regular people, many of whom told interviewers they'd never been political before but had suddenly been awakened to the idea that their country was in danger and they had to save it from mortal peril. Their voices were amplified by Fox News, which covered the protests relentlessly and even organized some of them, and by conservative donors who sought to turn the protesters' raw energy into political clout. On April 15, 2009, Tax Day, hundreds of protests were held all across the country.

Republican lawmakers rushed to style themselves Tea Party leaders. Sarah Palin sprinted to the front of the parade. The 2008 campaign had made her a political celebrity, and she was mulling a 2012 presidential campaign; in July 2009, she abruptly quit the Alaska governorship halfway through a single term to lead the Obama resistance full time.

The Tea Party purported to be about the Constitution, small government and fiscal discipline. Activists maintained that the "Tea" in "Tea Party" stood for "Taxed Enough Already." Donors such as the billionaire brothers Charles and David Koch insisted the movement was essentially libertarian, an expression of popular outrage at out-of-control government spending and regulations that tied the hands of individuals and businesses. The message could be selective, however. One protester carried a sign that read, "Get the Government's Hands Off My Medicare!"

Republican leaders suspected the Tea Partiers were not motivated entirely by a passion for cutting spending. In polls, large percentages of Tea Partiers said they believed the false "birther" conspiracy theory that Obama was actually born in Kenya. Political scientists who studied the movement would later conclude that the main thing that distinguished Tea Party followers from regular Republicans was high levels of racial resentment.

But at the time, journalists and political leaders largely took the Tea Partiers at their word, and both parties strained to show that they believed in cutting spending. This misunderstanding would prove consequential in the coming years, as Republicans kept trying to rein in spending and wondering why their base was not appeased—until Trump came along and gave them what they apparently really wanted: not spending cuts, but anger, nostalgia and racism.

In November 2009, the Tea Party held a rally on the Capitol lawn attended by Republican leaders, including Minority Leader Boehner. Banners depicted Obama as the Joker and Pelosi as the "Weasel Queen." Giant signs featured grisly photos of Holocaust victims, with the legend, "National Socialist Health Care, Dachau, Germany, 1945."

But while the GOP tried to co-opt the Tea Party, the movement professed to be nearly as angry at Republican leaders as it was at Democrats.

It was George W. Bush who had started the cycle of deficit spending and big-ticket bailouts, they noted. And now, despite what the Obama White House perceived as an unreasonable level of Republican obstruction, the Tea Partiers saw a GOP that had utterly failed to rein in a dictatorial and illegitimate president.

Any Republican who'd been nice to Obama was a target. Bob Bennett, a three-term Republican senator from Utah, had a long conservative track record. But activists seized on a picture of him standing behind Obama at the inauguration, looking suspiciously happy. Bennett was actually there to swear in the vice president, his duty as the top Republican on the Senate Rules Committee; whatever his policy differences with the new administration, he believed in the peaceful transfer of power. In May 2010, at the Utah GOP convention, the longtime incumbent came in third for the nomination to the Senate seat he'd held for nearly two decades. The Tea Party would go on to defeat numerous other establishment incumbents and candidates in that year's Republican primaries, nominating fringe or far-right figures in their stead and driving formerly moderate pols rightward. It was an object lesson in the dynamics of political movements: the more passionate they are, the harder they are to control.

❖ ❖ ❖

Back in Washington, the much-delayed passage of health care, while exhilarating to the Democrats, had left lawmakers exhausted and spent. The original plan—to have health care and energy legislation run on parallel tracks, and have both bills done before 2009 was out—looked laughable in retrospect.

It wasn't that they hadn't tried. While the health care fight wore on, a bipartisan team of senators worked behind the scenes on cap and trade, trying to come up with a version of the House bill that could get 60 votes. But by late April, the talks had fallen apart. Reid called Axelrod and bluntly informed him the Senate would not be bringing climate legislation up for a vote. It was exactly as the House Democrats had feared—they had been BTU-ed, taken a tough vote only to be hung out to dry.

There was one more major agenda item on the list: Wall Street reform, reorganizing the complicated tangle of regulations that governed the financial industry. Congressman Barney Frank worked with Senator Chris Dodd on the legislation, which brought transparency to the derivatives market, stiffened banks' capital requirements and created a new regulatory agency to oversee consumer credit. Obama signed the bill, which passed with 3 Republican votes in each chamber, in July 2010. It was another major accomplishment to add to the pile of things he and Pelosi had done together.

But it was also another complicated, compromised piece of legislation that managed to please no one. Consumer advocates charged that it didn't go far enough, while the same ungrateful banks who'd crashed the economy and begged for rescue two years earlier screamed that it was overly onerous. "Bringing transparency to the derivatives market" didn't do much to slake public anger at Wall Street—not when the executives still got their bonuses and nobody went to jail; not when the administration's feeble efforts to help home owners left out most people facing foreclosure; not when unemployment was still up over 10 percent. Obama, wary of being perceived as antibusiness, still shied away from bashing Wall Street, even as his onetime supporters on Wall Street turned on him for the raft of legislation that threatened their bottom line.

By the time health care was finished, it was April, and the midterm elections were just seven months away. The Democrats had spent so much time shooting for epochal reforms that they'd taken their eye off the thing voters cared most about, and Republicans had taken to taunting, "Where are the jobs?" The economy had stabilized, but growth was sluggish. Republicans argued that they were being proven right, that the stimulus had failed and what was really needed was spending cuts. Some of the White House's more conservative economic advisers agreed that it was time to turn to reducing the deficit, even as most liberals thought that this was the last thing the country needed—like telling a patient still healing from major surgery that he'd better start exercising if he wants to be healthy. The House passed several more pieces of economic legislation, including a bill that would open up to small businesses the credit that banks were still loath to extend, so businesses could start hiring again. But despite being backed by the Chamber of Commerce, the bill was blocked by Republicans in the Senate.

The White House worried that all the messy congressional action had taken a toll on the president's outsider brand. While the administration's congressional liaisons argued that Obama had to lead Congress if he wanted to achieve his goals, his political advisers thought he should distance himself. Speaking about congressional Democrats, Axelrod told a reporter, "The horse has been ridden hard this year, and just wants to go back to the barn." Another official described the political advisers' attitude more vividly: "Fuck whatever Congress wants, we're not for them."

The administration could view the midterms casually, since Obama wouldn't be on the ballot for two more years. But for the members of the House, the stakes were existential—and the White House didn't seem to have their backs. Pelosi and her strategists at the Congressional Campaign Committee begged the president to go out and campaign for them. They came up with a message he could use to subtly point out the disaster he'd inherited while staying positive and not seeming to make excuses. Obama, they said, should argue that Democrats wanted to keep going forward, while Republicans wanted to go back to the policies that had caused the collapse. Pelosi kept pestering the White House. When was the president going to start campaigning? Just as important, when was the party's biggest fund-raising asset going to start raising some money?

In May, Obama finally held his first fund-raiser of the season for congressional Democrats, a swanky, celebrity-studded, fifteen-thousand-dollar-per-person dinner at the St. Regis Hotel in New York City. And he finally served up the red meat Democrats were waiting for, bashing the GOP for refusing to help clean up the mess they had created. "After they drove the car into the ditch, now they want the keys back," he said, to laughter and applause. "No! You can't drive! We don't want to have to go back into the ditch! We just got the car out!"

Pelosi looked across the table at Chris Van Hollen, the Maryland congressman who was one of her favorites. Van Hollen was heading the campaign committee for the second cycle, and 2010 was shaping up to be a far less pleasant election for the Democrats than 2008. The line about car keys was something they'd come up with together. When Van Hollen heard it, he caught Pelosi's eye and flashed her a thumbs-up.

Pelosi had a very simple approach to messaging: you came up with a message and you hammered it. You said it over and over again, no matter how bored you were or how hokey and repetitive it sounded, and eventually people would hear. But Obama still found fund-raising distasteful, and partisanship at odds with his brand. He tended to go after the Republicans mostly at fund-raisers, behind closed doors—great for raising money, not so great for communicating with voters. And he still had a habit of referring derisively to "Congress" as the problem. No, no, no, Pelosi and Van Hollen would say. You mean congressional *Republicans*!

✧ ✧ ✧

There was some truth to the Republicans' critique that the White House was insufficiently focused on jobs. The administration argued that the climate and health care initiatives that followed the stimulus would make the economy more vibrant as it healed, but Obama's claim that the Affordable Care Act was, in fact, a jobs bill was too contrived to register. Liberals argued that the administration had been insufficiently bold, too cowed by bad-faith Republican critiques (and conservative Democratic senators) to reach for solutions that might have had more impact, such as breaking up the banks or having the federal government hire workers directly. Leaving banking regulation for last on the agenda of big-ticket items had made it a relative afterthought, illustrating that fixing the root causes of the economic crisis wasn't the top priority and allowing banks to marshal opposition and weaken the legislation.

Many of the GOP criticisms were disingenuous, attacking Democrats for the continued weakness of an economy Republicans had done nothing to help fix, or blaming Obama for the problems still plaguing health care even though most provisions of the Affordable Care Act weren't scheduled to take effect for four more years. (Pelosi had tried to get the administration to include more immediate people-pleasing measures in the bill.) Perhaps most annoying to Pelosi, the GOP had seized on the fact that the health care bill cut hundreds of billions of dollars from the Medicare budget, arguing that it hurt seniors. This was one of the Senate bill's cost-saving measures; it cut the amount Medicare paid to certain providers, but it didn't cut anybody's benefits. The Republicans, of course, had argued for some time that in order to balance the budget, Medicare needed to be made less generous. For them to accuse Democrats of sabotaging the program, something they'd done to make the bill more conservative, was galling in the extreme.

But the Obama White House didn't seem to have any way to counter the Republican attacks. It seemed constantly on defense, even as Pelosi, Van Hollen and many other Democrats begged the White House to go out and sell the party's many accomplishments. In the summer of 2010, Vice President Biden did go out on the road to tout stimulus projects, in what was dubbed "Recovery Summer." But with signs of actual economic recovery few and far between, the effort was pilloried as tone-deaf boasting.

The White House bridled at the criticisms. Obama had a lot on his plate. There were still two wars to manage—heeding Pentagon warnings about the chaos that could result from a precipitous pullout, the antiwar president had yet to bring them to a close. In April, an explosion on an offshore oil rig owned by BP caused millions of gallons of oil to spill into the Gulf of Mexico; the burst well spewed for days while officials watched helplessly before it could be brought under control. Then, in August, a lengthy controversy erupted over a plan to build an Islamic cultural center a few blocks from the site of the 9/11 attacks in Manhattan. Fox News had misleadingly dubbed it the "Ground Zero mosque." All these crises made it difficult for the president to drive a positive message. The White House press secretary, Robert Gibbs, later acknowledged, "If people turned on the television and saw stories and shouting about BP and the mosque, they'd be right to ask, 'Is anybody paying attention to what's important in my life?'"

❖ ❖ ❖

Jack Murtha didn't live to see health care reform passed. In early February 2010, two days after becoming the longest-serving member of Congress from Pennsylvania, he died of complications from gallbladder surgery.

The last days of Pelosi's old friend were spent in ignominy, as corruption investigations swept up the friends and family he'd helped with congressional largesse over the years. It would later be revealed that, at the time of his death, he was under FBI investigation. But to Pelosi he would always be her loyal mentor and ally, the crusty old chauvinist who made the other men take her seriously—and the principled marine who could not abide a callow commander in chief's misbegotten war. At Murtha's funeral near Johnstown, Pelosi recalled his twinkle-eyed smile, his compassion—and his distaste for long speeches.

Murtha's death was a reminder to Pelosi of how time had passed. Gone were the days of Tuesday night dinners among friends in the House—most of the group's members had moved on, from the House, from politics or from life. Politics had become less collegial with the constant need to fundraise and campaign. Pelosi had come to Congress as a forty-seven-year-old neophyte. Now, twenty-three years later, the circle of colleagues she could see as peers was shrinking, and she was the one the rookies looked to for guidance.

Murtha's death triggered a special election in May to fill his seat, and both parties poured money into the race. The Republican candidate declared he was running to stop "the Obama-Pelosi agenda" and repeal the Affordable Care Act. When the Democrat, a former Murtha staffer, eked out a narrow win, it gave the Democrats a glimmer of hope at a time when they badly needed it. "We are going to maintain our majority," Hoyer declared.

But Pelosi could feel trouble brewing. In 2006 and 2008, it had been easy to recruit candidates to challenge Republicans. But in 2010, Democrats were having trouble finding qualified candidates. It was clear that the public mood was turning against their party. Pelosi's 79-seat majority was so large that it had initially seemed impossible that the party could lose the House, even in a bad year. But now even that was in doubt.

In July, the White House's Gibbs said on *Meet the Press*, "I think there's no doubt there are enough seats in play that could cause Republicans to gain control. There's no doubt about that. This will depend on strong campaigns by Democrats." The remark seemed innocuous enough, but to beleaguered House Democrats who already felt abandoned by the White House it was infuriating: the administration seemed to be saying not only that they might lose, but that it would be their own fault if they did. That night, at a party Pelosi attended, donors kept asking her if it was true the House was already lost—they didn't want to throw good money after bad.

By the next day, the comment had Pelosi in a state that one colleague described as "nuclear mad." At Tuesday's closed-door meeting of the Democratic caucus, she let the members vent. Congressman Bill Pascrell of New Jersey enacted a dramatic reading of Gibbs's remarks, punctuating them with complaints about the White House. When he was finished, Pelosi said only, "I disagree on one point: I think you were too kind to Mr. Gibbs."

As the House Democrats saw it, the White House had asked them to take so many tough votes—the stimulus, health care, climate—and then let the Senate water down or decline to take up their legislation, leaving House members to answer for their positions on liberal bills that hadn't necessarily become law. The supposed geniuses in the White House had waffled and equivocated on jobs and housing, leaving the economy sputtering and Congress empty-handed on the issues most pressing to the electorate. And what had Obama done for them? He'd effectively dismantled the Democratic National Committee, creating a separate organization, Organizing for America, that didn't seem to do anything. He seemed mostly focused on saving the Senate: the president's schedule included twenty-four Senate campaign appearances, while he had done only four for House members.

Obama seemed unable to build public support for the many things he had accomplished with Congress. On health care, the latest poll-tested selling point was that the law was "bending the cost curve," a description no one really understood and which wouldn't fit on a bumper sticker. When Cabinet members went out into the country to announce new programs or tout infrastructure projects funded by the stimulus, they often forgot to notify the local members of Congress so that they could appear alongside them and get some good press back home.

The Democrats went off to the August recess with palm cards—miniature sheets of talking points—reading, "Democrats moving us forward, while Republicans take us back." After Labor Day, Obama tried a different theme, attacking the GOP as in bed with special interests—a line that resonated with few outside the liberal base. And then the money came flooding in. In January, the Supreme Court had decided *Citizens United v. Federal Election Commission*, which opened the door to unlimited "dark money" campaign spending. Pelosi watched in horror as tens of millions of dollars' worth of GOP attack ads went wall to wall in the election's final weeks. It was Big Business's backhanded tribute to Pelosi's effectiveness: they were especially aware of the threat she posed to their profits.

The GOP's closing message centered on the cut to Medicare spending in the health care law. Besides being misleading and hypocritical, the ad was effective at revealing what GOP voters really cared about in a time of scarcity: not the abstraction of the deficit, but the government benefits they believed were owed to them. The problem with Obamacare for these voters wasn't that it represented a socialistic intrusion; it was that it took something away from *us* to give it to *them*.

Pelosi appeared in more Republican ads than Obama in the election's final weeks. In September and October, the National Republican Congressional Committee aired 125 ads mentioning her and only 50 mentioning the president. Never in history had a congressional leader been the target of such a barrage—but focus groups substantiated the RNC's hunch: Pelosi just got a rise out of people. And "San Francisco values" was a handy proxy for the culture war.

The Republicans' congressional campaign committee had a template for it: they'd put up the Democratic incumbent's picture, then Pelosi's, then say what percentage of the time the incumbent voted with her. On I-95 in south Florida, billboards showed Congressman Ron Klein's head on a marionette, with Pelosi as the puppeteer. "Ron Klein votes with Pelosi 98%. Fire them both!" the ad read. Even Democrats not running for Congress got the Pelosi treatment: television ads tied her to candidates for state legislature, even a state agriculture commissioner. To combat the attack, one Democrat, in Alabama, aired his own TV ad declaring that he wouldn't vote for Pelosi for Speaker. By October, she barely campaigned in public outside California, appearing mainly at private fund-raisers. A *Washington Post* poll put her favorable rating nationally at just 29 percent, with 58 percent of voters viewing her unfavorably.

Pelosi never expressed anguish about the ads, even to her closest congressional allies, who were frustrated on her behalf. Her friend George Miller, a sincere sixties liberal whose father had served in the California State Senate, was a policy maven from a district just east of Pelosi's. With his soft blue eyes and big white mustache, Miller, passionate about education and the environment, was considered by many to personify Pelosi's liberal conscience. Now he groused to whoever would listen that the White House ought to be ashamed for not sticking up for Pelosi.

Unsentimental as ever, Pelosi sought no retribution against the dissenters. The Democratic Congressional Campaign Committee spent more than a million dollars on the Alabama congressman who'd aired the ad distancing himself from Pelosi, and showered funds on others who'd criticized her or refused to vote for Democratic legislation.

In the end, the election wave did not discriminate. It took out members who'd voted for the climate bill and members who'd voted against it, members who'd stuck with Pelosi and members who'd denounced her. By the time the votes were counted after November 2, Republicans had taken 63 seats, winning the majority with the biggest congressional shift since 1948.

❖ ❖ ❖

After the election, Pelosi disappeared from sight for a few days. No one knew what she was going to do. It seemed likely she would quit—that was normally what congressional leaders did when their party lost. That was what Gephardt had done after 2002, and what Hastert had done after

2006. The day after the election, she met with Hoyer for two hours, talking about what had happened. It was, they agreed, mostly the dismal state of the economy that had led voters to lash out at Washington—and the combination of Big Business money and White House lassitude hadn't helped.

"Nancy, you're the leader," Hoyer said. "What are you going to do?" She changed the subject, and he knew better than to press her further.

Heath Shuler, the former quarterback from North Carolina, had been telling people for months that it was time for Pelosi to go. He called her two days after the election and told her he understood. In high school and college, he'd been the champion football player everybody loved, but then he got to the NFL and flamed out. "They replaced me as starting quarterback," he said. "And I had two options. I could say, 'I'm not the problem—it's everyone else.' Or I could support the other guy taking my place. I decided to be a team player. And I'm asking you to be a team player."

When Shuler was finished with his little soliloquy, Pelosi replied coolly, "I totally understand. But you need to understand, Heath, that there are a lot of other members who are calling me and asking me to maintain the leadership role."

The Republican National Committee had taken down its "Fire Pelosi" banner and replaced it with one that read, "Hire Pelosi." A GOP spokesman snarked, "If House Democrats are willing to sacrifice more of their members in 2012 for the glory of Nancy Pelosi, we are happy to oblige them."

Pelosi was not about to give them the satisfaction. "They want to say, 'See, we chased Nancy Pelosi away,'" her friend Jan Schakowsky said. "Well, Nancy Pelosi doesn't get chased away."

21

Pelosi was at a crossroads. It could have been the end of her career. On the one hand, she'd now spent twenty-three years in a job she'd initially planned to do for no more than a decade. She'd risen so much higher than she could ever have dreamed; she'd shattered the marble ceiling; she was seventy years old, with nine grandchildren, living mostly apart from her beloved husband and keeping a schedule that would have worn out a twenty-five-year-old. No one would have begrudged the first woman Speaker for riding off into the sunset, leaving it to a new generation to resuscitate her party.

Staying on would be nearly unprecedented—not since Sam Rayburn in 1953 had a House Speaker accepted a demotion to minority leader. And the demotion would be a precipitous one, a dignity-swallowing step down from the exalted title of Speaker of the House. She would have to move from the Speaker's quarters on the second floor of the Capitol to the minority leader's offices down the hall, where Boehner's tenure had soaked the scent of cigarette smoke deep into the walls and curtains. Her staff would be reduced by one-third. (For all Pelosi's punctiliousness, staff management had never been a strength. Those who would be let go found out in a mass email.) Nor could she expect a soft landing: the Republicans who'd howled at how Pelosi had cut them out of the process when they were in the minority were not likely to turn around and play nice now that the situation was reversed.

Still, she hated the thought of leaving as a loser. She wasn't going to be bullied out of her rightful place by the GOP and its Big Business goons, with their $70 million in attack ads, or the moderates and cowards in her own party who'd fallen for the opposition's line. The next election in 2012 would be a presidential year, with the economy presumably healthier and Obama on the ballot to generate another surge in Democratic turnout. Democrats would have to pick up only 25 seats to make her Speaker again. On the geologic timetable of Congress, two years was a mere blip. Pelosi was a patient person. She could wait two years.

Pelosi felt that familiar combination of obligation (*somebody has to do this*) and self-assurance (*I'm the one who can do it*). Who else was there to do the job? Hoyer didn't have her toughness and, as a moderate, he wouldn't be able to rein in the caucus's left flank. Van Hollen she viewed as a future Speaker, but he wasn't ready yet. Heath Shuler certainly couldn't do it. She believed that no one else had her fund-raising ability, her knack for orchestrating complex legislation, her ability to keep the fractious caucus together.

Somebody had to stand up for liberal values, not just against the GOP, but against a Democratic White House and Senate that would sell them out without a second thought. Somebody had to protect the president from his own worst instincts and meager negotiating skills. Somebody had to protect the Affordable Care Act from the Republicans who had vowed to repeal it. Somebody had to protect Medicare and Social Security and all the other Democratic accomplishments of the last century from being negotiated away.

Without her, her allies implored, the party might fall apart. And without her, there would be no women at the leadership table. And so this was the moment Pelosi decided. She would not be someone who took one shot and then quit. She would be someone who stayed and fought. She would be a survivor. It was, she joked, using President Bush's old jargon for religious outreach, a "faith-based initiative."

And yet, even for the worst job in Washington, she would have to fight.

✧ ✧ ✧

On Friday, three days after the election, Pelosi sent a letter to the caucus announcing that she intended to stay on as leader of the Democratic minority. "As a result of Tuesday's election, the role of Democrats in the

112th Congress will change, but our commitment to serving the American people will not," she wrote. "We have no intention of allowing our great achievements to be rolled back."

Opinion leaders were aghast. Democrats, they said, were clearly failing to heed the message the voters had sent. "Sacrificing the unpopular Mrs. Pelosi," sniffed the *Wall Street Journal*, "might stand as a down payment on winning back the trust of the independent and suburban voters who fled Democrats this year." Hoyer considered running against her for leader, but stood down when his advisers concluded he couldn't beat her. Instead, Shuler announced he would run. He didn't think Pelosi should go unchallenged, and he still hoped he might convince her to step aside. He knew he probably couldn't get enough votes to beat her, but he suspected there was more angst brewing than his colleagues were willing to admit publicly.

Swing district Democrats bruised by the barrage of anti-Pelosi ads were similarly vexed—though many had been defeated and thus no longer had a vote in the caucus. "Nancy Pelosi was the face that defeated sixty-plus members," groused Allen Boyd of Florida, a conservative Democrat who'd lost his seat in the wave. Obama was noncommittal, issuing a statement from a spokesman: "The White House does not comment or get involved in leadership elections," it said. "But as the president has said before, he appreciates the work of the Speaker and the entire House Democratic leadership team who have been great partners in moving the country forward."

Pelosi's decision to stay was also news to Hoyer, whom she did not alert beforehand—and who would now have to run against Clyburn for the next post down, minority whip, or get squeezed out. For all that both Pelosi and Hoyer touted their cordial and productive partnership, she never seemed to miss a chance to make him sweat. (Some even wondered whether blocking Hoyer from becoming Speaker was part of the reason she chose to stay.) It soon became clear, however, that Hoyer had the votes to beat Clyburn easily, which was a problem in its own right. If Pelosi let that happen, Clyburn would be ousted from leadership, and Pelosi risked a backlash from the Congressional Black Caucus that could put her own position in peril. She brokered a deal that created a new position of "assistant leader" for Clyburn, allowing him to remain number three.

On November 17, two weeks after the election, the Democrats filed into the Capitol basement for another leadership election. The room had a funereal air. The dozens of members who'd lost their elections milled around the hallways outside like aimless ghosts. Pelosi rose to speak. She told those in attendance how she'd once led them out of the minority, and pledged to do it again. Her supporters pointed out her strength as a fundraiser and the unfairness of the attacks against her, and her ability to stand up to the White House, which they argued would sell out Congress even more without a strong leader to stick up for them.

"How can we fold on this woman," said Mike Doyle of Pennsylvania, "when she is not folding on us?"

In the vote of the Democratic caucus, they made Pelosi their leader again by a vote of 150–43. Then, in January, when the new Congress convened to elect the Speaker in the customary roll call vote on the floor, 19 Democrats didn't vote for Pelosi—the largest defection from a caucus leader since the Republican Speaker vote of 1923 went to nine ballots.

Pelosi smiled her frozen smile and held her head high as she handed the gavel to Speaker John Boehner, who kissed her on the cheek and wept.

✦ ✦ ✦

The new Congress opened on a tragic note. On January 8, 2011, Gabrielle Giffords, a moderate Democratic congresswoman from Arizona, was meeting with constituents in the parking lot of a Safeway in suburban Tucson when a gunman opened fire. First, he aimed point-blank at Giffords, shooting her in the head. Then he began firing indiscriminately. In the end, six people were killed, and Giffords was left in critical condition.

The shooting put Congress on edge and struck many as the tragic result of a toxic political climate, though it turned out that the shooter had no apparent political agenda beyond a deranged obsession with Giffords. House votes were suspended for a week, and Pelosi flew to Tucson. She was at Giffords's bedside when, four days later, the congresswoman opened her eyes for the first time after the shooting.

The top item on the new Republican majority's legislative agenda was fulfilling their campaign pledge to repeal the Affordable Care Act. A week before the election, Boehner boasted to Sean Hannity, "We're going to do everything—and I mean everything—we can do to kill it, stop it, slow it down." But any such effort would be an uphill battle considering that the Democratic president who considered the health care law his signature accomplishment was still in the White House, and Democrats still controlled the Senate.

The Republicans introduced Obamacare repeal on the first day of the session. They called their effort the "Repealing the Job-Killing Health Care Law Act," and the GOP voted for it unanimously. Pelosi knew better than to take for granted that these efforts would fail. Democrats might not vote for this kind of clumsy total repeal, but some in the caucus might be tempted by cleverer bills that rolled back only the more unpopular parts of the law, or Trojan horse GOP efforts to "improve" it. Over the coming years, there would be dozens of stealth attacks on the law by the GOP, and a major part of Pelosi's job would be spotting them, warning members that they were actually attempts to gut Obamacare, and keeping her flock in line against such bills.

But in 2011, the main drama on Capitol Hill was about dollars and cents.

It began even before the new Congress convened in January, during the December lame-duck session, when Pelosi was still Speaker. George W. Bush's tax cuts were set to expire at the end of the year. Democrats didn't want to see taxes go up on middle-class and low-income taxpayers, especially with the economy still mired in recession. And Republicans and their allies in Big Business didn't want the top rates to expire. For two years, Pelosi had urged the Obama administration to let Congress pass a permanent fix: given that all the tax rates would go up if they did nothing, the issue provided leverage to make Republicans come to the table and negotiate a deal, perhaps on a jobs bill. But the White House passed up the opportunity.

Now, in the wake of the midterm drubbing, with Congress in a December lame-duck session, the White House was eager to show it would be able to work with the new Republican majority. In early December, Vice President Joe Biden summoned Pelosi and her top deputies, including Chris Van Hollen, the top Democrat on the Budget Committee, to the White House's Roosevelt Room. There he presented them with a fait accompli: a deal Biden had worked out with Senate Republican leader Mitch McConnell that would extend all the Bush tax cuts, even those for the richest of the rich, for two years.

"I thought I was going to be at the table," Van Hollen protested. "We weren't at the table." Pelosi icily told Biden that if the administration wanted House Democrats to vote for his deal, he'd have to come to the caucus and sell it himself. Just then, Obama ducked into the room. Not to worry, he assured them—this was the last time he would compromise on taxes. But the lame-duck fiscal talks proved to be a sign of things to come under GOP rule.

There was something else Pelosi had been pushing for all year and wanted to get done now: repeal of "Don't Ask, Don't Tell," the ban on gays serving openly in the military. Obama had promised it in his State of the Union address, and Pelosi's House had put the repeal measure in the annual bill that funded the Pentagon back in May. What happened next was a source of great private amusement to Pelosi. The far-left antiwar flank of the Democratic caucus prided themselves on never voting for a defense bill, their protest against wars they opposed and a military-industrial complex they considered bloated and unaccountable. But this time, Pelosi informed them, in the name of LGBT rights, they were going to vote for a defense bill. No, the liberals insisted, the Republicans would carry the military funding bill, just like they always did. "Just watch," Pelosi said.

Sure enough, the very same Republicans who'd spent so many years portraying antiwar Democrats as unsupportive of the military now refused to vote to fund the Pentagon if it meant allowing gay men and women to serve. All but 9 GOP members voted against the funding bill. And many of the antiwar Democrats—Barney Frank, John Lewis, Anna Eshoo and other "100 percenters," as Pelosi thought of them—dutifully voted for it.

That was back in May. But the funding bill had gotten bottled up along with the rest of the budget. Gay rights activists had started confronting Obama publicly for failing to keep his promise. Now, in the post-election lame duck, the repeal finally passed. Pelosi signed it, surrounded by a few of the fourteen thousand soldiers who'd been discharged for being gay. Then she led the group in a chorus of "God Bless America."

✧ ✧ ✧

When budget talks got under way in January, Pelosi and her caucus were largely cut out again. Instead, the White House and Senate Democrats met with Boehner and the House GOP. They maintained that this was not a ploy to exclude Pelosi, noting that the Senate minority leader, McConnell, was also not included. But that was just an excuse: in fact, some in the administration thought compromise would be easier without Pelosi, with her reputation for rigid partisanship. While Obama himself always respected her, some of the "Obama bros," his arrogant young political aides, were dismissive. Behind her back, they called her "Nasty P."

But without Pelosi, the talks weren't going particularly well.

Of the 242 Republicans in the House, 87, fully one-third, were freshmen, many with no government background. This was a point of pride: they'd run against Washington, business as usual and the "career politicians" who were supposedly the cause of everyone's problems. They'd gotten elected thanks to the inspiration and furious energy of the Tea Party: one representative example was a pizzeria owner from northwest Illinois who'd been inspired to run by a Glenn Beck monologue and took out a Democratic incumbent by 10 points. Depending on your perspective, the freshmen were either a band of brave, patriotic citizen legislators or a bunch of angry amateurs with no clue, and seemingly no interest in, how Congress actually worked.

Boehner had figured the rowdy freshmen would settle down and learn the ropes once they got to Washington, just like he once had. Similarly, the Democratic Senate and president expected the GOP, with control of a mere half of the legislative branch, to negotiate and compromise like normal legislators in a normal lawmaking body.

As both Obama and Boehner would soon discover, to their shared chagrin, these were not normal legislators.

The new GOPers believed the Tea Party had sent them to Washington to slash government spending and reduce the budget deficit—and not to compromise. Boehner seemed powerless to placate them. Even bills he thought would be no-brainers, such as an extension of the Patriot Act, drew right-wing rebellions. Boehner's whip, Kevin McCarthy, hadn't even bothered to whip the Patriot Act renewal vote, because he didn't think he needed to—and then it was defeated in a floor vote. A failed floor vote was considered humiliating: no self-respecting leader would bring up legislation for which the votes weren't a sure thing. In her four years as Speaker, Pelosi had never lost a major floor vote except for TARP—an episode of Republican brinkmanship that, four years later, looked like a portent. Her skill at counting votes might have made getting bills through the House look inevitable for the majority. Boehner's Republicans would soon flamboyantly demonstrate that it was anything but.

In the session's first few months, Congress twice had to pass last-minute two- or three-week "continuing resolutions," authorizing agencies to maintain basically their current funding levels, to buy more time to come up with a budget agreement. The Tea Partiers kept threatening to shut down the government if they didn't get the spending cuts they demanded. Finally, at 10 p.m. on a Friday in April, with two hours to go until the nation's parks, food inspections, and cancer drug trials would start shutting down, the negotiators reached agreement. The package contained $38 billion in cuts the Democrats found painful. But it didn't go far enough for right-wing House Republicans. Boehner had to beg his caucus to support it—and, tellingly, the only thing that swayed them was when he recounted in exaggerated detail how mad he'd made Obama in their meetings.

When the spending bill finally came to the floor, 59 Republicans voted against it, as did Pelosi. It passed only because 81 Democrats voted for it.

This was the opening Pelosi had been watching and waiting for: a clear sign that Boehner couldn't control his own people. He couldn't even control his second-in-command, Eric Cantor, the majority leader, who had his eye on the speakership and was undercutting Boehner behind his back. The top two Republicans' relationship made Pelosi's strained partnership with Hoyer look like a love story for the ages. If Boehner couldn't keep his caucus together, it meant that, to get to 218, he needed Democrats—Pelosi's Democrats. That meant she had *leverage*.

Next time, if Boehner wanted her votes, he was going to have to go through her. Next time, she was going to get something in return.

❖ ❖ ❖

The Republicans had grander plans than grubby little short-term budget deals. These plans were personified by Paul Ryan, the chairman of the House Budget Committee.

Since arriving in Congress in 1999, Ryan, a doctrinaire Wisconsinite with a doleful gaze, had styled himself a policy wonk. Starting in 2008, he had drafted his own alternative budget proposals, portraying them as the lodestar of fiscal conservatism. Critics contended that they were gimmicky and vague, relying on technical sleight of hand to conjure unrealistic economic scenarios. But on one point the budgets were clear: Ryan was determined to solve the long-term insolvency of entitlement programs, primarily by turning Medicare into a voucher program.

Initially, Ryan's proposals were viewed as extreme and politically radioactive even by many Republicans, and they got nowhere. Newt Gingrich derided them as "right-wing social engineering." But by 2011, they had entered the GOP mainstream. Obama, who still cherished the dream of an opposition substantive enough to join in a real policy debate, praised Ryan's plans as "serious." In April 2011, the House Republicans passed the Ryan budget as a statement of their philosophical orientation.

At that moment, a special election was under way in upstate New York to replace a married Republican congressman who'd resigned after sending a shirtless photo to a woman he met on Craigslist. The seat should have been a slam dunk for Republicans, but their preferred candidate had to contend with a Tea Party radical running on a third-party ticket. Then Democrats went on the attack with the Ryan budget as their ammunition, charging that a vote for the GOP candidate was a vote to "end Medicare as we know it." Republicans countered, naturally, with ads showing Pelosi as a puppet master. But in a result that shocked Washington, the Democratic candidate won the seat.

To Democrats, it seemed that, in voting for the Ryan budget, the GOP had signed its own political death warrant. The 2012 election, Pelosi proclaimed, would be about one thing: "Medicare, Medicare, Medicare." In a caucus meeting, the new Democratic campaign committee chairman, Steve Israel, gleefully staged a showing of all the Republican ads from 2010 promising to protect Medicare. By exploiting Republican divisions and promising to protect seniors, Democrats believed they finally had a message that could win back the House and keep Obama in the White House: not with the poetry of hope and change, but with the cold hard prose of "Don't let them take this away from you."

Little did they know that behind the scenes Obama was already working to complicate that narrative.

◇ ◇ ◇

Obama and Boehner got along well personally. Each saw in the other a recognizable type: to Obama, Boehner was the kind of country-club Republican he'd dealt with in the Illinois Statehouse; to Boehner, Obama was your average uptight liberal know-it-all. Nothing better epitomized the contrast between the two men than a meeting at which Boehner had a cigarette and a Merlot while Obama drank iced tea and chomped Nicorette. But Boehner didn't share his party's derangement over the African American president. He endured a raft of angry calls and letters after he pooh-poohed birtherism on television, and another round of hate mail when, in June, he played golf with Obama.

At that golf game, Boehner and Obama teamed up to beat Vice President Biden and Ohio governor John Kasich, then had a beer at the clubhouse. The president and the Speaker hit it off well enough to want to keep talking. In August, the nation's credit limit, known as the debt ceiling, would need to be raised. This was a formality to allow for the borrowing of money Congress had already authorized to be spent, but nonetheless, the debt ceiling was inevitably a political football. The party out of power would often vote against it and use the occasion to grandstand about fiscal responsibility—Obama, as a senator when Bush was president, had done exactly that.

Pelosi had warned Obama that Republicans were not going to vote to raise the debt ceiling, and had urged him to get it done in the December lame-duck session. America's creditworthiness was too important to use as a bargaining chip, she said, and the president agreed. But Obama thought the very seriousness of the issue would bring the GOP to the table. He believed the party of fiscal responsibility would never allow the nation to default on its debt.

Obama and Boehner began hatching a secret plan. The debt hike, they thought, could be the occasion for a much bigger deal, a "Grand Bargain" to solve the nation's fiscal challenges. With the annual deficit north of one trillion dollars, virtually all of Washington agreed that something had to be done to balance the country's books. (A few liberals argued that that should wait until the economy was in better shape, or that the main thing wrong with the federal bottom line was not enough revenue—but they were largely ignored.) What if, the two men wondered, they could reach the kind of big, history-making agreement Ronald Reagan had made with Tip O'Neill? In a single stroke, they could solve one of America's biggest long-term problems. Perhaps even more important, they could prove that bipartisan cooperation was still possible, restoring trust in government and bringing sanity back to a toxic and gridlocked Washington.

Each side would have to slay one of its most sacred cows: Democrats would have to agree to reform entitlements, and Republicans would have to agree to increase taxes. Each man knew his party would pitch a fit, so the talks were kept secret for weeks, as staffers for the president and Speaker Boehner swapped memos full of figures. As they neared a preliminary agreement, in early July, they prepared to present the proposals to their parties.

But word leaked out ahead of time, and Democrats were predictably incensed to discover that the White House had put entitlements on the chopping block. On the eve of the Democratic leaders' meeting at the White House, Pelosi's caucus erupted. In the closed-door meeting, she let them vent for a while. Then she took the microphone for a speech that was more rousing than usual. "I want to let you know," she said, "that we stand for Medicare, and we stand for Social Security. And tomorrow I'm going down to the White House to represent you to the president. And so, I would just like to know, do I have your permission to go over there and say, 'We're not cutting Medicare, we're not cutting Social Security'?" The caucus meeting ended in cheers.

Pelosi said one other thing to the enraged Democrats, whose indignant quotes were already starting to appear in the press. "Say whatever you want about this deal," she said. "It's terrible, it's a disgrace. You get me more leverage by complaining about it. But don't say you're not going to vote for it. Because you just don't know."

At the White House meeting, Pelosi and Harry Reid both complained about being shut out of the negotiations. You're going to need our votes, Pelosi reminded Obama's budget director, Jack Lew. No matter what they say, the Republicans are not going to raise the debt ceiling. When Lew protested that the leaders were negotiating in good faith, Pelosi said, "Don't insult us. You guys don't know how to count." While the White House and Boehner futzed with billion-dollar line items, the number she cared about was the same as ever: how many votes do you have for this? For Boehner, she was confident it was fewer than 218.

The White House, Pelosi said, shouldn't take for granted that the Democrats would be there to pick up the slack without getting anything in return. "You better make sure that you—we—use the leverage," she said. "If you're going to ask for House Democrats to put the vote over the top, we want to make sure that our concerns are more fairly reflected." She insisted that any deal could not include cuts to Medicare benefits, though it could, as with the Affordable Care Act, tinker with the cost of the program in other ways.

At the same time, in a subsequent meeting with Obama, she made it clear that if he needed her, she would be there, even if it meant agreeing to entitlement cuts. For all the talk of Pelosi's inflexibility, she wasn't the one drawing lines in the sand; it was the Republicans who kept walking away from the table. She was forceful in front of the cameras—at one point, she held up a penny at a press conference to rail against Republicans for proposing "not one red cent" in taxes on the wealthy—but behind the scenes, she surprised White House officials with her willingness to deal. This, to her, was how negotiation was supposed to work: make your values and your position clear to the public and your caucus, get the other side to do the same, and then put the rhetoric aside, get together in private, work out the numbers and meet in the middle. You couldn't negotiate, as the president was trying to do, by pretending to agree with the other side, pretending *you* were actually in the middle. And you couldn't negotiate by making all your concessions up front.

With nobody counting votes, Pelosi knew that this was not a serious negotiation. Republicans, she saw, were just going through the motions, trying to get to "no" and blame it on the president when the deal fell apart.

Within a couple of weeks, that was exactly what happened. Rather than respond to Obama's last offer, the Speaker of the House disappeared. He then refused to return multiple calls from the president of the United States for a day and a half. Finally, he publicly announced that there was no deal to be had.

Each side blamed the other for the talks falling apart. They disagree to this day over whether it was Obama's fault for demanding more revenue at the last minute, or Boehner's for walking away from the table. Pelosi took the White House's side, but to her it didn't really matter; even if they'd made a deal, Boehner never could have gotten the votes from his caucus to pass it. "These people come to the table, they want it all their way," she vented to a colleague. "And then they can't provide two hundred eighteen?" To her, nothing they'd been discussing was real, because nobody was counting votes.

And so, on the eve of a national default that could have shaken the markets and sent the still-fragile economy into a new spiral, Congress took over the talks. (Obama called the situation a "crisis that Washington imposed on the rest of America," again blaming all of Congress rather than Republican intransigence.) The solution the congressional leaders came up with wasn't pretty: no entitlement reform, no new revenue, but the formation of a bipartisan "supercommittee" that would have ten weeks to come up with more than a trillion dollars in cuts and revenue. Failure to do so would trigger automatic across-the-board cuts to the entire federal budget. Pelosi, now at the table, secured some important concessions: the trigger would hit defense spending just as hard as domestic spending, and there would be no changes to Social Security, Medicare or Medicaid.

On August 1, Pelosi urged her caucus to vote for the deal even though they justly hated it. Congressman Emanuel Cleaver, a pastor from Kansas City, called it a "sugar-coated Satan sandwich." On the House floor, Pelosi said, "I urge you to consider voting yes, but I completely respect the hesitation that members have about this." She couldn't resist a shot at Boehner, who had, like her, been laboring to convince his people it was the best deal they could get: "I hear that our Republican colleagues have said they got ninety-eight percent of what they want in the bill," she said. "I hope that their votes reflect that."

Then a dramatic moment occurred: Gabby Giffords, missing from Congress since the assassination attempt that had left her with a severe brain injury, came to the House floor to cast her vote for the bill, earning a standing ovation from both sides of the aisle. The bill passed with 95 Democratic votes.

As they were leaving the floor, Pelosi's California colleague Dennis Cardoza confided, "Madam Speaker, the president of the United States is the worst negotiator who has ever owned that title!" Then he thought better of such possible hyperbole: "I mean, I didn't know Millard Fillmore. But he's the worst."

"Yeah," Pelosi said, "but he doesn't think so."

22

Obama and Boehner had hoped to make their Grand Bargain to show the public that Washington could work again. Their failure had starkly illustrated the opposite: a country in the midst of a crisis of governing.

The same day Congress narrowly avoided default, the Dow Jones average dropped 266 points, and a few days later, Standard & Poor's downgraded the United States' credit for the first time in history. Congress's approval rating, which had been declining for years, hit single digits; it was less popular, according to one poll, than root canals, traffic jams or head lice.

One might have expected everyone involved to emerge from the debt ceiling fiasco chastened. But far from a learning experience, the episode was a preview of the pattern that would define the remainder of the Obama presidency: a *Groundhog Day* cycle of crisis, featuring marginalized Democrats, recalcitrant Republicans, a White House unwilling or unable to strategize around them, and a government that could barely keep the lights on, much less solve any of the nation's pressing problems. Another recurring feature of this depressing cycle: Pelosi, the one leader with a track record of successfully working across the aisle and compromising, was still routinely cast aside. When she was able to force her way into the room, problems generally got solved. But it didn't seem to occur to the men in charge to invite her into the room the next time.

Lather, rinse, repeat. The debt ceiling debacle had occurred in August 2011. By mid-September, it was time for another government-funding bill. Pelosi thought what Republicans were proposing was too stingy, and she came out against it. But Boehner thought he had the votes, and he put it on the floor. Forty-eight Republicans joined the Democrats in voting against it, and it failed. At the Republicans' next party caucus meeting, Boehner simply crossed his arms and stared at his members. "Now what?" he said—a shocking admission of how totally he was at the mercy of a caucus he couldn't control. It was hard to imagine Pelosi ever putting herself in that position.

Pelosi kept prodding Obama to be more aggressive. She wanted him to take the gloves off and fight for what Democrats believed in. Exasperated by the failed negotiations and with his own reelection campaign on the horizon, the president finally seemed to be listening. His speeches increasingly invoked FDR and struck populist economic tones, attacking Republicans as the party of Big Business and the rich. He started talking less about changing Washington and more about raising taxes on millionaires and protecting Medicare and Social Security.

Launching his reelection campaign, Obama made the House Republicans and the Ryan budget the focus of his argument that his opposition was dangerously extreme. One liberal group made an ad showing a Paul Ryan look-alike pushing a wheelchair-bound grandma off a cliff. The Republicans played into this narrative when they nominated Mitt Romney, a multimillionaire financier, as Obama's opponent. And then Romney picked Paul Ryan as his vice presidential nominee. "Governor Romney chose the architect of the destruction of Medicare for his running mate," Pelosi crowed.

Obama also started to ease up on blaming all of Congress, rather than just Republicans, for problems rooted on one side of the aisle. When someone asked him what he would say to "Americans who just want both sides to stop fighting," the president answered, "There is oftentimes the impulse to suggest that if the two parties are disagreeing, then they're equally at fault and the truth lies somewhere in the middle. And an equivalence is presented, which reinforces, I think, people's cynicism about Washington generally. This is not one of those situations where there is an equivalence."

Pelosi projected confidence about the prospect of taking back the House—and becoming Speaker again—in 2012. But it soon became clear that this was unlikely. One reason was the map: Republicans' 2010 landslide had perfectly coincided with the Census, which in most states triggered a decennial redistricting process. The GOP in 2010 had won not just the House of Representatives but also hundreds of down-ballot elections at the state and local levels, and Republican governors and state legislatures used those victories to gerrymander their congressional maps, making it harder for Democrats to gain seats even when they got more votes. (Democrats, of course, did the same in the few states whose maps they controlled.)

Another reason for Democrats' political difficulties was the recession's lingering hangover. The economy continued to limp along, arguably in part because Democrats had shied away from pursuing more aggressive economic policies when they had the chance. Unemployment was still over 8 percent, and 70 percent of Americans thought the country was on the wrong track. Wall Street, however, had made a terrific comeback, and no major bankers had ever been prosecuted for causing the financial crisis. Anger pervaded the electorate, expressed in both the right-wing Tea Party and the left-wing Occupy Wall Street movement.

Some blamed Pelosi for her party's difficult prospects. When Heath Shuler, her star recruit turned critic, and other conservative Democrats decided to retire, they cited Pelosi as part of the reason, saying she was too big an electoral liability for them to overcome. The Supreme Court upheld Obamacare, but the legislation that represented Pelosi's and Obama's greatest achievement was still dismally unpopular and seen as a political millstone—only a third of Americans viewed it favorably. Pelosi still firmly believed that the law, many of whose provisions had yet to go into effect, was a major improvement that had changed the country for the better. But as health care costs continued to rise, the public blamed the Democrats for everything they still disliked about the system.

Obama, still beloved by the Democratic base and well-liked by swing voters, was an asset for the Democrats. But he was necessarily focused on his reelection fight. His campaign hoarded its resources and refused to contribute anything to the congressional campaign committees. Pelosi was understanding to a point. She wanted only one favor. In May, she would celebrate twenty-five years in Congress with a weeklong festival from New York to San Francisco, including public events, lavish fund-raisers, concerts with Bono and members of the Grateful Dead, and the naming of a street in Golden Gate Park in her honor. (Pelosi viewed it all with amusement: "I've exploited it to the hilt," she joked to reporters. "We've got music, we've got streets, we've got bridges. Very immodest.") An appearance from Obama was the only thing she asked from his reelection campaign. "After all I've done for you," she pleaded with his top campaign strategists. But they refused. Her toxic image might hurt him politically. She tried to call the president to take it up with him personally, but he didn't call her back.

✧ ✧ ✧

In November, Obama won reelection, not with the soaring themes of 2008 but with an unlovely tactical slog. Democrats barely held on to the Senate. Democratic House candidates got 1.4 million more votes than Republicans, but the party fell short of the majority, gaining just 8 seats.

As difficult and unexpected as Pelosi's decision not to retire in 2010 had been, after the 2012 election it was, in a way, even more wrenching. In 2010 she could tell herself she was only committing to two years in the minority. In 2012 she had to accept that she was probably signing up for four more years in that thankless position: anything could happen, but history suggested the 2014 midterms would not be kind to the president's party.

They were not likely to be fun years. A divided government that could barely keep its own doors open was probably not going to engage in any bold liberal policymaking. Obama had been criticized for biting off too much in his first two years, when he had Democratic majorities, but it was now apparent that those two years would be responsible for virtually all the legislative accomplishments of his presidency. In retrospect, they had left so much on the table. The 2009 cap-and-trade bill Pelosi had pushed was dismissed by environmentalists at the time for not going far enough. Now it looked like a distant dream, and climate change kept getting worse. The same could be said for all the other progressive legislation Pelosi had passed only to see it die in the Senate: card check for unions, the DREAM Act for young immigrants, antidiscrimination legislation for gays and lesbians.

The Congress in which Pelosi was signing up to serve another term was clearly destined for only more gridlock and conflict. Some of it could be attributed to a divided nation, with two parties that represented honest disagreements about issues. But there were plenty of issues where bipartisanship might have been possible if Republicans weren't simply determined not to let the Democrats win anything. There were Republicans who supported immigration reform, gun control, tax reform, and campaign finance legislation. But Boehner feared a right-wing rebellion if he allowed votes on any such measures, and his Senate counterpart, Mitch McConnell, had vowed to stymie Obama's agenda at every turn. Even issues that hadn't traditionally been partisan were now mired in legislative conflict: infrastructure funding, farm subsidies, the expansion of a Georgia port. Republicans blocked reauthorization of legislation that had previously been renewed unanimously, such as the Voting Rights Act and the Violence Against Women Act. Pelosi had been trying to convince Obama from the beginning that the GOP was simply not interested in compromise. Belatedly, he began to see that she was right.

Pelosi was an institutionalist who believed in Congress's ability to make people's lives better. She was a liberal pragmatist who believed bipartisanship was possible, if not necessarily a virtue in its own right. Practically alone among the congressional leaders, she could point to a record of making Congress work in the post-Gingrich age of polarization and institutional collapse. But the commentators who bemoaned the death of bipartisanship and the lack of strong leadership in Washington seemed incapable of recognizing the example of competence that stood right in front of their noses. Pelosi, who had brushed off the attacks on her as a distraction, now couldn't shake the public perception that she was part of the problem in Washington. The caricature that launched a thousand attack ads, the shrill partisan with extreme views, had taken hold.

Increasingly, at seventy-two, she was also viewed as a relic of the past and an obstacle to the Democratic Party's future. When a twenty-seven-year-old television reporter asked whether she'd thought about stepping aside in favor of "fresh blood," Pelosi's frustration bubbled over. "You always ask that question, except to Mitch McConnell," she said. The Senate Republican leader was only two years younger than she was. "So, you're suggesting that everybody over seventy step aside?"

She wasn't finished. "Let's, for a moment, honor it as a legitimate question, although it's quite offensive, but you don't realize it, I guess," she said. "You have to take off about fourteen years from me because I was home raising a family, getting the best experience of all in diplomacy, interpersonal skills." Her defensive response would do nothing to quiet the rumblings that she'd had her time and was stopping Democrats from turning the page.

Pelosi stayed. "I'm not here on a shift, I'm here on a mission," she liked to say. In the caucus elections, she was unopposed.

Within a few weeks, in the December 2012 lame-duck session, she was again getting the better of Boehner in another fiscal fight where he couldn't come up with a solution that would satisfy the conservatives in his caucus. Once again, Boehner's plans fell apart on the floor. In a Republican caucus meeting, announcing near tears that he didn't have the votes he needed, Boehner recited a prayer often used in twelve-step programs: "Lord, grant me the serenity to accept the things I cannot change, the courage to change the things I can, and the wisdom to know the difference." Once again, he needed Democratic votes to get to 218, forcing him to make concessions to Pelosi.

The same commentariat that was endlessly dismissive of Pelosi seemed to have bottomless sympathy for Boehner's plight, viewing him as the honorable victim of an intractable right wing he was powerless to appease. It was true he was in a pickle: if he cast aside the right-wingers and started openly dealing with the Democrats, he ran the risk of being deposed as Speaker. But Pelosi, when asked about Boehner's struggles at a press conference, had little patience for this perspective. "That's what we all take the job to do—to risk something, not just sit in office," she said.

When Bush wouldn't back down on Iraq, she noted, she'd stopped her more extreme faction from doing something irresponsible, even though she sympathized with them. "Do you know what it was like for me to bring a bill to the floor to fund the war in Iraq that was predicated on a misrepresentation to the American people?" she said. "It was very unpopular, and I have to tell you, I'm not sure I ever recovered amongst some on the left for that." But she'd found a procedural solution by splitting the funding bills in two so that Democrats could vote for the domestic spending but not the war, and Republicans could vote for the war funding but not the domestic spending.

"So, is the point that you don't want to put your members on the spot?" she said of Boehner's dilemma. "Figure it out. We did. Figure it out."

✧ ✧ ✧

Obama still pined for bipartisanship. Perhaps, he thought, his reelection would finally teach Republicans a lesson. Before the election, they might have thought that by blocking him at every turn, they could scuff his postpartisan sheen, make him seem ineffective and weak, and win back the White House. But the election proved that obstruction wasn't helping

Republicans politically. Maybe now the GOP, which was going through its own dazed reckoning with political failure, would decide to try something new: compromise. "We can break this fever," Obama said during the campaign, and make Republicans return to "common sense."

It did not take long to learn that this hope was misplaced. In December, a gunman killed twenty elementary schoolers and six adults in Newtown, Connecticut, shocking the nation, bringing the president to tears and spurring a bipartisan group of lawmakers to try to put together a modest package of gun control measures. The legislation failed. In March, the Republican National Committee released a report concluding that the party needed to back immigration reform to regain the presidency, giving a boost to bipartisan efforts to pass a major immigration bill. That failed, too.

Rather than wake from its fever dream, the GOP only seemed to sink deeper into nihilism. House Republican investigators chased phony scandals involving a 2012 terrorist attack in Benghazi, Libya, and the botched 2010 "Fast and Furious" gun-trafficking investigation. They voted to hold the attorney general in contempt of Congress for only partially complying with investigators' record requests, the first such charge against a sitting Cabinet member in history. House Republicans refused even to send negotiators to conference with the Senate on funding legislation, for fear that such talks might lead to a compromise.

And they kept trying to repeal Obamacare. Against all evidence, the right still thought it could somehow get rid of the Affordable Care Act while Obama remained in office. Without Pelosi, they might have had more success. In July 2013, dozens of House Democrats joined Republicans to pass a bill delaying the legislation's mandates on employers and individuals. The bill died in the Senate, but Pelosi was furious at her members' defection, which sent the message that there were cracks in her party's determination to defend the law. The defectors were sternly admonished not to do it again.

The Obamacare opponents seized on a new gambit. September 30, 2013, was the next government-funding deadline. What if Republicans refused to fund the health care law? Right-wing pressure groups and talk radio, bolstered by Tea Party politicians such as the newly elected senator Ted Cruz, hyped the idea. If the House defunded Obamacare, they argued, it would put pressure on the Senate, eventually forcing swing state

Democrats to go along. Obamacare was still standing, they contended, only because Republicans weren't fighting hard enough to destroy it.

This was a delusional argument, and Boehner knew it. But the right-wingers didn't believe him when he told them that. If he didn't let them get their way, they might throw him out of the speakership. Pelosi sympathized, in a way, with Boehner's plight. She certainly didn't agree with repealing the health care law. But she'd been in a version of his position when she was up against Bush, trying to keep the Democrats' campaign promise to voters to end the war even though they lacked the power to make the Republican president reverse the centerpiece of his foreign policy. In a private letter to Boehner, Pelosi outlined the strategy she'd used—the escalating series of votes, the wire-thin middle ground she'd tried to find between putting pressure on war funding and not abandoning the troops in the field. She had failed to stop the war, of course. But she'd succeeded in keeping the Democrats from falling apart. Now, she suggested to him, he could do the same with health care—placate the right wing with a series of show votes, knowing Obama would never sign a repeal of his biggest accomplishment. The letter was a remarkable gesture: one party's leader offering strategic advice to her political opponent to prevent an outcome that would damage the country.

To avoid a shutdown, Pelosi also offered to work with Boehner to come up with a budget bill that Democrats and moderate Republicans could team up to support. She met with Boehner to try to understand what she was going to have to do to make it happen. But when she asked him how many Democratic votes he thought he would need from her, he didn't answer. "Two hundred?" she said. "I'll give you two hundred votes." But again Boehner was silent. He had decided there was only one way to prove to the hard right that their idea wouldn't work, and that was to show them. When the House wouldn't pass a government-funding bill that included health care funding, parts of the government ran out of money and had to close.

The shutdown went on for sixteen days. Trash piled up in national parks, and government workers went without paychecks. Republicans' approval ratings plummeted, just as they had during Gingrich's shutdowns in the mid-1990s. Pelosi knew what Boehner was trying to do, to make his extremists learn the consequences of their actions, but she still professed shock that Republicans would allow their internal divisions to cause such havoc to the government and the economy. "This is really very serious," she said. "My Republican colleagues, this is the major leagues." It was, she said, "beneath the dignity of what we come here to do, unless what you came here to do was shut down government." Through it all, the Democrats, at Pelosi's insistence, stuck together. Pelosi had left town before the shutdown began to celebrate her fiftieth wedding anniversary with Paul. A week later, she called in to a caucus meeting from their anniversary party.

After two and a half weeks of shutdown, with another debt ceiling hike on the horizon, the Republicans surrendered. Independent analysts estimated the shutdown cost the economy $24 billion. One Republican congressman likened his colleagues to "lemmings in suicide vests" whose self-defeating actions "basically empower Nancy Pelosi." Their antics had gained them nothing: the bill that Boehner put on the floor to end the shutdown was *less* favorable to the GOP than the deal they'd been offered before they shut down the government. It passed with mostly Democratic votes.

The shutdown coincided with the opening of Obamacare's national online health care marketplace. The law had directed states to create their own "exchanges" like Massachusetts', where individuals without employer coverage could shop for insurance from competing private carriers. Many states, especially red states whose leaders opposed the law, declined to do so, and the federal government was supposed to create a marketplace for people to turn to instead. But when it opened, healthcare.gov was a disaster, crashing and glitching and leaving customers in the lurch.

Some Democrats were grateful that the Republicans' political catastrophe, the shutdown, had largely eclipsed their own debacle—a perfect proof point for the GOP's contention that government can't be trusted to solve problems better than the market. The shutdown's political aftershocks even prompted some to hope that Democrats could defy history and do well in 2014.

But most could see that this remained unlikely. With little hope for Democrats on the horizon, some longtime lawmakers decided they'd had enough—including some of Pelosi's closest friends. In January 2013, both George Miller, her right-hand man, and Henry Waxman, the legislative wizard who'd steered bills through the Energy and Commerce Committee, announced their retirements. It was understandable that the two veteran congressmen would want to move on after forty years in Washington. But their departures were also a symptom of how thankless their jobs had become. Serving in the House of Representatives, especially in the minority, no longer seemed to many like the noble calling of public service. Rather, it had become a job everybody hated, a frustrating, futile grind. It was as if Congress had sunk to meet the low esteem in which the public held it.

Pelosi would never admit it, but the feeling of powerlessness seemed to be wearing on her, too. In August 2014, violence in Central America led to a border crisis as thousands of underage migrants flooded the southern border, overwhelming the United States' scant resources for asylum seekers and child detainees. On the House floor, a Republican congressman, Tom Marino, accused Pelosi of not having the "strength" to solve the problem when she had the chance. "I did the research on it," Marino taunted. "You might want to try it, Madam Leader. Do the research. I did it. That's one thing you don't do."

When Marino finished speaking, Pelosi chased him across the floor, wagging a finger in his face, incensed. "You are an insignificant person!" she said repeatedly, as the presiding congressman banged the gavel and shocked colleagues pulled her away.

The midterms in November were a disaster beyond Democrats' pessimistic expectations. Obama, having belatedly realized the importance of congressional control to his legacy, went all out on the campaign trail for congressional Democrats, headlining dozens of fund-raisers. Pelosi fund-raised at her usual heroic pace. But all the campaign ads in the world couldn't remedy the sour public mood. Democrats lost 13 seats, which put them even further in the minority than they had been after 2010—the smallest Democratic minority since the Depression. Republicans also took the Senate, which gave them control of both houses of Congress for the first time since 2006. For the third time in a row, Pelosi's Democrats had failed to win the House.

❖ ❖ ❖

Pelosi insisted the 2014 election was not a "wave" but "an ebbing." But Democrats' frustrations boiled over.

On the caucus's post-election conference call, several members protested when she put most of the blame on events outside her control, such as voter suppression, which she cited as a cause of low Democratic turnout. Her explanations smacked of excuse making and denial. No one was being held accountable for failure. After three successive defeats, members wanted soul-searching and scapegoats, not exhortations to keep the faith.

"Where was the Democratic message in this campaign?" asked Jim Clyburn. "People couldn't tell you."

Pelosi was still unchallenged for Democratic leader, but Waxman's departure created an opening for the top Democratic spot on the Energy and Commerce Committee. The race was between Frank Pallone, who was third in seniority on the panel, and Anna Eshoo, who was fifth. Eshoo was one of Pelosi's closest friends—she was godmother to some of Pelosi's grandchildren, and Eshoo had run for Congress from a Bay Area district at Pelosi's urging. Pelosi pushed Eshoo's candidacy as hard as she could, issuing multiple endorsement letters on her behalf and buttonholing members in private. Even Waxman, who had left Congress in part because he was tired of Pelosi's fund-raising demands, thought Pelosi's efforts were excessive and ill-advised. Since Hoyer supported Pallone, the battle was seen as another proxy fight between the two frenemies leading the caucus. And when Pallone won, it was seen as a sign of Pelosi's diminished clout—and possibly diminished judgment.

With no Democrat willing to challenge Pelosi for leader, members who were disgruntled with her leadership had nowhere to turn. The septuagenarian troika of Pelosi, Hoyer, and Clyburn had frozen the top three positions in place for going on a decade, and there was no obvious successor to any of them. More promising junior members were giving up and moving on, like Steve Israel, who, despite his position in leadership, would soon quit politics altogether at the age of fifty-eight and become a novelist instead. Pelosi believed it was not her job to figure out who would come after her; after all, she had fought her way into leadership against the establishment's wishes. Nothing had been handed to her; why should she be expected to give a hand to anyone else? "They all have a baton in their duffel bag," she told an interviewer who asked about the next generation. "Any one of them could step forward." Perhaps, too, she calculated that anyone she groomed to succeed her could become a threat.

The issue of succession was a delicate one. Even bringing it up risked drawing Pelosi's formidable wrath. When another reporter asked her if she was thinking about stepping down, she delivered another accusatory tongue-lashing, pointing out McConnell's age and implying that the question was sexist. For good measure, she threw in the fact that she had never been on the cover of *Time* magazine, but Boehner and McConnell both had. "As a woman, it's like, is there a message here?" she said bitterly.

If some Democrats wanted to solve the succession problem, they would have to do it without Pelosi's knowledge. And so, after the 2014 debacle, Chris Van Hollen, the Maryland congressman who was Pelosi's longtime pet and protégé, began meeting in secret with a group of top Democratic members of Congress, including some of Pelosi's closest allies, to discuss the prospect of running for leader in two years. But then, in March, he got another opportunity. The senior senator from his state, Barbara Mikulski, announced her retirement, opening up a Maryland Senate seat for which he would be a top candidate.

Van Hollen was torn. He badly wanted to become Speaker of the House, but how long was he going to have to wait for Pelosi to leave? He went to Pelosi and told her he was thinking of leaving to run for Senate. She begged him to stay—but she would not give him the one thing he was seeking: some kind of indication that she was planning to step aside. Van Hollen pulled the plug on the leadership machinations and entered the Senate race instead.

It was fair to wonder whether Pelosi was becoming like the establishment she'd once challenged: powerless to cope with an adverse political climate, lacking what it took to win, stuck in old ways, preferring to cast blame rather than find a new way. She seemed brittle, tired and in denial.

Even her legislative skills seemed to be waning. In December, during the next post-election government-funding battle, Pelosi stood her ground—this time against the White House, which had come to an agreement on legislation with Boehner, McConnell and Reid. Pelosi, along with Senator Elizabeth Warren and the liberal grass roots, opposed provisions to loosen Wall Street regulations and increase campaign finance limits. She was also tired of supplying votes for Republican proposals and wanted to show Boehner he couldn't rely on Democrats to keep bailing him out just because they were too responsible to shut down the government.

To the very end, Pelosi was sure she was winning, even as the White House worked the phones to sway her members, urging them to get the battle over with so everyone could go home for Christmas. In a pre-vote caucus meeting, she excoriated Obama by name for selling out Democrats. The day of the floor vote, she said in a letter to her colleagues, "It is clear . . . that the Republicans don't have enough votes to pass" the bill. "This increases our leverage to get two offensive provisions of the bill removed."

But this time, her vaunted vote-counting ability failed her. Fifty-seven Democrats joined 162 Republicans to pass the bill over Pelosi's objections.

◇ ◇ ◇

There was nothing for Pelosi to do, in 2015, but keep on going.

Sometimes there were glimmers of hope: in March, she and Boehner worked out a deal to permanently fix a Medicare reimbursement formula, saving billions, in exchange for an extension of the Children's Health Insurance Program. Only after he and Pelosi had worked out an agreement did Boehner take the deal to his Republicans, boxing in the infuriated conservatives, who realized they were powerless to stop it. (The former Tea Partiers had rebranded themselves the Freedom Caucus, and were perpetually ineptly plotting to take Boehner down.)

The legislation passed with nearly 400 votes, and Boehner considers it his proudest achievement as Speaker, a small-bore version of the big entitlement-reform deal he and Obama had tried and failed to do before. "This is how Congress is supposed to work," Obama declared. With Pelosi at the center of the process, rather than consulted after the fact by the men who thought they knew better, something had actually gotten done, even in the toxic Congress of 2015.

Sometimes Pelosi could still be a crucial asset for the White House. In the spring, the administration neared completion on a long diplomatic process with Iran that would lift sanctions on the hostile dictatorship in exchange for a verified end of its quest for nuclear weapons. The potential agreement was highly controversial: Republicans and many Democrats joined Israel's leaders in viewing it as dangerous. It technically wasn't a treaty and didn't have to be approved by Congress, but Republicans were determined to pass a bill to stop it before it was even finished. It was up to Pelosi to round up enough Democratic support for the Iran deal to sustain a presidential veto of that legislation. It would not be easy. Of the 144 votes she would need, only 57 were initially committed to supporting the president's deal.

Recognizing that different Democrats could find different reasons to overcome their potential objections to the deal, Pelosi decided against the traditional route of drafting a single letter of support and getting members to sign on to it. Rather, she had each member who supported the deal write an individual letter, which she then collected in a binder. Working with the

White House, in the face of intense pressure from the Israeli government and the powerful U.S. Israel lobby, she won Democrats over, one by one, until there were enough of them to block a veto override. By September, she had delivered what her hometown paper the *Chronicle* called "the biggest foreign policy win of the Obama presidency." White House aides said Pelosi's support was crucial in rescuing an initiative that had drawn bipartisan skepticism.

But Pelosi couldn't always deliver for Obama. At the same time as the administration was nearing a deal with Iran, it was also wrapping up a long negotiation process on a new trade deal with Asia called the Trans-Pacific Partnership, which sought to isolate China by increasing the trading clout of its neighbors. Pelosi had a long history of ambivalence about trade: she'd regretted voting for NAFTA and had voted against other trade deals, including a Colombian pact negotiated by Obama. She'd opposed "fast track" trade negotiation authority when it was sought by Clinton in 1998 and Bush in 2002. But she was not a die-hard protectionist: she had supported other trade deals with South Korea and Panama, and generally believed that trade could be beneficial as long as it was fair and didn't compromise human rights. One former staffer described Pelosi's economic worldview as "skeptical internationalism."

The progressives in Pelosi's caucus, however, were dead set against TPP. Liberals such as Senator Elizabeth Warren called it a giveaway to multinational corporations. The anti-TPP lawmakers decided they could stop the deal. Pelosi warned the White House she doubted the votes would be there. But the administration was determined, and she was loyal. In deference to the president, she didn't take a position for or against the legislation and facilitated Obama's outreach to the caucus. On the day of the vote, Obama made his first visit in two years to a Democratic caucus meeting.

Outside the capital, a populist wind was blowing, and the trade deal had become a flash point for both parties. Donald Trump, the entertainer and businessman who'd become the unlikely front-runner for the Republican nomination, was campaigning passionately against it, casting it as an example of Obama's weakness. Bernie Sanders, the leftist senator making an insurgent bid for the Democratic nomination, was just as ardently against the pact as his liberal congressional colleagues. Public antipathy to TPP became so intense that even Hillary Clinton, the Democratic front-runner who'd helped negotiate the agreement during her tenure as Obama's secretary of state, disavowed it.

When it was clear that the votes weren't there for the legislation despite Obama's intervention, Pelosi came out against it, too, giving a passionate floor speech that contributed to its overwhelming defeat.

Never had Pelosi seemed so weak: ambivalent rather than decisive, following rather than leading her caucus, unable to perform her customary trick of moving mountains. As the 2016 presidential election loomed, she seemed like a spent force. Her dogged determination, the superhuman endurance that had kept her in the game for so long, began to look more and more like the stubbornness of someone who refused to acknowledge what everyone else could plainly see: her time was up.

23

THE RIGHT-WING ANGER THAT HAD SHUT DOWN THE GOVERNMENT AND paralyzed Washington was a fire raging out of control. John Boehner had tried to appease it, but it was never satisfied, and finally it consumed him, too.

September 24, 2015, should have been a glorious day for both Boehner and Pelosi. A year and a half earlier, Boehner had extended a long-shot invitation to Washington to the newly elected Pope Francis. To the happy surprise of the House's two Catholic leaders, the pontiff finally agreed to come and make the first-ever papal address to Congress.

The pope's visit came against the backdrop of—what else?—another congressional fight over government funding. Far from being chastened by the 2013 shutdown, the rabble-rousers in the Freedom Caucus had only grown bolder. In 2014, Boehner's deputy Eric Cantor unexpectedly lost his Republican primary to a local college professor who accused him of being soft on immigration—the first primary defeat of a majority leader in history, and yet more evidence that something other than government spending was fueling the rage on the right. When Boehner was reelected Speaker in January 2015, twenty-five Republicans didn't vote for him, nearly enough to force a humiliating second ballot.

The machinations against Boehner grew more and more overt. Egged on by their base, House conservatives wore their opposition to their weak Washington leaders as a badge of pride. Some even pointed to Pelosi as an example of the toughness and fighting spirit they craved. By July, the GOP rebels' ringleader, Mark Meadows of North Carolina, had taken the extraordinary step of filing a "motion to vacate"—a demand for another floor vote for Speaker, with the clear aim of forcing Boehner out.

As both the pope's visit and the government-funding deadline neared at the end of September, Boehner was in a bind. To get the spending bill passed, he would have to make a deal with Pelosi for Democratic votes. But making another deal with Pelosi could well be the last straw that clinched the conservative revolt and got him thrown out.

In a meeting with Pelosi, Boehner laid out the threat and asked for her help with a procedural trick to save his hide, if the motion came to the floor. The rebels' gambit rested on the assumption that Democrats would vote against Boehner, as they would in a normal Speaker vote. But if they voted "present" instead, Boehner would have the majority he needed to keep his job. Pelosi agreed to go along if it came to that: they had to work together, she thought, to protect the institution. "You can't have thirty people in your caucus decide they're going to vacate the chair," she said.

In the end, Boehner wouldn't need her help. The motion to vacate would never come to a vote. Pope Francis addressed Congress a few days after their meeting, delivering an urgent plea for "cooperating generously for the common good." He called on the lawmakers to embrace immigrants, heal the environment and end the death penalty. As the pontiff spoke, tears of joy streamed down Boehner's face. That night, the Speaker went home and told his wife he had made up his mind to quit.

The next day, he announced his departure in a press conference. A reporter observed that he seemed relieved. The Speaker broke into a smile and sang, "Zip-a-dee-doo-dah."

On his way out the door, Boehner worked out a deal with Pelosi to raise the debt ceiling and fund the government for two years. The conservatives could scream about it all they wanted. They couldn't touch him anymore.

❖ ❖ ❖

Outside Washington, the fire raged on. A few months earlier, Donald Trump had announced that he was running for president, gliding ridiculously down a gilded escalator in his eponymous tower on Fifth Avenue and ranting about immigrants being criminals and rapists to an audience of paid actors and passersby dragged in off the street. To the political class of both parties, his candidacy seemed like a joke that would quickly fade. But to everyone's shock, he surged to the front of the seventeen-candidate pack and stayed there, comfortably ahead of all the well-qualified governors and senators seeking the nomination. The same GOP base that had tormented Boehner and paralyzed Washington thrilled to Trump's insult-comic routine as he ranted about Mexicans and Muslims and insulted women and war heroes.

Republicans regarded Trump as a hostile invader, and in many ways he was. He thumbed his nose at the austere vision of Paul Ryan, who succeeded Boehner as House Speaker and quickly ran into the same obstacles. Rather than reining in spending by paring entitlements, Trump promised to protect Medicare and Social Security while building a border wall, humiliating Mexico and China, and barring foreign Muslims. Ryan had been the GOP's golden boy for years, the mascot of conservative intellectualism, the former vice presidential nominee with the bright political future. But tellingly, when Trump and Ryan feuded, Republican voters overwhelmingly took Trump's side. An early Trump endorser was Sarah Palin.

Despite Ryan and Trump's differences, to Pelosi, Trump and the House Republicans seemed more alike than different. It was House Republicans who for years had blocked immigration reform and proposed physical barriers on the southern border. It was House Republicans who called for a ban on refugees after a mass shooting by a native-born Muslim terrorist in Orlando. It was House Republicans who denied climate change and blocked even the most minuscule gun reforms. While the political world acted shocked at Trump's extreme outbursts, House Republicans, Pelosi contended, had been sounding many of the same notes for years—and while Trump was just a wandering bloviator, House Republicans were affecting the government's ability to function.

"Here's the thing that really gets me," Pelosi told a group of reporters in the summer of 2016. "They're worse than Donald Trump, or at least as bad. But they have power. He doesn't." It was, she added, "inconsistent for somebody to say, 'I don't like what Donald Trump has to say, but I'm going to support people who are acting upon what he says in the Congress of the United States, and have been doing so for a long time.'"

Democrats were also contending with an unexpected populist groundswell, as Senator Bernie Sanders, the self-proclaimed socialist long regarded as a Washington gadfly, mounted a strong challenge to Hillary Clinton's march to the Democratic nomination. To Pelosi, much of the anger on both sides of the electorate could be attributed to people's understandable angst at unchecked Wall Street greed and economic inequality—the lingering effects of the recession that the president had been too timid to take on aggressively and the gridlocked Congress had been too hamstrung to address. But only one party was stoking people's rage and directing it at immigrants and minorities.

Pelosi didn't take sides in the Democratic nomination fight. But for years, since shortly after Obama's reelection, she had been publicly cheerleading Clinton's potential candidacy for the breakthrough it would represent for women. She claimed also to welcome Sanders's candidacy, praising him for getting young people excited about politics. But she didn't doubt that Clinton would win the nomination—and beat Trump in November.

Pelosi didn't just think Clinton was going to win; she *knew* it. The Democrats' prospects for retaking the House were less rosy. It would take a gain of 30 seats; few analysts thought that many districts were conceivably competitive. Trump gave Pelosi hope. She called him a "gift that keeps on giving" for Democrats. But Clinton had chosen, maddeningly, to campaign on the idea that Trump was an anomaly and most Republicans were not so bad. The Clinton brain trust hoped this message would persuade moderate suburban Republicans to cross over, but it clashed with Pelosi's insistence that there was "not a dime's worth of difference" between Trump and the rest of the GOP.

The only way Pelosi would become Speaker again was if Clinton won in a landslide. Given the way Trump was acting, that seemed like a possibility. A decade-old outtake from the TV show *Access Hollywood* emerged in October that captured Trump boasting about his methods for attacking women: "When you're a star, they let you do it," he said. "Grab them by the pussy. You can do anything."

But as November neared, Clinton couldn't seem to put him away. Russian-hacked emails heightened Democratic divisions, demoralized Sanders supporters and reinforced voters' impression of Clinton sleaze. Trump seemed to lie with impunity. He conjured a hellscape of immigrant crime and refugee terrorism that stoked the deep-seated fears of old white people, and offered them instead the equally fallacious nostalgia of "Make

America Great Again." Clinton's cheery slogan "Stronger Together" was limp and unsatisfying by comparison.

U.S. intelligence agencies caught wind of election interference by America's Russian enemies and alerted Pelosi and other senior lawmakers. But McConnell balked at issuing a strong bipartisan warning about the threat, so the letter the leaders issued referred only to vague, unnamed "malefactors." A few days before the election, the FBI director, James Comey, issued a letter informing Congress that new evidence had caused him to reopen the investigation into Clinton's email security practices, bringing that trivial scandal back to the forefront of voters' minds. Pelosi, fuming, said privately that she considered Comey the best Republican operative in America.

By Election Day, she knew she would not be Speaker again, but she was gladdened by the prospect of Clinton's inevitable victory—and with it, the promise that a woman would finally be at the head of the table. In an afternoon interview with *PBS NewsHour*'s Judy Woodruff, she proclaimed, "We will, of course, retain the White House with the election of Hillary Clinton. I believe we will gain the United States Senate—it will be close, but we will gain the United States Senate—and we will pick up many seats in the House of Representatives." When Woodruff closed the interview by pointing out that Pelosi was the nation's highest-ranking woman politician, Pelosi grinned and looked at her Apple watch: "For the moment!"

❖ ❖ ❖

Trump's victory stunned everyone, including Trump. Democrats' world was turned upside down. The staff of the Democratic National Committee was given the next day off to grieve. Protesters spilled into the streets.

Pelosi was as dismayed by the result as anyone. She had even thought about retiring if Clinton won, since a woman would be at the table. But with Trump as president and Republicans in control of the House and Senate, it would take every trick in the book to prevent the GOP from undoing everything she'd fought for. This was not a job that could be left to an amateur. She thought back to 2005, when she'd led the Democrats out of the minority by battling an imperious president and his legislative minions. She steeled herself for another battle.

But if Pelosi was convinced her party still needed her, many Democrats weren't so sure. Trump had won because he promised to smash the establishment—to strong-arm the gridlock and beat the feckless politicians into shape. His followers thrilled to a vision of vengeance on the smug certainty of the permanent political class, the comfortable experts who thought they had the right to rule over everyone else. In Hillary Clinton, America (or at least the Electoral College) had just rejected a patronizing Baby Boomer elite with a dynastic vise grip on power. The decisive vote had come from non-college-educated whites in the heartland, who looked at her and saw something that made them react viscerally: the grating shrew, the demanding mother-in-law, the bitch who won't back off. Pelosi struck these voters similarly, as a rich and arrogant limousine liberal looking down on the unwashed masses from her San Francisco mansion (or DC penthouse), presuming to tell them how to live their lives. If the party wanted to win, Democrats grumbled, it had to change—not put that same kind of unlikable figure back on top.

Just like two years earlier, on the caucus's post-election conference call, there was much wailing and gnashing of teeth—but not from Pelosi. She saw it as her job to reassure her flock and psych them up for the fight ahead. She admitted no mistakes, took no responsibility, gave no sign of soul-searching or discombobulation. Democrats, she said, obviously cared about the working class and understood that the electorate was angry. That was not the problem. The problem was that their message hadn't gotten across. "We have to get out there and say it in a different way," she said.

Some of the shell-shocked members couldn't believe what they were hearing. "I think we're missing something," California congressman Scott Peters finally said. "We're just not hearing what's on people's minds."

Some Democrats thought it was time for a coup. Two dozen mostly younger members gathered at a swanky Italian restaurant on Capitol Hill to talk about what could be done. Pelosi had set the leadership elections for that same week, which would make it impossible for a challenger to gather momentum. The dissenters thought everyone needed more time to think things over. They signed a letter asking Pelosi to delay the vote until after Thanksgiving. In a tense and angry caucus meeting, Pelosi first resisted—"Don't lay this at my feet," she said—then relented and agreed to postpone the vote.

There was blood in the water. Another group of members, including some veteran lawmakers and ostensible Pelosi loyalists, quietly approached Joe Crowley, the vice chairman of the caucus, and pleaded with him to run against her. An affable, ambitious congressman from Queens, Crowley had started out a Hoyer protégé when he got to Congress in 1999, but managed to get into leadership after cozying up to Pelosi. When she had passed over some longer-serving members to put Crowley on Ways and Means, she told the ones who complained, "If you work as hard as he did, you can get there, too."

With his long service and deep relationships, Crowley, unlike the junior members, could have been a real threat. But the insurrectionists had to be careful: an unsuccessful coup would put them in Pelosi's dog-house, consigned to congressional Siberia. Just as she had with her children, Pelosi generally didn't punish members of her caucus; she didn't have to. They feared her too much to test her patience. The withdrawal of her usual graces, the chill of guilt and disapproval, was enough to keep people in line. Once, a colleague asked her why she hadn't punished a dissenter by taking away his spot on a committee. That, she said, would be counter-productive: "Now he's got to be with me on the next thing."

Crowley was serious enough to put out feelers and map out strategy, even installing a whiteboard in his office to tally potential votes. But nine days after the election, he concluded there wasn't a path to victory. He called Pelosi to let her know he wouldn't be challenging her. There was a brief silence on the other end of the line. Then she said, coolly, "Good decision."

The idea that Pelosi might go unchallenged was too much for Tim Ryan, another onetime disciple. The forty-three-year-old congressman from Youngstown, Ohio, a high school quarterback turned meditation enthusiast, had just watched the rural parts of his district swing mas-sively for Trump. He feared his party was becoming intolerable to the people he'd grown up with, in part because of its association with Pelosi. Ryan thought the Republicans' attacks on Pelosi were unfair—but they'd nonetheless been effective in turning off swing voters. With him rather than her as the face of the party, he reasoned, the GOP would have to start all over with their project of spending tens of millions to turn the Democrats' leader into a bogeyman. If Democrats wanted to win elec-tions, he told his colleagues, no matter how much they respected Pelosi, they simply couldn't afford to keep such a toxic figure in charge.

Ryan announced his challenge and began lobbying others for support in mid-November. (He called Pelosi to tell her, but she didn't call back.) Members told him privately that they shared his concern about the need for change, but they didn't dare express their dissent publicly. Ryan made a public push, appearing constantly on television in order to show colleagues what it would be like to have him speaking for the party. "I personally don't believe we can win the House back with the current leadership," he said in one of his many cable appearances.

Pelosi, in a letter to the caucus, announced that she already had the support of "more than two-thirds of the Caucus." She discouraged allies from openly campaigning for her, as it might show weakness. Pelosi's strength had always been the inside game—her mastery of the legislative process, her relationships with every caucus member—but Ryan's challenge made it clear that outside perspectives mattered more than she'd previously allowed. What good was all her fund-raising if it didn't buy victory? What good were her tactics if she couldn't secure the majority? No one, not even Ryan himself, was arguing that he'd do a better job than she at managing the caucus, negotiating with the new Republican president or shepherding complex legislation through the House. They simply believed he'd be better for the party's image. Pelosi had always ignored her public image as irrelevant to her effectiveness. But now her personal unpopularity threatened to make it impossible for her to continue in her job.

When the November 30 caucus election arrived, Tim Ryan gave a passionate speech, hoping he might move some disgruntled members at the last minute to change their votes on the secret ballot. Pelosi, in her pitch, pointed to her previous work going up against a GOP president and winning back the majority in 2006, making the case that she could do it again. "We've got President Trump trying to destroy many of the things Democrats have stood for over the years," said Congressman Elijah Cummings of Maryland. "We need our A team."

Pelosi won by a vote of 134–63. She hit almost exactly the two-thirds she'd claimed and cast that as a victory. But the many votes against her were a striking sign of her caucus's wavering confidence in her leadership.

Despite Pelosi's bravado, most analysts believed Democrats had virtually no chance of taking back the House until at least 2022. The Democrats were about to go into their biggest battle in decades—possibly the battle for democracy itself—with a badly wounded general. "Nothing's going to change," Congressman Kurt Schrader of Oregon said despairingly. "We're going to be in the minority for the next fifteen years." To critics, Pelosi seemed prepared to preside over an endless decline, zealously guarding a shrinking empire as the winds of change howled around her.

24

THE DAY AFTER THE 2016 ELECTION, NANCY PELOSI CALLED TRUMP Tower to talk to the newly elected president.

Some Democrats had been up all night crying. Hillary Clinton never appeared at her own Election Night "victory" party, waiting until morning to give a terse, wounded concession speech. Pelosi didn't have time to mourn: there was work to be done.

Trump, when she reached him, was naturally in a good mood. She was, characteristically, polite and formal. She congratulated him on his victory and said she hoped they could work together. Trump was effusive: "I think we'll get things done," he said. "I know what you do. You're somebody that gets things done. Better than anybody."

They talked about the work that lay ahead. Pelosi suggested Trump could benefit from a meeting with the Congressional Women's Caucus, and Trump said that sounded like something his daughter could do, handing the phone momentarily to Ivanka. When Donald Trump got back on the line, he and Pelosi talked about Clinton's concession speech, which Pelosi remarked "must have been very hard for her to do." Trump replied, "It would have been hard for me, too"—sounding more gleeful than empathetic.

Pelosi didn't want to look back at the election. The wound was too raw, and it was pointless to dwell on it. But she was still shaken by the loss of the supposed "Blue Wall," the reliably Democratic states of Michigan,

Pennsylvania and Wisconsin that had been the linchpin of Trump's victory. Clearly, Trump had seen something everyone else had been blind to. "What did you know?" she asked.

Trump replied, "I saw the hostility." To Clinton, to Obama, to Pelosi, to the whole changing social order, the indifferent world: he didn't have to say it. Pelosi knew immediately what he meant.

But to Pelosi, Trump wasn't hostile—far from it. His public tough-guy act tended to melt away in private; he craved approval and seemed desperate to be liked. "Don't forget, I was a supporter of yours, a good one," Trump said as their call came to an end. "I think you're terrific."

It was true that they were not quite strangers. In 2006, Pelosi's then-colleague Charles Rangel, the longtime Harlem congressman, arranged for her to visit the Manhattan developer and TV personality at Trump Tower. She successfully extracted a twenty-thousand-dollar contribution for the Democratic campaign committee. After the Democrats won and she became Speaker, he sent one of his signature notes, scribbled in Sharpie on a newspaper clipping about her swearing-in: "Nancy—you're the best. Congrats. Donald."

During his presidential campaign, Trump flaunted his past as a Democratic donor as proof that he understood the sleazy pay-to-play of politics. He knew the system, he said, because he'd been part of it, greasing the wheels to make sure his permits got approved and his taxes stayed low. Voters disgusted with the wheeling and dealing of the political world—the world Pelosi inhabited—thrilled to the mirage of a rich man who couldn't be bought.

When he won, no one knew what to expect from a Trump presidency, in part because no one had bothered to give it much thought. (This included Trump and his advisers.) His background suggested he was ideologically flexible: he'd been a Democrat and an independent, supported abortion rights and gun control and immigration, even called for George W. Bush to be impeached. He had won the Republican primary running as a different kind of Republican, vowing to protect Social Security and Medicare, build roads and bridges, and rip up NAFTA—he'd even said he favored single-payer health care.

For all his racism and sexism, all the nastiness and dirty tricks of the campaign, Trump appealed to many people as a builder, a deal maker, someone who wanted to get things done—to win. His hostile takeover of the GOP of McConnell and Boehner was the ultimate irony: the same voters who'd demanded uncompromising opposition became so frustrated with the years of Republican-caused Washington gridlock that they elevated a man the party establishment loathed, on the strength of his promise to blow up the whole sordid mess.

In Trump's hastily written victory speech, delivered at 3 a.m., after the race was finally called, he'd sounded a subdued and unifying note, vowing to "bind the wounds of division." Opinion makers speculated that Trump might be moved by the gravity of the office and start acting "presidential." Perhaps the loudmouth who'd bullied the Republican Party into submission in the election could do the same with the Republicans in Congress, making deals with Democrats to help the "forgotten man" who, both sides agreed, had been left behind by globalization and Wall Street greed. Perhaps Trump would be a Republican Pelosi could work with.

Three days after the inauguration, Pelosi and other congressional leaders filed into the White House for a social reception in the State Dining Room. Meatballs on toothpicks and pigs in a blanket were served. But the round of pleasantries quickly turned acrimonious. "You know I won the popular vote," Trump declared.

The lawmakers looked at one another in puzzlement. Trump's victory in the Electoral College was not in dispute, but Clinton had won the popular vote by nearly three million votes. Nonetheless, Trump insisted that millions of "illegals" had distorted that total. A golfing buddy, he said, had told him about standing in line to vote in Florida with a bunch of people who didn't look like they should be allowed to vote—they looked Latin American.

As the others shifted uncomfortably, looking down at their hors d'oeuvres, it was Pelosi who spoke up. "That's not true," she said. "There's no evidence to support that."

Trump insisted that it was true—"and I'm not even counting California." The conversation moved on—to health care, to China, to the size of the crowd at the inauguration, which Trump also insisted on lying about.

The meeting was a sign of things to come. In a single stroke, the president had shown himself to be an insecure, narcissistic liar who lived in an alternate reality, as well as someone who believed that only white people were truly American. His blustering, fact-free Twitter persona wasn't a pretense or a performance: he really believed the twisted conspiracy theories he harvested from the dark corners of the internet. Pelosi almost felt sorry for him, and worried about the prospects for collaboration. How could you get anything done with someone so divorced from reality?

The meeting established one other thing, too. Everyone else in that room may have been too cowed or embarrassed or polite to tell the new president he was full of it. But Pelosi gave it right back to him. She was the one who would not back down.

❖ ❖ ❖

Pelosi's number one mission was to protect the Affordable Care Act. In private meetings, she told colleagues it was the reason she'd stayed. The Republicans' number one mission was to destroy it.

At first glance, her task appeared nearly impossible: during the Obama administration, the House Republicans had passed more than sixty bills repealing all or part of Obamacare. (Pelosi kept track with a big white binder whose cover read, "Votes to Repeal or Undermine the Affordable Care Act.") Nearly all the repeal attempts had died in the Senate, before they could even reach Obama's veto pen. But with the House, Senate and White House all in GOP hands, there was theoretically nothing to stop them. Republicans had plenty of disagreements, but they all agreed on opposition to Obamacare.

Pelosi didn't waste a minute. Within a few weeks of the election, she convened a conference call with a coalition of health care advocates to begin planning grassroots actions in support of the law. *Don't agonize, organize.* They planned mass health care demonstrations across the country the weekend before Trump's inauguration. Pelosi attended the inauguration wearing a blue "Protect Our Care" button.

For all their apparent unity on the issue, Republicans had a problem: they'd spent years promising to "repeal and replace" the ACA, but they'd never actually come up with a replacement. Pelosi and other liberals believed that was because Republicans didn't actually want to fix the health care system—they really just wanted to pare back government programs and deregulate the insurance industry, but they didn't dare say that publicly. Another obstacle for the GOP was that, while the health care law had always been unpopular overall, many of its component parts, such as banning discrimination against people with preexisting conditions, were popular. And then there was the political truism that Republicans had discovered and mercilessly exploited in 2010 and beyond: any disruption to the health care system was easy to pin on the party in power.

Pelosi and her allies hatched a multipronged, coordinated strategy to thwart repeal. First was the public relations campaign: she seemed never to open her mouth without mentioning a Congressional Budget Office report that showed that repealing the law would cause thirty-two million people to lose health insurance and premiums to spike as much as 50 percent. She even brought it up in that first White House reception. Other Democrats were encouraged to follow suit and strongly discouraged from trying to introduce any alternative health care legislation of their own.

They were backed up by the grassroots groundswell of outside groups that Pelosi was helping coordinate. People with disabilities or sick children were at every Republican congressman's town hall, demanding to know why he wanted to take their health care away. Calls flooded into congressional offices. A conservative congressman from Alabama told a radio host, "I don't know if we're going to be able to repeal Obamacare now because these folks who support Obamacare are very active. They're putting pressure on congressmen, and there's not a counter effort."

Then there was the inside game: getting to Republican lawmakers. Almost half the GOP caucus came from states that had expanded Medicaid through Obamacare. Pelosi held a series of meetings with senior Democrats from those states to put pressure on their colleagues. She spoke personally with Republican governors who had expanded Medicaid, such as Nevada's Brian Sandoval and New Jersey's Chris Christie. Soon there was a rash of headlines about bipartisan opposition back home to what the House Republicans were trying to do.

As usual, Republican divisions helped Pelosi's cause. Republican moderates balked at the idea of a quick-and-dirty repeal that would take away insurance from millions. But conservatives protested any measure that didn't get rid of every part of the ACA, saying it wasn't a "full repeal." Trump wanted action, fast, and seemed as surprised as anyone by how unprepared his party was to put legislation on his desk—as if the president himself had been one of the GOP voters snookered by the "repeal and replace" promise.

The Republicans proceeded to do exactly what they'd falsely accused Democrats of doing back in 2009: they cobbled together legislation in a rush, in secret, without public hearings or bipartisan consultation, and tried to jam it through the House on a party line vote. But by March the effort faltered. Lacking the votes, Speaker Ryan had to pull the bill on the eve of the planned floor session. In a hangdog press conference that afternoon, Ryan moped, "I don't know what else to say other than Obamacare is the law of the land."

Pelosi joined a celebratory MoveOn rally on the Capitol grounds, where cheering supporters hoisted orange "Obamacare Saves Lives" placards and chanted, "Ho, ho, hey, hey, the ACA is here to stay." Pelosi was so happy, she told the crowd, she wanted to jump for joy—and then she did. The petite, impeccably put-together, seventy-six-year-old congresswoman bent down, took off her pumps, and jumped up and down.

The fight was not over, but Pelosi and the Democrats had shifted the momentum and the narrative. For the first time in its seven-year history, polls found, Obamacare was popular. Republicans realized they were in a lose-lose situation: pass a bill, and they'd immediately face a barrage of angry constituents and attack ads blaming them for taking away people's health care; fail to pass one, and they'd incur the wrath of the Republican base that had spent years cheering their promises of repeal.

In May, the House finally came up with a partial repeal bill it could pass on a party line vote. Pelosi predicted they would pay a political price: "This vote will be tattooed on them," she said. "They will glow in the dark. And we'll make sure that the public is aware." On the floor of the House, the Democrats taunted their Republican colleagues: "Na na na na, na na na na, hey hey hey, goodbye."

The president was jubilant at the partial victory, hosting the House Republicans in the Rose Garden even though the Senate had yet to take up the issue. Some Republicans groused that it seemed unwise to spike the football at halftime. A few weeks later, in keeping with his habit of hanging his allies out to dry, Trump called the bill, which would have left fourteen million uninsured within a year, "mean."

Pelosi, like a lot of people, might have been wrong about the 2016 election. But about Republicans' lack of positive agenda and inability to govern she was all too prescient. For all Boehner's weakness, Ryan, his successor, was starting to make Boehner look like a strategic mastermind.

Things were not going much better in the Senate. For years, the Republican majority leader, Mitch McConnell, had nurtured a reputation as a tactician, earning rounds of admiring press for his supposed legislative genius. Unlike Pelosi, McConnell's personal unlikability never seemed to factor into this narrative; his "accomplishments" consisted of blocking popular legislation, carrying water for Big Business, and twisting the rules of the Senate to ensure that Obama couldn't get anything done. McConnell had even refused to allow so much as a committee hearing on Obama's final Supreme Court nominee for nearly a year—and then boasted that this bit of procedural malfeasance had sealed the election for Trump by motivating social conservatives to vote. His proudest achievement to date was his longtime work to stop campaign finance reform. It was a rather profound commentary on Washington that this kind of obstruction and chicanery could get McConnell revered as a master of his art.

For all his vaunted tactical skill, when it came time to actually be a policymaker, to come up with a complex piece of legislation and usher it through his chamber, McConnell fell short. In July, he brought the Senate's health care bill to the floor. And Senator John McCain, in one of his last legislative acts before he died of brain cancer, cast the deciding vote against it.

Obamacare was still the law of the land.

✧ ✧ ✧

Even as Pelosi did everything in her power to block Obamacare repeal, she insisted she was willing to work with Trump in other areas. "I could be helpful to him," she told the *New York Times*. "We're not here to obstruct him."

She soon had a chance to prove it. Over the summer of 2017, Pelosi and Senate leader Chuck Schumer began strategizing for the upcoming debt ceiling deadline. It was virtually assured that Ryan and McConnell wouldn't have enough Republican votes to hike the limit. If Democrats were going to fill the gap, why shouldn't they get something in exchange? This was mildly hypocritical—Hoyer pointed out that they'd blasted Republicans for using the debt limit as a bargaining chip, and had sworn that Democrats would never do such a thing. But Pelosi and Schumer, in a bit of self-serving rationalization, insisted it was just a proposal, not an ultimatum.

Pelosi and Schumer, her new Senate counterpart since the 2016 retirement of Harry Reid, had a long history. The fast-talking New York senator, elected to the House in 1981, was a regular of the Tuesday night dinner group Pelosi joined when she arrived in Washington. Until George Miller left office in 2015, Schumer was one of his roommates, sleeping on a mattress on the floor of his scruffy Capitol Hill row house and paying below-market rent. Schumer was known for his political savvy and his endearing quirks, such as playing yenta to his staffers and keeping track of how many marriages he racked up. With his zest for publicity—Pelosi was one of many to joke that the most dangerous place in DC was between Schumer and a TV camera—he could hardly have been more different from the cagey Reid. Schumer's instinct was sometimes more to placate than to fight, which sometimes frustrated Pelosi, but they were in frequent contact and generally in agreement.

Pelosi and Schumer were vacationing separately in Italy in August 2017 as they prepared for post–Labor Day talks with the White House and Republicans. In conversations over the course of the break, they settled on their opening ask in the negotiations: a three-month debt limit extension, plus disaster relief for Hurricane Harvey, which had just devastated Houston. That would put the next debt ceiling deadline in December, around the same time as government funding would run out, providing the opportunity to negotiate a big package that they hoped would include immigration. On the eve of the talks, the administration had announced it was rescinding Obama's Deferred Action for Childhood Arrivals, or DACA, the executive action protecting young illegal immigrants from deportation. If Congress didn't act, the "Dreamers," eight hundred thousand young adults who'd been brought to the United States as children, would be subject to removal starting the following March.

The Republican leaders, Ryan and McConnell, preferred to extend the debt ceiling for a full eighteen months, to after the 2018 elections. Both sides figured they'd probably meet in the middle, with Trump's support lending strength to the GOP's position.

The Republican and Democratic leaders entered the Oval Office on September 6 to find Trump in an expansive mood, ready to deal. When Pelosi walked in, the president immediately called for his daughter—it was a seemingly Pavlovian reflex with him, when he saw the Democratic House leader, to think of the only other woman in his life whom he considered to be in possession of a brain. "You know my daughter Ivanka," he said, expecting Pelosi to appreciate the gesture. "She's like a Democrat."

They got down to business, and Trump listened to both sides make their case. Steven Mnuchin, the Wall Street gadfly turned Treasury secretary, argued that the stock market would fall if the debt limit weren't raised through 2018. Schumer peered down over the glasses perched on his nose and said he doubted the markets just happened to be counting on a debt ceiling increase that coincided with the midterm elections.

While the men bantered, Pelosi was like a broken record: Did they have the votes? If they did, she kept pointing out, they could do whatever they wanted. If they didn't, they had better negotiate. Gradually, after she had repeated herself several times, the men grew quiet as they realized she was right.

In truth, Trump was tired of dealing with Ryan and McConnell, who were always telling him what he couldn't do. (In their defense, many of the things he wanted to do were illegal or unconstitutional.) And so, the president suddenly cut off the discussion: "Let's just do that," he said, gesturing at the Democrats.

Pelosi and Schumer couldn't believe what they were hearing: the president, Mr. "Art of the Deal" himself, had completely sold out his supposed allies and given the Democrats everything they asked for. As the congressional leaders scurried out of the room, Trump called after Schumer that they should also try to do something on Chinese currency regulation. "Not without me!" Pelosi called. "I know more about China than everyone in this room."

Schumer rushed back to the Capitol to hold a press conference while Republicans seethed. "Chuck Schumer and Nancy Pelosi now have most of the cards for when we get to December," griped Republican senator Ben Sasse. "This is an embarrassing moment for a Republican-controlled Congress and a Republican administration."

Pelosi, for her part, couldn't quite believe it. She returned to her office in the Capitol still in shock. "They capitulated," she told her staff. "They took everything we asked for."

As Republicans stewed, Trump turned on cable news, where his turn to bipartisanship was being roundly praised. The morning after their meeting, he called Pelosi, sounding ecstatic. "The press has been incredible!" he said. He seemed to be enjoying making the dour Ryan and McConnell squirm: "Your two friends, not so much," he said.

Pelosi saw an opening to try to get more out of him. She turned to immigration—revoking DACA had caused widespread anxiety among

immigrants as well as the business community, and some in the Democratic caucus were angry that she and Schumer hadn't sought an immigration agreement as part of the deal they'd just made. She told the
president that although he'd announced he was keeping DACA in place
until March—ostensibly in order to give Congress time to replace it with
legislation—some people were worried that he planned to start deporting
people immediately. "If you could put something out—'When I say six
months, I meant six months,'" she suggested, with gentle finesse honed by
decades of charming arrogant men into unwittingly doing her bidding.

The president was eager to please: "I'll take care of it," he said.

She pressed further: it would also be nice to reassure people that the
administration had no intention of separating families, wouldn't it? "Don't
do that," she said. "We don't want to scare people."

Of course, Trump replied. "I agree with that."

While they were at it, she suggested, perhaps they could see about
passing the DREAM Act? The president said he was game for that, too: "I'd
love to do it quickly. Why should we wait six months?" As the call wrapped
up, she suggested he could make his commitment known on Twitter.

The call was a classic illustration of Pelosi's methods. While Trump
flailed around thoughtlessly, seeking above all to please his interlocutor and soothe his own ego in the moment, she was ticking off concrete
deliverables one after another, determined to leave nothing on the table.
She never went into an interaction without a plan, and she never missed
an opportunity to ask for more. Pelosi would always keep pushing until
she got a "no." This quality had not always endeared her to her Republican counterparts: Boehner regarded her as a nag and sometimes avoided
her calls because he knew she always wanted something. But it was also
why her caucus trusted her so completely in negotiations: they knew she
would fight until she'd gotten absolutely everything she possibly could,
and would never settle for less.

After the call, Pelosi went into a meeting of Democratic whips. Just
as she was working to sell them on the deal with Trump, Debbie Dingell
of Michigan piped up to say that the president had just tweeted something awfully interesting: "For all of those (DACA) that are concerned
about your status during the 6 month period, you have nothing to worry
about—No action!" @realDonaldTrump declared.

The deal still caused a small amount of heartburn in the Democratic ranks, where some liberals worried that any negotiations with Trump would "normalize" the president they loathed. Pelosi wasn't naïve enough to think that Trump had suddenly seen the light and was about to start governing responsibly. But she had no qualms about working with him to find common ground when possible. "I make no apology for doing that with the person who is going to sign the bill," she said. "It gives you great leverage."

Her deal making made her relevant again, proving that Republicans still needed Democratic votes to get almost anything through the House. And it put the lie to the Republican talking point that Democrats were interested only in obstruction, too blinded by Trump hatred to work constructively for the good of the nation. Pelosi had spent her career putting aside differences to negotiate with Republicans. She believed in coming to the table in good faith—as long as the other side did the same.

"Chuck and Nancy," as the president liked to call them, wondered how far they could push their luck. The following Wednesday, after the debt ceiling deal had easily passed both houses, they trooped over to the White House for dinner with Trump and a handful of administration officials and congressional staff. They dined at a rectangular table in the Blue Room. The White House chef had whipped up a meal of Chinese food—crispy honey-sesame-glazed beef with sticky rice.

After they'd discussed China, the Democrats tried to see how far they could get the president to go on immigration. Schumer proposed a package deal that would give legal status to the Dreamers and fund various border security measures—but not Trump's border wall. Democrats and Republicans alike assumed the wall was little more than a campaign gimmick, more a symbol than a real proposal; Mexico was obviously not going to pay for any such thing, which even the staunchest immigration opponents viewed as a costly and ineffective boondoggle.

Trump seemed interested in Schumer's gambit, but he wanted to know, "What's in it for me?" Schumer told him it was an opportunity to do something big on a bipartisan basis, potentially resetting the image of a presidency more interested in provocation than cooperation. It was only a few weeks since Trump had shocked the nation's conscience by equivocating about the organizers of a deadly white supremacist rally in Charlottesville, Virginia, saying there were "very fine people on both sides" of the racists' clashes with protesters.

Pelosi chimed in. The president wanted people to see him as a deal maker, didn't he? Well, if they worked something out on immigration, maybe they could also find ways to cooperate on fixing Obamacare, or tax reform.

At this point, all the men around the table started talking at once. Pelosi was, as usual, the only woman in the room. She tried to continue, but she was drowned out as they talked over her. Finally, she raised a finger. "Does anybody listen to women when they speak around here?"

The men fell silent. They let her finish.

The dinner seemed to have gone well. Trump had agreed to the Democrats' basic framework, with the wall left for another day. Pelosi and Schumer put out a statement that evening to put it on the record: "We agreed to enshrine the protections of DACA into law quickly, and to work out a package of border security, excluding the wall, that's acceptable to both sides."

The news of the supposed agreement caught Republicans by surprise. On Twitter and Fox News, conservatives excoriated the president and warned him that he risked alienating his base. Early the next morning, Trump tweeted that "no deal was made last night." The wall, he insisted, "will continue to be built." (No wall was actually under construction.) But he still sounded sympathetic to the Dreamers: "Does anybody really want to throw out good, educated and accomplished young people who have jobs, some serving in the military?" he tweeted. "They have been in our country for many years through no fault of their own."

Schumer remained optimistic. On the Senate floor later that day, a microphone caught him confiding to a colleague, "He likes us. He likes me, anyway . . . Oh, it's going to work out." The utterance encapsulated the difference between the Senate leader and Pelosi. Her deal making was based on common interests and the bottom line, not personal relationships. Schumer made deals by schmoozing; she made them by counting votes.

What happened next would define Trump's presidency. The Democrats had opened a door to a more cooperative path for the polarizing president. Polls showed support for the DREAM Act as high as 90 percent of the American public. If he had wanted to—if he had had the courage to rise to the occasion and lead—Trump could have teamed up with the Democrats not only on immigration but on all manner of broadly popular policies, from infrastructure to gun background checks to labor-friendly restrictions on trade. He could have forced the Republican Party that he had already shown he had a stranglehold on to go along. Pelosi and Schumer were willing to bring along their reluctant liberal colleagues, too, if that was what it took to get the things done that they cared about.

But Trump would not take the opportunity they offered. He backed away from the table on immigration, never to return. He chose the path of demagoguery and division, spurning the Democrats and casting them back into an opposing role. As the second year of his presidency dawned, that would only become more evident.

25

The day after Trump's election, American women woke up furious. They'd been sure this couldn't happen—sure that their country would never elect a man who had been captured on tape admitting to sexual assault, who'd been accused by more than a dozen women of everything from groping to rape, who clearly viewed women as objects of conquest. When he won, they were mortified, devastated—but mostly they were mad. And they wanted to do something about it.

Pelosi had spent decades trying to get more women to run for office. But many of them balked at the idea, in part because of how they saw her treated. "I couldn't subject myself to what they subject you to," they'd say. "I couldn't let that happen to my family." Pelosi could hardly blame them. She'd seen how women's opponents went out of their way to undercut the perception that female candidates were more trustworthy than men. Hillary Clinton's campaign was a good example of what could happen to a female candidate who got knocked off her ethical pedestal. A man might have been seen as having made an error in judgment for erasing some emails and giving some corporate speeches. When a woman did it, it proved she was corrupt through and through.

Over the years, Republicans had combed through Pelosi's personal finances and history, never coming up with much. From time to time, someone questioned whether one of her husband's investments constituted a conflict of interest, and each time, rather than argue or try to defend it or point out that Pelosi had no involvement in Paul's business, he would simply sell the asset in question, making the issue disappear.

The inevitability of this sort of invasive personal investigation, with the smallest things blown up into character attacks, gave women pause. It was one thing to answer criticism for one's political beliefs. But having one's integrity relentlessly questioned was not something many women thought they could handle, or wanted to. Pelosi viewed political power as the ultimate goal, something that had to be wrested away from the people, the men, who hoarded it. But she had limited success getting other women to see it that way.

This reluctance was the major reason that women's representation remained stuck at appallingly low levels. In "the Year of the Woman," 1992, the number of women in the House nearly doubled—to 47. After that, it inched upward only gradually. By 2016, Congress was still less than 20 percent female. Political scientists labored to figure out why. They determined that it wasn't because voters were too sexist to put women in power: when they ran, women tended to win elections about as often as men. The problem was that women didn't run. They didn't run for city council, didn't run for county commissioner, didn't run for dogcatcher—and thus, when it was time to find a candidate for Congress, there weren't many qualified women available. This idea was so well known it had a name: the "pipeline problem." And despite millions of dollars and hundreds of conference seminars devoted to it, it stubbornly refused to budge.

On November 9, 2016, the pipeline problem suddenly disappeared.

It was as if a switch had been flipped. In the two-year cycle leading up to 2016, Emily's List, the pro-choice women's political organization, was contacted by fewer than a thousand women interested in running for office. (The organization's name stands for "Early Money Is Like Yeast." Its founder sought to help women get ahead by seeding their campaigns with cash at early stages, the kind of cash men might have access to through establishment political machines, but women rarely did.) Such queries were unusual enough that there was no recruitment section on the group's website. Then, in November 2016, they started pouring in. Women were calling the main switchboard, sending unsolicited emails to the generic address on the website. *Here's my résumé,* they said. *I can't stand what's happening. What can I run for?*

They were women from all walks of life: social workers and air force pilots, executives and academics, teachers and prosecutors. Many had had jobs where they thought they could make a difference and serve their country without undergoing the degrading and intrusive popularity contest an election might entail. But with Trump's election, they suddenly felt called to do more. With a feeling recognizable to any woman who's watched her husband botch the laundry, they'd realized that the men were screwing everything up, and they were going to have to do the job themselves. By the end of the 2018 election cycle, Emily's List would hear from more than forty-two thousand women who wanted to run, for everything from school board to U.S. Senate.

America had seen waves of women's activism before—the suffragists, the temperance movement, the feminist movement—but never one so explicitly electorally focused. Clinton's campaign, which failed to galvanize women voters in any extraordinary way, was testament to the nation's lack of a real feminist identity movement. (For Clinton herself, the post-election activism was bittersweet: "I couldn't help but ask where those feelings of solidarity, outrage, and passion had been during the election," she wrote in her memoir *What Happened*.) But Trump's election changed that. While attendance at Trump's inauguration had been sparse, the following day, the streets in DC, across the country, and around the world filled with women, making the Women's March the largest single-day protest in American history.

Women would be the leaders of the anti-Trump resistance. A week into his presidency, when Trump issued a ban on visitors from several majority-Muslim countries, women were among the protesters who thronged the airports. In communities from Birmingham to Boise, women formed new grassroots groups and besieged their local Republican representatives. The largest of the new grassroots networks, Indivisible, reported that its members were about three-quarters female. Newly riled-up women made waves in other ways as well, speaking out against powerful abusers like Harvey Weinstein, powering the #MeToo movement and staging wildcat strikes in the women-dominated teaching profession.

Pelosi was as surprised by the women's activism as she was pleased. Usually, there would be a sort of lull the day after an election, win or lose, as people regained their bearings. But this time, her phone never stopped ringing. "This is urgent," the callers said. "What can we do to help?"

They'd realized what she already knew. "The minute they showed up, they saw their power," she said later. "And they continued to show up."

✧ ✧ ✧

By June 2017, the activist itch had found its first major political target: a special congressional election in the Atlanta suburbs. And Pelosi was in the middle of it.

The election was being held to fill the Georgia seat vacated by Tom Price, who'd been plucked from Congress to join the Cabinet as secretary of Health and Human Services. (Like so many of Trump's appointees, Price wouldn't last long: he resigned three months later, when it was revealed he'd spent hundreds of thousands of taxpayer dollars on unnecessary private jet travel.) The seat ought to have been reliably Republican. Price, running with token opposition, had won it by 23 points in 2016, and Trump won it by 2. The exurban district's voters were largely white, well educated and upper middle class—exactly the sort of voters who tended to prefer a traditional Republican candidate to Trump.

National Democrats ordinarily wouldn't have given such a district a second look. But thousands of local volunteers, predominantly women, rallied around the Democratic candidate, an earnest, clean-cut, thirty-year-old former congressional staffer named Jon Ossoff. When Ossoff got 48 percent of the vote in the first round of voting, almost enough to avoid a runoff, the race was suddenly on the national radar.

Newly minted activists all over the country showered Ossoff with donations. He would eventually raise thirty million dollars—an astronomical sum for a single House race, which combined with the two parties' spending would make it the most expensive in history. Hundreds of volunteers, including many out-of-work former Obama administration and Clinton campaign staffers, poured in from far and wide to help Ossoff get out the vote. The result wasn't particularly consequential; a single seat in Congress wouldn't change much in Washington. But the symbolic stakes were high: a victory in such unlikely territory would bolster the idea that Trump was politically weak. And liberals were desperate to feel like they were doing something to push back on Trump.

The national Republican Party, sensing danger, began pouring in millions to defend the seat. Its strategy was all about Pelosi. Ossoff avoided mentioning Trump, wouldn't commit to supporting Pelosi and positioned himself as a nonideological problem solver. But the GOP's ads portrayed him as Pelosi's best left-wing friend—a "rubber stamp for Nancy Pelosi's liberal agenda," someone who would "represent Nancy Pelosi" in Congress, who was funded by "Nancy Pelosi and members of the resistance movement." One mailer featured Pelosi peeling a rubber Ossoff mask off her head.

National Republicans were open about the fact that they considered Pelosi their best electoral argument, the only way they could convince discouraged and Trump-skeptical conservatives to get out and vote for the uninspiring GOP candidate, Karen Handel. They ran similar campaigns in other, less contested special elections, in Montana, Kansas and South Carolina. Pelosi's face was plastered on billboards and blanketed television ads. It wasn't a new strategy for the GOP, of course, but whereas previously she'd shared the spotlight with a Democratic president and his health care and economic policies, now she was virtually the sole focus. When the Georgia candidates debated, Republicans rented a trolley car, draped it with a "San Francisco ♥ Jon Ossoff" banner, and drove it around the venue.

Pelosi said the focus on her only proved that Republicans were out of ideas. But when Ossoff lost by 4 points, a fresh round of Democratic hand-wringing ensued about her being a liability for the party. Democrats had turned out at unprecedented levels for a special election, spurred by the desire to send a message against Trump—but Republicans had turned out just as robustly, erasing any enthusiasm gap. And what had spurred Republicans to vote was, apparently, Pelosi. Could Democrats afford to keep in place someone who was so powerfully galvanizing for the other side? "The Republican playbook for the past four election cycles has been very focused, very clear," Congresswoman Kathleen Rice of New York told the *Times*. "Is it fair? No. Are the attacks accurate? No. But guess what? They work. They're winning, and we're losing."

In a private meeting the morning after the special election, anxious Democratic lawmakers pressed the head of the Democratic Congressional Campaign Committee, Ben Ray Luján, on what the party planned to do to counter the GOP's anti-Pelosi messaging. Tony Cárdenas of California said they had to stop treating the topic as taboo out of loyalty and confront it head-on. Some of the anti-Pelosi faction renewed their calls for her to step down for the good of the party, and a few of them met privately with Tim Ryan to strategize.

Pelosi was defiant. Luján put out a five-page memo making the case that the Georgia race's close margin was a good sign and that the party was in a position to compete in "dozens and dozens" of more favorable districts. Pelosi sent a letter to the caucus arguing that "every effort was made to win" in Georgia and that Democrats were in the process of developing a persuasive economic message to take to voters in the upcoming midterms. When reporters peppered her with questions about whether she was hurting the party politically, she dismissed the attacks and pointed to her fund-raising clout.

"I think I'm worth the trouble," she said.

✧ ✧ ✧

But Democrats, in Washington and across the country, were clearly restless. Pelosi's stock of political capital within the Democratic caucus was at a low ebb thanks to the outside attacks and internal challenges to her leadership. Tim Ryan was still in talks with other insurgents about trying to remove her at the next opportunity. And Joe Crowley made no secret of the fact that he was lobbying colleagues for support, though he said it was only in the event that she didn't run again.

Pelosi's upbringing as a polite, ladylike 1950s Catholic girl had given her a sense of modesty; she was confident, but she didn't want to seem boastful. Now, however, something seemed to have snapped. The ends-focused operational leader realized that she couldn't count on anybody else to tell her side of the story in the face of the prevalent negative narrative about her. The attacks weren't hurting just her; they were hurting her party and its candidates.

The way she chose to address this challenge was typically Pelosi: straightforward, personal and rhetorically ham-handed. She had always gravitated to a stock set of highly repetitive slogans, many of them alliterative ("money, message, motivation," "proper preparation prevents poor performance"), using them as mnemonic devices to keep herself on message and prevent her brain from racing too far ahead of her tongue. Now a new, brazenly boastful set of lines began appearing in her interviews as she tried to drive home the strengths that she believed outweighed her weaknesses.

"I am a master legislator, I am a shrewd politician and I have a following in the country that, apart from a presidential candidate, nobody else can claim," she said.

"Self-promotion is a terrible thing," she said, "but evidently someone has to do it."

Another challenge to Pelosi was brewing in the liberal grass roots. Across the country, the left was on the march. Bernie Sanders's campaign had inspired a massive, youth-driven leftist movement that agitated for radical policies and generational change. Pelosi, to them, looked like part of the same out-of-touch, triangulating old guard that had produced Hillary Clinton's campaign. As recently as 2011, "socialist" was considered such a slur that a formal complaint was lodged against a Republican congressman who hurled it at a Democrat on the floor of the House. Now, following Sanders's example, people wore it proudly. The previously moribund Democratic Socialists of America organization had thousands of new members. New groups, such as the Justice Democrats, formed with the explicit goal of fielding liberal candidates to challenge moderate Democrats in primaries.

For various reasons, the Democratic Party had never been riven like the GOP with its own version of the Tea Party. When liberals challenged establishment Democrats in ideologically themed primaries, they mostly lost, as Sanders had to Clinton. The reason Republicans feared the right more than Democrats did the left could largely be explained by the parties' different ideological proportions. When pollsters asked people if they considered themselves liberal, moderate or conservative, about two-thirds of Republicans called themselves conservative, but the proportion of Democrats who called themselves liberal tended to be less than half; the majority of Democrats considered themselves moderate or even conservative. Still, just as the Tea Party succeeded in driving the Republican Party rightward, the left was now successfully pushing Democrats' dialogue in its direction. Not only was "socialism" now okay to say out loud, but candidates were talking about things like establishing single-payer health care, abolishing Immigration and Customs Enforcement, and providing reparations for slavery.

This trend shook the party in a little-watched June 2018 primary in Queens, New York, where a twenty-eight-year-old political newcomer named Alexandria Ocasio-Cortez challenged Joe Crowley, the ten-term Democratic congressman who was scheming to move up in the House leadership. Few thought Crowley, long the unquestioned boss of the local party machine, was in any trouble. Crowley hadn't had a primary challenger since 2004, and he assumed this challenge was nominal. He spent more time fund-raising for others, to rack up chits with his colleagues for a future leadership race, than tending to his own campaign. But his district's composition had changed under his feet, from being made up mostly of working-class Irish and Italians to being, by 2018, less than 20 percent white. Crowley's record was solidly liberal, but Ocasio-Cortez, an avowed democratic socialist, attacked him for not being left enough.

Ocasio-Cortez beat Crowley by nearly 14 points, out of fewer than 30,000 votes. The resounding victory shocked Washington. She was now virtually guaranteed to win the strongly Democratic district in November. Suddenly, a man who thought he had a good chance to become the next Speaker of the House was out of a job. When Crowley called Pelosi on Election Night to tell her what had happened, she sounded distraught.

In addition to destabilizing Pelosi's leadership team, Crowley's loss fed the narrative that the Democratic Party was hungry for fresh faces. Even though Crowley's defeat removed a potential threat to Pelosi, a spate of analyses speculated that the upset spelled trouble for her leadership. All across the country, the Democratic campaign committee was laboring to recruit the kind of appealingly moderate candidates they believed they needed in swing districts, while the left argued that bolder candidates were more electable. In the event, the pattern in Democrats' 2018 primaries wasn't that voters consistently chose liberal or moderate candidates; it was that they were disproportionately choosing women.

But it was the charismatic, outspoken, far-left Ocasio-Cortez who now threatened to become the party's most visible standard-bearer. Pelosi downplayed any larger significance of the result: "They made a choice in one district," she said. "Let's not get yourself carried away."

She moved quickly to bring the new voice into the fold. The day after the election, she reached Ocasio-Cortez by phone and told her how happy she was to have more young, progressive women in Congress. "There's a lot to do," Pelosi told her. "Thank you for your courage to run. This is not for the faint of heart."

❖ ❖ ❖

Back in Washington, Pelosi was, as always, looking for leverage. The moment of comity between Trump and "Chuck and Nancy" hadn't lasted. The December 2017 deadline they'd engineered came and went with no agreement as they tried to insist on a fix for the Dreamers. A court temporarily blocked Trump's attempt to end DACA, giving Democrats room to demand more without putting the vulnerable population at further risk. In January, Schumer even went so far as to offer Trump billions in border wall funding in exchange for a DACA deal. But Trump retreated to his nativist corner, complaining to lawmakers in an Oval Office meeting that the United States shouldn't have to accept immigrants from "shithole countries."

As another funding deadline approached in January 2018, Pelosi convinced Schumer it was time to take a stand, even if that meant shutting down the government—something the Democrats had sworn they'd never do. It would really be Republicans' fault, they reasoned: it was the GOP that was in the majority but unable to come up with a bill that could pass with Republican votes alone. Democrats had put a price on their own votes for a funding deal, saving DACA, and they had to show they were serious about it. "This is an important moment for our caucus, standing up for what we know is right," Pelosi told the Democrats. "We will not give up our leverage, for our priorities and for our Dreamers." The Republicans' proposal, she said, was "like giving you a bowl of doggy doo, put a cherry on top and call it chocolate ice cream."

Pelosi's caucus was on board. But Schumer's pitch to his own ranks was not as convincing. After three days of partial shutdown, the Republicans seemed to be winning the public argument, successfully accusing the Democrats of holding the government hostage for the sake of an unrelated demand on immigration. Schumer caved and agreed to a DACA-free deal, selling out the House and leaving Pelosi and her caucus furious.

"How do we know the Senate isn't screwing us?" Congresswoman Gwen Moore of Wisconsin demanded.

Hoyer replied, "They are."

In exchange for opening the government, McConnell had given

Schumer a promise to hold votes on immigration legislation. But the Speaker, Paul Ryan, made no such promise to Pelosi, probably because he knew as well as she did that if it were ever put on the floor, the DREAM Act would have enough Democratic and Republican votes to pass. Paul Ryan personally favored immigration reform, but he couldn't allow it to pass without endangering his own position—the picture of political cowardice.

On a chilly morning in February, immigration protesters flooded the Capitol. They packed the marble rotunda outside Pelosi's office and draped an enormous banner from the balcony above. The banner featured the face of a young Latina woman and the words "DREAM ACT NOW." Frustrated at her inability to help them, Pelosi decided she could at least show them they weren't forgotten. In her car on the way to work that morning, she called her staff and told them to send out an all-member request for Dreamers' stories.

At 10 a.m., she took the House floor, wearing a blue shirt under a cream-colored pantsuit and her usual four-inch heels. Lashing out at the Speaker's refusal to put immigration legislation on the floor, Pelosi said, "Why should we in the House be treated in such a humiliating way?" She wasn't quite sure, as she began, how long she would continue to speak. Under the House rules, top party leaders can talk as long as they want—as long as they don't sit down or take a break, even to go to the bathroom.

"We have a moral responsibility to act now to protect Dreamers, who are the pride of our nation and are American in every way, except on paper," she said. And then she began telling their stories, interspersed with Bible verses. The nine-year-old from South Korea. The five-year-old from Mexico. The thirteen-year-old from Brazil. She read their names and American hometowns into the *Congressional Record*, one by one. As the hours passed, her voice grew hoarse, but she kept going.

The cable networks and Twitter realized what was happening and tuned in. More stories flooded in from across the country; Pelosi's staff rushed to print them out and ferry them to her so she could keep going. At one point she asked for a rosary, and her friend Rosa DeLauro passed her one. The speech resembled a Senate filibuster—except that in the Senate, the filibuster can be handed off between senators, allowing the main speaker to take breaks as colleagues fill in. Pelosi was on her feet speaking, alone, the entire time.

When she finally sat back down, to a round of applause from her

colleagues, it was 6:11 p.m., eight hours after she had begun. Asked if anything like that had ever been done before, the nearest precedent the House
historian could find was a five-hour speech against a tariff proposal delivered by Representative Champ Clark of Missouri in 1909. Pelosi's appeared
to be the longest continuous speech in the history of the House.

Her stand inspired an outpouring of gratitude from immigrants and
their advocates across the country. For months afterward, young Hispanic
activists would approach her at events around the country to tell her how
her strength and passion had moved them to tears. But in practical terms,
the speech was no substitute for the coin of the realm, as Pelosi called it—
votes. Pelosi voted against the DREAM-free budget agreement, but it still
passed easily.

❖ ❖ ❖

Trump's Washington was consumed by chaos. There were too many scandals to count. The Cabinet was populated with corrupt, self-dealing government antagonists, from Price, the health secretary who resigned over private
jets; to Ryan Zinke, the secretary of the interior who, when he wasn't opening public lands to oil and gas drilling, was allegedly steering the agency's
policies to his own personal and political benefit; to Scott Pruitt, the Environmental Protection Agency administrator who denied climate change
while allegedly handing out favors to his family and lobbyist friends. The
president spent large amounts of his day watching Fox News and tweeting
insults at people, from the mayor of London to cable TV hosts to private
citizens. When the FBI wouldn't stop investigating the mounting evidence
that Trump's 2016 campaign had accepted help from the Russian government, he fired FBI director James Comey. And when Trump's own attorney
general and longtime ally, Jeff Sessions, wouldn't call off the special counsel
appointed to investigate the matter, Trump turned on him, too.

Jimmy Carter, the last U.S. president to own a private business, put his
Georgia peanut farm in a blind trust. But Trump refused to follow precedent and divest from his business empire; indeed, he seemed to view government coffers as his personal piggy bank. Articles and books streamed
out detailing the president's personal and political dysfunction—at one
point, he was moved to declare that, contrary to so many portrayals, he
was in fact a "very stable genius." The president's longtime personal lawyer
went to jail after revealing that he'd paid off Trump's mistresses to keep

their stories out of the press on the eve of the election, making the president himself an unindicted co-conspirator in a felony campaign finance case.

The administration's lawlessness threw a spotlight on the necessity of Pelosi's role. The founders had tried to create a government system of checks and balances, where the legislature, executive and judiciary reined one another in. Many of Trump's excesses, from the travel ban to the attempt to add citizenship to the Census, were indeed being stopped by the courts (though McConnell was working at a rapid clip to stack the courts with Trump-friendly judges). But in the legislative branch, while many Republicans harbored private qualms about Trump, the overwhelming majority were too cowardly to say or do anything publicly to stop him. It was only Pelosi and Schumer, with their near-powerless minorities, who stood between the lawless president and his dreams of authoritarian rule.

At least, Pelosi mused, the administration's recklessness was undercut by its incompetence. Even with control of the House and Senate, Republicans had proved unable to enact their promise of repealing Obamacare. Desperate for a signature accomplishment, in December 2017 the GOP hurriedly rammed a tax bill through Congress. But while Paul Ryan and other fiscal conservatives had long dreamed of large-scale tax reform that would simplify the bloated and confusing tax code and allow ordinary Americans to file their taxes on a postcard, the bill they came up with did not come close to that goal. Instead, it gave a massive tax break to corporations and the wealthy while blowing a $1.5 trillion hole in the deficit.

The tax bill proved how hollow the GOP's years of deficit-reduction demands had really been. Once they were in power, Republicans didn't care about balancing the budget at all—and neither did their voters. With his tirades against minorities, contempt for women and cruel policies toward immigrants, Trump seemed to be giving the party's base voters what they'd really wanted all along. He was more popular with his own party than almost any president in decades.

In March 2018, it was time again to negotiate a government-funding bill. It seemed unlikely at this point that Trump would ever agree to help the Dreamers. His rhetoric on immigration had become increasingly harsh, and he'd pushed for a Senate immigration bill so restrictive that even many Republicans wouldn't back it: it got just 39 votes.

On March 7, Pelosi called the White House and spoke to Trump. She urged him to push Republicans on DACA and advocate for a bipartisan House immigration bill. But the president was noncommittal. He asked her to come over for lunch the next day. Having now been through several time-wasting rounds of supposed deal making with a president who'd proven that his word could not be trusted, and with the Dreamers protected for the time being by court order, Pelosi decided this was going nowhere and declined his invitation.

Instead, she kept negotiating with congressional Republicans, determined to use her leverage to keep domestic priorities funded and stave off attempts at environmental and labor deregulation. She knew where the pressure points were: Republicans fervently wanted to increase military funding. Democrats would agree to that—if Republicans agreed to increase domestic spending, too. Paul Ryan, the supposed fiscal hawk, had no choice but to go along. He needed her votes.

By the time she had hammered out an agreement to present to her caucus, Pelosi had secured a laundry list of liberal victories. More than one hundred of the GOP's industry-friendly deregulation riders had been stripped away. New provisions were added to enable gun violence research and keep guns out of schools, the first legislative gun control action in at least a decade. The omnibus bill specifically prohibited spending on a concrete border wall and barred increases in immigration detention or interior ICE agents. Republicans dropped their bids to cut Planned Parenthood funds and change a crucial family planning provision, agreed to her demands for $380 million in election security funding and a $1.3 billion increase for the Census, and incorporated a fix to wildfire funding that the Obama administration had tried and failed for years to secure.

The failure to help the Dreamers was a bitter pill, but most Democrats agreed with Pelosi that, given the court order protecting them temporarily, no deal on DACA was better than a bad deal. The caucus was stunned at how successful Pelosi had been in the negotiations. This was a better budget deal than most of the ones they'd gotten when Obama was president. While Trump blundered and raved, it was Pelosi who was giving Washington a master class in the art of the deal—from what ought to have been the most powerless position in congressional leadership.

So embarrassing was the spending deal for conservatives that the president, upon signing it, proclaimed, "I will never sign another bill like this again." But it was the conservatives' own fault: by refusing to lend their votes to any compromise, they'd made themselves irrelevant and forced Paul Ryan to seek Democratic votes instead.

In April, the beleagured Ryan announced that he would not run for reelection.

✧ ✧ ✧

Back in 2006, Pelosi and Rahm Emanuel had determined that Democrats could win by running hard against President Bush and mostly ignoring policy. In 2018, though, she decided their strategy needed to be exactly the opposite.

Trump was already unpopular—he didn't need the Democrats to drive down his approval rating, which, unique among presidents, had never been more positive than negative. Trump also uniquely monopolized the news cycle, his cloud of perpetual outrage blotting out seemingly everything else. Hillary Clinton's campaign had thought people would vote for her because they were disgusted by Trump's character. But she was so busy attacking him that many voters never heard her positive message, all the policies she was proposing to make America a better place, and they concluded that nothing was at stake that really affected their lives. To many voters, Clinton seemed like the worse of two equally unpalatable choices. In 2018, the Democrats were determined not to make that mistake.

Pelosi and her strategists decided that voters' antagonism to Trump was already baked in. What they needed to hear, and wouldn't unless Democrats hammered it home with single-minded focus, was that there was a positive alternative, a party with real plans for improving people's lives. The Democrats workshopped ideas for months and came up with a package they called "For the People." The plan included proposals to break up corporate monopolies and use infrastructure spending to create jobs. But they boiled it down to a simple three-pronged slogan: lower health care costs, bigger paychecks, cleaner government. That last item could be understood to encompass everything from Trump's scandals to campaign finance reform.

Pelosi was also careful not to make Clinton's mistake of denigrating the Americans who had voted for Trump. When Clinton, late in the campaign, referred to half of Trump's supporters as "irredeemable" and belonging in a "basket of deplorables," it reinforced the impression of Democrats as smug, censorious, politically correct scolds. Pelosi didn't want to disrespect

Trump's voters; she just wanted to make them aware of what he was doing to them. She knew that might take time. "Did you ever know anybody who was dating a jerk?" she said. "Could you tell her? No. You have to wait until she figures it out for herself, hopefully before it's too late, or you'll just drive her into his arms."

The tax cut legislation presented a problem for the Democrats: it was an actual accomplishment, one that Republicans could use to convince conservative-leaning voters that Trump was delivering for them on policy even if they hated his tweets. So Pelosi set out on a mission to destroy it. She dubbed it the "GOP tax scam" and mentioned it at every opportunity. She traveled the country doing "GOP tax scam"–themed events. She called the bill "a monumental, brazen theft from the American middle class" that "raises taxes on 86 million middle-class households" and "hands a breathtaking 83 percent of its benefits to the wealthiest 1 percent of Americans." These talking points were, at best, highly misleading: in fact, the bill cut the taxes of 65 percent of Americans, though it was true the wealthy benefited disproportionately. But her disciplined messaging campaign worked. By 2019, less than 40 percent of Americans believed they'd actually gotten a tax cut.

Many voters also believed Trump was taking away their health care, though he'd mostly tried and failed to do so. Unable to repeal Obamacare legislatively, the administration was busy finding other ways to sabotage it, from refusing to advertise the exchanges' open-enrollment period to supporting a federal lawsuit to overturn the entire Affordable Care Act. The tax bill also included a provision eliminating the individual mandate penalty. The idea that Republicans wanted to bring back insurers' ability to discriminate against people with preexisting conditions resonated broadly with the public—so broadly that the GOP tried to turn it around and claim that it was Democrats who would throw people off their health care, by changing to a single-payer system. Few were fooled by this talking point.

There were signs the political winds were turning in Democrats' direction. In November 2017, Democrats won Virginia's gubernatorial election by an unexpected 9-point margin and gained an astonishing 15 seats in the state legislature—11 of the seat flippers were women, many first-time candidates. In December, Democrats won a U.S. Senate seat in Alabama after the GOP bypassed more palatable options to nominate a fire-breathing right-winger who was accused of having sexually assaulted teenage girls. Throughout the year, Democrats won little-watched special elections for state legislature seats in places like Oklahoma and Wisconsin. And in March 2018, a Democrat managed to win a Pennsylvania congressional district Trump had won by 20 points. Nearly 60 percent of the GOP's ads in that race were attacks on Pelosi—and so were 7 percent of the Democrats': to neutralize the "Pelosi issue," the Democratic candidate aired his own commercial promising voters he wouldn't support her in Congress. He won.

Republicans begged Trump to change his behavior and his message. But when he was supposed to talk about tax reform and the economy, he decided this was boring and discarded his prepared remarks to talk about immigration instead. He seized on a "caravan" of migrants making their way through Mexico toward the U.S. border, falsely depicting the ragged band of a few hundred desperate asylum seekers as a menacing horde of terrorists and invaders. He described Democrats as an "angry mob," conjuring dark images of '60s riots. Trump might have won only a single election in which he lost the popular vote, but the president trusted his own political instincts more than any pencil-necked consultant. And his instincts told him that fear, division and racial resentment were the way to rile up his most loyal voters.

In September, the Senate was in the process of considering Trump's second Supreme Court nominee, Brett Kavanaugh, when a scandalous allegation came to light. A high school acquaintance, Christine Blasey Ford, charged that Kavanaugh had pinned her to a bed, groped, mocked and threatened her at a long-ago party. Ford's accusation almost didn't see the light of day. She initially reached out to her Northern California congresswoman, Anna Eshoo, Pelosi's close friend. Ford was leery of going public, but thought her charge was something those considering Kavanaugh's nomination ought to know. Since it is the Senate that hears judicial nominations, Pelosi advised Eshoo to pass her along to Senator Dianne Feinstein, the Californian and top Democrat on the Judiciary Committee. When Feinstein failed to act on the information, Pelosi contacted Schumer, but still nothing happened. Ford's complaint might never have emerged had it not leaked to the press in the hearing's final days. Pelosi's frustration with Schumer for his handling of the matter caused a temporary rift between them.

The Kavanaugh hearings were a too-perfect distillation of the politics of 2018—a year when women, racked with pain and rage, repeatedly rose to protest the trauma that had forced them into years of terrified silence; a year that repeatedly revealed the extent to which American life was shaped by the privilege and prejudices of entitled men. From news anchors to studio heads to performers to politicians, these men had always gotten to decide what the public knew and to whom the laws applied. But in 2018, with their voices and their votes, women across the country decided they'd had enough.

The accusation didn't stop Kavanaugh from being confirmed, and the controversy inflamed the right enough to give Republicans a glimmer of hope on the eve of the midterm elections. Trump, naturally, mocked Ford and cast Kavanaugh as a near martyr. The GOP spent more than $100 million on more than 100,000 ads attacking Pelosi, an unprecedented and unrebutted onslaught. As November neared, Democrats fretted. What if, just as he had in 2016, Trump knew something they didn't about the political moment? What if his demagoguery succeeded in whipping up his personality cult, overpowering their own base's passion? What if Pelosi, with the visceral loathing she inspired, was simply too big a liability for Democrats to overcome?

26

On Election Day, November 6, 2018, Pelosi made her rounds: hair appointment, Judy Woodruff interview, visit to a college girlfriend—in a sad marker of the passage of time, the girlfriend was a grieving widow now.

Early in the night, she sat in a backstage room marked for VIPs at the Capitol Hill Hyatt as the jitters set in. The first few closely watched House races, long-shot districts in Kentucky and Tennessee, went to the Republicans, and the Senate and gubernatorial races in Florida were too close for comfort. Calls flooded in from donors and operatives desperate for reassurance that they weren't seeing a repeat of 2016. "This is heartbreaking," liberal commentator Van Jones declared on CNN.

But then the victories began to mount. A typical case unfolded in Virginia, where the Tea Party congressman who'd ousted the Republican majority leader in 2014 was unseated by a female former CIA agent in an exurban district Trump had won by 7 points. Abigail Spanberger's first-ever run for political office was buoyed by a new grassroots group called the Liberal Women of Chesterfield County. They had so pestered her opponent with their protests that he was caught on tape complaining, "The women are in my grill no matter where I go," and all but ceased appearing in public. In their only debate, he mentioned Pelosi two dozen times, even though Spanberger had promised not to support her. Nonetheless, Pelosi's leadership PAC spent half a million dollars boosting Spanberger, and she won.

Across the country, results like that one kept rolling in. At 9:33 p.m., Fox News was the first network to announce that the Democrats had won the House.

More than any other national election of her lifetime, 2018 was truly Pelosi's. There was no Democratic presidential candidate leading the ticket and determining the message. The Senate was not really in play. It was all about the House, where she was both the engine of the Democrats' strategy and fund-raising and the target of most of the Republicans' attacks. All across the country, women organized, women ran for office and women voted. Turnout set a midterm record. Pelosi's own demographic, college-educated white women, was the most decisive factor: after voting for Hillary Clinton by just 4 points in 2016, they voted for Democrats in 2018 by a 15-point margin. The effect of this massive swing was concentrated in suburban areas from Oklahoma City to Orange County, California. When the dust settled, after weeks of counting and recounting, Democrats made a 40-seat gain, well exceeding the 23 they needed to take the majority. It was the largest Democratic gain since the post-Watergate midterms of 1974. Twenty-four of the seat flippers were women. For the first time in history, the number of women in the House exceeded 100—and 89 of them were Democrats.

Pelosi took the stage in the Hyatt's basement ballroom around 11 p.m., looking out on the crowd of relieved, elated, tipsy Democrats. In her brief speech, she called for bipartisanship. "It's a new day in America," she announced, raising a fist.

Trump called right as she was leaving the stage. He'd just watched her speech on TV and appreciated the bipartisanship talk. Was he saying something about infrastructure? The cheering was so loud she could barely hear the president's voice. "Thank you, Mr. President," she yelled into the phone.

Pelosi's strategy had been vindicated, her opponents' discredited. The great gears of democracy's engine had turned, delivering a definitive verdict on the divisive president and empowering the House—her House—to rein in his destructive impulses. With the Senate remaining in Republican hands, it would fall to the Democratic Speaker to embody the Constitution's ideal of checks and balances.

Before the night was out, she had personally called every new member of the Democratic caucus.

◇ ◇ ◇

There was no time to rest and celebrate: Pelosi had another election to win before she could become Speaker. And while Tim Ryan's 2016 run against Pelosi had been a last-minute, improvised affair, this time her opponents had been organizing for months.

There was no one ringleader; Ryan was involved again, along with Kathleen Rice of New York and Ed Perlmutter of Colorado. But no one came to epitomize the effort more than Seth Moulton, a square-jawed, Harvard-educated, forty-year-old marine veteran who'd been one of the 2016 coup plotters. Moulton had just been elected to his third term in Congress, but what he lacked in experience he made up in self-assurance. His résumé was studded with successes: one of the nation's most prestigious prep schools; three Harvard degrees; four tours in Iraq, during which he'd starred in an award-winning war documentary; capped with his first run for office, in which he'd toppled an incumbent Democrat to represent a deep-blue Boston-area district. As a House member, he had few accomplishments to his name but could frequently be found on cable TV criticizing Pelosi and touting his own political strategy, which involved recruiting more military veterans to run as Democrats and serve as a "new generation of leadership."

Despite the midterm victory, the rebels were convinced that Pelosi had to go. From their perspective, little had changed since 2016: she was still standing in the way of the Democratic Party's progress and bottling up the House. Pelosi was seventy-eight, Steny Hoyer was seventy-nine and Jim Clyburn was seventy-eight, and the three of them had now ruled the Democratic caucus for fifteen years. How could Democrats convince people they were the party of youth and progress, of hope for the next generation, when their top elected officials were all born during the FDR administration? In election after election, American voters had unmistakably cried out for change, yet the Democrats insisted on giving them more of the same.

The rebels knew they weren't the only ones who felt this way. In whispered hallway conversations, they found plenty of sympathetic ears; after so many years of toil in the minority, everyone had some frustration, some gripe. Even some members thought to be Pelosi's allies would give them encouraging signals: *Don't tell her I'm saying this, but I'm glad somebody has the guts to do this.* Media organizations kept tallies of all the members and candidates who wouldn't commit to supporting Pelosi—lumping together the hard nos and the vague calls for "new leadership." The *Times* counted nearly sixty such statements. To the rebels, all those people and more seemed gettable.

But none of the rebels wanted to run against Pelosi themselves. And finding someone to do so proved difficult. When they put out feelers to Karen Bass of California, for example, Bass—a former Speaker of the California Assembly who respected the complexity of such a job—tipped off Pelosi instead.

Pelosi could win the late-November caucus vote with a mere majority of the 235 Democrats. But her campaign for the speakership wouldn't end there. She would also have to get 218 votes on the floor of the House come January 3. That meant she could afford to lose a mere 17 votes, less than 10 percent of the caucus.

The rebels resolved to blaze ahead without a Speaker candidate. They decided to put out a letter demonstrating that there were enough of them to be a real threat; that would embolden more of their colleagues to join the cause, and eventually, once they reached critical mass, a candidate would step forward. Or perhaps, they hoped, Pelosi would see the writing on the wall and step down.

✧ ✧ ✧

Pelosi knew what the rebels were up to, and she was planning a campaign like none she'd ever run before. In 2016, she'd barely campaigned against Ryan in order to demonstrate the natural depth of the caucus's loyalty to her. But this time she would need every single vote.

The decisive election victory had eased much of the angst, particularly among longtime members. No longer could they accuse Pelosi of not knowing how to win back the House, or of being a crippling burden to her party. The midterms also complicated the idea that Democrats needed to better appeal to blue-collar Rust Belt whites to succeed, and women's key role in the election made overthrowing the first woman Speaker a less appealing prospect. But only the members who had been around for at least a decade were familiar with her skills as Speaker, and they now amounted to less than 40 percent of the caucus. The others, particularly the freshmen, knew her mainly by her popular negative caricature. She would have to win them over.

The day after the election, Pelosi hand-addressed and signed a typed letter to each member of the caucus. That day she also got an endorsement she didn't expect—from Trump. "In all fairness, Nancy Pelosi deserves to be chosen Speaker of the House by the Democrats," he wrote in an early-morning tweet. "If they give her a hard time, perhaps we will add some Republican votes. She has earned this great honor!" Pelosi brushed off the compliment as well as the supposed offer. There was no way she was going to go begging for Republican votes to lead the Democrats.

Her staff made spreadsheets and plotted connections. Did this new member need fund-raising help to retire a campaign debt? Would that one who'd served in the Obama administration be swayed by a call from the former president? How about Bill Clinton, or Al Gore, or John Kerry, or the governor of their state? Where the rebels looked at the dozens of candidates' calls for new leadership as soft opposition, Pelosi saw the opposite: savvy politicians who'd left their options open, including the option to support her.

One possible source of opposition was on the left, where many regarded Pelosi as insufficiently revolutionary. Ocasio-Cortez, who'd gotten to Congress by mounting an insurgent challenge to the Democratic establishment, was the left's new darling. Millions of followers hung on her snappy Twitter comebacks and policy pronouncements. But Pelosi had courted Ocasio-Cortez early, bonding with the idealistic young politician over a July lunch in San Francisco, where she insisted that her heart was with the progressives, even if she couldn't always give them everything they wanted.

A week after the election, AOC, as she'd become known, joined a group of environmental protesters who staged a sit-in at Pelosi's office to demand climate action. But the confrontation quickly turned into a lovefest: Pelosi declared that she found the activists inspiring, told the police to leave them alone and affirmed her plan to reinstate the special climate committee that the GOP had eliminated. It was a canny move that defused the idea of a rift with the left. AOC praised Pelosi's commitment to grassroots organizing, and before long she announced her support for Pelosi as Speaker, noting that any alternative was likely to be less progressive, not more.

Pelosi proceeded to cash in a lifetime of accumulated chits from every part of the Democratic coalition. Unlike the typical inside-baseball caucus election, this one would be decidedly public-facing. Pelosi released endorsement letters from labor unions, environmental groups, Emily's List, gay rights advocates, abortion rights advocates, campaign finance reformers, gun control groups and the online grassroots collective MoveOn. Liberal celebrities like Barbra Streisand, Rob Reiner and Martina Navratilova praised her on Twitter, with Navratilova musing that it seemed odd that Pelosi was under pressure when Schumer wasn't. "A man loses and keeps his place, a woman wins and gets booted?!?" she wrote.

Pelosi showed up at meetings of every Democratic subgroup, from the freshman orientation of the Progressive Caucus, where she pointed out that she'd been a founding member, to the centrist New Democrats, where she argued that they mustn't become the left's version of the Freedom Caucus. She entered negotiations with the Problem Solvers, a bipartisan caucus that was demanding process reforms. (They considered themselves business-friendly centrists, while the left considered them corporate shills.) She scheduled twenty-minute meetings with every member of the caucus— "booked like a barber," her staff quipped—meetings in which she asked for people's priorities and aspirations but didn't directly seek their votes.

❖ ❖ ❖

The rebels were soon under siege. Their ragtag operation couldn't compete with the dozens of calls every uncommitted member was getting from donors, supporters and friends urging them to support Pelosi. Moulton had been sure that the twenty military veterans his Serve America PAC had helped get elected would return the favor and join his effort. But Pelosi had her own sources of sway with these freshmen. She had Ted Lieu, a California congressman and air force reservist, reach out on her behalf, as well as the progressive defense group VoteVets. In the end, few of Moulton's mentees joined his cause. When a reporter brought up Moulton in Pelosi's presence, she breezily declared, "I will be the Speaker of the House, no matter what Seth Moulton says."

The insurgents claimed they had enough commitments to stop Pelosi from getting to 218, but for nearly two weeks they wouldn't say who or how many. They were supposedly about to send out a letter, but days passed with no sign of it. Behind the scenes, the rebels were scrambling as the gesture they'd hoped would establish their strength instead threatened to demonstrate their weakness. On Twitter, liberals had branded them with the mocking hashtag #FiveWhiteGuys. Why, they asked, were the rebels targeting only Pelosi, when two male leaders, Hoyer and Clyburn, were just as old and entrenched? Tim Ryan protested that the criticism was unfair because there were "plenty of really competent females" who could replace Pelosi. That tone-deaf remark only made it worse.

The grassroots backlash against Moulton was particularly brutal. Many women looked at him and saw a familiar archetype: the younger male know-it-all who steamrolled them in meetings and got promoted over their heads. Could you even imagine, Pelosi's allies whispered, what people would say about a forty-year-old woman who thought she could single-handedly take out an accomplished male leader in the twilight of a storied career? (For that matter, could you imagine *anyone* crusading to get rid of a distinguished older man, who was scandal-free and still in command of his faculties, on the grounds that he wasn't likable?) Moulton suddenly found himself disinvited to meetings with major donors and targeted by potential primary opponents, most of them women. At a town hall in his Massachusetts district, dozens of protesters showed up to decry his anti-Pelosi push. "I almost feel like I'm targeted—I'm old and I'm a woman," one constituent said. When Moulton pleaded, "The majority of Democrats want this change," the crowd shouted, "No!"

On November 14, the rebels got a ray of hope. Marcia Fudge, a six-term Ohioan and former chair of the Congressional Black Caucus, told her hometown paper she was considering running for Speaker. Fudge's experience, gravitas and relationships would give the rebels instant credibility, and having a black woman as their nominal leader would defuse the "five white guys" attacks. Pelosi professed to be unbothered: "Come on in, the water's warm," she said. In fact, the water was hot. Reports soon spread about Fudge's refusal to cosponsor LGBT antidiscrimination legislation (on technical grounds) and a letter of support she'd written for an ex-judge convicted of beating his wife. It was a warning to other potential challengers that they would be similarly scrutinized.

Before the rebels could put out their letter, Pelosi's allies released their own, signed by sixty-one women. When the rebels' missive finally went public, it laid bare their failure to consolidate Pelosi's disparate dissenters. There were only sixteen signatories, and they didn't include five of the freshmen who'd promised not to support Pelosi during the campaign. Neither the hard left nor the caucus's moderates had joined in any numbers: only one signer was a member of the Progressive Caucus, and only one was a member of the Problem Solvers, who were negotiating separately with Pelosi for their proposed reforms.

Once the signatories were public, Pelosi began picking them off methodically. She met with Fudge for a forty-minute discussion in which she outlined the Speaker's responsibilities—the constant travel and fundraising, the endless meetings and negotiations, the thousands of relationships to maintain. Fudge agreed to drop her challenge in exchange for the chair of a subcommittee on voting rights. From the outside, it seemed like an awfully small price. But Pelosi couldn't give the rebels too much, lest she give the caucus rank and file an incentive to act out as well.

Another rebel, Brian Higgins, was an upstate New York congressman who had memorably called Pelosi "aloof, frenetic and misguided" and vowed to oppose her earlier in the year. The real source of his grievance, she knew, was that her staff had told Higgins his pet policy, allowing Americans over fifty to buy into Medicare, was unworkable. Pelosi met with Higgins, apologized for the slight and promised to seriously consider his ideas on health care and infrastructure. But in exchange for this vague commitment, he had to make a public statement of support. Higgins's letter announcing he would vote for Pelosi defended his reversal as a "principled stand," but to other wavering members it looked like a warning. Nobody wanted to go out on a limb for a doomed cause only to have to eat humble pie shortly thereafter.

By the day of the caucus vote, November 28, the rebels were in disarray. Pelosi's gains had sapped their confidence and created a sense of inevitability around her return to the speakership. Moulton realized he'd miscalculated and was in danger of being left out in the cold. Without consulting the rest of the group, he announced that they would negotiate with Pelosi, alienating those in the group who insisted their opposition was absolute. Meanwhile, Pelosi's talks with the Problem Solvers stretched on so long that she was late to the caucus election meeting, but she succeeded in getting a deal to secure their 8 votes, agreeing to new rules that would make it easier to move bipartisan legislation to a vote.

There was still no one but Pelosi running for Speaker, and she could have been elected by acclamation—essentially by default—as Hoyer and

Clyburn had been. But she wanted to give members a way to express opposition, so her staff crafted an unprecedented ballot featuring her name and
boxes marked "yes" and "no." This gesture was made out of calculation, not
magnanimity: it would allow members who'd pledged to vote against her to
say they'd kept their promise, giving them a pretext to support her as the
Democratic nominee in the crucial floor vote.

In the caucus meeting, a parade of members spoke on Pelosi's behalf,
starting with Joe Kennedy III, the charismatic, redheaded young heir to
the political dynasty. The last to speak was John Lewis, the revered hero of
the civil rights movement. "Nancy, Nancy, Nancy," he thundered. "Believe
in me. I would not lie to you. I've seen the struggle. I've been beaten, left
bloodied, left unconscious. I almost died on that bridge in Selma. But Nancy's been with us, and she will be with us now, tomorrow, and in the years
to come. I ask for you, I beg of you, I plead with you to go and do what
we must do, and cast your vote for Nancy Pelosi as the next Speaker of the
House."

Pelosi won the Speaker vote with 203 yeses, 32 nos and 3 ballots left
blank. It was short of 218, but a far cry from the 63 defectors she'd suffered
two years prior. And her whip count was already ticking upward: as they
streamed out of the meeting, some members told the press they'd now
fulfilled their pledge to vote against her and were prepared to support her
on the floor.

Immediately after the caucus vote, Pelosi summoned Moulton, Ryan
and Rice for their negotiating meeting. It got off to an awkward start when
Rice, who didn't know that Moulton had requested the meeting, thanked
Pelosi for calling it, only to have her shoot back, "I didn't ask for this meeting." Ryan tried to explain the rebels' case: "I know how capable you are,"
he said. "This is not about skill. It is about our brand."

But it was clear to Pelosi, and to many of the rebels, that she had the
leverage now; it was up to them to decide whether to try to get something
out of their fading effort. For the moment, she offered them nothing, and
they left empty-handed.

❖ ❖ ❖

Two weeks later, on December 11, with the Speaker race still unresolved,
Pelosi and Schumer went to the White House for their first post-election
meeting with the president. Another government-spending deadline

loomed. For two years, congressional leaders had slow-walked Trump's demand for a wall on the southern border, which even many Republicans viewed with skepticism. The two parties had already negotiated a deal to keep the government open, which included more than one billion dollars for border security, but it needed the president's support. GOP leaders and Trump's own staff tried to convince the reality-challenged president that a few miles of border fencing renovations would amount to the big, beautiful wall he had sought, hoping he might claim victory and move on. But Trump realized the lame-duck Congress was his last chance to wield his rubber-stamp House majority.

Only Schumer had been invited to this White House meeting, but he saw through the transparent attempt to divide and conquer the Democratic leaders and insisted on bringing Pelosi with him. They strategized in advance about how they would approach the conversation. Trump, they decided, lived in a bubble of ego-stroking conservative media, spineless congressional Republicans, and sycophantic staff. He lied and lied, and no one ever spoke up to contradict him. Their strategy would be to confront him with the facts.

When they entered the Oval Office, they found two high-backed maize-colored chairs arranged at the end of two gold brocade sofas, in front of a marble fireplace draped with holiday garlands. Trump and Pence took the chairs; Schumer sat at the end of one sofa, to Trump's left, while Pelosi sat across from him, on the other, next to Pence. According to the normal protocol for such meetings, the White House press pool would photograph the leaders together, then be shooed out of the room while they got down to business. But Trump, a skeptic of normal protocol, allowed the reporters and cameramen to stay and film the proceedings. He'd done this before, in Cabinet meetings and other negotiations, believing it put others off balance and created an appealing visual of a man in command of his power. But in this case, the result would not be what he hoped.

The conversation began blandly enough. Trump held forth for several minutes, lauding bipartisan progress on criminal justice reform and the farm bill and reading some talking points about border security. When he turned to Pelosi, she also sought to sound a cordial note—to a point. "Well, thank you, Mr. President, for the opportunity to meet with you, so that we can work together in a bipartisan way to meet the needs of the American people," she said. "I think the American people recognize that we must keep government open, that a shutdown is not worth anything, and that you should not have a Trump shutdown."

"Did you say 'Trump'?" the president snapped. "I was going to call it a Pelosi shutdown."

She ignored him and kept talking, trying to make the point that when it came to the border wall, the president's problem wasn't with the Democrats; it was with his own party. "You have the White House," she said. "You have the Senate. You have the House of Representatives. You have the votes. You should pass it right now."

"No, we don't have the votes, Nancy, because in the Senate, we need sixty votes, and we don't have it," Trump countered.

Pelosi kept insisting that he didn't have the votes in the House, either, or else the GOP would have funded the wall already. Trump argued that it was pointless to pass something in the House that would go nowhere in the Senate, while she continued to needle him, repeating her point over and over: "The fact is you do not have the votes in the House."

Trump turned to Schumer, who set out to make the case against the border wall. They argued pointlessly for a while, until Pelosi tried to bring the conversation back down to earth. "Unfortunately, this has spiraled downward," she announced. They had lost sight of the needs of the American people, who had just signaled in the midterms that they rejected Trump's agenda. "Sixty people of the Republican Party have lost—are losing their offices now because of the transition," she said, slicing the air with her right hand.

The suggestion that he was a loser was too much for Trump. He had spent the month since the election trying to cast it as a win because the GOP had expanded its Senate majority, though that was largely due to the fact that most of the Senate seats up for election happened to be in red states. "Nancy, we've gained in the Senate," he said. "Excuse me. Did we win the Senate?"

Schumer turned toward the assembled cameras with a smirk. "When the president brags that he won North Dakota and Indiana, he's in real trouble," the Senate leader deadpanned.

"I did!" Trump insisted. "We did! We did win North Dakota and Indiana." Pence sat silent throughout, hands on his knees, head swiveling from side to side like a spectator at a particularly slow and unpleasant tennis match.

"This is the most unfortunate thing," Pelosi said. "We came here in good faith, and we're entering into this kind of a discussion in the public view."

"It's not bad, Nancy. It's called transparency," the president snarled.

"It's not transparency when we're not stipulating to a set of facts," she said as he continued to talk over her, ranting about drugs and diseases coming over the border.

"I also know," Trump said, "that, you know, Nancy's in a situation where it's not easy for her to talk right now, and I understand, and I fully understand that." It was an allusion to her fight to regain the speakership, which had indeed weakened her leverage with her caucus, but it wasn't true, as he insinuated, that she refused to fund the border wall only because she feared a revolt from her base.

She interrupted him. "Mr. President," she said, waving a finger. "Mr. President, please don't characterize the strength that I bring to this meeting as the leader of the House Democrats, who just won a big victory." She pleaded again for a closed-door negotiation based on facts.

Schumer said they all ought to be able to agree that they didn't want to shut down the government, as Trump had repeatedly threatened to do. The meeting had now gone on for fifteen minutes, and Trump had grown increasingly agitated as it progressed; clearly, he was unaccustomed to dealing with congressional leaders who wouldn't lie down and do his bidding. Schumer continued to goad him, staring straight ahead with a serene smile, until Trump took the bait.

"I'll tell you what," Trump said. "I am proud to shut down the government for border security, Chuck, because the people of this country don't want criminals and people that have lots of problems, and drugs pouring into our country. So, I will take the mantle. I will be the one to shut it down. I'm not going to blame you for it."

It was an explosive declaration: the public debate during shutdowns generally revolved around which party was to blame for the failure to reach agreement. Republicans had already started preparing talking points to blame Schumer for the shutdown if it happened. Now the president had cut his own team off at the knees.

When the meeting ended, the two Democrats walked out of the White House's North Portico. They emerged into a blinding winter sun, and Pelosi put on her round-framed tortoiseshell sunglasses, a self-satisfied smile on her face. She and Schumer walked up to a stand of microphones set up in the White House driveway, where Schumer told the press that Trump had had a "temper tantrum."

When it was Pelosi's turn to speak, she simply said, "He does not have the votes in the House to pass whatever his agenda is with that wall in it."

Even as she spoke, the image was catching fire. The little grin, the rust-red coat, the sunglasses, the coolly collected woman who'd flustered the raging president without breaking a sweat—liberals on Twitter were passing around images and bits of video, calling Pelosi a "rock star" and more. They called her a gangster and set the slow-motion clip to hip-hop. "The new power suit for women. Red coat. Sunglasses. Nerves of steel," one woman tweeted. "NANCY PELOSI THROWS SHADE AT TRUMP (THEN DONS SHADES)," a CNN chyron blared.

In that moment, Pelosi went from bogeyman to icon. It was as if America, after years of fixation on her weaknesses, had suddenly woken up to her strengths. It wasn't just her impeccable style—the upright posture, the perfect chin-length bob, the chicly understated ensemble. It was what she'd done. Her calm but forceful presidential comeback—"please don't characterize the strength that I bring"—resonated with every woman who'd ever been belittled in a meeting, every liberal "resister" who longed to see Trump put in his place. (The line, too, was soon on T-shirts.) "Nancy Pelosi just did something that not a single Republican has had the guts to do in 2 years," a liberal commentator tweeted. "Stand up to Trump, in public, to his face." Everything about her—her toughness, her experience, her confidence, her power—had made her the match for the moment.

Returning to the Capitol, she marveled at the president's wall fixation. "It's like a manhood thing for him," she told her colleagues. She had tried, she said, to avoid stooping to his level, which she colorfully described as "a tinkle contest with a skunk." Instead, she said, "I was trying to be the mom."

❖ ❖ ❖

It was all over for the rebels after that meeting. They could tell that the temperature had changed.

Pelosi's ongoing negotiations with Ed Perlmutter, the moderate Democrat from Colorado, wrapped up the next day. She agreed to a new, retroactive four-term limit on top House leaders; counting her previous stint as Speaker, that meant she could serve no more than four more years. The deal secured 7 votes, which, combined with other commitments, put her safely over 218. It also rankled Hoyer; he still hoped to be Speaker one day and hadn't been party to the term limit agreement—once again, Pelosi had found a way to slip the knife in her supposed partner's side. (Clyburn held a more realistic view: that all three leaders were destined to leave their positions at the same time.)

After sealing the deal, Pelosi entered her next meeting laughing. She had, she said, planned to stay only one term anyway, so the "limit" she'd accepted had doubled her expectations. When a colleague wondered if she'd still been unwise to pin herself down, she said, "Let me tell you a story about Louis Quatorze."

The French king, she said, was about to sentence to death a peasant who'd poached on his land. "If you let me live," the peasant says, "I can teach your horse to talk!" The king says, "I'll give you one year." The peasant's friends are aghast at the absurd promise. But the man says, "In a year's time, the king might be dead, I might be dead, or the horse might talk."

Like her clash with Trump, Pelosi's fight for the speakership had ended up showcasing her strengths, demonstrating to newer members the qualities that made her excel at the job. "Our diversity is our strength," she said in an oft-repeated mantra. "Our unity is our power." It was a unity she had forged with great effort, but now she was prepared to wield it.

She would soon get the chance. It turned out Trump had been right: he did have the votes in the House but not in the Senate. The House passed a funding bill with five billion dollars to build the wall, while the Senate passed one without it. On December 21, at midnight, the parts of the government that hadn't been funded shut down.

Pelosi and her husband took their usual vacation in Hawaii over the holidays, while Trump stayed in the White House, sulking and tweeting. Paul Ryan made his forlorn final speech, the shuttered government a testament to his failures as he slunk out of office.

So this was how her second speakership would begin. Against a backdrop of collapse, it would fall to her to somehow restore the balance.

27

January 3 dawned, cold and sleepless but electrifying nonetheless.

At noon, the clerk called the House to order. Congressman Hakeem Jeffries of New York rose to nominate Pelosi for Speaker. A talented messenger who'd steered the passage of a bipartisan criminal justice reform bill, Jeffries, just elected caucus chair, was viewed as a potential future Speaker himself. In 2018, he was instrumental in crafting the "For the People" slogan that House Democrats had adopted for their campaign—saving them from Schumer's cringeworthy alternative, "A Better Deal."

Now Jeffries, a forty-eight-year-old black man with a bald pate and a lilting Brooklyn accent, stood amid the ranks of new and old members who sat on dark leather-and-wood chairs on the left side of the House floor. "The Scripture says that weeping may endure during the long night, but joy will come in the morning," he said. "Madam Clerk, it is with great joy that I rise today as directed by the House Democratic Caucus, to place the name of Nancy Pelosi in nomination to be the next Speaker of the United States House of Representatives."

On the right side of the floor, the shrunken group of Republicans, a nearly uniform horde of white men in dark suits, sat motionless, while the Democrats rose to applaud. Their side of the House was a riot of color, dotted with women's bright dresses. They were male and female, black and brown and white and Asian, gay and straight, young and old—AOC, at twenty-nine, was the youngest congresswoman in history. From above, a lei, a cowboy hat and a hijab could be seen. Many had brought their children—they cradled infants in their arms or shushed restless grade-schoolers. It was the most diverse Congress ever, including the first two Muslim women and the first two Native American women; straight white men made up less than 40 percent of the Democratic caucus (but more than 90 percent of the GOP's).

Pelosi, seated to Jeffries's left in her hot-pink sheath dress, stood and waved. Paul and the five Pelosi children watched from the front row of the Visitors' Gallery.

"Nancy Pelosi is a woman of faith," Jeffries said. "A loving wife. A mother of five. A grandmother of nine. A sophisticated strategist, a legendary legislator, a voice for the voiceless, a defender of the disenfranchised. A powerful, profound, prophetic, principled public servant, and that's why we stand squarely behind her today. Let me be clear: House Democrats are down with NDP—Nancy D'Alesandro Pelosi—the once and future Speaker of the United States House of Representatives!"

The reference to a hip-hop classic, "O.P.P.," was, the *Washington Post* wryly noted, "perhaps the first nod to a Naughty by Nature song in a nominating speech for House speaker."

The Republicans nominated their own leader, Kevin McCarthy. The clerk called the roll, and each member declared their vote. "Nancy 'No Wall' Pelosi!" hollered Veronica Escobar of Texas. "The lady who will truly make America great again, Nancy Pelosi!" said Steve Cohen of Tennessee. Fifteen Democrats cast votes against her, including Abigail Spanberger and Kathleen Rice, but not Tim Ryan or Seth Moulton. Three voted "present." In the final tally, Pelosi got 220 votes.

She strode down the aisle, beaming, pausing for handshakes and hugs. Reaching the well of the House, she accepted the gavel from McCarthy, holding it in front of her with both hands and swiveling from side to side, unable to suppress an enormous, gleeful smile. For decades, the Capitol had been her habitat and context. She knew its every nook and cranny—the hidden hideaways, the basement catacombs, the committee rooms and cloakrooms. It had been a place of triumph and a place of defeat, of ambition and frustration, of lofty aspirations and ugly compromises. To most Americans, it was an opaque or repulsive place, where greedy pols did greasy deals—or, worse, accomplished nothing at all.

But today it was her pedestal. She stood in front of a leather chair so high-backed it was level with the top of her head, a shiny American flag draped sideways behind it.

"Every two years, we gather in this chamber for a sacred ritual," she said. "Under the dome of this temple of democracy, the Capitol of the United States, we renew the great American experiment." She proudly observed that the House would have a woman Speaker, and a record number of women members, in the centennial year of women's right to vote.

"Two months ago, the American people spoke and demanded a new dawn," she said. "They called upon the beauty of our Constitution, our system of checks and balances that protects our democracy, remembering that the legislative branch is Article One, coequal to the presidency and to the judiciary."

For one day, at least, while chaos raged outside, it was possible to imagine the House as an exalted place: "America's town hall," Pelosi called it, "where people will see our debates, and where their voices will be heard." The Republicans sat stone-faced as she called for health care, green energy, gun control, LGBTQ rights and the DREAM Act—even when she quoted President Reagan praising immigrants. "You're not going to applaud for Ronald Reagan?" she asked incredulously.

At the end of her speech, she called the children up to join her—not just her own grandchildren but dozens of others rushed up and crowded around her as her raspy giggle echoed over the still-hot microphone. The oldest member of the House, a crusty eighty-five-year-old Alaska Republican named Don Young, read the oath of office, and she said, "I do," and blew a kiss.

"I now call the House to order on behalf of all of America's children," Pelosi announced, banging the gavel three times. She told the children they could go back and sit with their parents, but most of them wanted to stay up there with her.

✧ ✧ ✧

After the pomp and circumstance, her day was far from over. She had to administer the oath of office to every member individually, posing for a photo each time. For efficiency's sake, two identical swearing-in stations were set up in the Capitol's Rayburn Room, where the members formed two lines as Pelosi shuttled back and forth between them in her high-heeled shoes, somehow showing no hint of exhaustion. By the time the House reconvened to pass a bill to fund the government but not the border wall—the same legislation the Republican Senate had passed in December—it was nearly 11 p.m.

The message was clear: Republicans had left the government closed and walked off the job; Democrats, on their very first day, were working to reopen it, on terms the Republicans themselves had supported before the president changed his mind. But beyond symbolism, the bill had no effect. The Senate ignored it. McConnell, weary of the president's ever-changing whims, had essentially disappeared, declaring it was up to the White House and Democrats to figure out an end to the shutdown.

For the new members of Pelosi's caucus, the situation was befuddling and dismaying. They'd campaigned on getting things done for their constituents, only to find themselves spinning their wheels. They'd campaigned on a promise to rise above partisanship, only to land smack in the middle of a high-stakes partisan fight. They'd arrived in Washington eager to get to work, only to be told that, when it came to the shutdown, what they were going to do was . . . nothing.

They would not negotiate. They would not compromise. They would pass bill after useless bill to fund the government, but they would not give the president his wall or anything else in exchange for his bullying. To do so would be to legitimize the shutdown as a negotiating tactic, rather than an unacceptable violation of the people's trust. Pelosi pointed back to her tangle with George W. Bush over his Social Security reform plan, when the Democrats had held firm and refused to make a counterproposal, forcing Bush to defend it on the merits.

Trump wasn't helping his own cause: rather than express concern about the hundreds of thousands of federal workers who were going without pay, he alternately insisted, contrary to all evidence, that they supported the gambit, or he claimed they were all Democrats anyway. (The president had a habit of implying that he had no responsibility to help citizens who weren't his supporters: he'd even tried to withhold federal wildfire aid to liberal California.) The commerce secretary, Wilbur Ross, an investor worth $700 million, said he didn't understand why unpaid workers were going to food banks when they could just get loans. "Is this the 'Let them eat cake' kind of attitude?" Pelosi responded. "Or call your father for money?"

When she and Schumer met with Trump on January 9, Schumer accused the president of using federal workers as leverage and asked why he wouldn't open the government and stop hurting people. "Because then you won't give me what I want," Trump said. He turned to Pelosi and asked what it would take for her to come around. "In thirty days, will you be in favor of a wall?" he asked.

"No," she replied.

"What's the point?" he growled, slamming his hands on the table. "Bye-bye." The meeting was over.

Trump continued to peddle the idea that there was a crisis at the border requiring immediate action. He talked about declaring a national emergency, a troubling and unwarranted end run around the Constitution that demonstrated his authoritarian tendencies. As an emergency measure, the border wall made no sense: even if it were fully funded, it would take years to design it, acquire the land and build it.

Behind the scenes, some Democrats were going wobbly as the shutdown wore on. In caucus meetings, members from more conservative districts worried that their no-negotiation stance looked unreasonable. The Blue Dogs began circulating a letter calling for talks, while a group of freshmen pondered a similar move. But there was little public dissent. Even the public worker unions whose members were going unpaid urged the Democrats to stand strong. When the White House invited a group of centrist Democratic members to meet the president, in an attempt to peel them away from Pelosi's position, none of them went.

Poll after poll showed that the public overwhelmingly blamed Trump and Republicans for the shutdown. We are winning the argument, Pelosi assured the members. Just be patient, she said. And if you disagree, please keep it in the room—don't air it out in the press.

On January 16, with the shutdown already the longest in U.S. history, Pelosi sent a surprise letter to the White House proposing to postpone the State of the Union address scheduled for January 29. The letter was as cutting as it was subtle: "Sadly, given the security concerns and unless government reopens this week," she wrote, "I suggest that we work together to determine another suitable date after government has reopened for this address or for you to consider delivering your State of the Union address in writing."

The move showed the dividends of Pelosi's long experience. She could pull levers of power most people didn't know existed. Her caucus, which had received no warning, largely cheered the gesture. In a closed-door meeting, Clyburn introduced her with a quote from Sun Tzu's *The Art of War*. The president who thought he could do anything had run up against the master of structural power. In the words of the talk show host Samantha Bee, "Dude, I know it's driving you crazy that a woman turned you down, but this is the point in your life where you're actually going to have to learn that no means no. There will be no grabbing this podium until Nancy is good and ready."

Trump was uncharacteristically silent for twenty-four hours while Pelosi and a group of members prepared for an unannounced trip to Brussels and Afghanistan. Everyone but Pelosi had already boarded the bus that would take them to their military jet at Andrews Air Force Base when a missive from the White House landed. "Due to the Shutdown, I am sorry to inform you that your trip to Brussels, Egypt, and Afghanistan has been postponed," it began. (In fact, there was no stop in Egypt on the schedule.) Trump called the trip, a visit to service members in a war zone, a "public relations event," and said Pelosi could still fly commercial if she liked. Where her letter had dripped regal condescension, his reeked of petulance.

Conservatives crowed that Trump had one-upped Pelosi and put her in her place. But as the shutdown reached a month's duration, public anger grew. Unpaid air traffic controllers and airport screeners were calling in sick, which was leading to long lines, delayed flights and grumbling among the 1 percent. Republican senators were taking heat back home. In public statements and private conversations, they began to signal to McConnell that they couldn't hold out much longer.

On January 25, after thirty-five days, Trump caved. He signed a bill to reopen the government for three weeks, insisting that it was only a temporary reprieve to restart wall negotiations, but it was clear he had folded. On social media, liberals gloated about the humiliating retreat. "So basically, Nancy Pelosi dog walked Trump," one tweeted, to which the rap star Cardi B responded, "Basically." Congresswoman Karen Bass tweeted, "Speaker Pelosi should give the State of the Union since she's obviously the one running the country." Congressman Mark Takano tweeted a doctored cover of *The Art of the Deal*, with Pelosi's name and face in place of Trump's. "Fixed it," he wrote.

Pelosi took a different tone. In her subsequent press conference with

Schumer, reporters repeatedly tried to goad her into taking a victory lap, but she demurred. To those who knew her methods, it was clear what she was doing: trying to send a message to the president about how easy things could be if he just did things her way. Like a mother rewarding a toddler for good manners, she was trying to create positive reinforcement for good behavior.

Perhaps now Trump would realize that his power was not absolute, that the political climate in Washington had changed since the midterms, that he would have to deal with her if he wanted to get anything done. Perhaps she could, as she had with George W. Bush, work with him on goals they shared even as they fiercely opposed each other where they didn't agree. Perhaps she could domesticate him as she had so many others on both sides. But she was not naïve enough to be optimistic. Some children can't be taught.

That night, she and Paul and one of her college girlfriends had a quiet dinner at the chic Georgetown restaurant La Chaumière. When Pelosi got up to leave, the population of the restaurant, including the staff, burst into cheers.

The State of the Union transpired a week later than originally planned, on February 5. The Democratic women all wore white in honor of the suffragists. Pelosi, clad in a sleek ivory pantsuit, stood behind Trump as he gave his rambling, scripted address. When he got to the part about "the boundless potential of cooperation, compromise and the common good," she extended her arms forward and clapped, mouth twisted in a sardonic, close-lipped smile.

Pelosi maintained that her applause was in earnest, but that wasn't how people saw it. As with the picture with the red coat, the image of her clapping became an instant meme: "acres of shade dispensed by a skilled politician firmly in control," the *Times* called it. On Twitter, the comedian Patton Oswalt quipped that Pelosi had "invented the 'fuck you' clap," while Pelosi's daughter Christine said the gesture took her back to adolescence: "She knows. And she knows that you know. And frankly she's disappointed that you thought this would work." Whole essays were written about the clap's meaning, and many remarked on how starkly Pelosi's image had turned around since the election. Another meme that began circulating around this time pictured Trump wearing the signature white bonnet of the slave women of *The Handmaid's Tale*, captioned "OFNANCY." In a bar in DC, a box on the wall held a bottle of Taittinger champagne, the words "IN CASE OF PRESIDENT PELOSI BREAK GLASS" etched on the front.

But had Pelosi changed, or had the culture? She'd grown up in a world where women were supposed to be soft and gentle, but now America loved "bad bitches." A book called #GirlBoss was a smash best seller, one of many on the theme of unabashed female empowerment. Beyoncé sang, "Who run the world? Girls," and the song was a huge hit. Pelosi was profiled for a CNN series called "Badass Women of Washington." Forceful, confident, determined, unafraid to wield power—even a decade earlier, these qualities in a woman registered as frightening and repellent, but in 2019 the combination of femininity and aggression was greeted with "YASS KWEEN."

This new breed of woman, brash and brave and ballsy, was everywhere—including Congress.

◇ ◇ ◇

On a whim, they called themselves the Squad: four youngish freshwomen of color from liberal districts. They were AOC; Ilhan Omar, a thirty-six-year-old Somali American Muslim from Minneapolis; Ayanna Pressley, forty-four, the first black woman to represent Massachusetts in Congress; and Rashida Tlaib, a forty-two-year-old Palestinian American Muslim from Detroit. Idealistic, social media–savvy and extremely left-wing, they relished the sisterly solidarity they represented.

All four voted for Pelosi for Speaker, but as the congressional term got under way, they chafed at the constraints she imposed on the Democratic agenda. The climate committee AOC had praised her for creating was toothless, and AOC wasn't even on it. Its agenda didn't include the Green New Deal, a far-reaching, multitrillion-dollar plan to restructure not just the energy industry but the whole American economy. Pelosi referred to it as "the green dream or whatever they call it."

She voiced similar skepticism about Medicare for All, the single-payer proposal many liberals embraced. (Ironically, just when Obamacare finally became popular, liberals decided it wasn't good enough. Pelosi's view was that more had to be done to regulate the health care industry and shore up the Affordable Care Act, but that uprooting the whole health care system wasn't workable—or politically wise.) And she opposed the idea of abolishing U.S. Immigration and Customs Enforcement, the agency created by Bush in 2003, which liberals charged had become a brutal and lawless deportation force.

Whenever Pelosi took flak from the left, she would point out that Republicans had spent hundreds of millions of dollars calling her a "San Francisco liberal"—a label she was proud to own. "Come to my basement. I have these signs about single-payer from thirty years ago," she'd say. "But we have a responsibility to get something done." Progressives suspected she paid lip service to their ideals while using them as a foil when it suited her.

In February, Ilhan Omar tweeted that politicians' support for Israel was "all about the Benjamins baby," implying that Jewish interests were buying them off. It wasn't the first time she'd been accused of anti-Semitic language. Many of her colleagues were offended, and Pelosi immediately issued a statement denouncing the remark. Within hours, Omar apologized. But a few weeks later, she spoke about "the political influence in this country that says it is okay for people to push for allegiance to a foreign country," again inflaming Jewish sensitivities by echoing the historic accusation that Jews' patriotism was suspect because their first loyalty was to Israel. Several Jewish Democrats publicly criticized the remark.

Pelosi sought to defuse the issue with a House resolution condemning anti-Semitism, hoping to put the matter to rest and unify the caucus around a statement of indisputable shared values. But many black and progressive members thought it was unfair to single Omar out for rebuke and to implicitly validate Trump's disingenuous attacks—"It is shameful that House Democrats won't take a stronger stand against anti-Semitism in their conference," the president wrote on Twitter, despite his own history of equally blatant anti-Semitic allusions. The proposed resolution was rewritten to blandly condemn all kinds of bigotry, but this angered Jewish members who wanted a specific statement.

The issue was a potentially explosive one that threatened to pit Democrats against one another along racial and religious lines. Omar's statements were unfortunate and divisive, but Republicans were clearly seizing on them not out of concern but in order to drive wedges in the opposing party. Pelosi disliked all this; she wanted people to think Democrats were orderly and focused, committed to getting things done, legislating, and achieving results for their constituents. In fact, the House was drafting and passing legislation at a brisk clip, much of it bipartisan, but McConnell wouldn't put much of it up for a vote in the Senate, where he proudly called himself the "Grim Reaper" and devoted the schedule to ramming through judicial nominations to pack the courts with Trump loyalists.

The irony of Pelosi's position was that in the area she wanted to focus on, policy, she couldn't accomplish much beyond symbolism; in the area she wanted to downplay, oversight of Trump, she actually did have the power to do things with the House alone. At the same time as the House investigated Trump's many scandals, she was negotiating with the administration to revise NAFTA, seeking bipartisan deals on prescription drug pricing and infrastructure, and working to achieve a budget agreement—sometimes to howls from the left, which thought any engagement with Trump threatened to "normalize" his presidency and improve his political standing. It was the president, not Pelosi, who blew up negotiations and walked away from the table, only to then turn around and blame Democrats for getting nothing done.

Pelosi sought to refocus attention on the caucus's center rather than its fringe. Amazingly, the leader whom moderate Democrats had tried to drive out for being too liberal had become the party's moderating force. The experience of 2010 had made her keenly aware of the importance of protecting moderate members in conservative-leaning districts, who, unlike AOC, had delivered Democrats the majority and whose voters would punish them if they saw the party's agenda veering too far left. Thirty-one of her members in 2019 were elected from districts that Trump had won. It was true, of course, that the GOP would brand them all socialists and accuse them of liberal extremism whether or not it was the case. But it was an easier argument to rebut if Democrats didn't play into their hands.

AOC's far-left views were too much even for many progressives; her "wing" of the party, Pelosi told 60 Minutes acerbically, was "like, five people." But the idea that they should fall in line only further inflamed the liberal freshmen, who felt they were being marginalized. Tlaib accused Democratic leaders of using women of color as props, adding, "However, when we ask to be at the table, or speak up about issues that impact who we are, what we fight for & why we ran in the first place, we are ignored. To truly honor our diversity is to never silence us." When Trump accused Omar of disrespecting the 9/11 attacks, a distortion of her remark that Muslims shouldn't be held collectively responsible for something "some people did," liberals found Pelosi's condemnation of Trump's comment insufficiently vocal. More than two hundred progressive groups signed a letter of support for Omar.

It was against this raw-nerved backdrop that Congress prepared to respond to the Trump administration's request for money to deal with the border crisis. The situation was heartbreaking: children ripped from their families and kept in cagelike enclosures; families housed for months in frigid, dirty, crowded warehouses, shielded from public view by the private operators contracted to run them—even lawmakers couldn't visit or take photographs without permission. At least seven migrant children had died in custody, the first such deaths in a decade. The administration, one of its lawyers told a judge, did not believe that the statutory requirement of "safe and sanitary" conditions obliged it to provide detainees with toothbrushes or soap. Teenage refugees were responsible for caring for distraught, diaperless toddlers with no adult assistance.

Progressives didn't want to fund these detention camps; they wanted to eliminate them. But moderates didn't want to look weak on immigration. And if the camps had to exist, better that they have adequate provisions than not. Pelosi sought to broker a compromise that would fund the facilities while imposing restrictions on them to protect the children they housed, such as a three-month limit on detention, minimum health and safety standards, and a requirement that lawmakers be allowed to inspect them at any time. It was a stark illustration of the drawbacks of compromise, and also its necessity: powerless to stop the situation, Pelosi would try to improve it, even if that meant enabling a monstrous policy.

The plan was for the House to pass its bill first, and then Schumer and the Senate Democrats would lobby for McConnell to take it up. But the progressives were in a fighting mood, and Pelosi's negotiations dragged on into the summer as they refused to commit. As the July 4 holiday approached, some Democratic senators feared getting steamrolled, so they entered into negotiations with their Republican counterparts, coming up with a $4.6 billion bipartisan bill. By the time the House released the more liberal measure that Pelosi had labored to construct, the Senate bill already had broad bipartisan backing.

The House passed its bill after Pelosi pleaded with liberals to support it. The only Democrats who didn't vote for it were the four members of the Squad. Pelosi expected that Schumer would then play hardball, getting his caucus to oppose the Senate bill and force McConnell to make concessions. But Senate Democrats thought the bill they'd negotiated was good enough. They passed it with a strong bipartisan vote, jamming Pelosi, who had little choice but to bring up the Senate bill for a vote in the House.

Chaos broke out on the House floor on June 27, the day of the border bill vote. Members yelled at one another. The co-chairman of the Progressive Caucus, Mark Pocan of Wisconsin, dubbed the Problem Solvers, who lobbied for the Senate bill's passage, "the Child Abuse Caucus." The Hispanic Caucus called the bill "a betrayal of our American values" that would not be forgotten. It passed with more Republican than Democratic votes.

Pelosi was humiliated, and furious with Schumer. Republicans licked their chops at the specter of Democratic division; columnists pilloried Pelosi as falling victim to the same forces of division and absolutism as John Boehner and Paul Ryan had. (Some were honest enough to note that she had, despite the ugly fracas, gotten the policy in question passed, unlike her paralyzed predecessors.) A *HuffPost* headline asked, "What the Hell Is Nancy Pelosi Doing?"

✧ ✧ ✧

By Independence Day, everyone needed a vacation. Pelosi retreated to the vineyard in Napa she and her husband owned, where every summer she hosted an elite group of donors for an ideas conference. She marched in the San Francisco Pride parade. Afterward, over omelets, she gave an interview to the *Times*'s Maureen Dowd, who asked about the Squad. Pelosi said she considered them irrelevant, because they'd voted against the House bill. "All these people have their public whatever and their Twitter world," she was quoted as saying. "But they didn't have any following. They're four people and that's how many votes they got."

The Dowd column landed like a grenade. AOC fired back—on Twitter, naturally, where she now had nearly five million followers. "That public 'whatever' is called public sentiment," she wrote. "And wielding the power to shift it is how we actually achieve meaningful change in this country." Her chief of staff went further, criticizing Pelosi in harsh terms and equating moderates with segregationists—spurring a fresh round of outrage from the moderates, many of them people of color, who didn't appreciate being called racist.

The Pelosi-AOC exchange was a revealing glimpse into Pelosi's mindset. To her, only hard power mattered: the power of having the votes to pass legislation. Her perspective was understandable. As a woman in the 1970s, she couldn't make anybody listen to her voice, but as she found when she got to the library board, she could move them with her vote. It was her mastery of systems of hard power that had formed the basis of her career. She didn't really get Twitter—once, when a colleague showed it to her on his phone, she didn't know how to scroll through the tweets—but in a larger sense, she didn't believe soft power meant anything if it didn't result in votes. "Power is not influence," she'd once said. "They will have these magazine articles that have the hundred most influential people in the world. I'll look at it and think: 'That's interesting. That's influence; that's not necessarily power.'" In her mind, you earned power by doing the work of legislating, not building some nebulous "movement."

When Congress returned to DC the following week, the intra-Democratic sniping had reached fever pitch. It was going to take a dramatic gesture to bring them back together. Pelosi needed to take command.

She strode to the front of the caucus meeting in a sky-blue blazer and a strand of oversize pearls. "Understand what we are up against," she began. "Mitch McConnell would have been very happy if we passed nothing and nothing was done. He doesn't care about the children."

The room, which sometimes buzzed with gossip even when she was speaking, fell silent. "We are never satisfied," she continued. "But to have nothing go to the children—I just couldn't do that. I'm here to help the children when it's easy and when it's hard. Some of you are here to make a beautiful pâté, but we're making sausage most of the time."

A few people laughed. She continued. "This is a team. On a team you play as a team." But they had to keep the big picture in mind: a Republican Party that didn't believe in science or facts, that scapegoated immigrants, abandoned the environment and disdained basic governance. Democrats, she said, needed to respect one another's different backgrounds and political circumstances, because nothing was more important than keeping their majority so they could pursue their shared values.

"I take responsibility," she said. "You make me the target. But don't make our Blue Dogs and our New Dems the target in all of this, because we have important fish to fry. . . . We're a family, and we have our moments. . . . You got a complaint? You come and talk to me about it. But do not tweet about our members and expect us to think that that is just okay."

The fiery speech got a standing ovation, but the hurt feelings lingered. Then, a few days later, Trump waded into the fray. "So interesting to see 'Progressive' Democrat Congresswomen, who originally came from countries whose governments are a complete and total catastrophe, the worst, most corrupt and inept anywhere in the world (if they even have a functioning government at all), now loudly and viciously telling the people of the United States, the greatest and most powerful Nation on earth, how our government is to be run," he tweeted. "Why don't they go back and help fix the totally broken and crime infested places from which they came. Then come back and show us how it is done. These places need your help badly, you can't leave fast enough. I'm sure that Nancy Pelosi would be very happy to quickly work out free travel arrangements!"

Even for Democrats who already thought the worst of Trump, the naked racism—referring to four nonwhite American citizens, three of them native-born, as if they could not be true Americans—was shocking. (Not to mention the hypocrisy: Trump routinely painted a dismal picture of his country, and his mother and wife were immigrants. In one of his more perplexing habitual untruths, in 2018 and 2019 the president repeatedly stated that his father was also an immigrant, born in Germany, but Frederick Trump was actually born in New York to German parents.) Between this and "shithole countries," it seemed clear he believed that only white people deserved to be American, regardless of citizenship. Death threats against the Squad members flooded in as crowds at Trump's rallies chanted, "Send them back!"

Pelosi quickly responded to Trump's tirade: "When @realDonaldTrump tells four American Congresswomen to go back to their countries, he reaffirms his plan to 'Make America Great Again' has always been about making America white again," she tweeted. Suddenly Democrats were unified again (though some worried that Trump had succeeded in his goal of making the Squad the face of the party).

And Pelosi was back in control. In the next caucus meeting, she said, "The fact is, as offended as we are—and we are offended by what he said about our sisters—he says that about people every day, and they feel as hurt as we do about somebody in our family having this offense against them." A resolution condemning Trump's tweets passed with just 4 Republican votes.

Pelosi scheduled a meeting to mend fences with AOC, something her progressive allies had been urging her to do. The two women talked privately, then posed for a photo posted to Twitter. "We're good," Pelosi said.

Soon after that, the budget she'd negotiated overwhelmingly passed the House and Senate and was signed by President Trump. Working quietly for months with Treasury Secretary Mnuchin, she had succeeded in negotiating a two-year bipartisan agreement that lifted the debt ceiling, got rid of the sequestration spending caps and added $320 billion in new spending, the majority of it for domestic priorities. Months of negotiations culminated on an airport tarmac in Detroit, where she sat in seat 23D talking on her cell phone for the duration of a three-hour delay, working out the final provisions.

Compared to the Squad fracas, the budget received little attention—a crisis averted, an unglamorous triumph. Under Obama, Congress had gone years without passing a budget at all, relying on stopgap extensions instead. Unlike all the Washington squabbling, the budget would actually make a difference in people's lives. It soared through the House and Senate with more Democratic than Republican votes (including from two members of the Squad), and Trump quickly signed it into law.

28

To Democrats, Trump represented a crisis for the country—and also for their party. The issue of how to hold him accountable now increasingly divided them.

Trump had barely been in office a month before some members of Pelosi's caucus began calling for him to be impeached. Representative Al Green of Texas drew up and introduced articles of impeachment in October 2017. Tom Steyer, a San Francisco billionaire and longtime Pelosi friend and donor, started an online impeachment petition that quickly had millions of signatures, and he began spending tens of millions of dollars on pro-impeachment ads. Pelosi relayed a message to Steyer—*please cut it out, you're not helping*—but he didn't listen. The majority of impeachment petition signers, according to Steyer's data, were women over the age of sixty-five.

Publicly, Pelosi firmly dismissed talk of impeachment. She vividly remembered the Clinton impeachment, which she considered to have been a joke; she also recalled resisting the liberals' determination to impeach President Bush, whom they considered a war criminal. When Obama was president, Republican activists spent years demanding that their leaders impeach him, to no avail. Ever the institutionalist, Pelosi viewed impeachment as an extraordinary step that should be undertaken only in the most serious of circumstances, after other avenues were exhausted. She feared that a country already riven by partisanship would be thrown into a toxic, divisive cycle where every successive president was impeached by the opposing party, to the point where it became routine. And with Republicans controlling the Senate, there was little chance Trump would be convicted or removed; ever the instrumentalist, Pelosi didn't see the point of pushing for something that wouldn't have any tangible result.

That didn't mean the Democrats would ignore Trump's corruption. Since taking the majority, Pelosi had spearheaded the coordination of six different House committees charged with different investigations of the Trump administration, from the president's personal finances to the ties to Russia that were the focus of the special counsel's ongoing investigation. She hired a forty-year Justice Department veteran to head the House counsel's office, a secretive team of nine lawyers, and she personally oversaw its work as it picked cases to ask the courts to resolve, such as unanswered subpoenas and the attempt to put a citizenship question on the 2020 Census. The administration was violating norms on so many fronts that the counsel's office had its biggest workload ever.

But Pelosi's public rationales for not pursuing impeachment were conflicting. She insisted the Democrats would not impeach for political reasons, but also would not *not* impeach for political reasons. At the same time, she said she would move forward only if there were Republican support and public sentiment in favor—a fundamentally political standard. As evidence of Trump's lawlessness mounted, Democrats inside and outside Congress grew increasingly agitated that their party seemed to be avoiding its constitutional obligation to hold him accountable for his abuses of power.

Some Democrats believed Trump had been violating the Constitution since he took the oath of office. But many hoped a smoking gun would be delivered by the special counsel, Robert Mueller, the straitlaced Republican former FBI director appointed in May 2017 to investigate Russian election interference. The special counsel's office secured criminal convictions of Trump's former campaign chairman and his deputy, his former national security adviser, former personal lawyer, and a campaign operative who told an acquaintance the Russian government had stolen Hillary Clinton's emails, along with a bevy of Russian spies and trolls. Trump himself was identified as an unindicted co-conspirator in the felony campaign finance case involving hush money payments to two alleged mistresses. The prosecutor seemed to be circling ever closer to his ultimate target.

In court filings, Mueller's prosecutors outlined in meticulous detail the Russian government's nefarious plot to subvert American democracy and the Trump campaign's willing participation in the scheme. Mueller soldiered on despite Trump's increasing attacks on the "witch hunt" and attempts to derail the investigation, from trying to fire Mueller—Trump's White House counsel threatened to resign rather than do so—to getting his congressional allies to investigate the investigators, to encouraging witnesses to lie on his behalf, suggesting he'd pardon them if they got in trouble. Democrats breathlessly awaited Mueller's final report. Online boutiques sold "Mueller Time" T-shirts; grassroots activists made protest signs depicting Mueller in a superhero's cape. Some even fantasized that he might bring criminal charges against Trump, despite a Justice Department policy against prosecuting sitting presidents.

Mueller finished his investigation in late March and turned his report over to the attorney general, William Barr, who quickly sent Congress a mild four-page summary. The report, Barr said, "did not establish that members of the Trump Campaign conspired or coordinated with the Russian government in its election interference activities," and didn't come to a conclusion about whether the president obstructed justice. That, Barr said, was the attorney general's job, and he had determined that there was no crime.

Pelosi fielded calls about the letter from her granddaughter Bella's birthday party at a bowling alley in San Francisco. Perched on a chair, the Speaker, wearing a pink plastic lei, told her agitated committee leaders, "Be calm. Take a deep breath."

A month later, Barr released the entire, lightly redacted 448-page report. The document was dense and strenuously by the book, choked with legalisms—the opposite of the fiery, partisan, lascivious document Bill Clinton's investigators had produced. Yet it was far more damning than Barr had suggested. It laid out ample evidence of the Trump campaign's willing collaboration with Russia, saying it nonetheless fell short of the statutory definition of criminal conspiracy—in part because crucial evidence had been destroyed or withheld. It explained the legal elements of obstruction and outlined ten instances in which Trump's conduct seemed to fit them, but it declined to make a "prosecutorial judgment." "While this report does not conclude that the President committed a crime, it also does not exonerate him," the report read. The determination of criminality and consequences, Mueller wrote, was up to Congress—not, as Barr had stated, the attorney general.

Congress was in recess at the time, and Pelosi was briefed on the report while she was in Europe. When she returned, she convened an eighty-seven-minute conference call with the whole Democratic caucus, in which she again tried to calm the waters. There would be more subpoenas and more hearings, she said, but the House would not rush into anything. "This isn't about Democrats or Republicans. It's about saving our democracy," she said. As for impeachment, "If it is what we need to do to honor our responsibility to the Constitution—if that's the place the facts take us, that's the place we have to go."

Some members chafed at this; media whip counts of congressional impeachment support ticked upward. But most members who came out in favor of impeachment framed it as a personal position, not a criticism of Pelosi or her leadership. In private, she said they should follow their conscience and their district, but without casting judgment on colleagues who might feel differently.

Pelosi's caution was a stark contrast to Trump's approach: a barrage of lies, insults and distortions. He declared over and over that the report had exonerated him despite the fact that it had quite pointedly not done so. He depicted the report as a nothing burger and a dud despite its clear direction to Congress to pursue and act on its findings. He directed his administration to ignore and block all congressional subpoenas, despite Congress's well-established authority to oversee the executive branch and compel evidence and witnesses. He even sued his own accounting firm to stop it from providing his financial records to congressional investigators.

Trump's stonewalling was unprecedented. Other presidents had selectively resisted congressional requests, based on narrow legal arguments specific to the information in question. But none had ever been so brazen as to declare the whole process—in essence, the whole notion of constitutional checks and balances—illegitimate on its face. The process exposed Congress's troubling lack of recourse: it could compel evidence, but it needed the courts to enforce its requests, which could take months or even years. If an administration could ignore congressional subpoenas with impunity, tying them up in judicial appeals until they became moot, did Congress have any real oversight power at all? Some liberals called on the House to use an antiquated provision called "inherent contempt" to fine subpoena dodgers or even hold them prisoner. Frustration mounted at Pelosi's refusal to escalate—or to use the ultimate tool of congressional accountability, impeachment.

In a caucus meeting on the morning of May 22, Pelosi again pleaded for patience. Trump had just ordered former White House counsel Don McGahn not to testify before Congress, even though he'd cooperated with Mueller's investigation. Maxine Waters, chair of the Financial Services Committee, argued the Democrats had a "responsibility to impeach." But Cheri Bustos, a moderate from Illinois, argued that it was time to "let all this Mueller stuff go." The disagreement had mostly been polite to that point, but there was growing potential for a dangerous and unbridgeable rift among the Democrats.

Emerging from the meeting, Pelosi channeled her flock's frustration while still stopping short of endorsing impeachment. "The president of the United States is engaged in a cover-up," she told the assembled press.

Shortly thereafter, she went to the White House with Schumer and other leaders of both parties to continue their talks about infrastructure. A previous meeting on the subject had gone well—to the alarm of some fiscal conservatives, Chuck and Nancy had gotten the president on board with the idea of two trillion dollars in public spending. But this time, Trump did not shake hands or take his seat. Enraged by the "cover-up" comment, which he said was "terrible," he said he wouldn't make any deals until the "phony investigations" stopped. Before anyone else could speak, he stormed out of the room.

To Pelosi, the outburst seemed like a pretext to hide the fact that the president hadn't done his homework and come up with a funding plan for the infrastructure package. "I knew he was looking for a way out," she said.

The president's adviser Kellyanne Conway, a sycophant with a penchant for disingenuous spin, turned to Pelosi and said, "Respectfully, Madam Speaker, do you have a direct response to the president?"

Pelosi said if she wanted to respond to the president, she'd do so directly, not to members of his staff.

"Really great," Conway replied sarcastically. "That's really pro-woman of you."

Trump stalked out to the Rose Garden, where he stood at a lectern hung with a preprinted sign—not about infrastructure, but about the

Mueller investigation, validating Pelosi's hunch that he'd always planned to change the subject. "Mueller Investigation by the Numbers," it read. "2,800+ subpoenas. 675 days. 500+ witnesses." That much was true. "$35+ million spent. 18 Angry Democrats." Those points were false. The president proceeded to give a ten-minute diatribe enumerating his grievances. "I don't do cover-ups," he said. To a reporter who asked whether he respected congressional oversight, he responded, "What they've done is abuse."

Pelosi's tightrope walk was getting ever more perilous, while the president's attacks grew more unhinged. He called her "crazy" and said she'd "lost it." He circulated a video mash-up of her stammering during a news conference. He dubbed her "Nervous Nancy." Allies found the nickname laughable—of all the things to call the confident, steel-spined Nancy Pelosi, "nervous"?—but to some confidants she did seem more uncertain than usual. A planner, a strategist, a leader who saw around corners, she increasingly found herself trapped in a no-win situation, with no control over the endgame and no road map to a defined goal. She told friends she'd started wearing a mouth guard to bed because the president made her grind her teeth in her sleep.

Publicly, she responded with her typically devastating hauteur: "I pray for the president," she said.

In late July, two House committees brought Mueller to testify, even though he'd said he wanted the report to speak for itself. It was clear, thanks to the report's cautious language, Barr's deceptive rollout and Trump's muddying of the waters, that the public hadn't absorbed the gravity of its conclusions. Congressional Democrats hoped a day of testimony, carried live on all the networks, would showcase the truth. But as a witness, Mueller was a dud. Terse and stumbling, the seventy-four-year-old special counsel gave mostly yes or no answers and seemed at times unfamiliar with his own report, while Republicans succeeded in staging disruptive procedural stunts.

While Mueller was reluctant to elaborate on the president's misconduct, he was adamant about the danger of Russian election interference, telling the committees it remained a clear and present danger as the next election approached. (Trump had resisted his own administration's attempts to improve election security and repeatedly questioned the intelligence community's unanimous assessment of the ongoing danger, including in the public presence of Vladimir Putin, while McConnell blocked multiple bipartisan election security bills in the Senate.) Mueller's warning alarmed Democrats and rallied more members to the impeachment cause.

One of the members who had decided it was time for impeachment was Jerry Nadler of New York, chairman of the Judiciary Committee, which had the power to start the impeachment process. In caucus meetings, he and Pelosi sniped at each other, and he threatened to go rogue. She authorized him to refer to the committee's investigations as part of a possible impeachment process in legal filings, but he went further, publicly arguing that impeachment was already under way and lobbying colleagues to join him in pressuring her.

Still, she held the line. During the August congressional recess, she appeared at a banquet in her honor—the "Heart of the Resistance" Dinner—hosted by the San Francisco Democratic Party. She had barely begun to speak when a group of young activists rose in the back, standing on chairs and unfurling black fabric banners with white lettering. "TIME TO IMPEACH," they read. "WE CAN'T WAIT." A young woman shouted, "People are being killed by white supremacists!" A man cried, "We are your constituents!" As the rest of the crowd drowned them out with chants of "Let her speak," a burly labor organizer got in the activists' faces, and for a moment it seemed like they might come to blows before hotel security escorted the protesters out.

"It's okay," Pelosi said from where she stood at the front of the room. "I'm going to speak. I'm the Speaker of the House!" The crowd cheered and waved the Rosie the Riveter–themed "Speaker Pelosi" posters that came with their seats.

She went on with the speech as planned, making no mention of the I-word. "Our investigations are leading to litigation," she said. "We are winning in the courts. We will persist, because no one is above the law, not even the president of the United States. We will hold him accountable." But that was as far as she went.

As Congress trickled back to Washington after Labor Day, it wasn't clear how much longer she could hold her caucus at bay. Normally middle-of-the-road commentators mocked her assertion that Trump "practically self-impeaches every day" with his disregard for the rule of law, and called her feckless for refusing to use Congress's power to rebuke him. "At some point, Madam Speaker, history may show you had one critical chance to stop this slide toward populist authoritarianism," the conservative writer Andrew Sullivan opined. "And you decided you had better things to do."

✧ ✧ ✧

Then, in mid-September, everything changed.

At first the details were murky: vague reports of a whistleblower who'd gone through official channels to raise the alarm about some kind of misconduct by alerting the inspector general of the intelligence community. The inspector general found the complaint both credible and significant and forwarded it to the acting director of national intelligence—the Senate-confirmed director had quit in frustration a month before, leaving the position, like so many in Trump's Cabinet, vacant. By law, the acting director was supposed to turn the complaint over to the congressional intelligence committees, but instead he alerted William Barr's Justice Department, which told him not to forward it to its rightful recipients.

Congress caught wind of the whistleblower without knowing what the complaint was about. The chairman of the Intelligence Committee, Adam Schiff, a Californian and Pelosi protégé, called for the complaint's release as more disturbing details came to light. The complaint involved the president. It involved a conversation with a foreign leader, and some sort of "promise." It involved Ukraine, the American-allied former Soviet republic still at war with Putin's Russia.

The shocking allegation came into focus in anonymously sourced newspaper reports: Trump had tried to bully a foreign leader into publicly announcing an investigation of one of Trump's potential political opponents, Joe Biden, based on a debunked conspiracy theory involving Biden's son, using White House access and congressionally approved foreign aid as leverage. Trump had, in other words, apparently turned U.S. foreign policy into an instrument of his personal ambition, putting the nation's security at risk in the process. And he had done it the day after Mueller's testimony—seemingly believing himself immune from consequence as he proceeded to try to cheat in the next election in nearly the same way he'd been accused of doing in 2016.

Pelosi spent the weekend of September 21 at back-to-back funerals, first in Washington for Cokie Roberts, the veteran journalist and daughter of Pelosi's mentor Lindy Boggs, then in South Carolina for the wife of Jim

Clyburn. (It was a season of sadness and loss: within the next month, Pelosi's dear friend and colleague Elijah Cummings, chairman of the Oversight Committee, died at the age of sixty-eight, just three days before her beloved older brother Tommy died at ninety.) She knew it was finally time to act, and she began to strategize about how to begin impeachment. She called her most trusted colleagues and gauged the mood of the caucus. On Sunday, September 22, Trump all but admitted he'd done what he was accused of, telling reporters, in one of his customary shouted Q-and-As on the White House Lawn on the way to his helicopter, "The conversation I had was largely congratulatory, with largely corruption, all of the corruption taking place and largely the fact that we don't want our people like Vice President Biden and his son creating to [sic] the corruption already in the Ukraine."

"At this point," AOC tweeted, "the bigger national scandal isn't the president's lawbreaking behavior—it is the Democratic Party's refusal to impeach him for it." But AOC's wasn't the opinion Pelosi was concerned with. It was the Trump Country representatives. They, too, had begun to feel they had no choice but to act.

Virginia congresswoman Abigail Spanberger and six other freshmen members with military and intelligence backgrounds—five of them women, all from formerly Republican districts—conferred among themselves. They were, like the Squad, one of several freshmen cliques, drawn together by their shared experiences, helping each other navigate the confusing world of the House with text messages, dinners and family get-togethers. On Sunday, they started drafting a joint statement. The next day, they notified the Speaker that they wanted to talk to her. Pelosi was in New York, backstage at a United Nations event, when she joined their 5 p.m. conference call. The freshmen told her what they'd decided: they were about to publish in the *Washington Post* a joint op-ed calling for impeachment. It was posted online a few hours later. "We have devoted our lives to the service and security of our country," it read. "These allegations are stunning, both in the national security threat they pose and the potential corruption they represent." The authors' backgrounds as national security experts and swing-district moderates gave their position instant credibility. Within hours, the dribble of support for impeachment had become a flood.

That night, on the plane back to Washington from New York, Pelosi began drafting an announcement for the following day, writing in her looping cursive hand on a piece of loose-leaf paper. In the morning, she couldn't find it, and she thought she must have left it on the plane. But she knew what it was she planned to say.

Before she could make her statement, the president wanted to talk to her. On the morning of Tuesday, September 24, he reached her at her apartment in Georgetown at 8:16. He was in New York, about to give a speech to the UN General Assembly. The ostensible reason for the call was gun legislation—Democrats had passed multiple gun control bills, none of which the Senate had taken up, and Trump, who'd once seemed to support such policies, had proven unwilling to take on his party's Second Amendment absolutists. But it quickly became clear that this wasn't what he wanted to talk about. Instead, it was the still-unreleased whistleblower complaint.

Pelosi had been publicly calling for Trump to release the complaint, but he insisted to her that he wasn't the one holding it up. "Mr. President, you have come into my wheelhouse," she interrupted him, referring to her long tenure on the Intelligence Committee. If he wasn't holding it up, she said, he ought to get whoever was doing so to release it.

The president whined in typical fashion. There was "no pressure at all" to the Ukrainian president, he said. The call was "so perfect—literally, you would be impressed by my lack of pressure." Over and over, she told him this could all be cleared up if he just released the complaint. "Why would I say something bad?" he said. "It was one hundred percent perfect. I didn't ask him for anything."

"Mr. President," Pelosi said. "We have a problem here."

After twenty minutes, the conversation ended. She urged him one more time to release the complaint. "I have to go give a speech," Trump said, and hung up.

If she hadn't been certain before, the call sealed it. It was crystal clear that the president had no sense of right and wrong, and that he would keep putting the nation at risk if nothing were done. Even Nixon had had the good sense to know when he'd been caught. Trump was thumbing his nose at the Constitution, a document he didn't even understand. Nothing bothered Pelosi more than the time he'd said, "I have an Article Two, where I have the right to do whatever I want as president." Congress was Article One of the Constitution. It was supposed to be coequal to the president, with limited and defined powers for each. But this president believed he was a king to whom no rules applied. In the end, Pelosi's political conditions for impeachment evaporated in the face of the president's blatant behavior. She felt she had no choice. The announcement was scheduled for 5 p.m.

That afternoon, Pelosi met at 3 p.m. with the committee chairs, at 3:30 p.m. with the Democratic leadership, and at 4 p.m. with the entire caucus. (She'd found the statement she wrote on the plane, stuffed into a pile of papers, and refined it in a session with her speechwriter.) After their fractious summer, the Democrats were remarkably unified. There were no objections as she told them what she planned to do. Even some of the caucus's most electorally vulnerable members were convinced that impeachment was necessary, whatever the consequences. Meanwhile, in Pelosi's warren of offices in the Capitol, aides scrambled to set up a backdrop in a narrow hallway—a row of flags, a teleprompter, a simple wooden lectern bearing the gold House seal.

As the appointed time drew near, Pelosi was still in the caucus meeting. An aide repeatedly urged her to go upstairs and run through the speech just once before she went out and delivered it. Finally, she turned on him, saying, "I walk into rooms and read teleprompters all the time. That's what we'll do."

Then it was time. She strode out into history—a moment for which she'd be remembered, a step she didn't want to take but that might, perhaps, bring the republic back from the brink. Unlike many of her public announcements, at this one she would not be flanked by colleagues to share credit. She alone would be the face of this momentous decision.

A lifetime spent mastering one institution after another, the family, the Church, the party, Congress, the levers of power and engines of democratic governance, the chaos of popular democracy; all the victories and defeats, the confrontations and commendations, the halting steps toward progress—it had all come to this.

"The president must be held accountable," she said. "No one is above the law. Getting back to our founders, in the darkest days of the American Revolution, Thomas Paine wrote that 'the times have found us'—that the times found them to fight for and establish our democracy."

She was racing through the words on the teleprompter, a rhinestone flag pin affixed to her indigo dress, hands clasped tightly in front of her on the lectern. At this moment, the bright half smile on her face turned grave.

"The times," Pelosi said, "have found us today."

AFTERWORD TO THE PAPERBACK EDITION

Nancy Pelosi wasn't wild about my question. It was November 2019, we were talking about the then just under way impeachment of Donald Trump, and I'd asked if she thought it was the most important thing she'd ever do in elected office.

"I just really can't say," the Speaker said, after an uncharacteristically long pause. "I mean, it's—apart from declaring war, this is the most important thing that the Congress can do. So I guess you would have to say that this is the most serious. The most serious. I'm most proud of the Affordable Care Act, but this is the most serious initiative that I've been involved in, in my career."

As we sat there in Pelosi's Capitol office, in gold-clothed armchairs around a low table topped with a tasteful arrangement of hydrangeas, neither of us could have known what an eventful year lay ahead. Pelosi sat in her customary spot, her back to the window, where the sweeping view of the Mall was shrouded in wintry clouds. (Once, I'm told, President Obama accidentally sat in her usual seat, and she politely asked him to move.) Impeachment seemed destined to become the ultimate drama of Trump's tumultuous presidency, and perhaps a central part of Pelosi's legacy as well.

It was, she told me, a matter of principle: Congress is not supposed to defer to the president—any president. "You have to remember, we are a separate, Article One branch of government, coequal," she said. "So it's not a condescension from his side, 'Well, maybe I'll do what they want and maybe I won't.' No. It's the law. It's the Constitution."

That conversation in Pelosi's office was the culmination of more than two years of reporting. The inspiration for this book began when, in late 2017, I took a job at *Time* magazine and was assigned to profile the then–minority leader. Despite having been the first woman Speaker of the House, Pelosi had never been on the cover of *Time* or any other American newsmagazine, including *Newsweek* and *U.S. News*, which bothered her and her staff. The fixation struck me as petty—journalists know that coverage has much more to do with the improvised daily or weekly scramble to keep up with events than with any grand design; our job is to serve our readers in the moment, not satisfy some cosmic score sheet.

At that point, a year before the midterm elections that would return her to the speakership, her political stock was at a low ebb. Most stories about Pelosi focused on her advancing age, internal dissent in her party, and negative public perception. I try to approach all politicians respectfully but skeptically. But I admit I didn't expect to find her particularly compelling.

As I came to know and study Pelosi, I grew to appreciate her—as a leader, as a woman, as a historic figure, as a human of remarkable and specific talents. That's not to say I agree with her ideologically; I am not a Democrat or a liberal (nor am I a Republican or a conservative). But covering politics in this day and age is enough to make you yearn for leaders who seem to know what the heck they are doing. If this book has a thesis, it is that you needn't agree with Nancy Pelosi's politics to respect her accomplishments and admire her historic career.

I came around to her view on the magazine cover, too. Was it really a coincidence that the historic (mostly male) brain trusts of all those magazines had never seen fit to feature her? Was it really such a good idea, in retrospect, to make her the runner-up to Ben Bernanke for *Time* Person of the Year in 2009? Why were politicians like Pelosi and Hillary Clinton always held responsible for their reputations, but nobody ever asked Donald Trump, the most unpopular presidential nominee in the history of modern opinion polling, "Why do you think people don't like you?" Pelosi had done many important things in her career, but a powerful woman, it seemed, was defined less by what she had done than by how she made people feel.

It was striking, in my interviews, how many people—Obama administration officials, pundits, fellow members of Congress—volunteered that in retrospect they'd underestimated or underappreciated Pelosi. Covering Pelosi became an occasion for me to reflect on many of the themes that ran through my fourteen years of reporting on American politics: partisan polarization, congressional gridlock, the Republican civil war, the decline of governing, the erosion of institutions and, especially, women's representation in politics. Plus, of course, the rise of Trump.

In September 2018, on the eve of her party's sweep of the House, Nancy Pelosi finally made the cover of *Time*. It took 11,431 days from the date of her first election, compared to 5,788 for Newt Gingrich and 7,242 for John Boehner. My article wasn't wholly laudatory—I don't do one-dimensional puff pieces—but it sought to question the conventional narrative around Pelosi and reposition her for appreciation as a pioneering woman at a time of unprecedented women's political activism. I was proud of the piece. It isn't easy to put a fresh spin on a figure who's been in the spotlight for decades. Hardened political reporters I knew told me it changed their view of her. I got letters from women around the world who looked up to her, and from more than one Republican source who respected her game. (I also got an email saying it was an abomination before God for women to be in politics—from a woman.)

After the midterms, and especially after that moment with the rust-red coat, America seemed to see what I saw. The moment seemed ripe for Pelosi's extraordinary and underappreciated story to be told in a new way. Over the course of two years of reporting, I interviewed Pelosi in Baltimore, San Francisco, New York, a campaign swing to Houston, and multiple times in DC. I conducted more than a hundred interviews with critics and supporters, activists and operatives, current and former staff, and dozens of current and former members of Congress from across the political spectrum. Though Pelosi gave generously of her valuable time and gamely fielded all manner of queries, the characterizations in this book are mine, and she had no control over the final product.

As it turned out, far from being the biggest event of Trump's tenure, that first impeachment would not even be the biggest event of his final year in office—or his only impeachment. In December 2019, the House brought two articles of impeachment against Trump, for abuse of power and obstruction of Congress. Pelosi overruled many in her caucus to leave Robert Mueller's findings out of the impeachment articles, even editing mentions of them out of Judiciary Committee press releases. Her micromanagement extended to suggesting a smaller chair for the diminutive Judiciary chairman, Jerry Nadler, before the committee's televised hearings began, so he wouldn't look small on camera. In February 2020, the Senate proceeded to acquit Trump of the House's charges without calling a single witness, even though Trump's former national security adviser John Bolton had said he was willing to testify. A few months later, Bolton published a scathing book about his White House tenure that confirmed the Ukraine accusations along with numerous other allegedly impeachable acts. But rather than blame the Republicans who had enabled Trump and turned a blind eye to his misdeeds, Bolton faulted Pelosi and the Democrats for their handling of the impeachment process.

On the eve of the Senate's impeachment vote, Trump visited the House chamber to give his final State of the Union address. Pelosi extended her hand, but Trump turned away rather than shake it. She sat behind him, speed-reading the speech as he gave it, while Republican lawmakers chanted "Four more years!" and Trump staged a reality-show spectacle. At one point, the First Lady rose and draped the Presidential Medal of Freedom around the neck of the right-wing radio host Rush Limbaugh. When Trump was finished, Pelosi picked up her copy of the speech and theatrically ripped it apart. "He used the Congress as a backdrop for a reality show when he had absolutely no reality in his speech," she later explained. "I wish I didn't have to do that. I wish the speech were dignified and truthful. But it wasn't, and so that was the least I could do."

All the while, reports percolated of a deadly new respiratory virus originating in China. Starting in January, Trump administration officials began raising warnings privately and publicly about the potential for the disease known as COVID-19 to ravage the United States. Trump insisted it was nothing to worry about, and besides imposing a clumsy and ineffectual ban on travel from China, did little to prepare the nation for the calamity that was to come. By mid-March, large swaths of the country were in lockdown as the death count began its tragic rise. Pelosi sprang into action, negotiating with Treasury Secretary Mnuchin on legislation providing funding for free testing, paid leave, and expanded food stamps. At one point, Mnuchin boasted to her that his staff had been up until 4 a.m. putting the finishing touches on the Families First Coronavirus Response Act. "I'm not impressed," she retorted. "We do it all the time."

By April, as the pandemic claimed tens of thousands of lives and tens of millions of jobs, Congress had passed four massive bills with a price tag of nearly three trillion dollars to aid the sick, shore up the health care system, and ease the burden on workers and businesses—the biggest federal outlay in history, dwarfing the response to the 2008 financial crisis. The economic stimulus worked: even as workers were furloughed and industries ground to a halt, personal income went up and poverty went down, cushioning, at least temporarily, the pandemic's blow. Pelosi and the Democrats believed it was still not enough. In May, the House passed a bill with another three trillion dollars in aid for individuals and businesses, funding for state and local governments, and support for testing and tracing. But the Senate dismissed it, and the White House, belatedly recognizing Pelosi's success in policy terms in the earlier rounds of talks, stopped letting Mnuchin negotiate with Pelosi.

During lockdown, Pelosi again became the focus of ginned-up micro-controversies based on resentment of her lifestyle. In an effort to show her human side, she opened her freezer to display her plentiful stash of chocolate ice cream; critics seized on the expensive fridge and gourmet desserts to portray her as a latter-day Marie Antoinette. She went to the salon to get her hair done; a surveillance camera captured her briefly unmasked, spurring days of Fox News coverage of her alleged hypocrisy. Pelosi claimed she was set up by a hairstylist with a political agenda who had falsely assured her staff the visit was allowed under the guidelines in place at the time. Whether or not that was true, it was yet another iteration of a familiar phenomenon—the insane level of scrutiny applied to Pelosi's personal choices. It was hard to imagine a multi-day news cycle erupting if it had been Trump or Mitch McConnell getting his hair done.

Trump spent the summer undermining his own administration's scientists; by the fall, as cases rose to their highest level yet, he was rushed to the hospital as an outbreak spread through the White House. Still, he spent the weeks leading up to the election insisting the media were only going on about COVID because they wanted to hurt his reelection chances. In the end, Pelosi's party won the November election—and the first woman in history became vice president. But rather than expanding their majority as expected, Democrats lost seats in the House. Pelosi stayed on as familiar fights loomed. What lay ahead would not be the expansive mandate for a new New Deal, but another two years of partisan trench warfare—the messy, brutal, incremental work of legislating in a government, and a country, divided.

But Trump would not leave office quietly. Some combination of ego and delusion prevented him from conceding the election, and he spent two months whipping his followers into an aggrieved frenzy over the lie that the vote had been stolen. Judges he'd appointed himself rejected dozens of his spurious lawsuits, while craven Republican politicians and conservative media amplified the paranoia. On January 5, Democrats won two U.S. Senate seats in runoff elections in Georgia, putting them in the majority. On January 6, as Congress gathered to make Biden's election official, Trump told a crowd of thousands to march on the Capitol and "fight like hell." And they did.

The rioters penetrated the Capitol and the Speaker's office. While Pelosi crouched in a secure bunker, staff members hid under a conference table in the office suite. "Where's Nancy?" the rioters jeered, banging on doors as they went. A self-described white nationalist from Arkansas put his feet up on her desk and stole a piece of mail as a trophy. A woman from Pennsylvania stole a laptop. A lawyer from Americus, Georgia, wrote on Facebook, "The first of us who got upstairs kicked in Nancy Pelosi's office door and pushed down the hall towards her inner sanctum, the mob howling with rage. Crazy Nancy probably would have been torn into little pieces but she was nowhere to be seen."

Trump's first impeachment took months; the second took less than a week. The charge was incitement of insurrection. Ten Republicans joined the Democrats to support it, making it the most bipartisan impeachment in history. "The president of the United States incited an armed insurrection against America," Pelosi said. "The gleeful desecration of the U.S. Capitol, which is the temple of our American democracy, and the violence targeting Congress, are horrors that will forever stain our nation's history, instigated by the president of the United States." She wore the same striking black skirt suit and gold necklace as she had for Trump's first impeachment, sparking a wave of admiring commentary on her "impeachment outfit."

Since the original publication of this biography, I've frequently been asked what I think Pelosi's legacy will be. My answer is threefold. Her wish, as she told me that day in her office, is for her legacy to be the Affordable Care Act, and she will surely be remembered for that and other major policy accomplishments. Second, her effectiveness: congressional scholars such as Norm Ornstein of the American Enterprise Institute consider her one of the great legislators of the past century, on a par with former House Speaker Sam Rayburn and "master of the Senate" Lyndon Johnson; Pelosi's ability to make Congress work is all the more remarkable for the fact that it's come at a time of historic polarization and gridlock. And third, her achievement of being the first woman Speaker is still underappreciated. As I write this, she remains the only woman ever to lead a party in either house of Congress.

There's another image of Pelosi that recently became iconic. It's October 2019, and she is in the White House Cabinet Room, wearing a slender blue suit, standing and wagging a finger at Trump, who is seated across from her. The context was a closed-door meeting on Syria, where the president struggled to explain his surprise decision to pull out troops, abandoning America's Kurdish allies in the fight against ISIS and ceding the field to Russia. "All roads with you lead to Putin," Pelosi declared, prompting Trump to insult her as a "third-rate politician" before she and Steny Hoyer walked out. It was Hoyer who insisted that she leave rather than put up with the president's insults, but as they were on the way out Trump shouted at Hoyer, "Steny, you agree with me," according to two sources who were in the room.

The image of Pelosi standing and pointing was captured by a White House photographer. (She once confessed, in a 2014 interview, that she knows people think it's rude to point, but she's never been able to stop herself from doing it, or to trade it for the thumb-fisted gesture many politicians adopt instead.) It became public only because Trump himself mockingly tweeted it with the words "Nervous Nancy's unhinged meltdown." But it quickly went viral among Trump's critics, who saw the opposite: the Speaker with the steel spine, standing up to the petulant president while a roomful of men preferred to avert their eyes.

For Pelosi, being the only woman in a room of important men was a familiar dynamic, but in 2019 it resonated anew. A few weeks later, on CBS's *Face the Nation*, the host, Margaret Brennan, asked her, "Do you think it's different now, though, because you are so often the only woman in this room? I mean, that iconic photo of you after that recent clash at the White House with you standing up."

Pelosi pointed out that that had been the case throughout her career, starting with George W. Bush. Brennan, the second female host in the history of the prestigious Sunday political talk show (and the only woman currently hosting such a show), was in college during the Bush administration, when all the hosts were men. Back then, the question never would have been asked, even if anyone had noticed. I asked Pelosi about this notion—whether she'd noticed people responding to her differently than they used to as society's view of women evolved. But what interested her about the photo wasn't the way the image had captivated people—it was the mistake Trump had made in releasing it. "He doesn't understand what is not in his interest," she said in amazement.

I should have known that she would be thinking more in terms of strategy than of symbolism. This was a common pattern in our conversations: I would ask her about something having to do with how she is perceived, and rather than engaging with that subject, she would divert to something more concrete, more results-oriented, more *operational*.

For all the time I've spent on Pelosi, she remains somewhat opaque. I've tried to explain her methods, the way she thinks, the sources of her mastery. But she is a private person, and her inner life is fundamentally off limits. I've asked dozens of people who know her personally to tell me about the side of her that's not seen in public. They all said there wasn't one. Whether it's her personality or how she was raised, she's not someone who indulges in public introspection. As her daughter Christine once said, "She's not one who really injects her psychological being into a conversation. You're not going to get a quote from her that's going to be a deep, self-reflective summation."

I will end this book the way I ended my 2018 Pelosi profile, with a story she told me in one of our first meetings, one that, to me, encapsulates so much about her. Once, during her first stint as Speaker, she traveled to Afghanistan via Kuwait. The Kuwaitis treated her with elaborate deference, calling her "Your Excellency." As the military plane soared over snowcapped peaks, Pelosi heard the pilot say he was headed for Kabul. That's wrong, she said. You're supposed to be taking me to Bagram Airfield to see the troops.

But the pilot wouldn't take her word for it. He called the U.S. embassy in Pakistan. She could hear him on the radio: "Our instructions say to go to Kabul, but payload wants to go to Bagram." Narrating it to me, Pelosi cracked up at the memory: "In a few hours, I went from 'excellency' to 'payload'!"

Pelosi left the real punch line unspoken. In the end, it didn't matter what they called her. In the end, they did what she wanted.

January 2021

Illustration Credits

All images are courtesy of Nancy Pelosi with the exception of the following:

Nancy's yearbook photo from Trinity Women's College, 1962. Courtesy of Trinity (Washington) University

Pelosi at the 1984 Democratic National Convention, which she helped bring to San Francisco. © Bettmann Archive / Getty Images

Campaigning for Congress in 1987. © AP / Paul Sakuma

Declaring victory with John Burton on Election Night, 1987. © Allen Brisson-Smith / *San Francisco Chronicle* / Polaris

Advocating for LGBT rights in the 1990s. © AP / Barry Thumma

With President Bill Clinton, 1993. © White House / Consolidated News via Getty Images

With Steny Hoyer, 1997. © Christopher Ayers / CQ Roll Call via Getty Images

Pelosi emerging victorious from the Democratic caucus whip election, 2001. © AP /Joe Marquette

Pelosi at Farmfest in rural Minnesota, 2006. Not visible here: the jeans and cowboy boots she wore to the event. © Eric Luse / *San Francisco Chronicle* / Polaris

With Rahm Emanuel and Harry Reid on Election Night, 2006, when Democrats took the House and Senate. © AP / J. Scott Applewhite, File

Hoisting the gavel surrounded by grandchildren as she's elected Speaker in 2007. © Stephen Crowley / *The New York Times* / Redux

With President Obama at the Capitol, 2010. © Jim Watson / AFP via Getty Images

Signing the Affordable Care Act, 2010. © AP / Manuel Balce Ceneta

Watching President Obama sign the ACA. © AP / J. Scott Applewhite

Handing the Speaker's gavel to John Boehner, 2011. © AP / Charles Dharapak

Applauding President Trump's call for unity at the State of the Union, 2019. © Doug Mills / *The New York Times* via AP, Pool

Confronting Trump at a national security briefing, 2019. © Official White House Photograph by Shealah Craighead

Notes

Prologue

xi   **But there must have been something in the seltzer:** Pelosi told me she drank a Bai brand vitamin-infused sparkling water, which she didn't realize contains a small amount of caffeine.

xiii   **"You come at the queen, you best not miss":** Twitter user @meganeabbot.

xiii   **"that look when you just got finished man-handling a man baby":** Twitter user @mmpadellan.

xvii   **her husband of fifty-five years, Paul, would sometimes point out that she needed new clothes:** A popular legend has it that Paul buys her clothes. In fact, according to multiple sources, he doesn't shop for her, but he does give advice.

Chapter 1

Pelosi related much of this family history to me and in her memoir, *Know Your Power*. See Nancy Pelosi and Amy Hill Hearth, *Know Your Power: A Message to America's Daughters* (New York: Anchor Books, 2009). I am also deeply indebted to her previous biographers Marc Sandalow and Vincent Bzdek for the information in these early chapters. Most of the information not otherwise attributed here can be found in their volumes. See Vincent Bzdek, *Woman of the House: The Rise of Nancy Pelosi* (New York: Palgrave Macmillan, 2009); and Marc Sandalow, *Madam Speaker: Nancy Pelosi's Life, Times, and Rise to Power* (New York: Rodale, 2008).

2   **he grew, quite literally, into the role:** Mark Bowden, "Bossin' Around: How Things Got Done in Baltimore," *Baltimore City Paper*, June 29, 1979.

4   **long-standing rumors that D'Alesandro was tied to various Mafia figures:** In 1947, the FBI interviewed a witness who described then-mayor D'Alesandro as a "constant companion" of several local Mafia figures. In 1961, for the federal board appointment, federal agents reinterviewed the witness, who said that "his previous statements were based only on rumor and hearsay" and he had no personal knowledge of such ties.

6   **All she really wanted was to be in control of her life:** Interview with Nancy Pelosi, August 2019.

6   **Big Nancy was big and loud and rough around the edges:** Pelosi doesn't talk about her this way, but several people who knew Big Nancy described her to me thus.

8   **Everyone knew who she was . . . but she never acted as if she thought she was better than anybody else:** Interview with Steny Hoyer, September 2019.

Chapter 2

11   **A memory flashed in her mind:** Interview with Nancy Pelosi, February 2018.

11   **In 1967, thirty-eight-year-old Tommy:** "D'Alesandro Beats Sherwood and Carries Entire Democratic Ticket to Victory at City Hall," *Baltimore Sun*, November 8, 1967.

12   **Pelosi told the stunned real estate agent**: In her memoir, *Know Your Power*, Pelosi notes that her daughter Alexandra says this story tells you everything you need to know about her.

13   **Tattling and gossip were prohibited**: Interview with Christine Pelosi, August 2019.

Chapter 3

17   **It was, she realized later, a feminist gesture**: Interview with Nancy Pelosi, January 2018.

19   **Burton, hard-drinking and prone to fits of rage**: John Jacobs, *A Rage for Justice: The Passion and Politics of Phillip Burton* (Berkeley: University of California Press, 1997).

21   **Tommy and his friend Ted Venetoulis**: Interview with Ted Venetoulis, May 2019.

22   **Brown and Pelosi became friends**: Interview with Jerry Brown, August 2019.

26   **One of Cuomo's aides:** "Unionists Accused of Sexism in a Race to Lead Democrats," *New York Times*, January 29, 1985.

26   **Mitchell . . . had met Pelosi on fund-raising trips to California**: Interview with George Mitchell, July 2019.

Chapter 4

28   **The House's hard-charging liberal lion**: Jacobs, *A Rage for Justice*.

29   **When it was campaign season, she could be found in their campaign office**: Interview with Judy Lemons, June 2019.

30   **John resigned after five terms to seek treatment**: Interview with John Burton, August 2019.

36   **It was a difficult choice, but he'd worked with her**: Interview with Jim Hormel, May 2018.

36   **These flyers, targeted at Republicans, were Paul's idea**: Mark Z. Barabak, "House Honors Pelosi's 25 Years in Congress," *Los Angeles Times*, June 10, 2012.

Chapter 5

38   **John Burton was worried about her . . . But she wasn't worried**: Interviews with John Burton and Nancy Pelosi, August 2019.

40   **She seemed so elegant**: Interview with Judy Lemons, June 2019.

41   **"But we always managed to get there"**: Interview with Leon Panetta, August 2019.

42   **It didn't happen overnight**: Republicans took the South in presidential elections from Nixon forward, but it took them much longer to erode Democrats' Southern dominance in Congress and state and local elections.

Chapter 6

48   **There was not even a women's bathroom**: Women began wearing pants on the House floor in the 1990s. They didn't get a bathroom near the floor until 2011.

49   **A prominent woman lobbyist recalls**: Interview with the lobbyist in question, who spoke on condition of anonymity.

51   **The oldest continually operating military installation**: The Spanish established a fort at the Presidio in 1776, predating the fortification of West Point in 1779.

54   **Pelosi made a spreadsheet**: Interview with Judy Lemons, June 2019.

55   **As one writer marveled**: Marc Sandalow, whose descriptions of Pelosi's early legislative battles in *Madam Speaker* are vivid and invaluable.

Chapter 7

57   **Then she heard that a colleague had an intern**: Interview with Judy Lemons. The intern, a Chinese American named Chao, worked in then-representative James Jontz's office, according to Lemons.

61   **Pelosi sat at her desk in San Francisco**: Interview with Nancy Pelosi, February 2018.

62   **Pelosi . . . was being written up in the papers**: "Pelosi's Prominence in Party on the Rise," *Los Angeles Times*, July 14, 1992.

64   **The issue made her internationally known**: "Pelosi, Flogging the Anti-China Horse," *Straits Times*, August 21, 1994.

64   **"congressional freedom squad"**: E. J. Dionne Jr., "Pelosi: Good News for Human Rights," *Washington Post*, November 19, 2002.

65   **Pelosi never gave up the fight**: According to two sources who worked on the legislation.

Chapter 8

67   **"I am now a famous person"**: "Newt Gingrich, Maverick on the Hill; The New Right's Abrasive Point Man Talks of Changing His Tone and Tactics," *Washington Post*, January 3, 1985.

71 **"I've been on the Intelligence Committee"**: "How Nancy Pelosi Took Control," *American Prospect*, May 12, 2004.

74 **The retirement in late 1997**: Democratic caucus chair Vic Fazio announced in November 1997 that he would not seek reelection in 1998.

75 **In July 1998, Pelosi convened her closest friends for dinner**: Some accounts place this dinner in 1999, but Judy Lemons confirms it was almost certainly 1998.

75 **Hoyer was a politician**: Despite his aristocratic lineage, Hoyer had a difficult childhood. His father left when he was young, and his stepfather was an abusive alcoholic.

Chapter 9

80 **she hosted the dozen newly elected Democrats**: Interview with Steve Israel, who attended, June 2019.

80 **"I don't think these boys know how to win"**: Interview with George Miller, August 2019.

81 **Pelosi was accused of playing dirty**: Then-representative Ellen Tauscher made the accusation in a front-page article in *Roll Call*. Ethan Wallison, "Pelosi Denies Whip Threats: Tauscher Charges Intimidation," *Roll Call*, August 2, 2001.

82 **215 House Democrats**: This number includes nonvoting House members such as Eleanor Holmes Norton of Washington, DC, who can vote in caucus elections but not on legislation.

Chapter 10

87 **it suddenly hit her**: In her memoir, Pelosi describes imagining that "Susan B. Anthony, Elizabeth Cady Stanton, Lucretia Mott, Alice Paul, and all the other suffragettes and activists who had worked hard to advance women in government and life were right there with me," saying, "At last we have a seat at the table."

91 **Pelosi got twelve thousand calls**: "Anti-War Protests Get Louder in Calif.," *Washington Post*, October 14, 2002.

92 **Pelosi's personal crusade**: Interview with Dick Gephardt, who didn't see it as undermining him, and who regrets his position on the war, July 2019.

93 **a reporter traveling with Pelosi**: The *Chronicle*'s intrepid Marc Sandalow, who somehow survived.

94 **Women, scientists concluded**: Patricia Hirsch, Iring Koch and Julia Karbach, "Putting a Stereotype to the Test: The Case of Gender Differences in Multitasking Costs in Task-switching and Dual-task Situations," *PLOS ONE*, August 14, 2019.

Chapter 11

98 **"Decisions are liberating"**: Interview with Eric Swalwell, July 2019.

104 **"I can't be with you on this"**: Interview with Steve Israel, June 2019.

104 **In the wake of the Medicare vote**: "How Nancy Pelosi Took Control," *American Prospect*, May 12, 2004.

Chapter 12

This chapter relies heavily on *The Thumpin'*, Naftali Bendavid's excellent book about Rahm Emanuel and the 2006 House campaign. See Naftali Bendavid, *The Thumpin': How Rahm Emanuel and the Democrats Learned to Be Ruthless and Ended the Republican Revolution* (New York: Doubleday, 2007).

112 **"Never. Is never good enough for you?"**: A reference to Bob Mankoff's famous 1993 *New Yorker* cartoon.

Chapter 13

120 **"demanded" a "big fat jet"**: Emails about Pelosi with similar wording continue to circulate, according to Snopes.com.

121 **The story entered the public bloodstream**: "House Security Chief: Pelosi Didn't Ask for Plane; I Did," CNN.com, February 9, 2007.

121 **Republicans spent two full hours**: Faye Fiore, "On Capitol Hill, Pelosi Plane Dispute Stays at High Altitude," *Los Angeles Times*, February 9, 2007.

122 **When a bird flew**: Faye Fiore and Julian Barnes, "Pelosi Gets Nonstop Abuse Over Air Travel," *Los Angeles Times*, February 8, 2007.

122 **Alexandra drove down to Baltimore**: Andy Kroll, "The Staying Power of Nancy Pelosi," *National Journal*, September 11, 2015.

126 **He was notorious for . . . steering pork**: Jason Zengerle, "Murthaville," *New Republic*, September 1, 2009.

127 **"It was a terrible mistake":** Interview with Barney Frank.

130 **In one negotiation:** Michael Grunwald, *The New New Deal: The Hidden Story of Change in the Obama Era* (New York: Simon & Schuster Paperbacks, 2013), chapter 3.

Chapter 14

139 **The meeting-cum-therapy session:** Noam M. Levey, "Pelosi War-Bill Gamble Pays Off," *Los Angeles Times,* March 24, 2007.

139 **"With the Democrats back in power":** Jeff Leys, "Tap Dancing on Graves," *Counterpunch,* March 19, 2007.

140 **As the caucus applauded:** David R. Obey, *Raising Hell for Justice: The Washington Battles of a Heartland Progressive* (Madison: University of Wisconsin Press, 2007), p. 410.

Chapter 15

142 **On Thursday, September 18, 2008:** John Lawrence, "When America Stared into the Abyss," *Atlantic,* January 7, 2019.

144 **In growing cities like Las Vegas:** I lived in Las Vegas at the time and saw the effects of the crash firsthand.

145 **The Clintons' network of supporters took note:** Two sources who witnessed the incident, speaking on condition of anonymity, described it to me.

146 **In a March 2008 interview:** Steve Kornacki, "Nancy Pelosi's Not-So-Secret Support for Obama," *New York Observer,* March 17, 2008.

146 **Pelosi also got a call from Harvey Weinstein:** Nikki Finke, "Harvey Weinstein vs Nancy Pelosi: . . . But Why Not Accept His Offer to Find Funding for Michigan & Florida Dem Primaries?" *Deadline,* May 8, 2008.

149 **After the meeting ended:** This scene has been described in numerous congruent accounts, including Aaron Ross Sorkin's *Too Big to Fail* (New York: Viking, 2009).

151 **A Republican congressman narrated:** Tim Alberta, *American Carnage: On the Front Lines of the Republican Civil War and the Rise of President Trump* (New York: Harper, 2019), chapter 1.

152 **John Lawrence, her chief of staff, later wondered:** Interview with John Lawrence, February 2018.

Chapter 16

153 **What struck Pelosi more than anything:** Nancy Pelosi, interview by Charlie Rose, *Charlie Rose,* PBS, March 13, 2009.

154 **"We're going to do it":** Jonathan Alter, *The Promise: President Obama, Year One* (New York: Simon & Schuster, 2011), chapter 6.

154 **She thought of it in terms of paleoanthropology:** Unpublished Pelosi interview with *Time*'s Jay Newton-Small, 2009.

157 **One new member told Pelosi:** Interview with Steve Israel, June 2019.

157 **Once, in Berlin:** Interview with John Lawrence, April 2019.

157 **Members who traveled with her:** Interviews with Rep. Dan Kildee, D-MI, May 2019; and others.

158 **Once, a press aide:** Interview with the aide in question; the incident was previously reported in the *New York Times Magazine.*

158 **Harman found out:** Interview with former representative Jane Harman, September 2019.

159 **Pelosi was grooming him:** Interview with Nancy Pelosi, February 2018.

160 **"You told me you had my back":** Robert Draper, *When the Tea Party Came to Town* (New York: Simon & Schuster, 2013), chapter 17.

Chapter 17

Much of the reporting in this chapter is drawn from Grunwald's essential book about the stimulus, *The New New Deal.*

162 **Keynes supposedly said:** The authenticity of this quotation is disputed, but Keynes expressed similar sentiments in his writing.

163 **After the meeting . . . David Axelrod:** Interview with David Axelrod, August 2019.

164 **The Democrats would prefer:** Interview with Rob Nabors, June 2019.

165 **The president complained privately:** Alter, *The Promise,* p. 326

166 **After their first meeting with Obama:** Bob Woodward, *The Price of Politics* (New York: Simon & Schuster, 2012), chapter 1.

168 **Charlie Dent . . . was one of a group:** Holly Bailey, "Barack Obama's Nancy Pelosi Problem," *Newsweek,* February 27, 2009.

170 **Later, Obama himself would wonder**: Alter, *The Promise*, chapter 8.

170 **"Mr. Fifty Yard Line"**: According to a source who heard this description from a senator.

Chapter 18

172 **Obama's team had drawn up a schedule**: Interview with Phil Schiliro, May 2019.

174 **Waxman had done it because**: Interview with former representative Henry Waxman, May 2019.

174 **Obama summoned Waxman to the White House**: Henry Waxman, *The Waxman Report: How Congress Really Works* (New York: Twelve, 2010), p. 227.

175 **He paraded CEOs**: Bryan W. Marshall and Bruce C. Wolpe, *The Committee: A Study of Policy, Power, Politics, and Obama's Historic Legislative Agenda on Capitol Hill* (Ann Arbor: University of Michigan Press, 2018), chapter 2.

176 **Another senior Blue Dog**: Draper, *When the Tea Party Came to Town*, chapter 8.

176 **She approached a longtime ally, Collin Peterson**: Interview with Rep. Collin Peterson, June 2019, corroborated by former representative Henry Waxman and others.

177 **Jim Clyburn, the Democratic whip**: Interview with Rep. Jim Clyburn, August 2019.

178 **One of the Democratic nays**: Ryan Lizza, "As the World Burns," *New Yorker*, October 11, 2010.

Chapter 19

179 **All day, Pelosi had been in meetings**: Staff of the *Washington Post, Landmark: The Inside Story of America's New Health Care Law and What It Means for Us All* (New York: PublicAffairs, 2010), chapter 2.

182 **"stone tablets"**: Matt Bai, "Taking the Hill," *New York Times Magazine*, June 2, 2009.

183 **"What are we supposed to do"**: Interview with David Axelrod, August 2019.

184 **When other Democrats would bring up**: Interview with a former Pelosi staffer, speaking on condition of anonymity.

184 **"Does the president not understand"**: Alter, *The Promise*, chapter 22.

184 **But time was short**: Jonathan Cohn, "How They Did It," *New Republic*, May 21, 2010.

185 **Pelosi was furious with the Senate:** Two sources to whom she vented privately at the time.

186 **Pelosi took the hairsplitting position**: Jennifer Steinhauer, "In Pelosi, Strong Catholic Faith and Abortion Rights Coexist," *New York Times*, September 21, 2015.

186 **Early in her career**: Interview with former representative Pat Schroeder, August 2019.

187 **She promised two California members**: Faye Fiore and Richard Simon, "She Had to Leave Left Coast Behind," *Los Angeles Times*, November 9, 2009.

188 **Then it was the House's turn**: Two sources who were in the room, corroborated with slight differences by contemporaneous reporting in *Politico*.

189 **Waxman piped up**: Interview with Henry Waxman, May 2019, and other sources who were in the room.

190 **At a meeting in the Oval Office**: Interview with Nancy Pelosi, February 2018, and others who were in the room.

191 **Pelosi even told colleagues**: Two sources close to Nancy Pelosi.

192 **Pelosi demanded that Reid**: Interview with former senator Harry Reid, July 2019.

193 **At a caucus meeting, a liberal congressman**: Interview with former representative Jared Polis, June 2019.

193 **It was Republicans who would look unreasonable**: Marshall and Wolpe, *The Committee*, chapter 3.

Chapter 20

195 **It was a fund-raising gambit**: Interview with then-RNC communications director Doug Heye, May 2019.

196 **A Republican candidate in Texas**: Alex Isenstadt, "GOP Casts Pelosi as Health Care Villain," *Politico*, March 17, 2010.

197 **"You know what, I'm in the arena"**: Nancy Pelosi, interview by Charlie Rose, *Charlie Rose*, PBS, March 13, 2009.

199 **Reid called Axelrod**: Interview with David Axelrod, August 2019.

201 **Axelrod told a reporter**: Lizza, "As the World Burns."

201 **Pelosi and her strategists**: The descriptions of the 2010 congressional campaign in this chapter are largely drawn from David Corn's terrific book *Showdown: The Inside Story of How Obama Fought Back Against Boehner, Cantor, and the Tea Party* (New York: William Morrow, 2012).

203 **Robert Gibbs, later acknowledged**: Ibid.

204 **In July, the White House's Gibbs**: Jonathan Allen and John Bresnahan, "At W.H., Pelosi Leverages Tension," *Politico*, July 14, 2010.

204 **At Tuesday's closed-door meeting**: Paul Kane, "House Democrats Hit Boiling Point; Obama Tries to Quell Uprising," *Washington Post*, July 15, 2010.

206 **The Republicans' congressional campaign committee**: Jonathan Allen, "Rage Against Pelosi a Drag on Dems," *Politico*, January 13, 2010.

206 **Her friend George Miller**: Interview with George Miller, August 2019, who publicly expressed similar sentiments at the time.

207 **"Nancy, you're the leader"**: Draper, *When the Tea Party Came to Town*, chapter 8.

207 **The Republican National Committee had taken down**: Paul Kane and Perry Bacon Jr., "Pelosi Declines to Step Aside," *Washington Post*, November 6, 2010.

Chapter 21

208 **For all Pelosi's punctiliousness**: Interview with a former Pelosi staffer.

209 **Pelosi felt that familiar combination**: A former staffer described her as always being driven by this combination of motivations.

209 **a "faith-based initiative"**: Karen Tumulty and Paul Kane, "Pelosi's Crusade: 'Win It Back,'" *Washington Post*, June 27, 2011.

210 **"Sacrificing the unpopular Mrs. Pelosi"**: "The Pelosi Minority," *Wall Street Journal*, November 6, 2010.

210 **Hoyer considered running**: Jake Sherman and Anna Palmer, *The Hill to Die On: The Battle for Congress and the Future of Trump's America* (New York: Crown, 2019), pp. 38–39.

210 **Pelosi's decision to stay was also news to Hoyer**: According to two sources close to Hoyer.

212 **Vice President Joe Biden summoned Pelosi**: Woodward, *The Price of Politics*, chapter 8.

213 **"Just watch," Pelosi said**: Interview with Nancy Pelosi, January 2018.

214 **Behind her back**: According to two sources.

216 **The 2012 election, Pelosi proclaimed**: Draper, *When the Tea Party Came to Town*, chapter 16.

217 **Boehner didn't share his party's derangement**: Alberta, *American Carnage*, chapter 4.

218 **Pelosi said one other thing**: Interview with Nancy Pelosi, August 2019.

220 **As they were leaving the floor**: Draper, *When the Tea Party Came to Town*, chapter 22.

Chapter 22

223 **She wanted only one favor**: According to two sources.

225 **the expansion of a Georgia port**: Carl Hulse, "A Consensus in Washington, but No Action," *New York Times*, April 25, 2014.

226 **"That's what we all take the job to do"**: Billy House, "Pelosi to Boehner: 'Risk Something,'" *National Journal Daily*, December 12, 2012.

227 **The defectors were sternly admonished**: Anna Palmer and John Bresnahan, "Dem Frosh Defy Pelosi," *Politico*, August 2, 2013.

228 **In a private letter to Boehner**: Interiew with former Boehner chief to staff Mike Sommers, May 2019.

228 **She met with Boehner**: Interview with Nancy Pelosi, August 2019.

230 **On the caucus's post-election conference call**: Emma Dumain, "House Democrats Look for Answers, Accountability after Midterm Losses," *Congressional Quarterly*, December 12, 2014.

231 **who had left Congress in part**: Interview with Henry Waxman, May 2019.

231 **"They all have a baton"**: Melinda Henneberger, "Pelosi Almost Endorses Clinton, Almost Accuses GOP of Racism," *Congressional Quarterly*, January 13, 2016.

232 **And so, after the 2014 debacle**: Robert Draper, "'You'd Have to Be Insane Not to Conduct Some Soul-Searching,'" *New York Times Magazine*, May 20, 2015; confirmed by my reporting.

233 **Boehner considers it his proudest achievement**: Tim Alberta, "John Boehner Unchained," *Politico*, November/December 2017.

234 **By September, she had delivered**: Carolyn Lochhead, "How Pelosi Rallied Dems to Preserve Iran Nuclear Deal," *San Francisco Chronicle*, September 10, 2015.

234 **One former staffer described**: Interview with former Pelosi policy director Amy Rosenbaum, October 2019.

234 **The anti-TPP lawmakers decided**: Trade deals generally pass in two parts, with Republicans supporting "trade promotion authority," authorizing the president to negotiate the deal, and

Democrats supporting aid to affected U.S. businesses and workers known as "trade adjustment assistance." The liberals stopped TPP by withholding their votes for this latter piece.

Chapter 23

237 **Boehner laid out the threat**: Alberta, "John Boehner Unchained."

238 **Despite Ryan and Trump's differences**: Carolyn Lochhead, "Pelosi: House GOP Like Trump," *San Francisco Chronicle*, July 4, 2016.

239 **Pelosi didn't just think**: Interview with Nancy Pelosi, January 2018.

239 **But Clinton had chosen**: Ruby Cramer, "How a Decision in May Changed the General Election," *BuzzFeed News*, September 22, 2016.

240 **In an afternoon interview:** Sherman and Palmer, *The Hill to Die On*, p. 35.

240 **Trump's victory stunned everyone**: He later claimed he expected to win all along, but my and many other reporters' sources at the time said he did not.

240 **She had even thought about retiring**: Interview with Nancy Pelosi, January 2018. Some of her colleagues are skeptical of this claim, noting that she never said anything to that effect before the election.

241 **The decisive vote had come**: Nate Cohn, "Why Trump Won: Working-Class Whites," *New York Times*, November 9, 2016.

241 **Just like two years earlier**: Robert Draper, "A Post-Obama Democratic Party in Search of Itself," *New York Times Magazine*, November 1, 2017.

241 **Two dozen mostly younger members**: Victoria McGrane and Astead W. Herndon, "Dems, Including Some from Mass., Rebel in House," *Boston Globe*, November 15, 2016.

241 **Another group of members**: Interview with Joe Crowley, June 2019, and others who added details and corroborated.

242 **Once, a colleague**: Interview with Steve Israel, June 2019.

242 **Crowley was serious enough**: Sherman and Palmer, *The Hill to Die On*, pp. 38–40.

243 **No one . . . was arguing**: Amber Phillips, "Why 63 House Democrats Voted to Oust Nancy Pelosi," *Washington Post*, November 30, 2016.

243 **Tim Ryan gave a passionate speech**: Jim Newell, "How Nancy Pelosi Won (and Spun)," *Slate*, November 30, 2016.

Chapter 24

245 **"I think we'll get things done"**: Edward-Isaac Dovere, "Nancy Pelosi Has Trump Right Where She Wants Him," *Politico*, November/December 2017.

245 **Pelosi suggested Trump**: Matt Flegenheimer and Maggie Haberman, "'You're the Best,' Trump Once Told Pelosi. Can They Deal Again?" *New York Times*, May 1, 2017.

247 **Three days after the inauguration**: Glenn Thrush, "Trump's Voter Fraud Example? A Troubled Tale with Bernhard Langer," *New York Times*, January 25, 2017.

248 **Pelosi almost felt sorry for him**: Carolyn Lochhead, "Pelosi Says She Finds Trump 'Insecure,'" *San Francisco Chronicle*, January 26, 2017.

248 **Within a few weeks of the election**: Interview with Christine Pelosi, August 2019; Heather Caygle, "Trump's Obamacare Stumble Empowers Pelosi," *Politico*, March 27, 2017.

249 **They were backed up**: David Weigel, "Left Out of AHCA Fight, Democrats Let Their Grass Roots Lead—and Win," *Washington Post*, March 24, 2017.

249 **Pelosi held a series of meetings**: Heather Caygle and John Bresnahan, "Pelosi Battles GOP to Save Obamacare—and Her Legacy," *Politico*, March 8, 2017.

251 **Over the summer of 2017**: Sherman and Palmer, *The Hill to Die On*, pp. 115–16; confirmed by my sources.

252 **Pelosi and Schumer were vacationing**: Sheryl Gay Stolberg, "'Chuck and Nancy,' Washington's New Power Couple, Set Sights on Health Care," *New York Times*, September 20, 2017.

252 **When Pelosi walked in**: Sherman and Palmer, *The Hill to Die On*, pp. 121–24.

253 **Republican senator Ben Sasse**: Peter Baker and Sheryl Gay Stolberg, "Energized Trump Sees Bipartisan Path, at Least for Now," *New York Times*, September 7, 2017.

254 **The deal still caused**: Sean Sullivan and Anne Gearan, "Trump Deal Signals Openings, Risks for Democrats," *Washington Post*, September 9, 2017.

256 **Finally, she raised a finger**: Ashley Parker, "Trump and Democrats Strike DACA Deal. Yes? No? Sort of? Trump's World Can Be Confusing," *Washington Post*, September 14, 2017.

Chapter 25

258 **Pelosi had spent decades**: Interview with Nancy Pelosi, January 2018.

259 **Such queries were unusual**: Interviews with Emily's List president Stephanie Schriock and staff, June–July 2018.

260 **her phone never stopped ringing**: Lisa Mascaro, "For Political Street Fighter Nancy Pelosi, There's New Power in Opposing Trump," *Los Angeles Times*, May 11, 2017.

261 **Its strategy was all about Pelosi**: John Wildemuth, "Pelosi in Hot Seat after 4 Dem Losses," *San Francisco Chronicle*, June 29, 2017.

262 **In a private meeting**: Alexander Burns and Jonathan Martin, "Democrats Seethe After Georgia Loss: 'Our Brand Is Worse Than Trump,'" *New York Times*, June 21, 2017.

265 **When Crowley called Pelosi**: Sherman and Palmer, *The Hill to Die On*, p. 250.

265 **she reached Ocasio-Cortez**: According to an aide with knowledge of the call; Ocasio-Cortez later corroborated this account in a television interview.

266 **"How do we know"**: Sherman and Palmer, *The Hill to Die On*, p. 212.

268 **For months afterward**: I personally witnessed several instances of this on a trip with Pelosi to Houston in February 2018.

269 **On March 7, Pelosi called**: According to an aide with knowledge of the call.

272 **"Did you ever know anybody"**: Nancy Pelosi at public event in Houston, February 2018.

272 **in fact, the bill cut**: Ben Casselman and Jim Tankersley, "Face It: You (Probably) Got a Tax Cut," *New York Times*, April 14, 2019.

273 **To Pelosi's frustration**: According to two sources familiar with the episode.

Chapter 26

275 **On Election Day**: Sherman and Palmer, *The Hill to Die On*, p. 347.

278 **When they put out feelers**: According to two sources familiar with the incident.

279 **Her staff made spreadsheets**: According to four people involved in the campaign, which was based outside Pelosi's congressional office with a group of trusted political advisers.

280 **Liberal celebrities**: Elise Viebeck, Mike DeBonis and Erica Werner, "Fight for House Speaker Explodes into National Political Campaign," *Washington Post*, November 17, 2018.

280 **But Pelosi had her own sources**: John Bresnahan, Rachael Bade and Kyle Cheney, "Pelosi Cranks Up Campaign to Win Over Freshmen," *Politico*, November 13, 2018.

281 **Moulton suddenly found**: According to a source who spoke on condition of anonymity, Pelosi is rumored to have encouraged the primary challenges.

284 **Only Schumer had been invited**: Interview with Chuck Schumer, December 2019.

287 **"Nancy Pelosi just did something"**: Twitter user @JuddLegum, author of the progressive newsletter *Popular Information*.

288 **Clyburn held a more realistic view**: Interview with Jim Clyburn, August 2019.

288 **After sealing the deal**: According to two sources in the room.

Chapter 27

289 **In 2018, he was instrumental**: According to two sources involved in the Democratic Policy and Communications Committee, which Jeffries co-chaired.

293 **When she and Schumer met**: According to a Pelosi aide's meeting readout, corroborated by others in the room.

293 **some Democrats were going wobbly**: Rachael Bade, Heather Caygle and John Bresnahan, "'She's Not One to Bluff': How Pelosi Won the Shutdown Battle," *Politico*, January 25, 2019.

295 **That night, she and Paul**: According to a source who happened also to be dining there.

295 **Whole essays were written**: Wesley Morris, "The Meaning of the Scene: When Pelosi Clapped at Trump," *New York Times*, February 20, 2019.

300 **Some were honest enough**: Megan McArdle, "Democrats, Welcome to Your Very Own Tea-Party Problem," *Washington Post*, August 20, 2019.

301 **She didn't really get Twitter**: According to a Democratic staffer who witnessed this.

301 **"Power is not influence"**: Kelsey Snell, "Nancy Pelosi Wants the Speaker's Gavel Back. And She Needs Hillary Clinton's Help to Do It," *Washington Post*, July 27, 2016.

301 **She strode to the front**: According to a Pelosi aide's meeting readout, corroborated by others in the room.

303 **She sat in seat 23D**: According to a source who was on the flight—her office later gave a different seat number, perhaps referring to a seat change when others debarked during the delay, but my source was seated in her row for the flight itself.

Chapter 28

304 **She vividly remembered**: Nancy Pelosi described the Clinton impeachment thus in a December 2019 interview. She claims Republicans never viewed Clinton as a legitimate president because they considered him low-class.

305 **she personally oversaw**: Interview with House counsel Douglas Letter, November 2019.

306 **Online boutiques**: Spotted in the wild at protests and Democratic events across the country in 2018–19.

306 **Pelosi fielded calls**: Robert Costa, "Pelosi Urges Democrats to Take a 'Deep Breath'—and Takes Charge of Her Party," *Washington Post*, March 28, 2019.

307 **When she returned**: According to a Pelosi aide's readout, corroborated by others on the call.

309 **to some confidants she did seem**: According to three sources close to Nancy Pelosi.

309 **She told friends she'd started**: "Pelosi Says Public Doesn't Support Impeachment," Associated Press, August 23, 2019.

310 **she appeared at a banquet:** I attended the banquet; Pelosi's staff knew there would be an impeachment protest outside the event but were blindsided when the protesters made it in to her speech.

Acknowledgments

Like having a child or being a member of Congress, writing a book is something people tell you is hard, but you can't comprehend the difficulty until you do it yourself. (I've done two of those three things, and studied the third pretty closely.) I couldn't have done this without the help and support of so many people.

First and foremost, I benefited from the generous cooperation of Nancy Pelosi and the assistance of her staff. Her deputy chief of staff and fierce protector Drew Hammill provided essential guidance and labored to convince the skeptical Speaker that helping to define her legacy was a worthwhile project. Pelosi gave generously of her valuable time and gamely fielded all manner of queries, however meandering, incoherent or challenging. The characterizations in this book are mine, and she had no control over the final product, but her contributions were essential and I am grateful for her trust.

I conducted more than a hundred interviews with Pelosi's friends and family, critics and supporters, activists and operatives, current and former staff, and dozens of current and former members of Congress from across the political spectrum. Most of my sources aren't quoted in the text of the book; I've tried to weave together their accounts in a narrative rather than journalistic style. There are hundreds more people I wish I could have spoken to, but we don't all have the luxury of Robert Caro's deadlines. I have tried to channel Pelosi's perspective without presuming to speak for her.

Where I have characterized her state of mind, it is based on her statements, to me or in her memoir; contemporaneous public comments; or views she shared with friends, staff, colleagues and others I consider reliable. Any error or misconstrual is, of course, entirely my fault.

I'm deeply indebted to Pelosi's previous biographers Marc Sandalow, Vincent Bzdek, and Ronald M. Peters Jr. and Cindy Simon Rosenthal. I drew heavily on their accounts of Pelosi's early life and career. Sandalow's *Madam Speaker* in particular is the essential text for any Pelosi watcher. I'm also deeply grateful to the beat reporters who pound the marble floors of Capitol Hill every day, giving the citizens of this country the insight they need into the workings of our great democracy. It's corny, but it's true. Much of this book is merely a second draft of the first draft of history they produce every day. Many of them also generously advised me as I worked on this project, helping me understand the institution and its history, customs and players.

My editor at *Time*, Alex Altman, is the best in the business. It was he who assigned me to profile Pelosi when I started at *Time* back in 2017, and he who transformed that piece, and so many others, from a loose pile of interesting sentences to a real, big-time magazine profile. This book would not exist without him. I'm grateful to *Time*'s DC bureau chief Massimo Calabresi, whose journalistic rigor inspires me on a daily basis. I'm indebted to Edward Felsenthal, *Time*'s editor in chief, for giving me the best job in journalism— and then letting me take off in the middle of an intense year for political news to write this book. I'm proud to work for *Time*, a publication that has meant so much to so many for going on a hundred years, and excited to see what the future holds under the visionary stewardship of our owners, Lynne and Marc Benioff. (Disclosure: the Benioffs are close friends of the Pelosis and have donated to Nancy Pelosi's campaigns, but they were not involved in any part of my coverage of Pelosi or my decision to write this book.)

My brilliant agent Howard Yoon believed I had a book in me for many years before I found a way to prove him right. When the right subject finally did come along, I wasn't even smart enough to recognize it—for that, I have my wonderful editor at Henry Holt, Serena Jones, to thank. Together with her colleague Madeline Jones (no relation), she gave me the support and confidence I needed to write my first book. I'm thankful to my research assistant, Susan Weill, who also fact-checked, along with Barbara Maddux, Harriet Barovick and the eagle-eyed Hilary McClellen.

I'm grateful to many friends and colleagues who served as sounding boards and supplemental editors, none more so than Elizabeth Drew, the legendary Washington journalist who has been a friend and mentor to me for many years. Her analytical rigor, sharp eye for detail and political acumen improved this book tremendously. Elizabeth, who is still writing and reporting essential pieces at the age of eighty-four, belongs alongside Nancy Pelosi in the pantheon of formidable DC women as far as I'm concerned.

I've buried the lede and left the most important people in my life for last. I'm lucky to come from a strong and loving family; my dad, Rick Ball, taught me to appreciate ideas and beer and a good laugh, and my mom, Joan Winn, raised me to value myself and others. Matt Ball has ten inches and at least a hundred pounds on me, but he'll always be the best little brother in the world.

My husband, David Kihara, is the love of my life. We've been on an incredible journey ever since we met eighteen years ago, and the adventure is just beginning. His love, patience, support, encouragement, insightful editing and delicious cooking have kept me alive and nourished me, literally and figuratively, through an exceptionally tough year. Baby, I couldn't have done this without you, but together, we can do anything.

Our children have to put up with me whether they like it or not, but I'm grateful to them nonetheless. They've challenged me and broadened my world, making me a stronger, more flexible and more compassionate person. Ben, Miri and Teddy, I love you and I'm so excited to watch you grow up. Even if sometimes I want to put you out in the rain and shrink you back down into babies.

Index